The Release Train Engineer Handbook

Transform your Agile Release Train (ART) with practical, result-driven approaches

Glenn Smith

Tim Jackson

Gez Smith

The Release Train Engineer Handbook

Copyright © 2025 Packt Publishing

Portfolio Director: Pavan Ramchandani
Relationship Lead: Tejashwini R
Content Engineer: Mohd Hammad
Technical Editor: Vidhisha Patidar
Copy Editor: Safis Editing
Indexer: Tejal Soni
Proofreader: Mohd Hammad
Production Designer: Salma Patel
Growth Lead: Priya Bhanushali

First published: November 2025

Production reference: 01311025

Published by Packt Publishing Ltd.
Grosvenor House
11 St Paul's Square
Birmingham
B3 1RB, UK.

ISBN 978-1-83620-523-4
www.packtpub.com

Foreword

If you asked a SAFe® organization about the most significant change in adopting this new way of working, certain aspects would likely emerge, such as PI Planning for creating alignment, organizing around value to eliminate bottlenecks and speed up flow, or perhaps the introduction of a regular cadence to synchronize key activities. But it can be guaranteed that most, if not all, would also mention the role of the **Release Train Engineer (RTE)**. The role of the RTE has become synonymous with SAFe, and there is good reason for this. In short, they play a pivotal role in scaling Lean and Agile practices; as such, we owe a huge debt of gratitude to all those who have fulfilled this role.

In SAFe, the **Agile Release Train (ART)** represents the team of Agile teams tasked with developing products that *release* value and delight customers. In most cases, 100+ individuals from all different functions of the organization collaboratively realize this goal. Another way to think about it is that the ART is a system of work. And as W. Edwards Deming taught us, "...*a system needs to be managed.*" Not *managed* in the traditional sense of the word, but rather someone needs to have responsibility for ensuring the smooth and effective operation of the ART. This person is the RTE. Given its paramount importance, additional guidance and support for those fulfilling this role are always welcome. With that in mind, I was delighted when I heard that Glenn Smith, Tim Jackson, and Gez Smith were writing this book.

Although the book as a whole should be viewed as a necessary text for all current or aspiring RTEs, three things in particular grabbed my attention as I read it. The first is the topic of *becoming an RTE*, which is tackled in *Chapter 2*. In our SAFe training and the accompanying Framework articles, there never seems to be enough time to cover the critical question of "Where do good RTEs come from?". This book provides the answer, recognizing, of course, that RTEs can come from many diverse backgrounds. Starting with an example of a typical job description, the authors take the aspiring RTEs and the organization employing them on a practical journey. They identify both the qualities and core knowledge required, in addition to the ongoing development needed for success.

Of particular importance is the fact that they do not shy away from some of the most common pitfalls that may be experienced when an individual transitions from an existing role to this new, and often very different, role as a Lean-Agile coach and servant leader.

The second standout quality of this new book is the breadth of coverage. It covers the most common elements of the life cycle of the RTE role—and more. Rather than simply focusing on some of the most common responsibilities, such as preparing for and facilitating PI Planning, and executing the PI (all of which it does superbly well), it starts the story even earlier. It begins with the critical role the RTE plays in helping to launch the ART itself, and then extends the storyline to include the complexities of working with Solution Trains, when, as the authors reflect, *"sometimes, 125 people just isn't enough to build and maintain large complex solutions."* This breadth accurately reflects the true breadth of the role across the organization, and it is wonderful to see it fully recognized here.

Finally, and perhaps most importantly, this book is a practical guide built on a wealth of first-hand experience. I feel very fortunate to have known the authors for many years and, through conversations, have benefited from their insights and learned from the multitude of SAFe® implementations that they have led and been a part of. *The Release Train Engineer Handbook*, with its embedded tips and techniques, ensures that the wider SAFe community, including current and future RTEs, can also benefit in the same way. Thank you, Glenn, Tim, and Gez.

Andrew Sales

SAFe® Chief Methodologist

Contributors

About the authors

Glenn Smith is a seasoned business agility consultant and trainer with over 25 years of experience helping organizations bring better products to market faster. As a certified **SAFe® Practice Consultant Trainer (SPCT)**, one of only a select few globally to achieve this certification, Glenn has guided numerous enterprise-scale organizations through successful transformations, regularly achieving dramatic improvements, including 50% gains in delivery predictability and 80% reductions in time-to-market. His journey from software engineer at Motorola through to founding Nimbility has given him deep practical experience across all levels of organizational change, from team-level agility to enterprise-wide business transformation.

Drawing on his extensive experience working with clients in defense, finance, education, and technology sectors, Glenn offers a notably pragmatic approach to organizational change. His unique perspective—that of a practitioner who has navigated these challenges firsthand—combined with his talent for making complexity feel simple and approachable, sets him apart in the field. His philosophy centers on avoiding one-size-fits-all solutions, instead crafting tailored approaches that address each organization's specific challenges while empowering leaders with the skills, tools, and processes they need for sustainable success.

Tim Jackson is an experienced **SAFe® Practice Consultant Trainer (SPCT)** with over 20 years of hands-on experience in Agile delivery, leadership development, and large-scale transformation. He began his career as a developer and tester in small start-ups before transitioning to consultancy in boutique consultancies and global agencies.

His passion for Product Management emerged while serving as director for mobile health at a medical device company. Tim has channeled his customer-centric approach into leading Agile transformations across complex, highly regulated industries, including pharmaceuticals and aviation.

Today, Tim helps people and organizations achieve their goals through consulting, coaching, and training. He is a certified Executive Coach with the **International Coaching Federation (ICF)** and the **European Mentoring and Coaching Council (EMCC)**, and he blends these disciplines to support leaders and teams in building resilience, alignment, and sustainable high performance.

Whether guiding leadership teams through Lean Portfolio Management, coaching executives to unlock their potential, or training the next generation of Agile change agents, Tim's focus remains constant: enabling people to thrive and organizations to deliver lasting value at scale.

Gez Smith began his Lean-Agile journey 20 years ago, using *The Toyota Way* and Scrum to grow a start-up from a bedroom company to working with 10 Downing Street and The White House. Along the way, he became a Product Owner, which was his first insight into how little he knew. A feeling that has only grown the more he has learned. Years later, he moved into financial services, including a spell as Global Head of Agile at HSBC, where he first used SAFe® to help thousands of people around the world get more value delivered more easily. Along the way, he picked up two master's degrees and also became a **SAFe® Practice Consultant Trainer (SPCT)** and a **SAFe Fellow**. Outside of the day job, he enjoys blogging, podcasting, and writing, having previously written books on digital engagement, Agile marketing, and Agile HR. He is a regular speaker at conferences, events, and meetups around the world. In short, he likes having ideas and sharing them with other people to see whether they find them useful too, which is why he contributed to this book.

About the reviewer

David Richardson has over 25 years of experience leading complex, large-scale programs, primarily within government, where he has helped major departments navigate transformational change with clarity and confidence. He combines strategic foresight with a pragmatic approach—breaking down complexity into simple, actionable steps that deliver tangible, customer-focused outcomes. Known for inspiring teams and fostering lasting commitment, David brings both rigor and humanity to delivery.

A trusted adviser to the UK Cabinet Office, David serves as a **High-Risk Project Review Team Lead**, providing expert analysis on the delivery confidence of the government's most critical and high-profile programs. His recommendations guide senior leaders on the interventions needed to strengthen delivery and improve outcomes across the public sector.

Since moving into consultancy in 2015, David has applied the lessons and insights gained from his public sector experience to support organizations across both public and private sectors in adopting and embedding new ways of working. An active Agile practitioner and coach, he collaborates with the **Association for Project Management (APM)** to advance understanding of the human dimensions of transformational delivery. He is a **SAFe® Practice Consultant**, one of the first **Chartered Project Professionals** globally, and has served as a judge for APM's annual Project Awards, recognizing excellence across the profession.

I'd like to thank the authors for inviting me to assist with their book, which is a treasure trove of advice and tips for established and aspiring RTEs, based on their extensive experience.

Acknowledgements

We (Glenn, Tim, and Gez) would like to thank the following people who were kind enough to offer their time, hard-earned lessons, and tips for inclusion during the writing of this book:

- Darren Wilmshurst, Cprime
- Maarten Sterrenburg, Connected Movement
- Isabella Reggio, Nest
- Annette Gomez, CVS
- Sam Ervin, Scaled Agile, Inc
- Hao Li, Allianz
- Stuart Griffith, www.cogna.now
- Thorsten Janning, KEGON
- Ali Hajou, Avant Edge

A special thanks to the following for enabling us to reshare or build some of our work on their content to make this book richer:

- Scaled Agile, Inc., for SAFe® imagery and registered trademark
- Dave Gray, Xplane, for Empathy Maps
- John M. Fisher, C2D Ltd, for Fisher Curve

SAFe® and Scaled Agile Framework® are registered trademarks of Scaled Agile, Inc.

Table of Contents

Part II: The RTE and the Agile Release Train   89

Chapter 6: Event Logistics for PI Planning 141

Part III: Beyond the ART   285

Chapter 11: Working with a Solution Train   287

Chapter 12: Connecting the RTE to the Portfolio 321

Preface

The **Release Train Engineer** (**RTE**) is one of the most pivotal—yet often misunderstood—roles in modern organizations. It's part servant leader, part systems thinker, part coach. The RTE helps others find clarity amid complexity, guiding people through the rhythms of delivery while maintaining a focus on the human side of change. In many ways, the RTE is the quiet conductor of a huge orchestra, helping each section play in tune while ensuring that the music connects with the audience it's meant to serve.

What makes the role so fascinating is that it sits at the intersection of structure and empathy. The RTE is there to make things work, yes—to ensure that planning events run smoothly, that dependencies are managed, and that flow is maintained—but also to nurture trust, build capability, and help people think differently. The most effective RTEs understand that their actual impact lies not in what they control, but in what they enable. They create space for teams to think, speak, and grow; they listen more than they direct; and they hold the tension between delivery and development with grace. Good RTEs excel at processes, great RTEs excel at processes and people.

This book was written to help you do exactly that. It isn't another course manual or certification guide; those already exist and do their job well. Instead, this book draws on lived experience: years of facilitating, coaching, and learning by doing across multiple industries and contexts. Between us, we've been privileged to work with RTEs, leaders, and teams from sectors as varied as pharmaceuticals, aviation, defense, technology, and government. We've also interviewed practitioners and coaches from around the world, people who've generously shared their stories, missteps, and moments of insight. Their voices and experiences run through these pages, offering a perspective that goes well beyond theory.

We've designed this book to be practical and supportive, something you can keep beside you as a companion. You'll find checklists, reflection prompts, and simple tools to help you pause, think, and act with intention. Some sections will invite you to look inward, to explore your coaching stance, your mindset, and your relationship with change. Others will focus on the outward work of alignment, flow, and facilitation. Whether you're preparing for PI Planning, leading an Inspect & Adapt workshop, or helping leaders connect strategy to execution, we hope this book provides you with both the language and the confidence to lead with purpose.

You can read it cover to cover, or dip into whichever chapter speaks to the challenge you're facing that week. It's deliberately modular, so you can return to it time and again as your journey unfolds. In many ways, it's less of a textbook and more of a coaching conversation—a space to pause, reflect, and reframe. If there's one thing we've learned, it's that every RTE's path is different. You'll find your own rhythm, your own voice, and your own way of helping others thrive.

At its core, this book is about people. Behind every feature, every dependency, and every metric, there's a story—a person trying to do their best work in a complex environment. The RTE helps connect those stories into something meaningful. We hold the space where teams can be brave, where ideas can surface, and where progress can happen without fear. In that sense, the RTE isn't just a facilitator of delivery; they're a coach for change, helping an organization learn how to learn.

About SAFe®

Much of what we discuss in this book is grounded in the **Scaled Agile Framework® (SAFe®)**, which provides a structure for applying Lean-Agile principles across large enterprises. SAFe® provides us with a shared language and patterns, but what makes it truly powerful is that it's dynamic. It continues to evolve as the global community learns, experiments, and grows. Some of the details you read here may change over time, but the underlying principles—flow, systems thinking, relentless improvement, and servant leadership—have proven to be enduring. They're the anchor points we return to again and again, both as practitioners and as coaches.

We've worked closely with our friends at **Scaled Agile, Inc.** to utilize some of their visuals and frameworks, which help bring the concepts to life. You'll find references and signposts throughout to point you toward the latest articles and resources. But it's worth remembering that SAFe's strength lies in its evolution. As coaches and leaders, we must stay curious and open to change, checking in regularly with the SAFe site for the most up-to-date insights.

The SAFe toolkits are now part of SAFe Studio, and you'll need a license to access them along with the full articles. In our view, it's a worthwhile investment. The materials are thoughtfully developed and grounded in years of practical application. If you're serious about growing in your RTE journey, the resources available at www.scaledagile.com can be invaluable companions.

One gentle caution: during our research and coaching work, we've encountered a wide range of online materials—and increasingly, AI-generated summaries—that reference older versions of SAFe. While much of that content remains useful, it can sometimes lack the depth or nuance of the latest guidance. SAFe is a framework, not a rulebook; however, when in doubt, always refer back to the source. The official SAFe site remains the single point of truth.

Ultimately, SAFe® gives us the foundation, but it's the RTE that brings it to life. It is the people who transform guidance into growth, theory into trust, and change into capability. This book is here to help you do just that.

So, whether you're preparing to step into the RTE role for the first time or are deep into your coaching practice, we invite you to approach these pages with curiosity and compassion. Use them to challenge yourself, to reflect on your impact, and to refine how you help others succeed. Because in the end, being an RTE isn't just about running a train, it's about assisting people to move forward together.

Who this book is for

RTEs come from diverse backgrounds, and success in this role isn't limited to a specific profile. Throughout this book, we'll explore how individuals with varied experiences can thrive as RTEs. Whether you're a new RTE seeking practical advice, a manager or leader aiming to support your teams and Agile Release Trains (ARTs), or an aspiring RTE curious about the role, this book is designed to meet you where you are and guide you forward. We've distilled insights from a wide range of successful RTEs to provide valuable perspectives, regardless of your starting point or current position.

What this book covers

Chapter 1, Introducing the RTE Role, defines what an RTE really is and isn't. You'll explore how this role sits at the crossroads of leadership, delivery, and facilitation, and how to approach it through a coaching lens.

Chapter 2, Your Initial Journey to Become an RTE, helps you understand the mindset shift from project management or team-level agility to system-level leadership, as every RTE journey starts differently. You'll reflect on your motivations and map your personal learning path.

Chapter 3, Interacting Within the Scaled Agile Framework® as an RTE, explores how the RTE role connects with the broader SAFe ecosystem—from Product Management and System Architecture to Business Owners and Scrum Masters. You'll learn how to balance guidance with autonomy.

Chapter 4, Understanding the RTE's Role in Launching an Agile Release Train, walks you through the preparation, facilitation, and coaching aspects that turn a collection of teams into a cohesive system. Launching a new ART is one of the most exciting and challenging experiences an RTE can have.

Chapter 5, Pre-PI Planning: Creating and Understanding the Backlog, describes the work before the big event that sets it up for success. You'll explore how to help teams and Product Managers build meaningful backlogs, manage dependencies, and ensure alignment to business outcomes.

Chapter 6, Event Logistics for PI Planning, gives you practical guidance on creating the conditions for effective PI Planning, both operationally and emotionally, from setting the agenda to designing collaboration spaces (physical or virtual).

Chapter 7, PI Planning: Day 1, teaches you that Day 1 is where the magic begins. You'll learn how to facilitate with energy and presence, manage dynamics in the room, and keep the focus on outcomes rather than obstacles.

Chapter 8, PI Planning: Day 2, explains how, as plans come together and confidence votes are taken, your role as RTE shifts from organizer to coach. This chapter explores how to help teams commit to realistic plans and leave inspired, not exhausted.

Chapter 9, Executing the PI, describes how, once the planning is done, the real work begins. You'll discover how to maintain flow, foster continuous improvement, and sustain alignment throughout the PI—even when things get tough.

Chapter 10, Coaching ART Improvements, focuses on mentorship and coaching—how to identify potential, and build capability and teams. Great RTEs don't just deliver; they develop others.

Chapter 11, Working with a Solution Train, explains how, when complexity grows beyond a single ART, you step into the world of Solution Trains. You'll learn how to apply the same principles of flow and alignment at an even larger scale.

Chapter 12, Connecting the RTE to the Portfolio, demonstrates how to align ART execution with portfolio priorities, striking a balance between strategic intent and delivery realities. We'll explore how RTEs contribute to organizational learning and cultural evolution beyond the ART alongside the Lean-Agile Center of Excellence (LACE).

Appendix A: Preparing for the SAFe® RTE Exam, provides practical guidance, reflection questions, and study tips to help you approach the exam with confidence and context for those seeking certification.

Appendix B: Building Confidence in PI Planning, offers coaching advice and conversation starters to overcome some of the harder-to-resolve concerns people may raise.

To get the most out of this book

Each chapter in this book builds on the next, but you don't have to read them in order. You can jump straight to the topic that resonates with your current challenge or curiosity.

Disclaimer about AI usage

The authors acknowledge the use of AI tools, including ChatGPT and Claude, during the development of this book. These tools were used to generate some initial outlines, refine the text for a consistent tone of voice across the three authors, and create a few images. All core ideas, technical content, and examples were created by the authors and further refined by a professional publishing team.

Download the color images

We also provide a PDF file that has color images of the screenshots/diagrams used in this book. You can download it here: https://packt.link/gbp/9781836205234.

Conventions used

There are some stylistic conventions used throughout this book.

> Warnings or important notes appear like this.

> Tips and tricks appear like this.

Get in touch

Feedback from our readers is always welcome.

General feedback: If you have questions about any aspect of this book or have any general feedback, please email us at customercare@packt.com and mention the book's title in the subject of your message.

Errata: Although we have taken every care to ensure the accuracy of our content, mistakes do happen. If you have found a mistake in this book, we would be grateful if you reported this to us. Please visit http://www.packt.com/submit-errata, click **Submit Errata**, and fill in the form.

Piracy: If you come across any illegal copies of our works in any form on the internet, we would be grateful if you would provide us with the location address or website name. Please contact us at copyright@packt.com with a link to the material.

If you are interested in becoming an author: If there is a topic that you have expertise in and you are interested in either writing or contributing to a book, please visit http://authors.packtpub.com/.

Share your thoughts

Once you've read *The Release Train Engineer Handbook*, we'd love to hear your thoughts! Scan the QR code below to go straight to the Amazon review page for this book and share your feedback.

https://packt.link/r/1836205236

Your review is important to us and the tech community and will help us make sure we're delivering excellent quality content.

Free Benefits with Your Book

This book comes with free benefits to support your learning. Activate them now for instant access (see the *"How to Unlock"* section for instructions).

Here's a quick overview of what you can instantly unlock with your purchase:

PDF and ePub Copies

Next-Gen Web-Based Reader

Free PDF and ePub versions

Next-Gen Reader

Access a DRM-free PDF copy of this book to read anywhere, on any device.

Use a DRM-free ePub version with your favorite e-reader.

Multi-device progress sync: Pick up where you left off, on any device.

Highlighting and notetaking: Capture ideas and turn reading into lasting knowledge.

Bookmarking: Save and revisit key sections whenever you need them.

Dark mode: Reduce eye strain by switching to dark or sepia themes.

How to Unlock

Scan the QR code (or go to packtpub.com/unlock).
Search for this book by name, confirm the edition,
and then follow the steps on the page.

*Note: Keep your invoice handy. Purchases made directly
from Packt don't require one.*

Part 1

The Release Train Engineer Role

In this first part of the book, we'll introduce you to the **Release Train Engineer** (**RTE**) role and its place within the **Scaled Agile Framework®** (**SAFe®**). We'll begin with a review of the role, followed by an exploration of the mindset shift from traditional project management to being a servant leader at scale for the RTE to be successful. We'll finish by introducing you to how and when the RTE interacts with the framework.

This part of the book includes the following chapters:

- *Chapter 1, Introducing the RTE Role*
- *Chapter 2, Your Initial Journey to Become an RTE*
- *Chapter 3, Interacting Within the Scaled Agile Framework® as an RTE*

1

Introducing the RTE Role

In the delivery-focused world of the **Scaled Agile Framework® (SAFe®)**, the **Release Train Engineer (RTE)** is an essential figure, steering the **Agile Release Train (ART)** toward success. As a servant leader and coach, the RTE helps multiple agile teams orchestrate their efforts, ensuring seamless value delivery while creating a culture of continuous improvement and collaboration. This chapter covers the multifaceted role of the RTE, exploring their responsibilities, challenges, and the skills required to excel in this position. We will explain what the RTE role is, why it's a critical role in SAFe, and how it compares to traditional roles, so you can understand the context of the RTE and the value the role can bring.

In this chapter, we will explore the following:

- What does an RTE do all day?
- The importance of the RTE role in SAFe®
- RTE vs Scrum Master and traditional **Program Management Office (PMO)** roles

Free Benefits with Your Book

Your purchase includes a free PDF copy of this book along with other exclusive benefits. Check the *Free Benefits with Your Book* section in the Preface to unlock them instantly and maximize your learning experience.

What does an RTE do all day?

One of the big challenges of a role in any agile framework is the killer question: "So what does your role actually involve?" You can understand why business people want to see a return on their investment, and very often, their biggest investment is in people. So, unless they can understand why these people are there, they may decide that they should not be.

The same problem occurs in any agile framework. Scrum Masters often get asked similar questions, and happily, the answer that applies to them also applies to RTEs, just scaled.

A Scrum Master's job is to deliver a high-performing team. Getting a group of people to collaborate, communicate, and deliver ever better results in ever better ways. Not only that, but they're also interested in what goes on around the team, helping to make sure that they have everything they need and facilitating the clearing of blockers out of the team's way.

If the Scrum Master's job is to deliver a high-performing team, then the RTE's job is to deliver a high-performing team of teams. In many ways, it is a similar role to a Scrum Master, just scaled up to a team-of-teams level.

This simple comparison does not make the role simple, however. The effort involved in being a great Scrum Master is often significantly underestimated. Getting complicated human beings, each with different skills, backgrounds, experiences, and life goals, to act as one single, united high-performing team can be incredibly challenging.

Now try getting *multiple teams* full of people like this to become a single, united, high-performing team of teams. The level of challenge involved just got considerably bigger.

It is for this reason that a good RTE always holds in their mind the following mantra:

> *Grant me the serenity to accept the things I cannot change, the courage to change the things I can, and the wisdom to know the difference.*
>
> —*Reinhold Niebuhr*

But how can they know this difference? The answer lies in your organizational context. In any given context, there will be things you can do and cannot (yet) do. There will be things you can change and things you cannot (yet) change.

This book will give you a comprehensive overview of all the different things an RTE could spend their days doing, along with heaps of examples of how these things work in real-world practice. However, your context matters, so please don't treat this as a comprehensive list of things you *must* do. Too often, Scrum Masters and RTEs go badly wrong when they become the process police—telling people what a framework tells them they must do and berating them when they don't follow the framework perfectly, all while ignoring what the people and teams are saying they actually need help with.

Not only does this sort of approach fail to win the battle of hearts and minds, which is so important when trying to use servant leadership approaches such as influence and persuasion, but it also mistakes a framework for a methodology. A methodology tells you what to do. A framework gives you a collection of tools and techniques to help make situations better, depending on the context.

A good analogy for this is a hardware store or a DIY shop, the sort of place you would visit for supplies when you're looking to improve your home. The store is full of different tools, paints, gardening equipment, and so much more, and it's up to you to choose the appropriate things to create the improvement you're looking to make. You wouldn't go into a hardware store, buy one of everything, and try to use it all at the same time. The result would be chaos, and probably a lot of damage too. Imagine trying to mow your lawn with a chainsaw. Similarly, trying to use all of the tools at the same time would likely be dangerous and cause you to burn out with stress.

The same is true of frameworks. They are collections of tools and techniques that have been proven to work in certain contexts and to solve certain problems, and you have to know which bits of them to use to solve which problems in which contexts. Use the wrong one in the wrong context, and it can cause harm. Try to implement them all at the same time, and you can cause yourself harm, too.

So, as you read through this chapter, always bear this idea in mind: There are many, many things a good RTE can do. A great RTE, however, knows when to use which tool in the framework, and when not to, in order to solve only a small selection of the most important problems, at one time.

You don't need to do all of it at once.

That said, what sorts of things does an RTE do to deliver a high-performing team? Let's take a look:

- Facilitating ART events, such as **Planning Interval** (**PI**) Planning, ART Syncs, and System Demos
- Supporting PI execution through making progress visible, risk management, and optimizing flow

- Driving relentless improvement by collating and analyzing data from team retrospectives to look for patterns, organizing **Inspect and Adapt (I&A)** events, tracking metrics, and running assessments
- Supporting the change more broadly via coaching others on the train, delivering training (whether formal or informal), building understanding across the wider enterprise, and modeling servant leadership behaviors

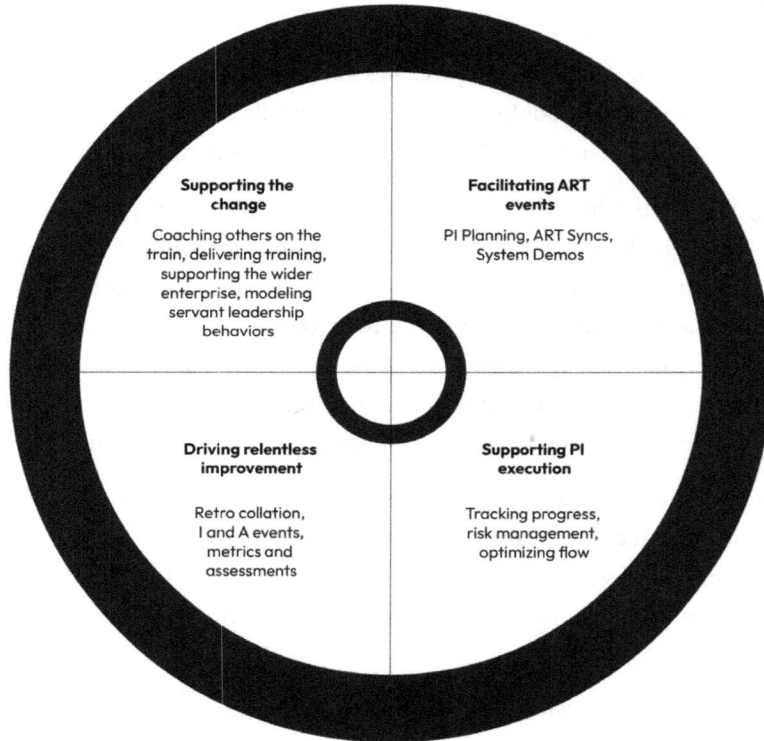

Supporting the change

Coaching others on the train, delivering training, supporting the wider enterprise, modeling servant leadership behaviors

Facilitating ART events

PI Planning, ART Syncs, System Demos

Driving relentless improvement

Retro collation, I and A events, metrics and assessments

Supporting PI execution

Tracking progress, risk management, optimizing flow

Figure 1.1: Things that an RTE does

We'll look at each of these elements in turn next.

Facilitating ART events

One of the primary responsibilities of the RTE is to facilitate ART events, including PI Planning, ART Syncs, System Demos, and I&A workshops.

To start with, though, what is facilitation? Facilitation often gets seen in two different ways. One is more effective than the other.

The simple version of facilitation is to see it as just an admin role:

- Are some people on the ART having a meeting? Ask the RTE to book the meeting room and send everyone a diary invite.

- Do these people have any good ideas in the meeting? Get the RTE to take the minutes and email the round-up of the actions afterward.

- Has senior management asked for status updates on delivery? Get the RTE to chase everyone to update their tickets in the tooling system and export a report to add to a PowerPoint deck.

This version of the RTE role is more common than it should be, and it usually results in one thing: no one seeing the value of the RTE, to the point that they get sidelined, and sometimes even sacked. The RTE sometimes even speeds this journey up by becoming so demoralized by what they are being asked to do that, to a greater or lesser degree, they *give up* and wait for their inevitable demise.

If this *admin* version of facilitation holds so little value, in contrast, the true version of facilitation can hold huge amounts of value.

In this version of facilitation, the RTE is hugely busy, hugely active, always observing, listening, watching, and noticing, to spot problems before they escalate, to connect people who would benefit from closer collaboration, to make sure that the right information is getting noticed by the right people at the right time. The list could go on and on. The best way to think of an RTE facilitating well is to see them as the conductor of an orchestra. They're not sitting in the orchestra playing any of the instruments. They're up at the front, watching the whole orchestra, keeping time for them, bringing people in, fading them out, telling them when to bring their instrument forward and when to fade it more into the background.

A great RTE conducts the people and teams on the ART to help them create beautiful music together, acting as one united orchestra, aligning around the music they're playing and how they're playing it. Just like a conductor, at the end of the performance, the RTE may be exhausted from the effort this facilitation took. Even still, they will be hugely satisfied with the triumph of the people they were conducting, and the rapturous reception and standing ovation from the people for whom they were performing.

Why is coffee the most helpful tool in an RTE's toolbox?

People often ask us what the best tool is for agile ways of working. Given that agile is all about collaboration with other people, we generally reply, "The best agile tool is video conferencing, the second best is the telephone." After all, how else do we meet the requirement of the **Agile Manifesto** to focus on *individuals and interactions over processes and tools*?

However, there is a tool that is even better than video conferencing or the telephone, and that is coffee. Coffee is what so often brings people together to talk face to face, which is a result that video conferencing and the telephone can only hope to imitate.

By inviting people for a coffee on a regular basis, the RTE can network themself across the whole ART and beyond, and stay much better connected to what is truly happening on the ground. Building social relationships through having coffee with people can also pay dividends later on, too, as the RTE builds their network of influence and support, ready for them when they need them.

You don't even need a reason for having a coffee with someone. Even if you don't fully see how, building social relationships across the ART and beyond can be hugely valuable in ways you may never have expected.

PI Planning

PI Planning is one of the most important events in SAFe®, and is often the one that brings the most value to organizations in the shortest amount of time. As such, there are whole chapters of this book dedicated to exploring how to prepare for it and how to run it. In short, though, it is where all of the teams within the ART come together to plan their work for the upcoming increment, acting as a single, aligned *team of teams*.

The RTE plays a crucial role in this event, not just managing logistics and setting the agenda, but ensuring that the team of teams produces and commits to a valuable set of objectives that the broader enterprise is keen to see delivered over the next 8 to 12 weeks. The RTE does this through multiple points during the event. At the start of the first day of PI Planning, the RTE introduces the event, reviews the purpose, agenda, and working agreements, and facilitates sessions where business context, product vision, and architectural vision are presented. During the event, they facilitate the regular sync meetings between team breakout sessions. To close out the first day, they facilitate presentation of the draft plan reviews and facilitate the management review and **Problem Solving workshop** that happens at the end.

On the second day, the RTE oversees planning adjustments, more syncs between team breakouts, final plan review presentations, and risk **ROAM**ing—the act of categorizing risks as either **Resolved**, **Owned**, **Accepted**, or **Mitigated** before culminating in a confidence vote and planning retrospective.

ART Syncs

A risk with PI Planning is that people confuse it for more traditional planning approaches and think that once the plan has been written, teams can just be left alone to deliver for the next 8 to 12 weeks of the PI. This couldn't be further from the truth. Once teams head off into delivery, they continually make small choices, changes, and revisions to what they planned to do based on what they learn through actually doing the work. This is not a problem. In fact, it is a good thing. The Agile Manifesto (https://agilemanifesto.org) tells us to *Welcome changing requirements, even late in development*, while *principle 3* of SAFe® (https://framework.scaledagile.com/safe-lean-agile-principles/) tells us to *"Assume variability; preserve options."*

Change is unavoidable, often leading to outcomes different from expectations. A poor RTE resists this shift, demanding adherence to the original plan at all costs. A good RTE monitors these changes and strives to align the teams with them. In contrast, a great RTE cultivates a network of teams capable of managing variability effortlessly by themselves, allowing them to adjust to the new plan seamlessly as if it were the previous plan. One key technique for this is ensuring regular sync meetings across the ART. On smaller ARTs, this may be a single meeting to bring together key players to check how aligned the work of the ART still is, making adaptations as new information emerges. On larger ARTs, this meeting may get split into a meeting for Scrum Masters, looking at how the work is going, and a meeting for Product Management and Product Owners, looking at what is being delivered.

Whatever the scenario, ensuring that these meetings happen and are well run and valuable to all attendees is a key opportunity for an RTE to build a high-performing and collaborative team of teams that can effortlessly handle any variability the world throws at them.

System Demos

If PI Planning looks at the *To Do* of an ART, and the Syncs look at the *Doing*, then the Demos look at the *Done*.

Getting agile teams to demonstrate their work shouldn't, in theory, be difficult. The whole root of agile is centered around continually inspecting and adapting what you deliver and how you deliver it. Getting feedback on what you've done to help you decide what to do next, getting it as often and as quickly as possible.

However, in some traditional enterprises, demos can provoke a surprising amount of resistance. At times, people are so used to filling in PowerPoint-based reports and **Red**, **Amber**, **Green (RAG)** statuses that they don't see the value of actually demoing working things to real people. In other organizations, it takes so long to build and integrate different parts of the systems being delivered that having *something to demo* every two weeks feels like an impossible ask. Others lack the psychological safety needed for people and teams to put their work up for public scrutiny, warts and all.

Regular, integrated demos are so essential to the success of SAFe® as an approach, however, that facilitating these events is a cornerstone of what an RTE should be delivering. Without them, how can we say that the work of the teams will integrate, that it remains aligned, and that what is being delivered is what the enterprise actually sees as valuable?

I&A events

Each PI closes with an I&A event for the ART. This event is made up of three parts, where the ART as a whole demos all of its progress over the last PI, then has the business value of its objectives assigned to create its predictability measure before holding an ART-level retrospective to identify process improvement activities to try out over the forthcoming PI.

All of this will require careful facilitation by an RTE. These parts may seem fairly straightforward on the surface, but how do you ensure that the PI System Demo, potentially the only one with very busy senior stakeholders in attendance, is living up to the SAFe core value of transparency and not just presenting good news? How do you ensure that the actual business value points assigned to the objectives are fair and representative of the team's work, ensuring the team isn't demoralized by scores that seem unfair? Most difficult of all, how do you simultaneously handle a retrospective for upward of 125 people, ensuring that all voices are heard without descending into arguments, and potential action items are recorded without descending into wishful thinking?

The I&A event can take significant amounts of facilitation, and it is the RTE that is at the heart of it.

Supporting PI execution

Beyond facilitating events, the RTE is deeply involved in the execution of the PI. They assist in facilitating the realization of objectives through the delivery of features and enablers, coordinating the removal of impediments, managing risks that could derail the ART's progress, and, above all else, optimizing the flow of work across the teams on the ART.

Tracking progress

An RTE needs to be careful with tracking the progress of the ART, not because it's a bad thing to do, but quite the opposite—it's an essential activity. However, the things that get tracked become what the teams focus on, so the RTE needs to ensure that they're tracking the right things. Team-level user story tracking is likely to be a level below which the RTE should concern themselves. Tracking the delivery of ART-level features and enablers is likely the right level of things to be tracking, but there is a risk that features themselves might sometimes not hold any value, at least not without other features being delivered alongside them. For this reason, we tend to prioritize tracking of the team and ART objectives. It is these that people have committed to in PI Planning, it is these that have had their business value assigned by the relevant business owner, and it is these that deliver the outcomes the business wishes to see achieved. Remember that we want to track outcomes, not outputs. Spend time monitoring the outcomes achieved, and less time tracking the delivery of the outputs that might achieve those outcomes.

One other element to remember is that an RTE's job is to help ensure that people and teams are focused on relentless improvement, so including an element of tracking backlog items generated from each Problem Solving workshop can be an extremely important element in achieving relentless improvement, too.

Risk management

Risk management is an often-overlooked element of an RTE's role. After all, we may have a department in the enterprise called *Risk*, and so shouldn't it be their job to worry about risks?

In short, no. Different enterprise risk management models exist, but a common one is the **three lines of defense** model. The first line of defense is the people on the ground doing the work. The second line of defense is then the risk team, which helps set the standards for the first line to follow, while the third line of defense is an audit team that checks the work of the second line risk team. As a result, the primary defenses against organizational risk sit with the teams doing the work, and it is the RTE's job to support those teams.

SAFe® has its own model for risk management called ROAMing, which we referred to earlier in the *PI Planning* section. However, teams often need to be encouraged to capture risks as they move through PIs, and helped with the formats used for capturing and storing them, which are usually unique to an enterprise. The RTE also needs to ensure that risks are tracked, updated, and reported in whichever cadence is most useful for the context.

A lot of this activity doesn't come naturally to teams doing the work, but it can have considerable positive impacts when handled well. A great RTE should be well-versed in risk management and how it works in their organization. They should help others minimize risks and continuously improve both what they deliver and how they deliver it.

Optimizing flow

Version 6.0 of SAFe® was semi-informally known as the **Flow Release**, as the framework made a significant shift to focus on promoting flows of work within an organization. Therefore, a vital responsibility of the RTE is to optimize the flow of value through the ART. There are lots of different ideas, principles, and practices that can contribute to promoting the flow of work, but ones especially relevant to an RTE include establishing pull- rather than push-based systems, making sure teams are matching their load to their capacity, reducing wait times, and removing cross-team dependencies.

Value stream identification or value stream mapping?

The idea of a **value stream** (the series of steps that work moves through from the initial idea to *done*) is an integral one to the concept of **flow**. However, there is sometimes confusion between the terms **value stream identification** and **value stream mapping**. So, what's the difference?

Value stream *identification* is the (relatively) simple act of identifying the steps in the delivery process, surfacing where value streams exist. It identifies the different stages, people, teams, and so on that work moves through from its initial concept to being live and in use by end users. It's a technique for which SAFe has a dedicated toolkit to use to run a workshop around. It is the typical starting point when initially designing ARTs within an organization. This way, we can bring together all of the teams involved in a type of flow of value into a single ART to help create alignment and minimize things that can slow down flow, such as dependencies, handoffs, and rework.

On the other hand, value stream *mapping* is a technique used to understand how well work is flowing through the value stream. It involves tracking work through the end-to-end delivery - gathering data on how long a piece of work is spent being actively worked on at each stage and how long it sits waiting to be worked on. A comparison between the time an item spends being worked on and the time it sits waiting to be worked on can show the overall flow efficiency of the value stream, and help identify bottlenecks and other delays that can then be removed to increase the flow.

In short, value stream identification identifies the different parts of a value stream. Value stream mapping actively looks at how well work flows through that value stream in reality.

Driving relentless improvement

Relentless improvement sounds like a good thing. Making improvements is good, so doing it all the time must be really good. It isn't even just *a SAFe® thing*. The idea of continuously inspecting and adapting what you deliver and how you deliver it is there in *Scrum*, it's there in *Lean*, it's there in *principle 12* of the Agile Manifesto:

> *At regular intervals, the team reflects on how to become more effective, then tunes and adjusts its behavior accordingly.*

The sad reality is that meaningful improvement activity in large organizations can sometimes be rare. Given that it is an RTE's job to drive relentless improvement, this is something an RTE needs to be conscious of, along with the reasons behind it. If improvement activity sounds so good, why do so few people do it?

The main reason is that improving something means changing something, and changing something is hard. In hierarchical organizations, things such as process design, team structures, workflows, tooling, environments, technology strategy, and so on are seen as under the control of senior leaders, with those impacted by the decision unable to influence them. Even though the people on the ground often most directly experience the impacts of poor decisions in these areas, they often have the best ideas for how to solve these problems, too. People and teams end up in a situation of *learned helplessness*, and just put up with the issues, all while idly dreaming of being a senior leader one day who could actually fix these problems.

In heavily regulated environments, organizations often dictate processes, policies, and procedures in order to feel in control of how people comply with the requirements the regulator gives them to meet. As a result, challenging and wanting to change how something is done is seen as a huge and fundamental risk to the organization's survival, so any such activity is, in reality, heavily discouraged.

There is also the very simple fact of inertia. In organizational systems that make it difficult to get things delivered, people work so hard to get anything done that they just don't have the time and headspace to try and improve things. Or perhaps their working environment is so difficult that they've just checked out of engaging with it, so they don't see the point of trying to improve anything anymore. The problem with inertia, though, is that organizational systems are subject to the second law of thermodynamics, just like everything else in the universe.

If you don't know it, the second law of thermodynamics introduces the concept of entropy. Put simply, things degrade over time. So, if you set an organizational process, the process won't stay at that level of performance forever. Over time, it will start to degrade. Shortcuts will be found. People will find reasons why they don't have to follow the process anymore. As a result, at the very least, you need relentless improvement activities to stand still, let alone reach escape velocity and reach even higher levels of performance and success. With that said, how do you square this circle and help create the relentless improvement that organizations so often desperately need, but so rarely achieve?

It's hard to draw precise boundaries around which RTE activities are *relentless improvement* and which fall into other categories, as the idea of relentless improvement is so integral to how a great RTE approaches anything they do. However, some definite activities can help the RTE build a culture of relentless improvement across those they serve and the wider organization as a whole.

Pattern identification

SAFe® promotes systems thinking. That means not looking at individual parts of an organization or process, but looking at how those parts join together into broader systems, in which the parts interact with each other in different, sometimes unexpected, ways. In systems thinking, the focus is far less on "Are employees performing well?" and much more on "Have we created an organizational system that enables people to bring their best selves to their work?". As W. Edwards Deming said,

> *The people are already doing their best, the problems are with the system. Only management can change the system.*

Deming wrote that many years ago, in the days before SAFe, and we would argue both that management in large organizations has often proven itself to be relatively ineffective in improving organizational systems and that the RTE role is ideally placed for stepping into this gap that many organizations experience.

The RTE works across multiple teams, which together form a system. Therefore, the RTE's job is to help optimize the wider system, taking a step back or a *helicopter view* of what is going on and looking for areas for improvement.

One important way to do this is to look for patterns in data, in behavior, and in problems that are emerging. Are many different teams all running into the same issue? Does work always tend to slow down in one part of the value stream? Are there consistently crisis meetings to deal with issues in production? People stuck in the detail of this work often don't have the time, visibility, or influence to notice these wider patterns. The RTE should have all of those things, and is perfectly placed to work on improving the wider system as a whole.

Problem Solving workshops

Once the RTE has spotted patterns in problems, however, how do they address them? Well, the temptation is to be the *senior leader* who drives forward their resolution personally. But to do so would be to miss the point of what it is to be an RTE.

It is not the RTE's job to fix problems. It is the RTE's job to make sure that problems are being fixed. This is a significant difference.

There are some problems that the RTE can fix themselves, and fix relatively quickly, and in these cases, they should do so. If person A doesn't know who to approach to get something done, then the RTE can connect them with the right person. If many people struggle to know who to speak to about different things, perhaps the RTE can put together a *Who's Who?* guide for the ART and the broader ecosystem around it. If a problem can be fixed quickly and simply, then all is good.

However, there are a number of risks of the RTE being the only person who solves problems. The first is burnout. If every problem comes to the RTE, the chances are that they will soon become overwhelmed, burned out, and ultimately, less capable of fixing any problems at all. The second risk is that if the RTE assumes responsibility for problems, others on the ART may feel less empowered to manage their own environment and shape their own future. It reduces their sense of autonomy, which harms our approach to *principle 8* of SAFe®:

> *Unlock the intrinsic motivation of knowledge workers.*

The third risk is related to a SAFe principle as well, *principle 9*:

> *Decentralize decision-making.*

If an RTE tries to solve a problem, they apply just their brain to the problem. If everyone on the ART collaborates to solve a problem, they apply upward of 125 brains to the problem.

Which approach do you think is more likely to lead to better solutions to problems?

It is for exactly this reason that one of the key events on an ART is the Problem Solving workshop. We'll talk more about this later in the book, but the workshop is, in essence, a retrospective held across everyone on the ART, to address issues that are typically bigger than a single team can fix. Following a well-proven approach, the teams work through problems to identify their root causes, then identify solutions (or more accurately, *countermeasures*) to address the root cause problems, before planning them in as activities in the subsequent PI Planning event.

In this way, these workshops are instrumental in promoting a culture of relentless improvement and ensuring that the ART evolves and adapts to meet changing needs.

Metrics and assessments

Lean-Agile approaches are typically empirical approaches. That is, they use the scientific method to look at objective facts about how things are before deciding how to improve them. A key component of this, therefore, will be data, which, in turn, can be used to create metrics and assessments.

Data, metrics, and assessments have to be handled carefully. Their usage is only as good as the quality of data that goes into them, and if people are creating inaccurate data in the first place, the decisions taken on that data will likely be suboptimal.

In addition, setting metrics can change behavior in both positive and negative ways. For example, some organizations set targets to have zero bugs in production. Typically, this just causes people to stop reporting bugs in production, meaning the bugs have greater production impacts than before. A metric set for teams to increase their velocity typically just causes them to increase their story point estimates, so a piece of work that previously added 20 points to their velocity now adds 30 points to it with no additional effort. As an RTE, it is always important to think through the impact a metric might have on human behavior, and how people might try to *game* the metric to paint an alternative picture of reality.

There is also an issue around psychological safety. In organizations where people fear personal repercussions from things going badly or being seen to go badly, people collecting data, promoting metrics, and running assessments can be viewed suspiciously or even with downright hostility. We know of more than one occasion where HR has been called in to stop assessments after people have made formal complaints.

Empirical approaches using robust data to evaluate the status and decide where to go next are hugely valuable and at the heart of Lean-Agile approaches. We only advise you of these risks so that you can be aware of them.

Finally, only capture data if it will lead to a decision. Collecting it for the sake of collecting it, generating no insights or improvements, is a form of waste.

Quality standards

High-quality work is essential to the smooth flow of work. This isn't the time to deeply consider flow accelerators and how they all fit together, but for now, just consider these simple examples:

- Team A does a piece of work and passes it to Team B. The work does what Team B needs it to do, so they do their work and pass it to Team C. The work does what Team C needs, so they do their work and pass it on to operations to run in production. Operations run the work in production, and it sits there working with zero production issues.

- Team A does a piece of work and passes it to Team B. The work doesn't work as Team B needed it to, so they pass it back to Team A to fix. Team A has already started work on a new piece of work, so they have to put that down, remind themselves what the last piece of work was, and fix it before passing it back to Team B. Meanwhile, Team C sits there with nothing to work on.

- Team A does a piece of work and passes it to Team B. The work doesn't work as Team B needed it to, but their manager tells them to ignore the bugs and just get on with it. Team B passes the work on to Team C, now with additional bugs introduced by Team B because of workarounds they had to implement, caused by Team A. Team C does their work and passes it on to operations to run in production. Operations try to run the work in production, but it keeps on creating big production issues, which Teams A, B, and C have to be pulled into fixing at random times, interrupting the next things they were delivering.

Which of these scenarios has the smoothest flow and gets the most work delivered?

Without high-quality work, we regularly experience delays, increased costs, confusion, and harmful customer impacts.

An RTE can impact quality standards on their ART in various ways, but one important method is by ensuring that teams and ARTs establish clear **definitions of done**. These definitions serve as the repository of quality standards that must be met for any work to be deemed complete and ready for delivery to customers.

Supporting the change

Sometimes, a new RTE gets to not just do the role but to support the organizational change activity that is moving to SAFe® and creating new training. We find this a particularly exciting and invigorating part of the transformation (but then we are biased as change agents). If you get the opportunity to be involved in such an endeavor, we encourage you to embrace it.

There are four key disciplines you can apply during such an activity.

Coaching others on the train

If the RTE's job is to deliver a high-performing team of teams, then coaching people on the ART is a key aspect of this. Coaching itself is a huge field of study that we cannot cover in detail here, but for now, the important elements to remember are as follows:

- Meet people where they are, not where you'd like them to be. If someone is beginning their agile journey, help them make small steps that deliver value for them early, rather than handing them a textbook and telling them to read it from start to finish.
- Simplify jargon where possible, using language that *includes* rather than *excludes*.
- Help them solve their problems, and ensure they are actually their problems, not problems you expect them to have.
- Avoid becoming the *process police* and enforcing every framework element with a rod of iron from Day 1. Change is a matter of both hearts and minds, and telling people that they're *doing it wrong* is not the way to win friends and influence people.
- Know when to propose solutions to problems, and when to help people uncover the solutions themselves.
- Remember that failure is a very impactful way to learn, so leave space for it where it is safe to do so.

Delivering training

Another way to support the change is to run formal training sessions, often using the licensed SAFe courses provided by Scaled Agile, Inc., assuming you are a certified **SAFe Practice Consultant (SPC)** with a current, non-lapsed certification. The agile world is full of arguments about the value or otherwise of externally provided, certificated training, but we can only speak from our own experience. In the right circumstances and provided by the right people, formal training can really help.

In terms of the circumstances, there are some important things to look out for when rolling out a successful training approach. Typically, we want to train people as close as possible to them using the skills they learn in their everyday practice. Training 1,000 people and then only launching one 100-person ART every 3 months is likely a waste of time, as by the time the final people get to experience PI Planning, their training in it will have taken place years ago. The quick start approach SAFe® recommends, where you launch an ART in a week, with two days of training followed by two days of PI Planning, may seem rapid compared with the pace of some organizations, but it can be hugely effective.

A more difficult but no less important issue can be ensuring that the people attending the training see the value of attending. More than once, we have been caught up in situations where the training has become *sheep-dipping* of people. Tell everyone that they must attend a two-day course whether they want to or not, set targets around the number of people trained to date, and try to make the class sizes as big as possible to hit the targets as quickly as possible. No one enjoys this approach, no one benefits from it, and no one learns anything. The irony is that Lean-Agile approaches are all about pull rather than push. People pull work toward themselves rather than having it pushed onto them. Ideally, the people you are training should have pulled themselves onto the training, rather than had it pushed into their diaries.

Supporting the wider enterprise

We've covered many of the points in this topic already in different ways, but never forget that the limits of an RTE's work are never just the boundaries of their ART. If we're applying systems thinking to our work, then the ART is likely just one component of a wider organizational system. The ART will be influenced by this wider system, just as the ART will influence this system in return.

A great RTE will make time to understand this wider system and understand why it behaves as it does. This can take time and a degree of treading carefully as you go, but an RTE should never be afraid to meet with, talk to, and influence those in the wider organization, just as they do with the people and teams on their own ART.

The only thing to call out here is the risk of the RTE getting pulled into so many conversations external to their ART that their own ART starts to suffer and derail. Changing organizations can become addictive, and there is often far more work to do than one person can do alone. Remember that as you coach others to limit their own **Work-in-Process (WIP)** and focus on delivering the most valuable work that takes the shortest amount of time, you also need to apply these disciplines to yourself.

Modeling servant leadership behaviors

At the heart of the RTE's role is the philosophy of servant leadership. Servant leadership is one of the schools of thought in the academic field of leadership studies. Its creation is credited to Robert Greenleaf, who famously said,

> *The servant-leader is servant first. It begins with the natural feeling that one wants to serve. Then conscious choice brings one to aspire to lead. The best test is: do those served grow as persons: do they, while being served, become healthier, wiser, freer, more autonomous, more likely themselves to become servants? And, what is the effect on the least privileged in society; will they benefit, or, at least, not be further deprived?*
>
> —*Greenleaf, R. K. (1977). Servant Leadership, p. 27.*

Larry Spears then went on to build on the work of Robert Greenleaf, and set out 10 key characteristics of servant leaders (*Spears, L.C. (2010). Character and Servant Leadership: Ten Characteristics of Effective, Caring Leaders*):

- Listening
- Empathy
- Healing
- Awareness
- Persuasion
- Conceptualization
- Foresight
- Stewardship
- Commitment to the growth of people
- Building community

As seen from the preceding excerpts, unlike traditional leadership models that emphasize power, hierarchy, authority, and control, servant leadership focuses on empowering and supporting people and teams to reach their full potential. The RTE embodies this mindset, prioritizing the needs of the ART and those on it, while creating an environment where self-organizing and self-managing teams can thrive.

But what does this mean in practice?

The day-to-day practice of servant leadership can, of course, vary depending on your context. However, some typical examples include the following:

- Listening more than talking, and providing a safe space for people to share their concerns
- Supporting people to solve their own problems, rather than telling them what you think the solution is
- Doing what people and teams need you to do, not getting them to do what you want them to do
- Seeing team members as people, not resources
- Encouraging the growth, development, and learning of people on the ART, even if that means less focus on *delivery*
- Persuading people of new ideas based on empirical evidence, rather than *pulling rank* and insisting that your way is correct
- Understanding and empathizing with the *whole person* for each person on your team, dropping, to some degree, the professional mask you each wear in the workplace
- Creating a psychologically safe space for people to challenge each other in a constructive way, resulting in them ganging up on the problem, not each other

To some people, these sorts of ideas sound like fluffy, hippy nonsense that gets in the way of *driving teams forward* or *rolling up your sleeves and delivering*. However, the journey to being a great RTE over time often uncovers multiple moments where you realize just how important, impactful, and relevant the preceding ideas actually are.

A personal anecdote

Years ago, Gez was in one of his first professional roles at a small tech start-up. Being a small company, the specific role each person held was blurry, but in essence, he was driving the delivery of a number of different products for the company. At the time, he felt like he knew what the products needed to look like, how they needed to be delivered, and what each person in the team needed to do in order to deliver what he wanted them to deliver. The team members sometimes didn't seem that happy with him or what he said, but that didn't matter; as far as he was concerned, it was clearly them not understanding the complete picture and what needed to be done. The more upset and disillusioned they became, the more apparent it seemed to him that the increasing lack of progress was entirely their fault. If only they'd listen to him more!

Over time, though, team members started to develop some quite good ideas—sometimes by suggesting them, sometimes by just telling him that they'd already implemented them. As they did so, he realized that perhaps he didn't hold all of the answers, and maybe these resources on the team were capable of good ideas, too. The more he listened to their ideas, or just allowed them to get on with implementing what they thought was the best thing to do, the better things became.

Eventually, a fundamental truth struck him. He had one brain, while these 10 team members had 10 brains between them. Ten brains can do far more thinking than one brain, especially when they work together collectively to solve problems. Ultimately, there was no way he could ever know better than this team because he had only 10% of their thinking power.

So he learned to let go and use his one brain to support whatever those 10 brains needed to be successful. Unsurprisingly, his projects started to be much more successful, too, and his customers grew both happier and greater in number until he found himself not working for small organizations on small projects but instead working directly for two different Prime Ministers of the UK.

It was then that he discovered the true value and importance of servant leadership.

Having offered an introduction to the role of the RTE, let's look at how the role compares and contrasts with other roles in SAFe®.

The importance of the RTE role in SAFe®

Great RTEs are hard to find. The RTE sits right at the heart of SAFe; the RTE needs to be charismatic enough to facilitate events with hundreds of people. They need to be able to manage relationships with senior stakeholders and help unblock issues that lots of clever people have already tried to address. They need to be able to coach teams and people to deliver more value and, at the same time, create a culture of psychological safety.

They might not manage Scrum Masters, but as the chief Scrum Master for the train, they need to be able to lead. If you're going to lead, you need to have a vision for where you want to go and how you'll get there. The RTE will also have to translate what is going on with the business and work closely with the system architect and Product Management to realize their vision.

The RTE has to be able to navigate the tools and systems to understand where they can make improvements using the flow accelerators.

The RTE will also work closely with the PMO or the Value Management Office (VMO) to ensure that they are reporting on all the most important metrics and that everything is rolling up to the portfolio.

RTE vs Scrum Master and traditional Program Management Office (PMO) roles

Having explained what the RTE role is, it is useful to highlight how the role is different from other roles within the organization that you might already be familiar with. One of the dangers in any agile framework or methodology is the immediate analogy that people make between old and new roles; for example, the Scrum Master is just like the team lead. Knowing and being able to call out differences will enable you to differentiate this critical new role.

RTE vs. Scrum Master

Isn't the RTE just a scaled Scrum Master? With SAFe® being a fractal model, going from the team to the ART level, the direct equivalent of the Scrum Master is the RTE. In some respects, this is true, but the RTE will take a broader, more holistic view.

Both roles, when executed well, come from people with similar servant leadership characteristics and a desire to see people grow through coaching and development. In addition, the purpose of both roles is to enable the teams to deliver successfully, optimizing the ways of working from start to finish.

The Scrum Master has a narrower focus. While the Scrum Master serves both the team and ART, it does so through the lens of the mechanics of delivery. They care about how their own and other teams operate and deliver.

By comparison, the RTE takes a zoomed-out view of the entire ART. The RTE looks inwardly at how the team of teams is performing and looks outwardly into the organization for coordination, optimization, and impediment removal. From an economy-of-scale point of view, it makes sense that you have a single person who takes the lead beyond the ART.

As part of this outward view, the RTE commonly thinks beyond the mechanics of delivery, getting involved with such topics as budgets, reporting, and staffing profiles.

When working within the ART, the RTE typically works through the Scrum Masters and Product Owners. Sometimes, we use the analogy that the Scrum Masters are the RTE's lieutenants.

RTE vs. PMO or Program Manager

You are likely familiar with what a PMO and Program Manager do, as most enterprises have them as part of their current working practices, working to help align delivery across multiple initiatives. However, when looking at the SAFe® big picture, they do not see themselves featured. The lack of a home creates anxiety, resulting in either them resisting the move to SAFe, or trying to find an equivalent role they could do.

It is this role matching where they land on the RTE. It's easy to say that the roles have similarities, but as has been outlined already, there is a mindset change required to be successful in the role, and mindsets do not change overnight. This mindset change results in behavioral changes and the intent of how they interact.

Does this mean that everyone in your existing PMO, as well as Program Managers, need to wrestle for the few RTE jobs? No, because in large enterprises, particularly in the earlier stages of transformation and in a government or regulated environment, there will always be coordination or reporting beyond the ART, portfolio, or even the organization.

While the RTE in some instances assists with these, and in some organizations they do, there will sometimes be economies of scale by having others outside the ART doing them, giving the RTE time and capacity to focus. Examples include the following:

- As an escalation route for issues and risks.
- People capacity and capability management. Aligning skills and utilization across the ART. Looking forward to future capability demands based on the solution roadmaps.
- Coordinating and implementing minimum viable reporting on actionable metrics.
- Managing the ART budgets, particularly in a fixed or annual funding cycle, ensures that future funding demands are captured and approved by appropriate fiduciaries.

At the heart of Agile and SAFe is the value of transparency. So, it is not surprising that the ART should clearly articulate progress, performance, and issues it needs help with. The RTE is best positioned to do this on behalf of the ART.

The following table summarizes the differences in focus between the PMO Lead, Program Manager, and RTE.

PMO Lead	Program Manager	RTE
Track delivery	Manage delivery	Facilitate delivery
Track	Decide	Enable
Ask/tell	Tell/ask	Ask and guide
Focus on what is being done	Focus on what is being achieved	Focus on how it is being done
Conduit for reporting; a repository of data, tools, and templates	Use data to drive delivery	Use data to improve delivery
Focused on representing the work of the teams	Focused on driving the delivery of the teams	Focused on supporting the teams

Table 1.1: Comparing the PMO Lead, Program Manager, and RTE roles

As you can see, there are similarities and differences between these existing roles. In *Chapter 2*, we will explore in more detail various previous backgrounds and roles that RTEs might come from, exploring the pros and cons they bring.

Summary

In this chapter, we have begun to introduce the RTE role, noticing that it is one of the most important roles in the entire framework. As we have seen, the closest comparison to the RTE role is that of Scrum Master, with both roles delivering high-performing teams or teams of teams. Like a Scrum Master, an RTE is a change agent skilled in influence and persuasion, helping reshape collaboration and delivery. A great RTE knows a framework is a collection of tools for different jobs and that organizational change is ongoing, not a final destination. Imposing too much or wrong change at the wrong time can cause resistance, burnout, and failure.

Within the RTE role, we saw that there are four primary categories of activity that an RTE undertakes: facilitating ART events, supporting PI execution, driving relentless improvement, and supporting the change.

When it comes to facilitating ART events, we distinguished between two types of RTE: one that merely runs the administration of the events, and a better type that proactively and skillfully facilitates the events in achieving successful outcomes.

A great RTE doesn't just use ART events for keeping the train on the tracks; they proactively support delivery throughout the PI itself, tracking progress while ensuring the focus is on outcomes rather than outputs, ensuring that risks are being managed appropriately, and above all else, optimizing the flow of work across the teams from funnel to done. Nothing builds confidence like delivery.

This work is supported by the RTE's focus on relentless improvement, not just ensuring that teams are continually inspecting and adapting how they work, but operating at a higher level, looking for patterns in problems across teams, and helping to optimize the delivery system as a whole, carefully using data and metrics as appropriate, and ensuring the quality remains high at all times.

All these elements are enabled by the RTE's role in supporting the move to more Lean-Agile ways of working across the organization, be it through coaching, training, or modelling behaviors. Great RTEs exemplify how a new world can look, paving the way for others.

Finally, we compared the differences between an RTE and other roles such as a Scrum Master, Program Manager, or member of a PMO. We saw that while their focus areas can sometimes be similar, the importance of an RTE lies in how they approach the work, maintaining a system-level view rather than getting lost in the details, focusing on the how more than the what, and above all else, guiding and supporting rather than controlling and directing.

With the outline and boundaries of the RTE now explored, in the next chapter, we will move on to examine how people become RTEs, looking at a typical job description for the role, some common career paths people take before becoming an RTE, and the knowledge, skills, and experience you will likely need to gather in order to become a great RTE.

References

Here, you can find the links to expand your knowledge about the specific concepts not covered in this book but referenced in this chapter:

- Agile Manifesto: `https://agilemanifesto.org`

- Greenleaf, R. K. (1977). *Servant Leadership*, p. 27

- SAFe® principles: `https://framework.scaledagile.com/safe-lean-agile-principles/`

- Spears, L.C. (2010). *Character and Servant Leadership: Ten Characteristics of Effective, Caring Leaders*, The Journal of Virtues & Leadership, Vol. 1 No. 1, pp. 25–30

Get This Book's PDF Version and Exclusive Extras

UNLOCK NOW

Scan the QR code (or go to `packtpub.com/unlock`). Search for this book by name, confirm the edition, and then follow the steps on the page.

Note: Keep your invoice handy. Purchases made directly from Packt don't require one.

2

Your Initial Journey to Become an RTE

So, did *Chapter 1* pique your interest in becoming an RTE? It is a fun, dynamic, and challenging role for sure, but one that positively impacts the outcomes of the organization and the lives of those on the **Agile Release Train (ART)**. The challenge most organizations face is that they will not have an existing role directly related to the RTE. Therefore, finding someone to fill the RTE role without additional competency development is unusual.

Whether you aspire to be an RTE or aim to develop a staff learning and development pathway toward it, this chapter outlines the steps—guiding you through self-development, gaining experience, and achieving certification—to give you the confidence to perform the role and become genuinely competent.

In this chapter, we will explore the following:

- The RTE job description
- Building basic knowledge
- Grounding yourself in SAFe® and the mechanics of the ART
- Exploring the RTE role

The RTE job description

Let's start our journey by reviewing a typical advert for an RTE role and exploring the skills and capabilities needed. We will also reflect on the usual starting points from which those who become an RTE will come.

Job Overview

We seek a dynamic and experienced SAFe® **Release Train Engineer** (**RTE**) to join our growing team. As the RTE, you will be at the heart of our **Agile Release Train** (**ART**) and responsible for guiding and optimizing the flow of value using the **Scaled Agile Framework®** (**SAFe®**). This pivotal role involves facilitating Agile events, managing risks, and driving relentless improvement to ensure successful PI Planning and execution.

Key Responsibilities

- **Facilitate PI Planning**: Coordinate and lead **PI Planning** events, ensuring clear alignment between ART stakeholders and teams.
- **Coach Agile Teams**: Provide servant leadership to Agile Teams, Scrum Masters, and Product Owners to foster a collaborative environment and maximize team performance.
- **Risk Management**: Track and manage risks using the ROAM technique, ensuring risks are addressed and mitigated throughout the PI.
- **Continuous Improvement**: Drive continuous improvement through Inspect and Adapt workshops and support relentless improvement across the ART.
- **Flow Optimization**: Use flow metrics and tools such as Kanban to improve the flow of value across the ART, helping to reduce bottlenecks and optimize delivery times.
- **Foster Transparency**: Enhance visibility through regular synchronization events such as ART Syncs, system demos, and PI Reviews.
- **Promote DevOps and Continuous Delivery**: Champion automation, built-in quality, and DevOps practices to streamline delivery and ensure alignment with Lean-Agile principles.

Skills & Qualifications

- **SAFe Certified RTE**: A current SAFe RTE certification is required.
- **Agile Expertise**: Deep understanding of SAFe principles, Lean-Agile practices, and Agile frameworks (**Scrum, Kanban**).
- **Leadership**: Strong servant leadership skills, capable of inspiring and coaching teams while focusing on collaboration and empowerment.
- **Problem-Solving**: Proven ability to identify and resolve complex issues hindering ART progress.
- **Communication**: Exceptional verbal and written communication skills to facilitate effective collaboration between cross-functional teams and stakeholders.

Experience
• Experience with scaling Agile using SAFe® in large organizations • Familiarity with DevOps pipelines and tools • Minimum of 5 years working in Agile environments, preferably in large-scale software development projects • Strong organizational and planning skills with attention to detail • A software development, engineering, or Product Management background is a plus

Table 2.1: A typical advert for the RTE role

So, if you want to become an RTE or recruit internally and externally, this chapter will help you and them on their journey.

We won't delve into the role's myriad details, as *Chapter 1* has already covered them. However, as the job advert shows, the position demands a broad range of skills and experiences that might not align with traditional roles within your organization. This may prove not easy to find in a single individual.

Therefore, when organizations recruit internally for an RTE, there will typically be some requirement for upskilling to fill in the gaps in capabilities. Looking externally isn't always an easy answer, as good RTEs are in short supply. Be prepared for some development needs when considering this route.

Where do RTEs come from?

Good RTEs often come from diverse backgrounds. During organizational transformations, we're frequently asked where staff can fit into new roles such as RTEs. However, the necessary mix of capabilities and mindset means there's no straightforward answer.

One of the aspects that distinguishes a good RTE from a great one is organizational networking, which includes political nous, situational awareness, and strategic thinking (understanding the context), along with deep organizational knowledge. All organizations have *shadow systems* within them. These are the methods by which things get done, and often differ from the organizational chart. If the RTE isn't aware of these informal networks, having someone who can guide them will expedite their effectiveness.

When people join an organization from outside, they don't have the necessary knowledge, networks, and connections. They may know the theory and how these things have worked elsewhere, but they will take time to learn how the organization works. Developing rather than hiring has trade-offs, and like most things in life, there is never a silver-bullet easy answer.

So that you can consider the potential starting places, we've outlined some of the more common positions that we find RTEs originating from and explored the generic pros and cons these starting points bring. This isn't an exhaustive list, but it will help you reflect on the journey to becoming a competent RTE.

Program and Project Managers

Program or Project Managers are not a bad starting point, as there is a reasonable overlap with the RTE job description. They are often the first port of call to source an RTE, as they understand delivery from the team to the broader organization.

Even in an aligned, mature, Agile enterprise, many moving parts and differing demands must be addressed. With battle-scarred experience, they have gained the political acumen to navigate the enterprise and overcome the quirks of working in a large organization.

The biggest potential challenge is the mindset shift from command and control to servant leadership. The RTE plays a supportive role, helping remove barriers and developing the team's competencies as they work toward a common goal. Consequently, if they have a more traditional project mindset, numerous behavioral traits need to be adjusted. If this is the case, assigning a guide or mentor will speed up the mindset change.

> **Isabella's story—one Program Manager's journey with Agile.**
>
> As a Program Manager, Isabella had spent many years applying traditional project management approaches to programs and transformations. Coming from a finance and operations background rather than technology, she quickly recognized the applicability of SAFe® across many disciplines when she first encountered it as part of an enterprise change program she was involved in.
>
> As part of the change program, she had the opportunity to be a Scrum Master for a team on a new ART. She recognized that she had to learn to apply Lean and Agile thinking beyond mere theory and overcome the little project management voice in her head. She became an excellent Scrum Master, developing a deeper appreciation for the role and the principles she had studied during her Agile training.

With her experience in managing programs and her ability to see the bigger picture, it was no surprise that she stood out and was selected as an RTE on an ART shortly after. Upon assuming the role, she delivered a humbling introduction at the start of PI Planning, saying she would do her best but recognized that old habits are deeply ingrained and that she might falter. She encouraged the ART to hold her accountable, promising to do the same for them when they slipped up, too.

It wasn't all plain sailing. She initially struggled with Product Management, not feeling comfortable knowing whether the backlog was suitably crafted and later being able to guide new Product Owners.

When we interviewed Isabella for this book, she recalled that SAFe® helped her examine what was going on, connect the dots, and put it together in a way that was working. She told us, *"I think I had to really go outside of my comfort zone, deep-dive, and learn a lot of new things."* Being prepared to learn and invest time and practice was crucial for Isabella, and it became apparent to her when stakeholders around the ART were not doing so.

She went on to say that to be successful, an RTE needs to overcome the challenges of behavior change and the importance of open communication, collective effort, and adherence to new ways of working while learning.

Avoid the trap of simply relabeling your existing people and processes

Sometimes, during some SAFe rollouts, we have found that organizations wish to utilize their existing internal personnel to fill their new RTE roles, and we have encouraged this. However, their approach is merely to rename their existing Project and Program Managers as RTEs and consider the job done.

These individuals have merrily continued to use their project and program management approaches, showing little interest in how SAFe, or any Agile methodology, might propose alternative methods. In one memorable instance, the SAFe adoption began to falter within a single PI, as the Program Managers started drafting and disseminating reports regarding the *percentage completion* of each PI objective rather than assessing them based on the value they delivered to the business. One RTE even began their **draft plan review** at their first PI Planning by stating, *"Remember, we're not an ART,"* and subsequently discussed all the work they were committing their teams to deliver, which exceeded the teams' capacity to deliver.

Changing the names but not the practices quickly misses the point of the introduction of SAFe®. To keep the change activity honest and successful, have the support of someone who knows what good looks like and understands the underlying principles that drive the practices outlined in the framework.

Scrum Masters

Experienced Scrum Masters who want to develop themselves and challenge themselves with more responsibility have much to offer the RTE role. They have the right mindset and values needed to operate successfully. They also understand the Lean and Agile principles and can coach people to success.

However, they may lack experience operating at scale or working across the wider organization. Do they have the contacts and ability to navigate outside the world of SAFe to serve the ART well? Depending on their experiences, they could have lived a sheltered life in the organization and might not have had exposure to the financial and procedural practices of the corporate world. These are learnable but can be overwhelming if you are new to them. Consider getting a mentor with this broader enterprise experience to short-circuit this learning.

A word of warning

You need to ensure they don't have the agile chip on their shoulder and cannot enact change. We have experience with those where everything that's wrong with how the team works is the fault of the unnamed *them*, or it all has to do with *leadership*, a signal of not taking ownership. While this can be because that person has been put in a position with no power or influence, they could also be ineffective at change management and influencing others.

Therefore, it is useful to understand how they have operated before and what their worldview is during an interview or similar to test this.

Lean-Agile coaches

Like Scrum Masters, extensive corporate awareness can be a weakness, depending on their experiences. Like the Scrum Master, though, they should have the right mindset and values to operate successfully. If they are a **SAFe Practice Consultant (SPC)**, they will also have a strong working knowledge of the practices of SAFe across many roles within the ART.

Coaching is a vital aspect of the RTE role, but equally important is the ability to execute tasks, which may sometimes involve setting a direction and driving change. A coach may face difficulties making progress without the flexibility to combine coaching and leadership. Knowing when, as a leader, to establish the direction of travel and next steps rather than adopting a more facilitative coaching approach, letting the team decide, enhances their effectiveness.

Technical Leads/Managers

You might think that having a technical background would be helpful to an RTE. While having some domain knowledge is advantageous in some situations, they risk using it to get stuck in the details and not take the step-back view they need to.

They will understand the intricacies of the development processes and the strengths and weaknesses of the **continuous delivery pipeline**, so they should have lots of ideas for improving things. If this isn't you, your System Team will have it covered, so don't worry.

Again, Managers, such as Project or Program Managers, will need to consider the challenge of moving from a telling to a supportive mindset and associated behavioral changes.

So, the ideal sweet spot for finding good RTEs is a combination of existing organizational knowledge and networks and a willingness to consider that there might be new, better ways of doing things.

Now that we know the role's shape and potential sources of candidates, let's examine what someone moving into the RTE role needs to know and be able to do, should you be in a position of needing an RTE, rather than being one.

Developing RTEs

The first step is to choose people as RTEs with experience assisting with large-scale deliveries across more than a team or two. Think of Program Managers more than Project Managers. Being an RTE isn't an entry-level role; it requires some previous experience to be done well. Before embarking on the role, people should at least have practical hands-on experience in getting things done at scale, which will provide a whole host of transferable skills for an RTE role.

The next thing to do is not rush them into an RTE class, but start with a more generic and introductory SAFe® class. We recommend **Leading SAFe** as the best overview of the framework, PI Planning, and its different roles and events. Once they have attended Leading SAFe, consider putting them through some other SAFe courses, too. Incidentally, this tip also applies to Scrum Masters, team coaches, and other roles where people will coach and support colleagues.

Within the online Scaled Agile platform, **SAFe® Studio**, an online framework and knowledge ecosystem, there is a self-paced, online SAFe Release Train Engineer Essentials class designed to bridge the gap in the framework articles. It provides coverage of the introductory topics, and an RTE will find it helpful in the early days.

The intention is that if RTEs are going to be coaching and supporting people in other roles, such as System Architects, Product Managers, and teams more broadly, then they should learn what those roles are being recommended to do. So, once your prospective RTE has taken a Leading SAFe course, consider putting them through some other relevant SAFe courses, such as Product Owner/Product Manager, SAFe for Architects, SAFe Scrum Master, and SAFe DevOps.

In short, if you want to help someone become a great RTE, you should first teach them some of the other roles in the framework so they will know more about the people and work they will support.

Another excellent way for people to learn is by giving them the opportunity, if they desire, to conduct training themselves. Teaching something is a compelling way of increasing your knowledge of it. Not only does teaching require you to learn things, but repeating those things in class after class will help cement your knowledge and consider the topics from different angles—not to mention the huge benefits you get from having random strangers ask you left-field questions about the framework regularly. You often have to go and research these questions, causing you to learn yet more things.

It's one thing to know the theory; it's a different thing to understand it deeply. For this, we need to gain hands-on experience in the various elements of the RTE role, which we'll move on to look at next. Before we do, though, consider one final point about training. Good trainers know the material that they're teaching. Great trainers have directly experienced the ideas they teach in real life. This allows them to introduce the concepts and bring them to life with *war stories* of what they tend to look like in practice. So, don't see training and practicing as separate things. Great RTE trainers are great RTE practitioners, and great RTE practitioners are often great RTE trainers, if this is something they want to do.

Building basic knowledge

To take a holistic view of what a successful RTE needs to know and be able to do to enable the flow of valuable work, we need to go back to the beginning and remind ourselves of the core of Lean and Agile, so our foundations are strong. This is helpful if you are looking to develop the capability for your organization or want to improve your own skills to do the role.

The underlying Lean-Agile principles are the bedrock of the RTE's context.

Lean and Agile foundations

It is critical that the RTE has a deep, well-rooted understanding and is welcoming of the principles and practices of agility. We truly want the RTE to be agile rather than do Agile. The RTE holds a critical position as a leader within the agile organization, and without them embodying the mindset and behaviors we want the train and broader organization to adopt, the business outcomes desired from using the Agile way of working will not be achieved.

Knowing the heritage of Lean and Agile will help an RTE build mental models upon which everything else is constructed and enable their narrative when supporting the change activity in Agile adoption.

Our suggested background reading includes the following:

- *Agile Manifesto* (`http://agilemanifesto.org/`): This is where it all started: the 2001 meeting of the leading minds at the time, which defined the now famous **Agile Manifesto** and a set of 12 guiding principles to empower a focus on delivery over the process. While crafted in the language of software, reading it today, 20+ years later, substituting *software* for *solutions* expands it, showing it is just as relevant in other disciplines, be that cyber-physical or business processes.

- *The New New Product Development Game, Harvard Business Review* (`https://hbr.org/1986/01/the-new-new-product-development-game`): This article inspired Ken Schwaber and Jeff Sutherland, the co-authors of the Scrum framework, to believe that there was a better way for team collaboration and product delivery to operate. It describes how a cross-functional team (here, rugby players) works together toward a common goal in short, focused periods, getting points, being aligned to a common goal, and winning the game.

- *Lean Thinking, Womack and Jones* (`https://www.simonandschuster.co.uk/books/Lean-Thinking/James-P-Womack/9780743231640`): This seminal book documented the ways of working of the Japanese manufacturing base, known as Lean. The awareness raised by the book took Lean from an obscure concept with little awareness outside of car manufacturing to a broader, particularly Western, audience in many industries.

In SAFe® and the industry globally, Scrum and Kanban are the most popular Agile methodologies. Consequently, RTEs will need to have a reasonable understanding of the practices, the values and principles which underpin them, and typical optimization patterns.

As the ART coach, the RTE, directly or through the Scrum Masters, has to be able to support flow optimization. In organizations new to agility, the RTE might not be able to rely on the Scrum Masters having deep experience or knowledge in these working practices. Even if the RTE is lucky enough to have Agile Coaches or support through the **Lean-Agile Center of Excellence (LACE)**, they need to be able to support the ART in improving and know how to do it so that, collectively, the ART works in unison.

The SAFe framework website is a sensible starting point to learn about the basics of both Scrum and Kanban. Plus, you cannot move for content introducing you to the basics of Scrum and Kanban on the internet.

Some have conflated the practices that many bundle as Scrum with the essence of Scrum. Consequently, we recommend you read the latest *Scrum Guide* (https://scrumguides.org/) and observe how much it doesn't tell you to do compared to the common assumptions about what Scrum is.

To learn more about Kanban, we recommend reading David J. Anderson's book, *Kanban*, which some refer to as the *blue book* because of its now well-recognized front cover. Being comfortable with Kanban is a core skill for the RTE, as it's possible to explain SAFe through the loosely linked hierarchy of Kanbans from the portfolio down to the team.

Family relationship builder—the refrigerator Kanban

Having learned the basics, why not apply it to the team you work with today, or use it at home? We've heard about many successful family Kanban boards on the refrigerator door at home. You'll be surprised how much you get done, and your loved ones will appreciate all the jobs they've been nagging you to do to get done, too. If we ever meet, you can thank us later!

Grounding yourself in SAFe® and the mechanics of the ART

Having laid the foundations of Lean and Agile, we can build upon them to understand SAFe. The first port of call will be the body of knowledge that is the SAFe framework website, www.scaledagileframework.com.

However, many people find learning in an experiential, curated way helpful. To this end, the first formal training class we recommend is *Leading SAFe® with SA* certification. During the two days of learning, you will be introduced to SAFe, the role of leading an Agile organization, and the underlying principles behind the practices. You will then experience the core SAFe practices.

Key capabilities

One way of describing the RTE role is that of an enabler. They enable teams, with the support of the Scrum Masters, to be the best they can be. They enable the ART to align and think with a hive mind. They enable the broader organization, particularly during a transformation, by standing between the ART and legacy processes and policies that hinder flow.

Enabling is leading without telling. Three core capabilities are needed to perform well in enablement: **servant leadership**, where you set a vision and support others in working toward it; **facilitation**, where you hold the room together, being present but not influencing; and **coaching**, where you support the growth of others, believing that they alone know what is best for them and how to improve.

Servant leadership

Even the title **Servant Leader** tells you the priority that you should take. Servant first, leader second. Enabling the ART is to serve the ART. To serve the ART, the RTE will paint the picture of the vision of the future and the goal the ART is working toward, but then support and serve the ART to reach that goal in the best way they can. Those on the ART know best, as there are 120 of them and one RTE. Brain-power maths says 120 wins every day!

Knowing it when you see it

I [Glenn] remember quite clearly when I saw my first true demonstration of servant leadership. I was working for a digital agency on a project for a university as the Agile Coach and team Scrum Master. At one point, we needed to purchase a software license that the team required to complete the project. They had asked me, and with the shackles of large corporate command and control still in place, I rang the founder and asked for permission to buy it. His response was an awakening for me. He asked questions. "Is it the right thing for the client and the project?" and "Does the team think it's the right thing to do?" and lastly, "Why are you asking me?"!

From this experience, the theory of servant leadership I had been reading about became real to me.

In the same way that you would expect a good Scrum Master, when probed about something on behalf of the team, to say, "I'll ask the team," the RTE at the ART level should say, "I'll ask the ART." This simple and somewhat subtle change in response to providing an answer demonstrates the mental shift required to be a servant leader. In practice, the RTE will coach those they ask to reflect on options and their pros and cons. This approach of not having all the answers is a suitable proxy for the correct mindset of a Servant Leader.

In addition to our suggested reading, we recommend you find a good example of an RTE and observe how they work and what they say and do to learn first-hand what it means. The two original thought leaders in this space are the following:

- Robert Greenleaf (`https://www.greenleaf.org/`)
- Larry Spear (`https://www.spearscenter.org`)

Facilitation

A practical skill to enable the ART is the ability to facilitate. There are two elements to this: facilitating conversations so people gang up on the problem, not each other, and facilitating a group working session, such as a workshop or PI Planning.

The former requires deep listening skills and conflict management, whereas the latter enables conversations and thoughts to progress to a desired end without interfering with the group's process. For now, we will focus more on the latter.

A good facilitator generally stays neutral to the content of the work but owns the process of helping the group reach its destination. Therefore, you need to be aware of the power you bring, as you command a presence standing at the front of the room. If you are not careful, you can move from facilitating to directing.

To remind ourselves of this, Michael Wilkinson, founder of Leadership Strategies, writes about it in *The Power of the Pen* (`https://www.leadstrat.com/the-power-of-the-pen/`). In a situation where you are documenting what the group is saying, if, as the facilitator, you change their words as you write them, you are no longer neutral. You also signal that you do not value their words and inputs. If you are to summarize, asking for confirmation that you captured their intent keeps the power with the group, not you.

Remember also that the RTE job spec clarifies that the RTE will facilitate PI Planning. If the ART has 10–12 teams in attendance, Business Owners, and others (such as shared services) present too, the room can easily reach 140 people. So, you had better feel comfortable not only being in front of a room with 140 pairs of eyes staring at you, but also having the presence to guide those people through the process. But don't worry if the performance element of PI Planning makes you uncomfortable—presentation skills or even an evening theater class can help prepare you for this.

As you start your journey as an RTE, the benefit of PI Planning is that the agenda and process have already been scripted for you in SAFe®, enabling the focus on executing the event.

Coaching

Last but not least, one of the three core capabilities to enable ART is coaching. People development math shows that a 5% improvement in 100 people will always be better than a 100% improvement in a single person. Therefore, the RTE needs to enable improvements within the ART and those who interact with it.

Like servant leadership and facilitation, coaching is the skill of helping, through empowerment, someone or some people to improve. Enabling this development, in the purest coaching sense, does not include telling them the answers, but rather guiding them to find the resources they need to satisfy their goals, honoring our desire to lead, not tell.

A popular and simple to use coaching process is the **GROW model**, which stands for **Goal, Reality, Options,** and **Will or Way Forward**. It is a popular and simple coaching process. It provides a structured approach for a coach to facilitate the conversation of improvement:

- **Goal**: Ensure the end state is clear and specific to the person looking to make a change. As an RTE, you will have set the vision for the ART, so help them align the objective with the overarching needs of the ART.
- **Reality**: Understand the current context, the challenges, and the opportunities of the situation, enabling a deeper understanding.
- **Options**: Enable the coachee to see the possible options of how to reach the desired goal.
- **Will or Way Forward**: This approach makes changes possible by clarifying and instilling confidence in the coachee's desire to change, using discrete steps to make the change happen.

Now that we've covered the foundational elements, it's time to explore the RTE role itself.

Exploring the RTE role

Since **SAFe® 6.0**, the framework has introduced responsibility wheels, which articulate in a consumable format what the role needs to achieve for many elements, including the RTE.

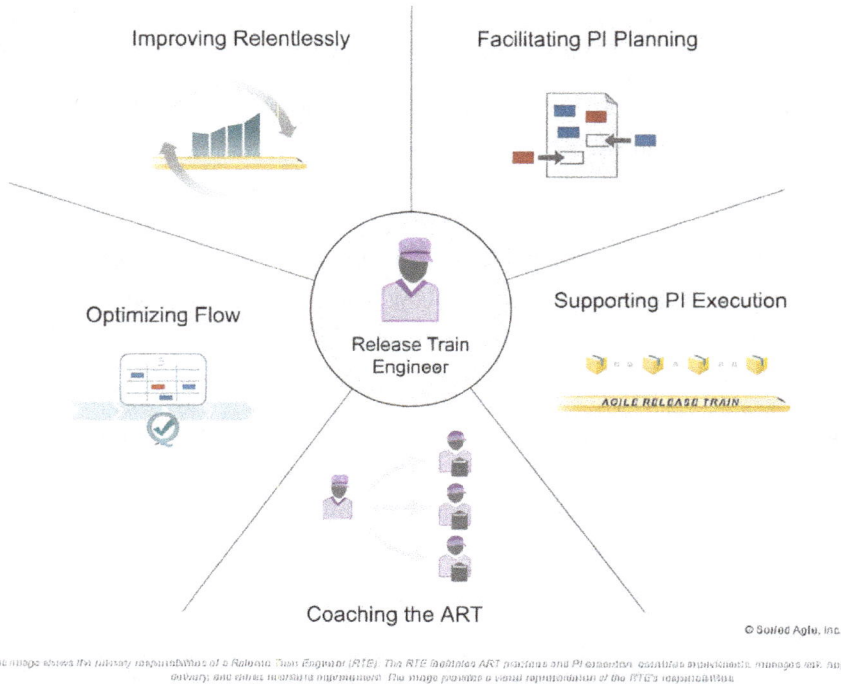

Figure 2.1: The SAFe RTE responsibility wheel (Image source: `https://scaledagileframework.com/release-train-engineer/`)

The framework clearly describes these, and we encourage you to reflect on these elements and consider the additional reading offered to deepen your understanding.

A paid SAFe Studio account (typically available after training, through an enterprise license, or paid subscription) includes an introductory e-learning course, *SAFe Release Train Engineer Essentials*, to accompany the public-facing framework guidance. This self-paced course covers the basics of performing the RTE role and provides many additional learning elements.

Gaining experience leading to certification

The SAFe® Release Train Engineer certification course has been designed to work slightly differently from those for other SAFe roles. Other classes are designed to introduce you to a topic, gain the core knowledge, and then, following an exam to validate your learning, provide certification.

The SAFe RTE class is designed not just to teach, which it does as well, but also to emphasize encouraging you to reflect and collectively learn through the shared experiences of the cohort. Consequently, RTEs should only attend once they have experienced the role for at least one PI, ideally a minimum of two to three PIs.

> While the class can be run internally in a private setting, there is value in going to a public version. Doing so provides a diversity of thinking and experiences from RTEs from other organizations. Our experience is also that people find it helpful to understand that the challenges they experience are not unique and are familiar to others.

Getting practical experience

At this point, having consumed a lot of knowledge, it is time to apply it. As Destin Sandlin says in his *Smarter Everyday, Backwards Bicycle* video (https://www.youtube.com/watch?v=MFzDaBzBlL0), *"Knowledge does not equal understanding."* It is through the application of knowledge that both your understanding and skill in applying it develop.

So, how do you gain that experience without already being an RTE? While this is not an exhaustive list, we've included a range of activities you could do to get hands-on experience and start building your understanding and skills:

- Shadow an RTE.
- Step in for the RTE, helping to facilitate some elements of key activities:
    - PI Planning
    - Facilitating ART Syncs
- Inspect & Adapt (I&A)
- Participate in communities of practice:
    - RTE, more to learn from others
    - Scrum Master and Team Coaches, to develop coaching and facilitation skills

- Coach small groups of Scrum Masters.

- Get a mentor—someone who can provide regular feedback and help you identify opportunities for growth.

- Review data in tooling and create hypotheses to improve. Practice data analysis and improvement cycle.

- Work with the LACE. Practice the leading, not telling, suite of skills through your organization's LACE.

- Read Paul Aker's *2 Second Lean*, and embed the behavior in your day-to-day life. This will tune your personal radar to see waste and the improvement processes to overcome it (`https://paulakers.net/books/2-second-lean`).

Summary

In this chapter, we have explored the role through the lens of what organizations will advertise it as in a job advert. Knowing an employer's requirements helps you develop your knowledge, skills, and experiences to fulfill the role.

We explored the basic knowledge needed to be successful, starting with the founding principles of Lean and Agile, which act as the role's bedrock. Providing yourself with a stable base of knowledge and understanding will enable you to be successful. With the foundations in place, we examined how to grow your knowledge of team-level processes, specifically Scrum and Kanban, before introducing the scaling practices that SAFe® provides. Finally, we outlined the journey to gain experience, the benefits of studying to gain experience, and the benefits of learning from others.

Now that you have this fundamental knowledge, *Chapter 3* looks at how the RTE works within the framework more specifically.

References

Here, you can find the references to expand your knowledge about the specific concepts not covered in this book but mentioned in this chapter:

- Manager Tools. (n.d.). *Manager Tools podcasts on coaching*. Retrieved [Month Day, Year], from `https://www.manager-tools.com/map-universe/coaching`

- Whitmore, J. (2002). *Coaching for performance: Growing people, performance and purpose*. Nicholas Brealey Publishing. Retrieved from `https://www.performanceconsultants.com/resources/coaching-for-performance-book/`

- Wilkinson, M. (n.d.). *The power of the pen*. Leadership Strategies. https://www.leadstrat.com/the-power-of-the-pen/

Exercise

Create your personalized development plan: As an adult professional, you own your personal development plan as you become and master the RTE role. A good starting point is to reflect and feel free to seek external help to act as a mirror on your current capabilities against those of the RTE role. Perform a gap analysis, which can guide your personalized action plan to improve.

Consider using this tool to support your reflection: https://agilityhealthradar.com/safe-rte-health-radar-assessment-2/.

Get This Book's PDF Version and Exclusive Extras

UNLOCK NOW

Scan the QR code (or go to packtpub.com/unlock).
Search for this book by name, confirm the edition,
and then follow the steps on the page.

*Note: Keep your invoice handy. Purchases made
directly from Packt don't require one.*

3

Interacting Within the Scaled Agile Framework® as an RTE

By now, we've established what the **Release Train Engineer (RTE)** is and where they come from. But knowing the role's definition isn't enough—we need to dive deeper into the real work of an RTE: the interactions, the collaborations, and the influence they have across the **Agile Release Train (ART)** and beyond.

At its heart, the RTE role is about people. Yes, we deal with flow, processes, and governance, but ultimately, we are here to create an environment where teams and stakeholders can thrive. That means working with a wide variety of roles within **SAFe®**—**Scrum Masters**, **Product Managers**, **System Architects**, **Business Owners**, and many more. But it doesn't stop there. RTEs also build bridges across the wider organization, ensuring alignment at every level, from the **Agile Teams** up to the portfolio.

If you think about a high-performing sports team, there's more to success than just talent on the field. There's coaching, leadership, strategy, and support behind the scenes, making sure everything runs smoothly. In many ways, the RTE plays that behind-the-scenes role, ensuring that the ART functions as a cohesive unit rather than a collection of independent teams.

In this chapter, we'll explore the many interactions that an RTE has and why they matter. We'll look at how we collaborate with our immediate ART leadership team, how we support Agile Teams, and how we scale our influence beyond the ART to the Solution Train and portfolio levels. This chapter will lay the groundwork for understanding the full scope of the RTE's relationships, with later chapters offering deeper, hands-on guidance on working effectively with each of these groups.

In this chapter, we will explore the following topics:

- The RTE and the ART
- The definition and role of an ART
- Your first team
- The RTE and organizational support structures in SAFe®

Let's begin by looking at the RTE's first and most essential relationship: the ART itself.

The RTE and the ART

SAFe is a **fractal model**. We take the ideas and principles that work with teams and then scale them to higher levels. So, as an RTE, we take inspiration from the Scrum Master and Team Coach roles and apply that to the ART. In essence, we take what works for a team and apply similar ideas to a team of teams.

There is no shortage of literature on coaching, but still, we find that all too often, it is that discipline that gets lost for RTEs. Many organizations don't seem to value the role of coaching, although this seems to be changing within the community. Over the years, businesses and leaders tend to see those who are focused on delivery, rather than those who help optimize delivery, as being of more value.

However, if you look at other industries (we often pull from sports teams as they are accessible for most people), you can see the impact a coach can have on teams and the people and culture that surround them.

The story of Coach Carter

When explaining Agile concepts, I [Tim] often draw from movies. For the RTE, my movie of choice is *Coach Carter* with Samuel L. Jackson. In *Coach Carter*, and I don't think I'm giving away any spoilers in saying this, Samuel L. Jackson plays a basketball coach for a high school team. What I find interesting about the movie is the different roles he must play as a coach with all the stakeholders. To the team, he must motivate and inspire them. Many of the players have grown lazy over the years. A level of arrogance has crept in and become a bitter root, primarily due to their celebrity status within the school. Coach Carter needs to instill a work ethic within the team. For Carter, the goal goes far beyond basketball; it is about what their talents can unlock, which is the actual prize for the players.

The ultimate goal is to become college players so they can have a shot at a better future. Yes, Carter needs to do many things you would expect a coach to do. He runs drills to get them in shape: *"I cannot teach you the game of basketball unless you are fit enough for me to do so."* He runs plays, drawing inspiration from fictional girl-friends—communicating in a language that high school boys understand. You can probably guess what happens in the movie, but the point is not the fairytale ending, but the journey that the team and the people that surround them go on to reach for something that they never felt possible.

The movie is a wonderful example of how a coach interacts with different people. Change is hard, and everyone needs something slightly different. It is fascinating to see how his behavior differs, given his ultimate goal. As a result, he has to build relationships with all sorts of characters, such as the parents and the other teachers. He makes tough decisions when the team doesn't meet their commitments, all with a higher purpose.

Now, let's consider how *Coach Carter* relates to the RTE and how we must communicate in SAFe®. Just like Carter, the RTE wears many hats and tailors their approach depending on who they're working with. With teams, the RTE creates the space for focus, rhythm, and growth, fostering a mindset of continuous improvement and collective purpose. With Product Managers and System Architects, they challenge thinking, remove obstacles, and ensure the right conversations happen at the right time. With leadership, they translate day-to-day realities into strategic insight and hold the mirror up when commitments aren't matched by delivery.

Coach Carter doesn't just run drills, and neither does the RTE. You're not just managing events or chasing reports. You're helping individuals and teams see what they're capable of, even when they don't yet believe it themselves. You balance inspiration with accountability, encouragement with challenge. And most importantly, you never lose sight of the higher purpose, delivering value in a way that grows people, builds capability, and moves the enterprise forward.

But while intent and leadership matter, scaling that across dozens or even hundreds of people introduces a new kind of challenge—one not just of motivation, but of communication, coordination, and complexity.

The complexity of scaling

We know that the more people we have within a team, the more challenging it can be to communicate effectively. Although it seems obvious, we find visualizing the number of lines of communication helpful with stakeholders. We often use the following diagram, which shows the complexity and the number of connections in groups of people:

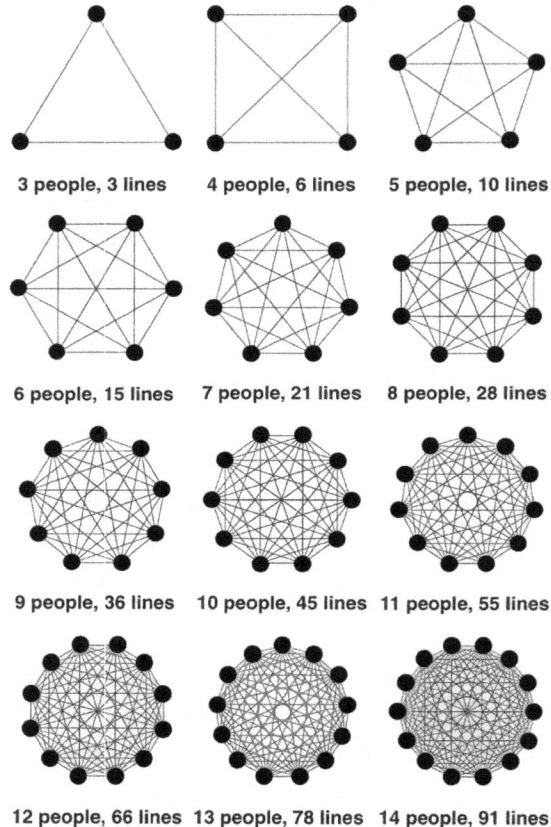

Figure 3.1: Lines of communication

If you've got a team of three people, then you've only got three lines of communication. A team of 4 people, and we're up to 6 lines, but by the time we have 50 people (a small ART), we've got 1,225 lines of communication between all of the people in that team. If you're interested, you can use the following formula to calculate it for your team:

$$N = N^*(N\text{-}1)/2^*$$

Simply put, as W. Edwards Deming said, the system must be managed; it will not manage itself, and so we have to find a way to make sure that everyone knows what everyone else is doing. Not only that, but with that degree of inherent complexity, just imagine how easy it is for people to miscommunicate, especially with complex information.

Our goal is to create a construct that will not only help us streamline communication but will enable us to maintain a sense of team and allow us to develop strong relationships with the people that we're working with on a day-to-day basis. If we get that right, everyone will understand the collective priorities and be able to make informed decisions about what they should do next. We also need to do this in a way that inspires and motivates them and maintains the sense of team that you get from working closely with just a handful of people.

One of the main thought leaders we draw from for inspiration is Robin Dunbar, a British anthropologist who researched primates' brains. He established that there is a certain number of interpersonal relationships that a human brain can sustain. Based on the previous formula, he noted that social communities break down after 150 people, 11,175 lines. We can see that throughout history, with villages, platoons, churches, and so much more. Therefore, we must consider how we will bring all these people together to maintain productive relationships with one another.

Like Coach Carter, you won't be able to do this alone. You'll need support from those around you to ensure that people feel motivated and engaged. The complexity doesn't stop there, either. We also need to consider all of the people with whom the ART will have to interact to get work done.

As an RTE, here are some of the most common people that you'll work with on a day-to-day basis:

- **Team level:**

    - **Scrum Master/Team Coach:** Servant leader for Agile Teams, ensuring a reliable application of Scrum or Kanban as a team-level approach to getting work done, involving holding a mirror up to the team, the removal of impediments, managing the inter-team dependencies, and facilitating team-level events

    - **Product Owner:** Represents the customer within the team, or even better, connects real end users directly to the team, while prioritizing the team backlog to maximize value delivery and accepting the work of the team as done

    - **Agile Team:** A cross-functional group of people responsible for delivering features in iterations or a flow-based system, combining developers, testers, and other roles needed for value delivery

- **ART level:**

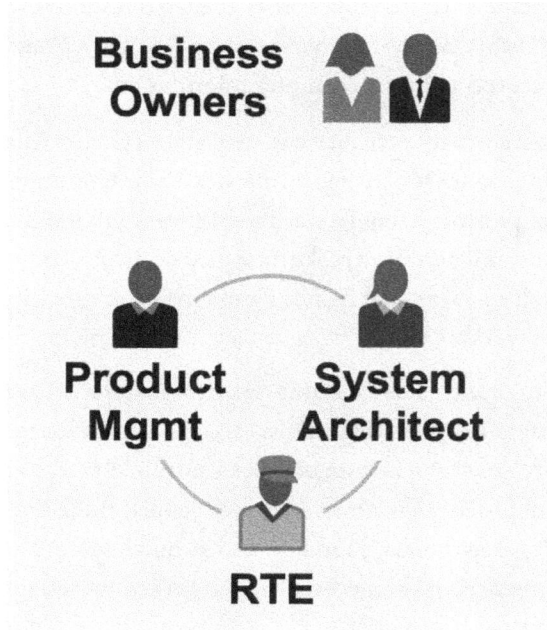

Figure 3.2: Key ART level leadership roles (© Scaled Agile, Inc. Source: `https://` `framework.scaledagile.com/safe-6-0-configurations/`*)*

- **Product Management:** Owns the ART backlog, working with Product Owners in teams and Business Owners more broadly to define and prioritize features based on business value

- **System Architect:** Provides technical direction, ensuring alignment with architectural standards and scalable solutions across the ART

- **Business Owners:** High-level stakeholders responsible for business outcomes, often the people who are paying for the work, while offering direction and making key decisions during ART events

- **Large solution:**

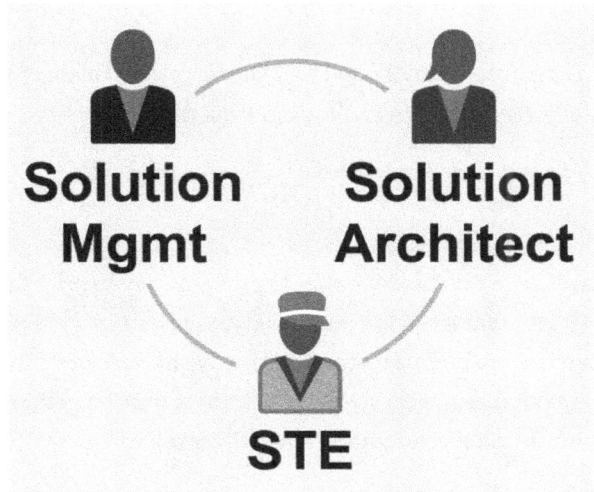

Figure 3.3: The Solution Train leadership triad (© Scaled Agile, Inc. Source: `https://framework.scaledagile.com/safe-6-0-configurations/`*)*

- **Solution Train Engineer (STE):** Coordinates multiple ARTs involved in delivering complex solutions, ensuring that large-scale solutions are aligned across all ARTs

- **Solution Architect:** Provides architectural guidance at the solution level, ensuring large systems' technical integrity and scalability

- **Portfolio:**

  - **Lean Portfolio Management (LPM):** Aligns the portfolio's strategy with execution by funding value streams, spreading work across investment horizons, and prioritizing epics

  - **Epic Owners:** Drive the development of large-scale business or technical initiatives (epics), working across teams to define, implement, and deliver

  - **Value Management Office (VMO):** Supports and facilitates the LPM capability, supporting oversight and governance of the portfolio

Before we go into more detail, let's look at what an ART is, and then we'll unpack those roles, clarifying their responsibilities so that you're equipped to work with them effectively.

The definition and role of an ART

> *The Agile Release Train (ART) is a long-lived team of Agile Teams that incrementally develops, delivers, and often operates one or more solutions in a value stream.*
>
> —*Scaled Agile Framework®*

What does that mean in practice? We should probably have a prize for the number of times we say that SAFe® is a fractal model. When teaching, we say it in every lesson. We're taking the idea of a team and scaling it up to build a team of teams. We like the term *tribe*; it captures the essence of what we're trying to achieve with an ART. We want to bring together teams that would otherwise be alone, to communicate, collaborate, and deliver together.

Not all teams have to be part of an ART, but when we're operating on the same value stream, we will likely run into significant dependencies. Rather than tripping over each other, we want to ensure that we collectively understand what all the teams are doing and that we're all pulling in the same direction. We're trying to build a simple, collective system of delivery, and as W. Edwards Deming said, *"Left to themselves, components become selfish, independent, competitive profit centers, and thus destroy the system."*

By forming a long-lived team of teams, we can start to break down some of the barriers that are inevitable if we're thinking in silos. It doesn't matter how good your team is; if you're pulling in a different direction from everyone else, you will slow things down. Therefore, our goal is to communicate where we're going effectively and then, as a team, play a part in delivering value to the customer's benefit.

PI Planning and the Planning Interval

The way that we align everyone in SAFe is by taking the familiar idea of a Sprint or an iteration and scaling it up to work with the team of teams. We want to ensure that all the teams are planning together on a regular cadence. Similar to a **Sprint** in Scrum, we create a timebox that we're going to plan for, but this time for our team of teams, the ART. Typically, our timebox will be 8–12 weeks, which starts with bringing everyone together for a big high-level planning event called **PI Planning.** We'll talk more about that in *Chapter 5*.

Before we go into more detail, though, we should have a look at the people that you're going to be working with on a day-to-day basis.

Your first team

One of our favorite books about teams is *The Five Dysfunctions of a Team* by Patrick Lencioni. In this book, Lencioni emphasizes the importance of considering the concept of your *first team*. When thinking about agility at scale, or any enterprise transformation, you will interact with lots of different teams, from LPM to the Agile Teams developing the solutions.

We know from Robin Dunbar that the number of social connections you can meaningfully maintain is limited, so it's important to prioritize the relationships you will need to focus on as an RTE. Your *first team* consists of the people with whom you're going to build the closest relationships. We're now going to have a look at some of those roles to understand their world a little better.

The ART leadership SAFe® roles

As an RTE, your first team will be composed of Product Managers and System Architects. You will have to work closely with these people to ensure that all aspects of Agile at Scale are successful. You will need to work with them to refine the backlog, coach the ART in executing the PI, and build strong bonds. This is important not only for facilitating various events but also for coaching the ART to help them improve and ensuring that the flow of value to the customer is enhanced.

Product Management

Product Managers have a tough job. Their role is to define desirable, viable, feasible, and sustainable solutions that meet customer needs. They are also responsible for supporting development across the product life cycle and ensuring that the products deliver value to the customers and the business. As there will always be more work to do than there is time, money, or inclination to do so, the Product Managers need to say "no," or at least "not yet," which inevitably makes people upset that their request is not being progressed.

Top tip: empathy maps

One of the best tools to better understand your customers is the empathy map, but there is so much more to it than just understanding your customers. You can use the empathy map to empathize with just about anybody; we're all people, after all. In this case, we can take the idea and apply it to the different roles in SAFe®.

To show you how this works, we'll start with the empathy map of our good friends, the Product Managers.

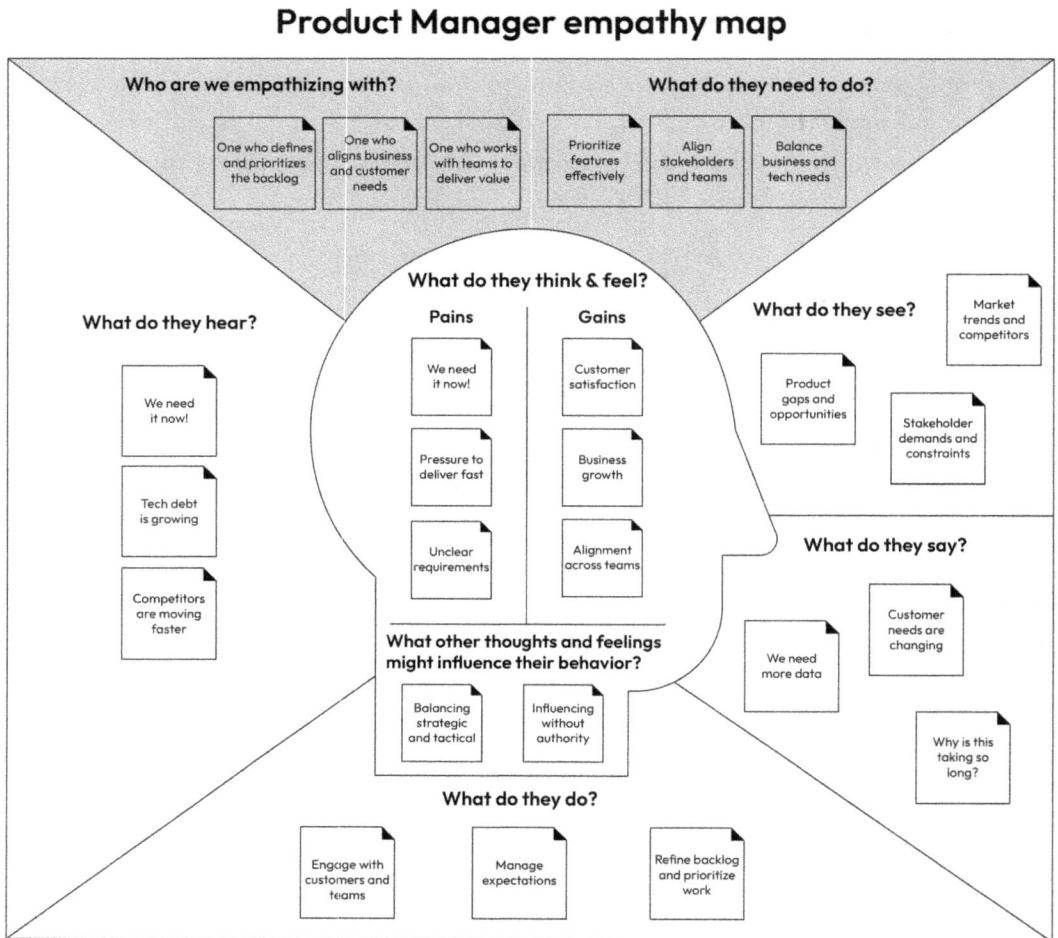

Product Manager empathy map

Who are we empathizing with?

- One who defines and prioritizes the backlog
- One who aligns business and customer needs
- One who works with teams to deliver value

What do they need to do?

- Prioritize features effectively
- Align stakeholders and teams
- Balance business and tech needs

What do they think & feel?

Pains
- We need it now!
- Pressure to deliver fast
- Unclear requirements

Gains
- Customer satisfaction
- Business growth
- Alignment across teams

What do they hear?

- We need it now!
- Tech debt is growing
- Competitors are moving faster

What do they see?

- Market trends and competitors
- Product gaps and opportunities
- Stakeholder demands and constraints

What other thoughts and feelings might influence their behavior?

- Balancing strategic and tactical
- Influencing without authority

What do they say?

- Customer needs are changing
- We need more data
- Why is this taking so long?

What do they do?

- Engage with customers and teams
- Manage expectations
- Refine backlog and prioritize work

Figure 3.4: Product Manager empathy map (inspired by Dave Gray, Xplaner.com; online empathy map here: `https://gamestorming.com/empathy-mapping/`*)*

The responsibilities of a Product Manager include the following:

- **Defining customer needs**: Product Managers work closely with customers to understand their needs and priorities. They use design thinking tools to bring in the customer's perspective and ensure that the products meet their requirements.

- **Creating product roadmaps**: Product Managers own the product roadmap and use it to deliver valuable products. They strategize and provide clarity to the teams by prioritizing features and defining the direction for product development.

- **Collaborating with stakeholders**: Product Managers work closely with Product Owners, stakeholders, and other teams to define features and acceptance criteria. They refine the product backlog for PI Planning and support teams by answering questions and providing guidance.

- **Supporting teams**: Product Managers support the development teams by sharing metrics, communicating the product vision, and helping with prioritization and trade-off decisions. They collaborate with architects, engineers, solution management, Business Owners, and subject-matter experts to build and demo required functionality.

- **Continuous value delivery**: Product Managers consider technical support, legal compliance, and customer feedback to create a continuous flow of value. They also make decisions about retiring products that are no longer valuable.

Your interactions with the Product Owner go far beyond the events in which you and they participate. The Product Manager plays a crucial role in defining and delivering valuable products that meet customer needs and align with the business goals established by the portfolio. The quality of the ART's backlog is one of the critical elements to enable the delivery of integrated value.

The Product Manager has to collate the many demand signals from across the organization and customer, as well as review feedback, telemetry, and market data. As a critical friend, the RTE will challenge them to keep a focus on the highest value items, as well as ask powerful questions to help unblock thinking. You can also review early drafts of **features** through the lens of deliverability. At times, your support can play the role of a *bad cop* when stakeholders are becoming overbearing, particularly during the **Weighted Shortest Job First (WSJF)** prioritization sessions.

In *Chapter 5*, we will go into considerably more detail on how the RTE can support the creation of an effective backlog.

In the RTE's working agreements with the Product Manager, both parties need to agree on who will facilitate the Product Owner Sync, unless the ART has replaced it with a combined ART Sync. Assuming this responsibility allows the Product Manager to concentrate on the content of the conversations and to be actively involved. Attempting to do both simultaneously is challenging and requires practice. Participating in this session also gives you the opportunity to pose relevant questions that aid in improving Product Management capability. Product Managers have **content authority** over the ART backlog. They take the ultimate responsibility for its content, prioritization, and the mix of **business features** and **enabler features**. Consequently, the RTE doesn't have control over what is in it. This doesn't mean you are passive about what is in the backlog. You do care about how the features are defined to support the smooth flow of business value. You also care that an effective Product Management approach is being enacted that solicits market and stakeholder inputs and robustly prioritizes work.

To this end, consider these questions to guide your interactions with Product Management:

- How will the feature hypothesis be validated and measured in production?
- Are the candidate features for the following PI aligned with the portfolio's **strategic themes**?
- How much involvement have the Business Owners had with respect to the backlog creation and prioritization? Do they know, if not accept, the sequencing?
- Could the feature be divided to simplify delivery, eliminate dependencies, release value sooner, or obtain feedback sooner?
- If the WSJF prioritization has been overridden, is there a sensible argument for doing so?
- Have the System Architect, InfoSec, tech leads, Product Owners, Business Owners, and so on been involved in refining the backlog?
- How has feedback (from the customer, telemetry, and Business Owners) been incorporated into the backlog?
- What is the level of uncertainty or risk in the backlog that puts in jeopardy the delivery predictability?
- What relationships is Product Management struggling with that I can help facilitate?
- What metrics might help create, refine, or validate the backlog hypothesis?
- Are features well constructed using the agreed-upon format for the ART, with acceptance criteria that clarify their scope?

System Architect (SA)

The SA is responsible for defining and communicating a shared technical and architectural vision for the solutions developed by the ART. Their role is to ensure that the system or solution being developed aligns with its intended purpose and supports the delivery of business value. They work hand in hand with Product Management. As we like to say, architecture is the other side of the same coin as Product Management. Neither party can work independently and without collaboration if a successful delivery is to be achieved.

System Architect empathy map

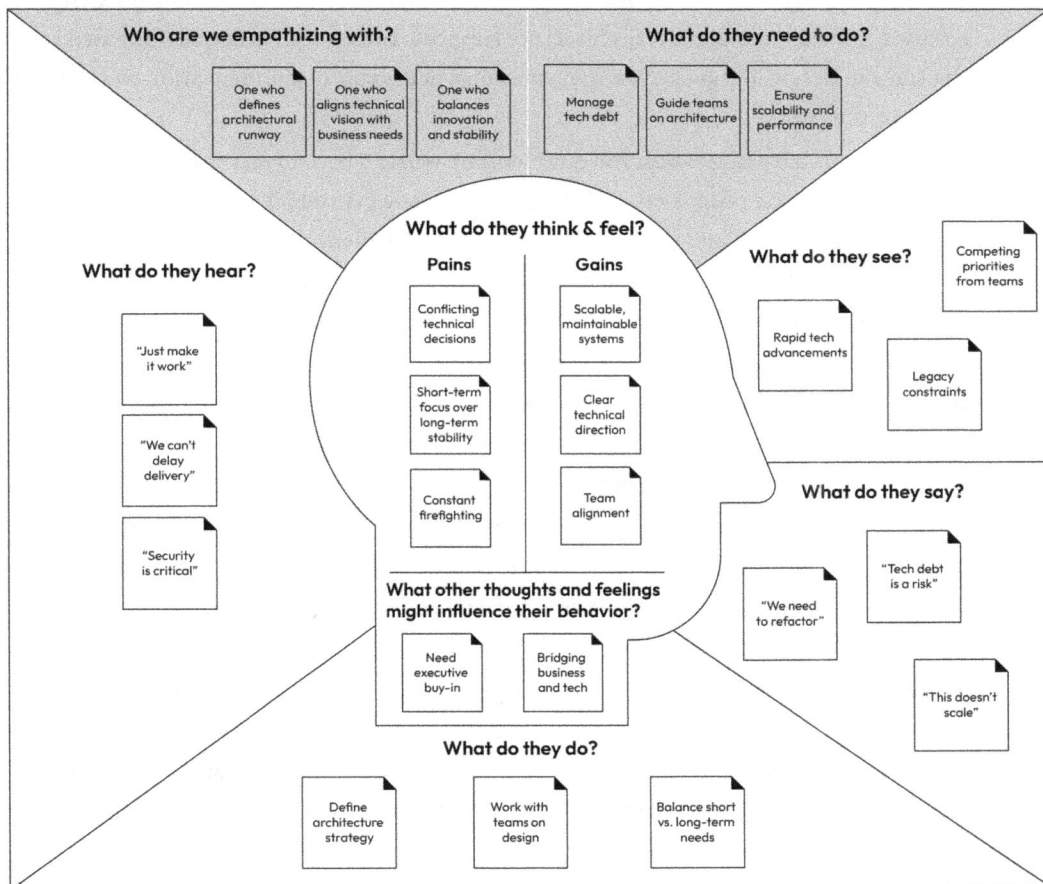

Who are we empathizing with?
- One who defines architectural runway
- One who aligns technical vision with business needs
- One who balances innovation and stability

What do they need to do?
- Manage tech debt
- Guide teams on architecture
- Ensure scalability and performance

What do they think & feel?

Pains
- Conflicting technical decisions
- Short-term focus over long-term stability
- Constant firefighting

Gains
- Scalable, maintainable systems
- Clear technical direction
- Team alignment

What do they hear?
- "Just make it work"
- "We can't delay delivery"
- "Security is critical"

What do they see?
- Competing priorities from teams
- Rapid tech advancements
- Legacy constraints

What other thoughts and feelings might influence their behavior?
- Need executive buy-in
- Bridging business and tech

What do they say?
- "Tech debt is a risk"
- "We need to refactor"
- "This doesn't scale"

What do they do?
- Define architecture strategy
- Work with teams on design
- Balance short vs. long-term needs

Figure 3.5: System Architect empathy map (inspired by Dave Gray, Xplaner.com; online empathy map here: `https://gamestorming.com/empathy-mapping/)`

The responsibilities of an SA include the following:

- **Defining and communicating architecture vision**: The SA presents the architectural vision to teams during PI Planning and provides guidance on implementing the vision during the PI execution. They ensure that the system design issues encountered by teams during implementation are addressed.

- **Participating in solution definition**: The SA is often closely involved in defining the solution as part of Design Thinking. They provide critical insights into the technological and implementation capabilities of the train, ensuring that solution ideation is effective.

- **Defining system non-functional requirements (NFRs)**: The SA defines NFRs for the solution and ensures that the architecture supports these requirements. They also assist the train in determining specific measures and necessary instrumentation to safeguard and monitor NFRs.

- **Ensuring capacity allocation for enablement work**: The SA works with Product Management to allocate proper capacity for architecture work, which occurs while preparing for each PI boundary and during PI Planning itself. Unless they have a perfect working relationship with the Product Manager, the RTE might need to arbitrate this conversation. It does not harm to be the devil's advocate either.

- **Aligning architecture with business priorities**: The SA defines enablers and the architectural runway to support the intended features. They continuously define, adjust, and support the journey of advancing architectural capabilities. They also participate in solution definition and ensure alignment with the reality of implementation.

- **Collaborating with various roles and teams**: The SA collaborates with Product Management, Product Owners, Scrum Masters/Team Coaches, the System Team, and Shared Services to ensure that the system design evolves in line with the shared architectural intent and the practical reality of implementation.

- **Evolving system design with teams**: The SA supports architectural experiments and spikes to validate architectural ideas with minimal development effort. They collaborate with teams on optimal system design, providing ongoing coaching and participating in technical **Communities of Practice (CoPs)**. They also align the architectural intent with the reality of implementation.

Overall, the SA is critical in aligning ART teams to a shared technical direction, elaborating the system architecture, validating technology assumptions, evaluating implementation alternatives, and creating the continuous delivery pipeline.

It is essential that the SA and the Product Managers work well together, and as the RTE, you may have to help manage conflicting priorities. It can be far too common to see the two roles working in an adversarial manner. There are a few tools in the SAFe® toolbox, such as WSJF and capacity allocation, that will help you facilitate conversation on the work, depersonalizing the conversation. We'll cover them in more detail in a later chapter when we look at backlog refinement.

As one of the primary responsibilities of the RTE is to optimize flow, the SA is a key person to work with. The architectural design can have a considerable impact on the number of dependencies created while delivering a feature and how easy it is for the feature's value to flow through the **continuous delivery pipeline**. You may need to coach them on why this is important, and to encourage them to attend the *SAFe for Architects* course, which demonstrates how to undertake architecting for the continuous flow of value.

Areas and questions to consider are as follows:

- How does the balance between deliberate and emergent architecture impact the ART's deliverability?
- Consider the balance of enablers to features. Is the balance correct? Are we linking enablement to the release of business value? Is there enough investment in architecture to not build up technical debt?
- How do I foster a close working relationship between the SA and Product Management?
- How is the System Team and SA working together?
- Is the architectural vision defined in a way that is aligned with the strategy themes, is easy to understand, and is communicated and understood by the ART and Business Owners?
- What is the SA doing to address technical debt?
- What is the SA's relationship with teams? Do they collaborate regularly? Do they have access to support when they need it?
- How is the SA getting feedback and incorporating it into the vision and backlog? What measurements are being used?
- What bottlenecks exist because of the solution design? How can the SA help optimize the process flow or solution design?

Business Owners

The role of the Business Owner is to have primary business and technical responsibility for **return on investment (ROI)**, governance, and compliance. They are key stakeholders who evaluate fitness for use and actively participate in ART events and solution development.

It doesn't matter which framework you're using, whether you're an **Agilist** or working in a more traditional Waterfall organization—if you're reading this book, your context is likely that you are at least seeing ad-hoc Agile within your organization or planning on starting your journey toward business agility soon. In *Chapter 2*, we discussed the origins of RTEs, as well as how they integrate with the business. It is often this aspect of the role—particularly how RTEs work within the business—that those with a background as Program Directors and Managers tend to find somewhat unsettling.

The idea of decentralizing decisions can be uncomfortable if you're used to calling the shots, but stakeholder management for complex programs is a skill that all RTEs need to have in spades.

> **The importance of stakeholder engagement**
>
> I [Tim] remember my first day studying **PRINCE2 (short for Projects IN Controlled Environments)** back in the day; the tutor claimed that the thing that matters most for the success of any project is stakeholder engagement. This is as true in Agile as it is in Waterfall. If we don't have strong relationships with the business to ensure that we're building the right thing—whatever that may be—for our customers and the business, then we're doomed to fail. As an RTE, you will have to work closely with the movers and shakers in your business and get them to a place where they can play their critical role. If they're disengaged, then they may not be intellectually or physically present for key events such as PI Planning and System Demos. The lack of feedback can result in catastrophe.

To work effectively with Business Owners, we need to step into their world—understanding their challenges, priorities, and what drives their decisions. They are responsible for business outcomes, governance, and ensuring that the ART delivers value. But they often juggle competing demands, face pressure from executives, and may not always be fully engaged with Agile ways of working.

Using an empathy map helps us see things from their perspective. It allows us to anticipate their concerns, tailor our communication, and build stronger relationships. Let's explore what a Business Owner thinks, feels, says, and does to better understand how we can collaborate effectively.

Business Owner (BO) empathy map

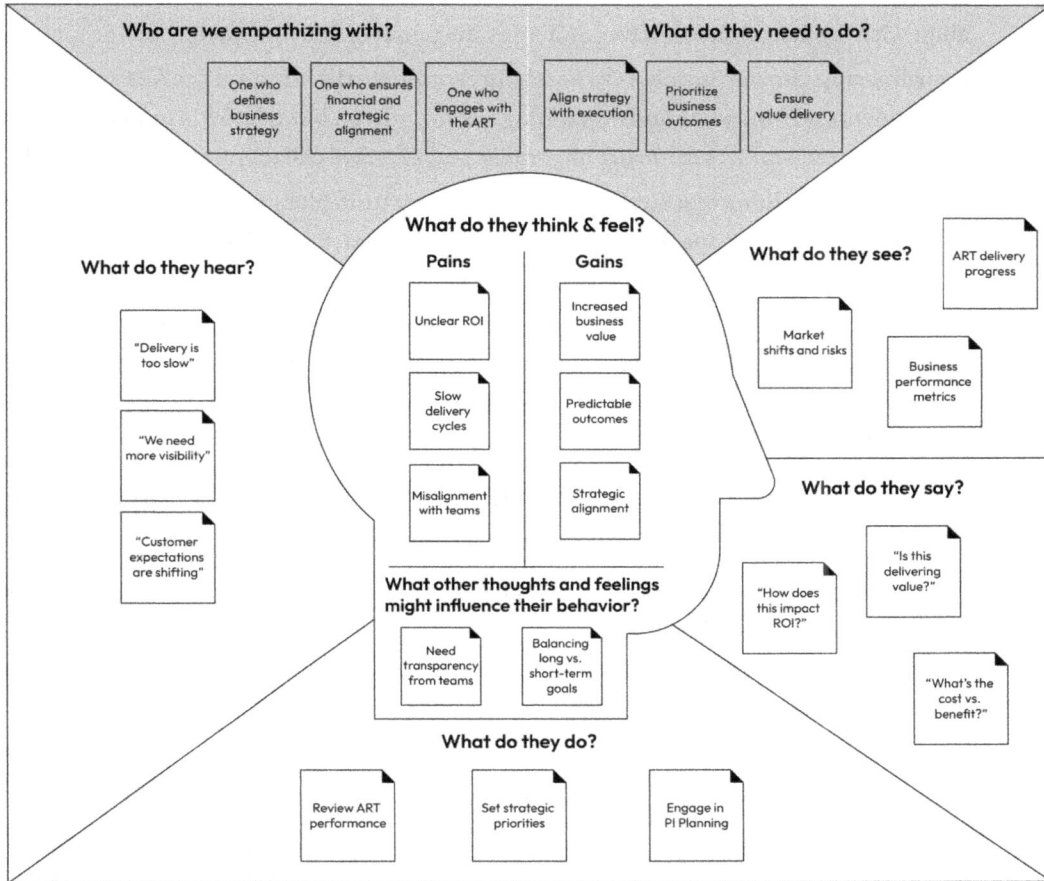

Who are we empathizing with?

- One who defines business strategy
- One who ensures financial and strategic alignment
- One who engages with the ART

What do they need to do?

- Align strategy with execution
- Prioritize business outcomes
- Ensure value delivery

What do they think & feel?

Pains
- Unclear ROI
- Slow delivery cycles
- Misalignment with teams

Gains
- Increased business value
- Predictable outcomes
- Strategic alignment

What do they hear?
- "Delivery is too slow"
- "We need more visibility"
- "Customer expectations are shifting"

What do they see?
- ART delivery progress
- Market shifts and risks
- Business performance metrics

What other thoughts and feelings might influence their behavior?
- Need transparency from teams
- Balancing long vs. short-term goals

What do they say?
- "How does this impact ROI?"
- "Is this delivering value?"
- "What's the cost vs. benefit?"

What do they do?
- Review ART performance
- Set strategic priorities
- Engage in PI Planning

Figure 3.6: Business Owner empathy map (inspired by Dave Gray, Xplaner.com; online empathy map here: `https://gamestorming.com/empathy-mapping/`)

Responsibilities of a Business Owner include the following:

- **ROI and business outcomes:** They are ultimately responsible for business outcomes and ensuring that the solutions developed by the ART deliver value and meet the needs of the customers and the business.

- **Governance and compliance:** Business Owners ensure that the development and delivery of solutions comply with relevant regulations, policies, and standards. They also provide oversight and decision-making on spending, audit, compliance, and measurement for their value streams.

- **Solution evaluation**: Business Owners evaluate the fitness for use of the solutions being developed by the ART. They provide feedback and guidance to ensure that the solutions align with the business objectives and meet the needs of the customers.

- **Coordinating efforts**: Business Owners help coordinate the efforts of the ART with other departments and organizations, spanning organizational boundaries. They collaborate with other stakeholders to ensure alignment and effective collaboration.

- **Participating in planning**: Business Owners participate in planning activities, help eliminate impediments, and speak on behalf of the development, the business, and the customer. They play a crucial role in approving and defending a set of PI plans.

- **Providing leadership**: Business Owners are leaders who guide the ART to optimal business outcomes. They lead by example, communicate the vision for SAFe® adoption, and actively engage with the teams and stakeholders to drive the cultural change needed for the adoption of SAFe.

It's important to note that the specific responsibilities of a Business Owner may vary depending on the organization and the context in which SAFe is implemented.

Sometimes, Business Owners act in a hierarchical manner, demanding that their requirements be worked on and escalating when they are told "no" or "not yet." This is a perfect time for the RTE to step in and help them manage expectations and elevate a potential escalation, which will ultimately only create tension and distraction.

The power of cadence and synchronization

Often, those wanting things to be worked on, through a history of not getting them done, or at least not done in a timely fashion, can become animated when the Product Owner or SA says "no" or "not yet."

As the ART is synchronized and operates on a known cadence, it becomes easier to stop the *do it now* requests. You can explain the process to the person wanting work to be done, showing how to submit it, and how the Product Management transparently prioritizes and sequences the work—how and when the demand signals reach the ART, and when it will be planned and delivered.

Through having a clearly defined process, with the predictability SAFe provides, you remove all the uncertainty that existed in previous ways of working.

Finding the correct number and mix of Business Owners for your ART can be challenging. We find the sweet-spot is three to five; it's definitely not one, and double-digits will likely cause too much distraction. Some characteristics you might want to consider when helping to find Business Owners are as follows:

- Do they have the time? A good Business Owner can easily spend 25% of their time working directly with the ART. From providing intelligence from the demand side of the organization to Product Management and the SA, to attending prioritization sessions, to being in key ART events such as PI Planning and the **Inspect & Adapt (I&A)**, and offering fast feedback on partially completed work, it all adds up.

- Are they prepared to honor the process? You don't want them accepting the plan in PI Planning and then, the next day, complaining they are not getting what they want.

- Do you have the right mix of Business Owners? Look to have diversity in the group such that customer demands, delivery, and operations are being represented and considered.

Now that we've covered the leadership roles, let's have a look at how we interact with the teams.

Working with people at the team level

Other than your first team, the ART leadership, you will work closely with teams. Our goal is to decentralize decision-making and act as a servant leader to encourage alignment across teams. You will have to create and support a culture of trust and transparency, making yourself available for teams to approach with questions and feedback.

Here is a summary of some of the most important activities:

- **Removing impediments:** The RTE works closely with Scrum Masters to identify and remove impediments that hinder team progress. They escalate issues that require higher-level support and facilitate problem-solving to keep teams on track. When they do, record the issue in a visible location, honoring your commitment to transparency. An impediment **Kanban board** is a perfect place. We've also seen leaders put them on their office door with sticky notes, so it's clear they have ownership of it.

- **Coaching and Lean-Agile practices:** The RTE coaches leaders and teams in Lean-Agile practices and mindset. They provide guidance on implementing SAFe® principles, help teams adopt Agile practices, and support continuous improvement efforts.

- **Facilitating ART-level events**: The RTE facilitates ART-level events such as PI Planning, ART Sync, and Scrum of Scrums. They ensure that these events run smoothly, encourage collaboration, and help teams align their work toward common goals.

- **Metrics and workflow optimization**: The RTE tracks metrics and works with Scrum Masters and teams to optimize workflow and reduce waste. They collaborate with teams to identify areas for improvement, implement changes, and measure the impact of those changes.

They play a crucial role in supporting teams by providing guidance, removing impediments, facilitating collaboration, and promoting continuous improvement. They work closely with teams to ensure that they have the support and resources needed to deliver value effectively. How much you get directly involved with teams depends on the experience and needs of the Scrum Master for the team.

Scrum Masters

You are going to rely heavily on your Scrum Masters; if the ART leadership is your first team, then the community of Scrum Masters and coaches will make up your second. The ninth Lean-Agile principle in SAFe® is *Decentralize decision-making*; therefore, you're going to have to be cognizant of what should be left to the teams, and what you need to take on as an RTE.

The role of a Scrum Master/Team Coach is to serve as a servant leader and coach for an Agile Team. They facilitate team events and processes and support teams. Think about what other teams need to know and where you need to take the reins.

For the vast majority of improvements at a team level, the Scrum Masters and coaches will be doing a lot of the heavy lifting. Your role as an RTE is to look at the bigger picture and decide what you need to put in place to integrate any data that you need to coach the flow of value for the ART as a whole.

Scrum Masters are key partners for the RTE, acting as servant leaders for their teams while driving continuous improvement across the ART. They balance coaching, facilitation, and problem-solving, often navigating team dynamics and organizational challenges.

By mapping their perspective, we can better understand their pressures, motivations, and how to support them in fostering high-performing teams. Let's explore their world through an empathy map.

Scrum Master/Team Coach empathy map

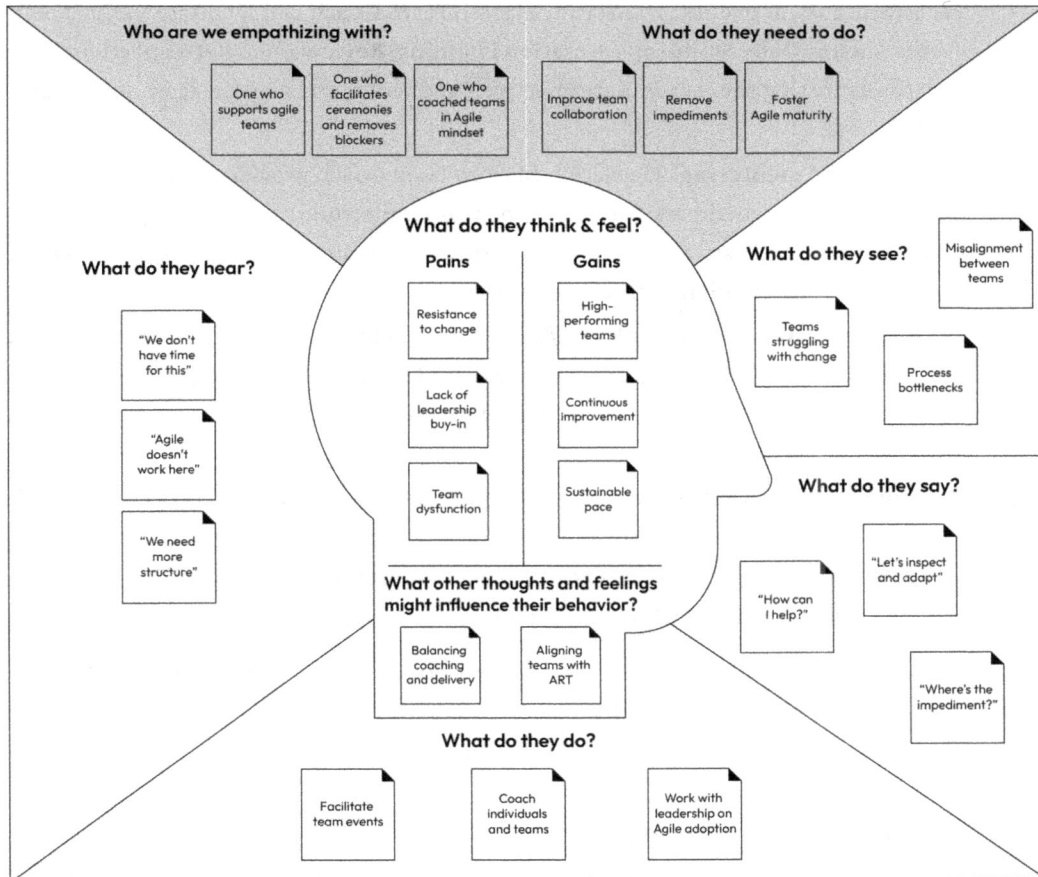

Who are we empathizing with?

- One who supports agile teams
- One who facilitates ceremonies and removes blockers
- One who coached teams in Agile mindset

What do they need to do?

- Improve team collaboration
- Remove impediments
- Foster Agile maturity

What do they think & feel?

Pains
- Resistance to change
- Lack of leadership buy-in
- Team dysfunction

Gains
- High-performing teams
- Continuous improvement
- Sustainable pace

What do they hear?

- "We don't have time for this"
- "Agile doesn't work here"
- "We need more structure"

What do they see?

- Misalignment between teams
- Teams struggling with change
- Process bottlenecks

What other thoughts and feelings might influence their behavior?

- Balancing coaching and delivery
- Aligning teams with ART

What do they say?

- "Let's inspect and adapt"
- "How can I help?"
- "Where's the impediment?"

What do they do?

- Facilitate team events
- Coach individuals and teams
- Work with leadership on Agile adoption

Figure 3.7: Scrum Master/Team Coach empathy map (inspired by Dave Gray, Xplaner.com; online empathy map here: `https://gamestorming.com/empathy-mapping/`*)*

Here are some key aspects of the Scrum Master/Team Coach role:

- **Servant leadership**: The Scrum Master/Team Coach acts as a servant leader, supporting the team in self-organization, self-management, and meeting their goals. They prioritize the needs of the team and help remove any obstacles that may hinder their progress.

- **Facilitating team events**: The Scrum Master/Team Coach can facilitate various team events, such as **Daily Stand-ups**, **Iteration Planning**, **Reviews**, and **Retrospectives**. They help to ensure that these events are effective, productive, and help the team stay focused on their goals.

- **Coaching and mentoring:** The Scrum Master/Team Coach provides coaching and mentoring to the team members. They help the team understand and adopt Agile practices, such as Scrum, Kanban, and XP. They also guide the team in continuous improvement and finding ways to enhance their performance.

- **Supporting ARTs**: The Scrum Master/Team Coach supports the ART in delivering value. They collaborate with other teams and stakeholders to ensure alignment and effective coordination. They also help the team understand and follow the agreed-upon Agile processes.

- **Enabling high-performing teams**: The Scrum Master/Team Coach plays a critical role in building high-performing teams. They foster an environment for continuous flow, collaboration, and relentless improvement. They support the team in achieving their goals and help resolve any conflicts or challenges that may arise.

An ART will unlikely become high performing without skilled Scrum Masters and the RTE working together. Consider them a vital ally for you. They help the team deliver value, promote Agile practices, and enable the team to become high-performing and self-sufficient.

> **Working with Scrum Masters**
>
> We spoke to Scaled Agile, Inc.'s RTE, Sam Ervin, for advice on how an RTE and the Scrum Masters can best work together. This was his advice:
>
> - Regularly check in with Scrum Masters to understand what they need from you and how you can best support them
> - Ask Scrum Masters for their recommendations on how you can engage with the teams effectively
> - Empower Scrum Masters to take the lead and own their responsibilities, rather than trying to do their job for them

- Encourage teams and Scrum Masters to step outside their defined boundaries and interact with other parts of the organization
- See yourself, as the RTE, as a gardener rather than a chess master—one where you create the environment for teams and the Scrum Masters to thrive, rather than trying to control everything

As Sam Ervin references, a Scrum Master needs to create a strong functioning team, but they must not be singularly inwardly focused. Encouragement goes only so far. You may need to remove silos and barriers that exist that hinder this collaboration. Being creative, too, means making connections with parts of the organization or other teams that, at first glance, do not look like they are part of the same group.

Story from the field

Let me (Tim) tell you a story. I was working with an ART a few years ago. I was brought in as the RTE temporarily; the ART had been running for a few PIs, and unfortunately, they weren't getting the results they hoped. After some digging, I realized that one of the main issues was the contracting for one of the teams on the ART. At a high level, they were a supplier and were contracted for specific deliverables. That isn't the end of the world, albeit far from ideal. The issue in this case was that the team was doing a fabulous job on their deliverables, but many of the teams depended on them to deliver their work. When talking to the Scrum Master, we realized their hands were somewhat tied; they had to deprioritize other teams' work to ensure that they got paid. Following the money is usually an excellent place to start if you want to get to the root of the problem.

As the RTE, I had to find a way to break the cycle, and I was well placed to do just that. I had a good relationship with one of the Business Owners for the ART, and we worked with the supplier to change our agreements and our way of working. We started out with low predictability, but we could see things improve after just a few weeks. I often tell this story for a couple of reasons. Firstly, it is an excellent example of systems thinking; it doesn't matter how well one team performs if the ART suffers. Secondly, as an RTE, you need to have the support of the decision-makers who can effect change within the business.

The balance between giving the Scrum Masters space and stepping in can be a fine line. The following are data points to consider when evaluating the best course of action:

- Team predictability
- Employee **Net Promoter Score (NPS)**
- ART and team execution measurements
- Scrum Master observed behaviors one-to-one or when facilitating groups
- Servant leader behaviors, such as whether they have an *I'll ask the team* style response when someone asks whether the team can do something
- Contribution level beyond their own team

Product Owners

Product Owners maximize the value delivered by the Agile Team. They ensure that the team backlog is aligned with customer and stakeholder needs. The Product Owner represents the needs of customers and the business within a particular solution domain. They work closely with the Product Manager to balance the needs of multiple stakeholders and continuously evolve the solution. The responsibilities of a Product Owner include connecting with the customer, defining and prioritizing the team backlog, ensuring alignment with PI objectives, removing obstacles, and facilitating communication between the team and the business. They play a critical role in driving the success of the Agile Team and delivering value to the customers.

By stepping into their shoes, we can better appreciate their challenges and motivations, helping us work together more effectively. Let's explore their perspective through an empathy map.

Product Owner (PO) empathy map

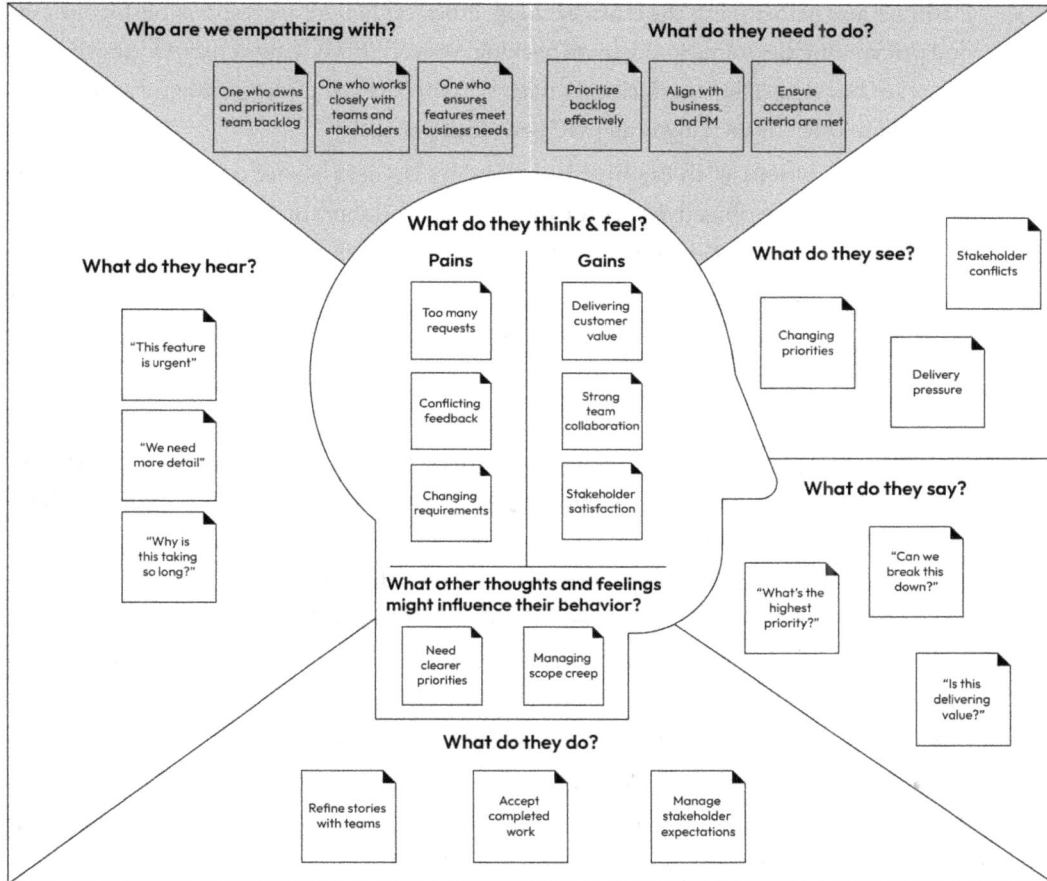

Who are we empathizing with?

- One who owns and prioritizes team backlog
- One who works closely with teams and stakeholders
- One who ensures features meet business needs

What do they need to do?

- Prioritize backlog effectively
- Align with business, and PM
- Ensure acceptance criteria are met

What do they think & feel?

Pains
- Too many requests
- Conflicting feedback
- Changing requirements

Gains
- Delivering customer value
- Strong team collaboration
- Stakeholder satisfaction

What do they hear?
- "This feature is urgent"
- "We need more detail"
- "Why is this taking so long?"

What do they see?
- Stakeholder conflicts
- Changing priorities
- Delivery pressure

What other thoughts and feelings might influence their behavior?
- Need clearer priorities
- Managing scope creep

What do they say?
- "Can we break this down?"
- "What's the highest priority?"
- "Is this delivering value?"

What do they do?
- Refine stories with teams
- Accept completed work
- Manage stakeholder expectations

Figure 3.8: Product Owner empathy map (inspired by Dave Gray, Xplaner.com; online empathy map here: `https://gamestorming.com/empathy-mapping/`*)*

The responsibilities of Product Owners include the following:

- **Defining and prioritizing the team backlog**: Product Owners are responsible for defining and prioritizing the items in the team backlog. We call this having content authority over the team backlog. They work closely with stakeholders to understand customer needs and ensure that the backlog is aligned with those needs.

- **Ensuring alignment with PI objectives**: Product Owners ensure that the team backlog is aligned with the objectives set for the PI. They collaborate with the Agile Team and stakeholders to define clear objectives and prioritize work accordingly.

- **Removing obstacles**: Product Owners help remove obstacles that may hinder the team's progress. They work closely with the Scrum Master and other stakeholders to address any issues or impediments that arise during the development process.

- **Facilitating communication**: Product Owners act as a bridge between the Agile Team and stakeholders. They facilitate effective communication, ensuring that the team understands customer needs and stakeholder expectations. They also provide regular updates on progress and gather feedback from stakeholders.

- **Validating and accepting work**: Product Owners validate and accept completed work items. They ensure that the delivered solutions meet the defined acceptance criteria and align with customer expectations. They also provide feedback to the team for continuous improvement.

- **Collaborating with the Agile Team**: Product Owners work closely with the Agile Team, participating in team events such as Daily Stand-ups, Iteration Planning, Reviews, and Retrospectives. They provide guidance, answer questions, and ensure that the team has a clear understanding of the work to be done.

- **Continuous learning and improvement**: Product Owners continuously learn and improve their skills and knowledge. They stay updated on industry trends, customer needs, and market dynamics to make informed decisions and drive the success of the Agile Team.

For the most part, the Product Owners will be working with Product Management. They play a critical role in maximizing the value delivered by the Agile Team and, therefore, the ART. They are responsible for ensuring that the team backlog is aligned with customer needs, removing obstacles, facilitating communication, and validating the delivered solutions. So, as an RTE, you may need to work with them quite closely when coaching ART and getting them ready for PI Planning.

One coaching opportunity you have with Product Owners is guiding them on the creation of team backlog items that are well understood, easy to release, broken down to reduce dependencies across teams, and open to continuous refinement through productive conversations. You may need to bring the SA in to support the breakdown or to take a holistic approach as they consider ways to support the team in the delivery of the backlog.

> **Anti-pattern: Product Owners only look at the team level**
>
> While the Product Owners primarily have a team focus, they are part of the broader Product Management function. Consequently, while they serve the team, they also serve the ART and work with Product Management to help refine and elaborate features. In some situations, Product Owners take a view that they only care about the team and want to be spoon-fed features from Product Management, criticizing the quality and not being prepared to help improve them.

This is an anti-pattern because, in the scaled environment you work in, they serve both the team and the ART. This behavior can stem from many years of traditional working methods, having been instructed not to ask questions and to simply comply with directions. As the RTE, you will need to help the two parties come together to work effectively.

Large solution-level roles

When building large complex solutions, we may scale our fractal model to accommodate hundreds or even thousands of people. A large solution in SAFe® refers to the development of complex and comprehensive solutions that require coordination and collaboration across multiple ARTs and teams. It involves the integration of various components, subsystems, and technologies to deliver a complete solution that meets the needs of the customer. If an ART is a team of teams, a **Solution Train** is a team of a team of teams.

Key characteristics of a large solution in SAFe® include the following:

- **Involvement of multiple ARTs**: Large solutions require the collaboration of multiple ARTs, each responsible for different aspects of the solution.

- **Cross-functional teams**: Teams from different ARTs work together to develop and integrate the various components of the solution.

- **Complex dependencies**: Large solutions often have intricate dependencies between different components, requiring careful coordination and synchronization.

- **Compliance and regulatory considerations**: Large solutions may need to adhere to specific compliance and regulatory requirements, adding complexity to the development process. While this can be the case in a single ART, it's a more regular occurrence at this level.

- **Extended value streams**: The value streams associated with large solutions span multiple ARTs and involve various stakeholders, including customers, suppliers, and partners.

SAFe provides guidance and practices for managing large solutions, including the use of Solution Trains, Solution Management, and Solution Architect roles. These roles and practices help ensure effective collaboration, alignment, and delivery of value in the development of large and complex solutions.

The Solution Train Engineer

Like the RTE, the **Solution Train Engineer** (STE) is a servant leader and coach who facilitates Solution Train events and processes, coordinates the work of ARTs and suppliers, and supports ARTs in delivering value. They play a crucial role in leading Solution Trains through the delivery of large solutions by coordinating the end-to-end value stream and ensuring efficient development and delivery.

By understanding their perspective, we can better support their challenges and foster stronger connections between the ART and the wider Solution Train. Let's explore their world through an empathy map.

Solution Train Engineer (STE) empathy map

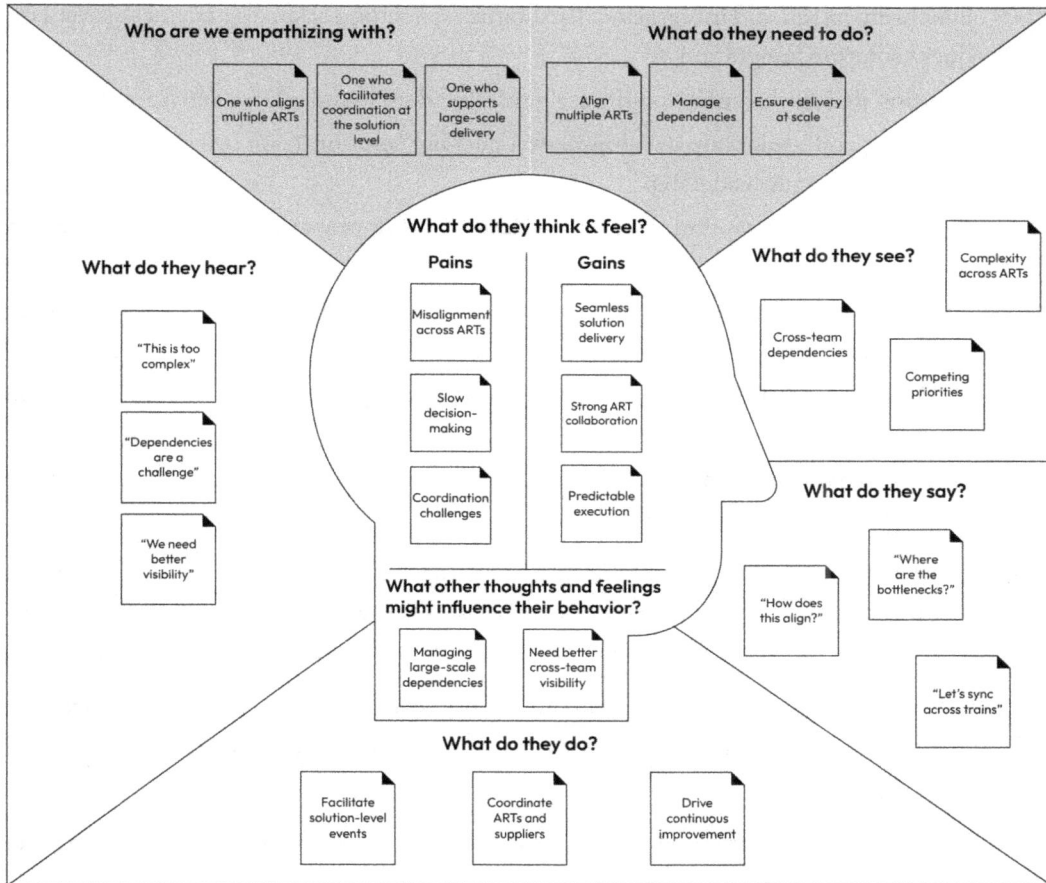

Figure 3.9: Solution Train Engineer (STE) empathy map (inspired by Dave Gray, Xplaner.com; online empathy map here: https://gamestorming.com/empathy-mapping/)

The responsibilities of the STE include the following:

- **Synchronization and integration**: Facilitating synchronization events and ensuring frequent solution integration
- **Solution delivery events**: Coordinating solution demos and release activities
- **Coaching and leadership development**: Coaching Solution Train stakeholders and promoting Lean-Agile leadership
- **Flow optimization**: Optimizing flow by addressing flow properties and improving system design
- **Solution definition and metrics**: Supporting solution definition and gathering feedback and metrics
- **PI Planning coordination**: Assisting with PI Planning logistics and defining Solution Train PI objectives
- **Delivery alignment**: Coordinating large solution delivery and maintaining alignment among Solution Train participants

The STE works closely with the RTE and the ART, as well as other stakeholders, to ensure effective collaboration and the successful delivery of capabilities. Together, you will provide guidance, support, and coaching to teams and help foster a continuous delivery culture within the Solution Train.

The RTE is to the STE as the Scrum Master is to the RTE. Reflect on what the Scrum Masters do and behave that makes your life easier, then think about how you can scale this when you are working with the STE.

In the same way, the RTE encourages the Scrum Masters not to be insular and to work with other teams. The RTE needs to work with peer RTEs and the STE for the benefit of the whole Solution Train. In the specific context of your situation, think about how you can best represent your ART, maintaining a systems thinking approach in events such as the Solution Train RTE Sync or Solution Train Sync.

Portfolio-level roles

Let's start by understanding what we mean by a **portfolio** in SAFe®.

> *A SAFe Portfolio is a set of value streams that delivers a continuous flow of valuable solutions to customers within a common funding and governance model.*
>
> *—Scaled Agile Framework®*

A SAFe® portfolio explores options, communicates the approach to achieving strategic themes, and allocates Lean budgets to pursue the portfolio vision. It operates within the context of the enterprise and influences the overall enterprise strategy by collaborating with other portfolios to improve overall flow. The SAFe portfolio consists of multiple **development value streams** (**DVSs**) that have their own Lean budgets and are responsible for maintaining and evolving solutions. The portfolio is defined by its purpose, context, and the structure chosen to achieve its goals.

Lean Portfolio Management

The role of LPM in SAFe aligns strategy and execution by applying Lean and systems thinking approaches to strategy and investment funding, Agile portfolio operations, and governance. LPM ensures that the entire portfolio is aligned and funded to create and maintain the solutions needed to meet business targets. LPM is responsible for coordinating and supporting decentralized ART execution, fostering operational excellence in Agile portfolio operations, and providing oversight of spending, audit, compliance, measurement, and reporting through Lean governance practices.

The people fulfilling the LPM function have various roles and titles and often reside in different parts of the organization's hierarchy. They hold strategy and investment funding responsibilities, ensuring that the overall business outcomes are achieved and that strategy is effectively communicated and aligned with execution.

The LPM team will no doubt need your help when planning epics and **minimum viable products** (**MVPs**) that are going to be delivered by your ART. In most cases, you will be working with the Product Managers to understand what your team will need to deliver and the wider context in the portfolio.

By understanding their perspective, we can collaborate more effectively, ensuring that portfolio decisions enable, rather than hinder, Agile delivery.

Let's explore their world through an empathy map.

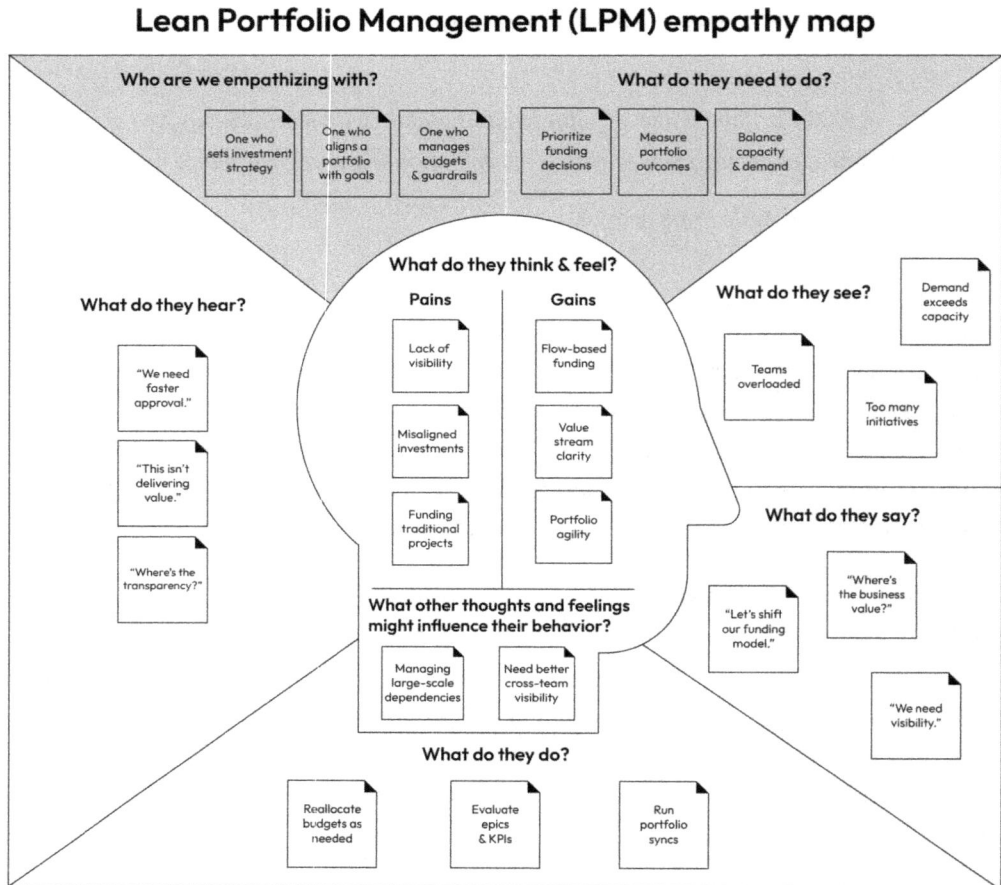

Lean Portfolio Management (LPM) empathy map

Who are we empathizing with?
- One who sets investment strategy
- One who aligns a portfolio with goals
- One who manages budgets & guardrails

What do they need to do?
- Prioritize funding decisions
- Measure portfolio outcomes
- Balance capacity & demand

What do they hear?
- "We need faster approval."
- "This isn't delivering value."
- "Where's the transparency?"

What do they think & feel?

Pains
- Lack of visibility
- Misaligned investments
- Funding traditional projects

Gains
- Flow-based funding
- Value stream clarity
- Portfolio agility

What do they see?
- Demand exceeds capacity
- Teams overloaded
- Too many initiatives

What other thoughts and feelings might influence their behavior?
- Managing large-scale dependencies
- Need better cross-team visibility

What do they say?
- "Let's shift our funding model."
- "Where's the business value?"
- "We need visibility."

What do they do?
- Reallocate budgets as needed
- Evaluate epics & KPIs
- Run portfolio syncs

Figure 3.10: Lean Portfolio Management (LPM) empathy map (inspired by Dave Gray, Xplaner. com; online empathy map here: `https://gamestorming.com/empathy-mapping/`*)*

The responsibilities of the STE include the following:

- **Strategy and investment funding**: Establishes Lean budget guardrails and allocates budgets to value streams rather than projects, enabling decentralized decision-making.
- **Lean governance**: Provides lightweight, principles-based oversight that empowers value streams while ensuring appropriate fiduciary and regulatory compliance.
- **Agile portfolio operations**: Coordinates value streams, manages portfolio flow, and maintains the portfolio Kanban to visualize and limit work in progress.
- **Portfolio vision and roadmaps**: Defines and communicates strategic themes and portfolio vision, and maintains roadmaps that connect strategy to execution.

- **Enterprise architecture alignment**: Ensures that the architectural runway supports both current and future business needs across the portfolio.

- **Value stream identification and funding**: Identifies, defines, and funds long-lived value streams that deliver solutions to customers.

- **Portfolio metrics and reporting**: Establishes and monitors Lean portfolio metrics to assess flow, outcomes, and the achievement of strategic objectives.

The Enterprise Architect

The role of the Enterprise Architect is to establish the technology vision, strategy, and roadmap for the portfolio. They provide the overall technical direction and guidance for the organization, ensuring that individual program and product strategies align with business and technical objectives.

Now, let's have a look at some of their challenges using our friend, the empathy map.

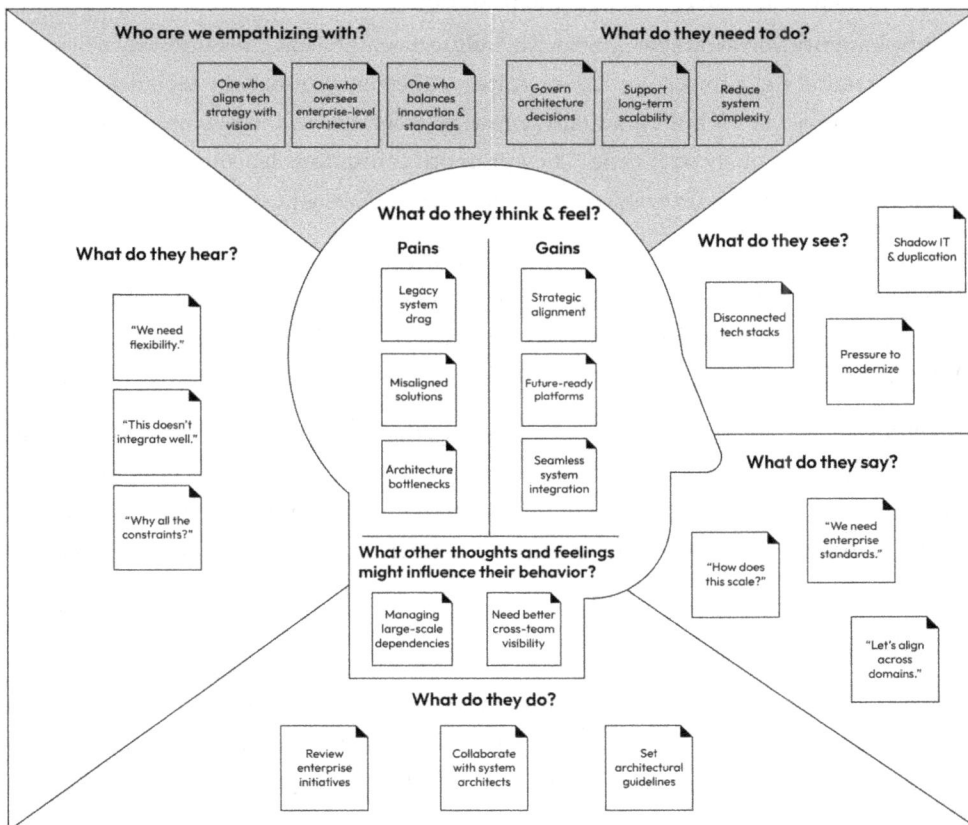

Figure 3.11: Enterprise Architect empathy map

The responsibilities of the Enterprise Architect include the following:

- **Aligning business and technical strategies**: Enterprise Architects are critical for understanding the connection between new technology trends and business. They help the organization identify, evaluate, and respond to opportunities and trends in its broader ecosystem. They ensure that the enterprise's complexity is governed to make innovation easier and facilitate change.

- **Infrastructure strategy**: Enterprise Architects develop and maintain plans for infrastructure, ensuring the reuse of configuration patterns, common physical infrastructure, and knowledge sharing across ARTs and Solution Trains. They provide direction for the development and deployment of infrastructure, including internal IT systems.

- **Inter-ART collaboration**: Enterprise Architects promote standard design and infrastructure practices to simplify and align architecture across different ARTs. They encourage active discussion and sharing of both standard and variable architectural designs among the ARTs to maintain innovation and flexibility.

- **Implementation strategy**: Enterprise Architects emphasize the importance of an active, incremental Agile implementation strategy. They ensure that the technical foundation for business epics is built gradually, allowing architecture and business functionality to grow synchronously over time. They promote continuous learning, fast feedback, and refactoring to maintain architectural flexibility for future business needs.

Overall, the Enterprise Architect helps in aligning business and technical strategies, guiding infrastructure and inter-ART collaboration, and driving an active, incremental implementation strategy. They provide the vision, evolution, and communication of the enterprise's technical architecture, enabling the organization to deliver valuable solutions effectively.

We expect the SA on the train to spend more time with the Enterprise Architect than the RTE will, but this doesn't mean the RTE won't engage. You may invite them to PI Planning to support the briefings or be available to have conversations with the teams. Alternatively, as you look ahead on the ART PI roadmap, you may want to discuss the implications of future work if it spans other ARTs and value streams.

Epic Owners

Epic Owners drive large-scale initiatives, working across teams and ARTs to turn big ideas into valuable outcomes. They navigate strategic priorities, stakeholder expectations, and technical feasibility—all while ensuring their epics deliver measurable business value.

By understanding their perspective, we can better support their journey from concept to execution, helping them align with the ART's ways of working. Let's explore their world through an empathy map.

Epic Owner empathy map

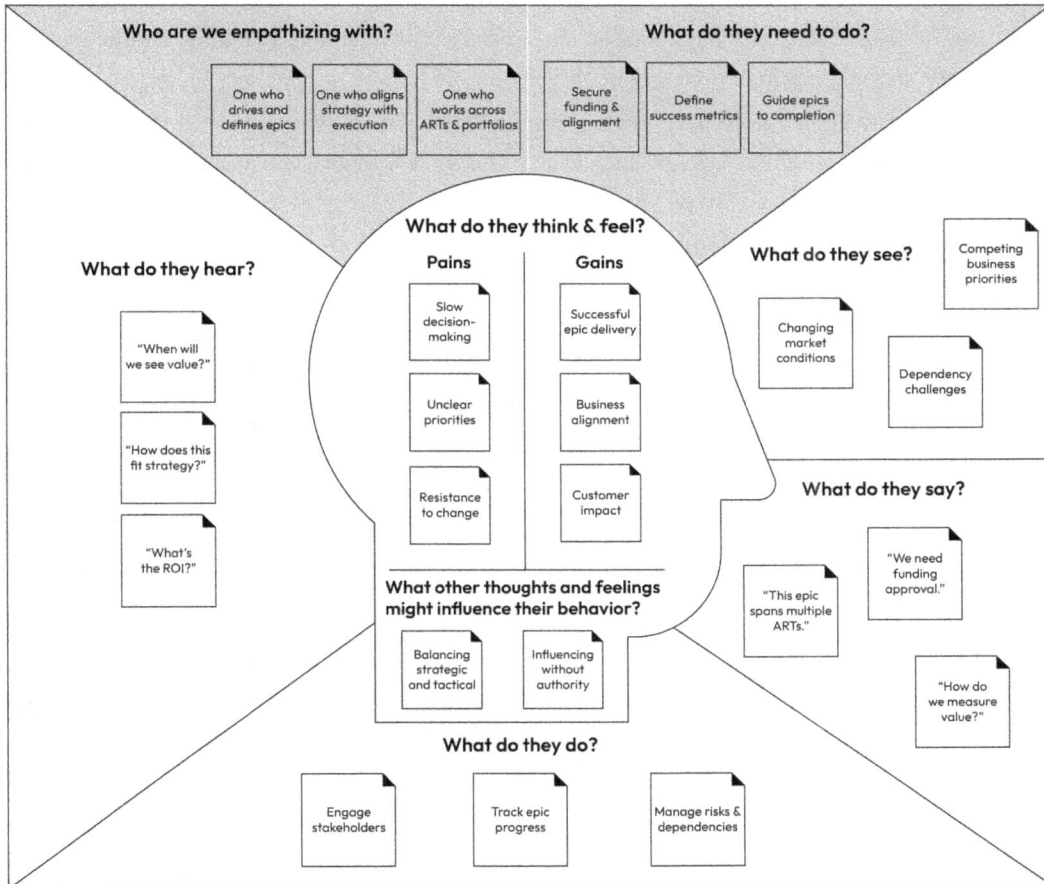

Figure 3.12: Epic Owner empathy map (inspired by Dave Gray, Xplaner.com; online empathy map here: `https://gamestorming.com/empathy-mapping/`)

Epic Owners have several responsibilities:

- **Collaborate and analyze**: Epic Owners work with various stakeholders to analyze epics and create Lean business cases. They collaborate with Enterprise Architects to coordinate enabler epics that support the technical considerations for business epics.

- **Present Lean business case**: Epic Owners present the Lean business case to LPM for a *go* or *no-go* decision. They focus on the merits of the business case and collaborate with LPM to make optimal investment choices.

- **Initiate MVP development**: After approval, Epic Owners work with ARTs to initiate the MVP development activities. They follow the **SAFe® Lean Startup** strategy to evaluate the business outcome hypothesis.

- **Coordinate epic development**: Epic Owners coordinate the implementation of the epic across value streams. They collaborate with Product and Solution Management, System and Solution Architects, and Agile Teams to decompose the epic into features and capabilities. They also participate in PI Planning, System Demos, and Solution Demo activities.

- **Coordinate with business units**: Epic Owners coordinate and synchronize epic-related activities with sales, marketing, and other business units. They ensure alignment and collaboration across different departments.

- **Monitor progress and integration**: Epic Owners understand and report on the epic's progress to key stakeholders and LPM. They facilitate the implementation of the epic through the continuous delivery pipeline and ensure its integration into the roadmaps of ARTs.

The role of the Epic Owner continues until the ARTs have sufficiently integrated the epic into their roadmaps and the Epic Owner's expertise or coordination is no longer required. As the Epic Owner may come from the demand side of the business and have little awareness of how the product is delivered, the RTE can guide them on the ways of working within the ART and coach them on appropriate behaviors when working with teams.

Having examined the relationship the RTE has with key roles in and around the ART, you will notice a constant theme emerging: a good RTE excels at the process, while a great RTE excels at both the process and the people, creating an environment where people can thrive and create meaningful and valuable work. In the next section, we will introduce two groups of people who may not be in direct daily contact with the RTE but are both valuable allies and supporters of the ART, working across the portfolio.

The RTE and organizational support structures in SAFe®

Successful ARTs depend on various organizational support structures to maintain alignment, promote efficiency, and encourage continuous improvement. Within the SAFe® framework, the **Lean-Agile Center of Excellence (LACE)** and the **Value Management Office (VMO)** offer this support. The LACE focuses on instigating Lean-Agile transformation and nurturing an Agile culture, while the VMO ensures that LPM principles are applied to value delivery throughout the organization. For an RTE, comprehending and collaborating with these teams can significantly improve your capability to facilitate ART operations effectively. This section will briefly discuss the roles of LACE and VMO.

The RTE and the LACE

The LACE is a small Agile Team dedicated to implementing the SAFe Lean-Agile way of working. The LACE team has various responsibilities, including managing the transformation backlog, facilitating the transformation, coaching leadership, supporting LPM, and fostering Lean-Agile learning.

The LACE team operates as an exemplar Agile Team and helps drive the adoption of Lean-Agile values, principles, and practices within the organization. They collaborate with various stakeholders, provide guidance, and support the organization in its Lean-Agile transformation journey.

As an RTE, you may sit on and serve the LACE, or call upon their services to support you within the ART. The LACE is not just there during the transformation; they are an enduring group available to guide and coach the organization to be successful. For example, you might call upon them to facilitate the I&A on occasion to enable you to take off the facilitator hat and become actively engaged in the improvement process.

We will look in more detail at the RTE and the LACE in *Chapter 13*. Again, let's understand the view of the LACE member through their empathy map.

Lean-Agile Center of Excellence (LACE) empathy map

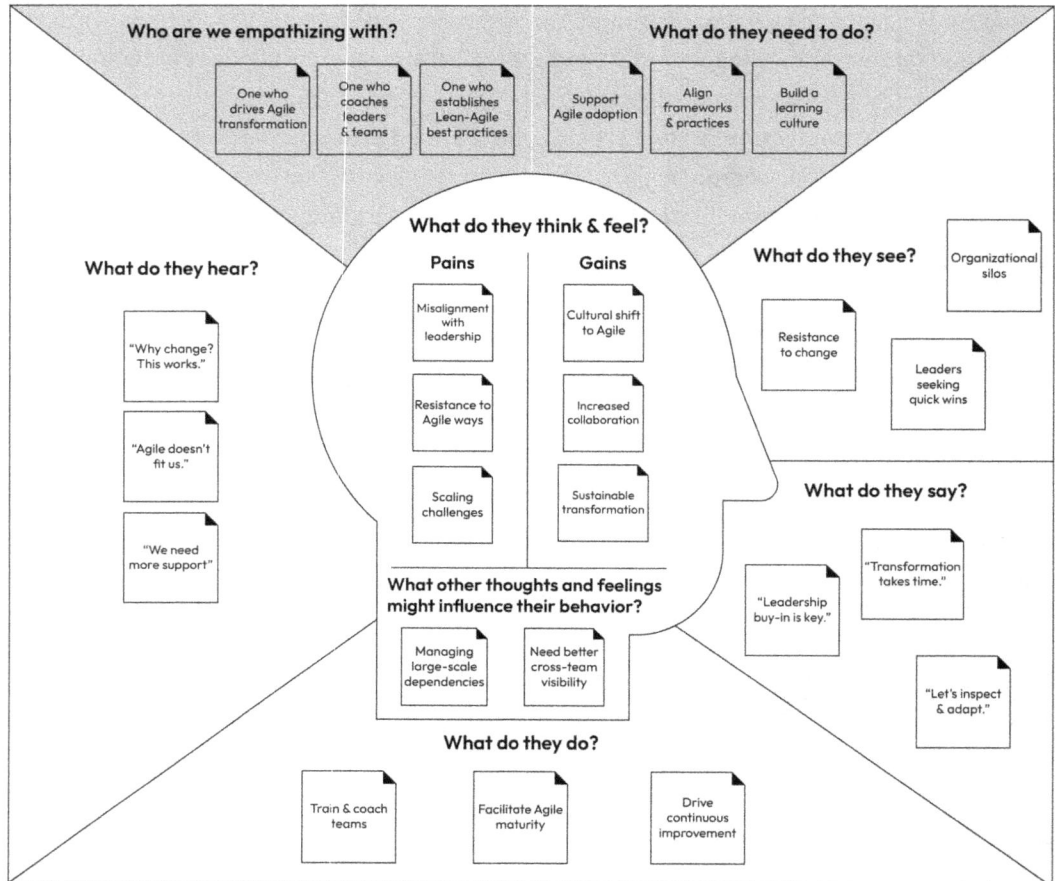

Fig 3.13: Lean-Agile Center of Excellence (LACE) empathy map (inspired by Dave Gray, Xplaner. com; online empathy map here: `https://gamestorming.com/empathy-mapping/`)

The main responsibilities of the LACE, the internal change agents and experts, include the following:

- **Managing the transformation backlog**: Prioritizing the backlog of transformation initiatives, impediments, and improvement opportunities to ensure the organization focuses on the most valuable changes.

- **Facilitating the transformation**: Coordinating and facilitating the end-to-end transformation effort to ensure alignment across initiatives, manage dependencies, and help the organization navigate the complexities of large-scale change.

- **Coaching leadership**: Providing executives and senior leaders with coaching and guidance to help them understand their role in the transformation and develop the Lean-Agile leadership behaviors needed to sustain change.

- **Supporting LPM**: Establishing and evolving LPM practices by assisting portfolio stakeholders as they implement strategy and investment funding, Lean governance, and Agile portfolio operations.

- **Fostering Lean-Agile learning**: Encouraging continuous learning for individuals, the organization, and the solution.

- **Being an exemplar Agile team**: Operating as a model Agile team that demonstrates Lean-Agile principles and practices in daily work, becoming a living example for others to follow.

- **Communicating the transformation vision**: Creating alignment and a desire to change through a compelling vision of the future.

- **Facilitating workshops and events**: Supporting the transformation through key events and ongoing execution activities.

The RTE and the VMO

The VMO is an organizational function in SAFe® that is responsible for facilitating the LPM process and fostering operational excellence and lean governance as part of a Lean-Agile transformation.

The VMO is a cross-functional business team with specific skill sets that support others in delivering value. Its main role is to connect the three dimensions of LPM (**strategy** and **investment funding**, **Agile portfolio operations**, and **Lean governance**) and ensure they are in constant alignment.

The VMO focuses on outcomes and value generation, and it works toward embedding long-lasting, stable teams in value streams. It also facilitates continuous feedback loops from customers and teams to drive continuous improvement.

There is more guidance on the VMO in *Chapter 12*. For now, their empathy offers some insight into their perspective.

Value Management Office (VMO) empathy map

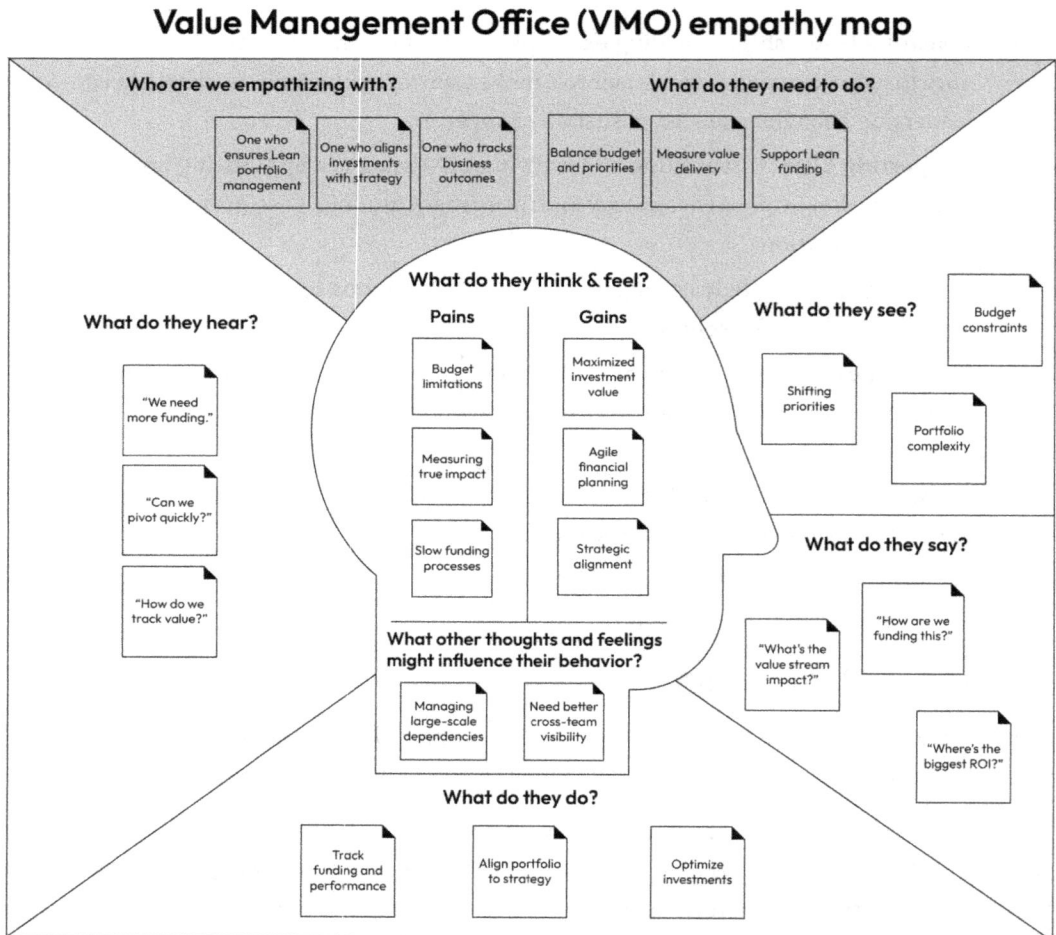

Fig 3.14: The VMO empathy map (inspired by Dave Gray, Xplaner.com; online empathy map here: https://gamestorming.com/empathy-mapping/)

The main responsibilities of the VMO are:

- **Enabling strategy and investment funding**: Aligning portfolio investments with strategic objectives and coordinating stakeholder engagement to ensure solutions receive appropriate funding to meet business targets.

- **Applying lean governance:** Providing lightweight oversight of spending, compliance, and performance metrics to replace traditional project governance while enabling faster decision-making and reducing funding friction.

- **Coordinating agile portfolio operations:** Synchronising cadence-based events and facilitating collaboration across value streams, Business Owners, and Enterprise Architects to ensure smooth flow and informed investment decisions.

- **Supporting the transformation:** Promoting continuous improvement, communicating the LPM governance model, and ensuring practices evolve as the organisation matures to drive sustainable Lean-Agile adoption.

- **Fostering operational excellence:** Identifying and eliminating waste, breaking down silos, and enhancing cross-team collaboration to improve efficiency and organisational responsiveness to change.

Summary

In this chapter, you've explored the intricate web of relationships that define the RTE role within SAFe®. You've learned that, at its heart, the RTE role is about people—creating an environment where teams and stakeholders can thrive while delivering value. The chapter has mapped out how you'll interact with critical roles across multiple levels: from your *first team* of Product Managers and System Architects at the ART leadership level to Scrum Masters and Product Owners at the team level, up to Solution Train Engineers and Epic Owners at higher levels of the organization.

Understanding these relationships is crucial because your effectiveness as an RTE depends on your ability to collaborate with and influence people across the organization. The complexity of communication in large teams, with potentially thousands of interconnections, means you cannot succeed alone. You must build bridges, facilitate alignment, and coach diverse stakeholders to maintain a sense of team cohesion.

You've also learned that the RTE role is a fractal extension of the Scrum Master role, taking principles that function at the team level and scaling them up to serve a team of teams. We introduced the concept of empathy maps, gaining insight into what motivates each role, the challenges they face, and how you can support them most effectively. Our maps are merely the starting point. As you become acquainted with the real people in your organization, document the reality you discover for the specific individuals you work with.

SAFe®'s success hinges on balancing the needs of various stakeholders while maintaining a focus on delivering value to customers. As an RTE, you play a crucial role in this balancing act—advocating for teams when necessary, coaching leaders on Lean-Agile principles, and ensuring that organizational structures support rather than hinder progress delivery.

These lessons are important because they prepare you to navigate human dynamics with empathy and purpose. Like Coach Carter in the movie, an effective RTE knows that real success comes not just from following processes but from inspiring people to reach for something they never felt possible. By understanding the roles you'll interact with, from their motivations, challenges, and responsibilities, you'll be better equipped to build the relationships that power high-performing ARTs.

In the next chapter, we will build upon this foundation of relationships to explore how the RTE is involved when launching a new ART.

References

Here, you can find the references to expand your knowledge about the specific concepts not covered in this book but mentioned in this chapter:

- Lencioni, P. M. (2002). *The five dysfunctions of a team: A leadership fable. Jossey-Bass.*

Get This Book's PDF Version and Exclusive Extras

UNLOCK NOW

Scan the QR code (or go to packtpub.com/unlock).
Search for this book by name, confirm the edition,
and then follow the steps on the page.

Note: Keep your invoice handy. Purchases made directly from Packt don't require one.

Part 2

The RTE and the Agile Release Train

Building on *Part 1*, which introduced the RTE's role and core knowledge, this part looks at the day-to-day work of the RTE within the **Agile Release Train** (**ART**). We begin with the crucial moments of launching an ART and preparing for PI Planning, before stepping into the rhythm of PI Planning itself. From there, the focus shifts to the execution phase—where the RTE not only supports processes and ceremonies, but also fosters the people side of delivery, helping teams collaborate, adapt, and continuously improve. Processes keep the train on the tracks, but people make it move—the best RTEs excel at both.

This part of the book includes the following chapters:

- *Chapter 4, Understanding the RTE's Role in Launching an Agile Release Train*
- *Chapter 5, Pre-PI Planning: Creating and Understanding the Backlog*
- *Chapter 6, Event Logistics for PI Planning*
- *Chapter 7, PI Planning: Day 1*
- *Chapter 8, PI Planning: Day 2*
- *Chapter 9, Executing the PI*
- *Chapter 10, Coaching ART Improvements*

4

Understanding the RTE's Role in Launching an Agile Release Train

Launching an **Agile Release Train (ART)** is one of the cornerstones of using the **Scaled Agile Framework® (SAFe®)**. Without ARTs, SAFe still has many valuable elements, but ARTs tend to be the first and most impactful thing from which an organization using SAFe gets value. But how do you do it, and more specifically, what is your role as an RTE in the launch of an ART? You cannot do it all; others will need to help as well. So, which areas should you focus on more specifically? Let's move on to look at key areas of RTE involvement in an ART launch, including how to identify the shape of an ART, prepare those involved, and engage the wider community around you.

It's important to understand what is involved in doing this properly, should you need to. Alternatively, if you've inherited an ART and it's not working perfectly, you can validate whether these issues occurred as part of the diagnosis process.

In this chapter, we're going to cover the following main topics:

- The Implementation Roadmap and the RTE
- Value stream identification
- Facilitating ART readiness
- Getting the right stakeholders engaged

The Implementation Roadmap and the RTE

When it comes to implementing SAFe®, it is well worth understanding the **SAFe Implementation Roadmap**. Developed over a number of years, based on numerous real-life experiences out in the field, it sets out a logical series of steps you might look to follow when rolling out SAFe across an organization, or at least a part of an organization, if the organization happens to be very large. The following figure illustrates it.

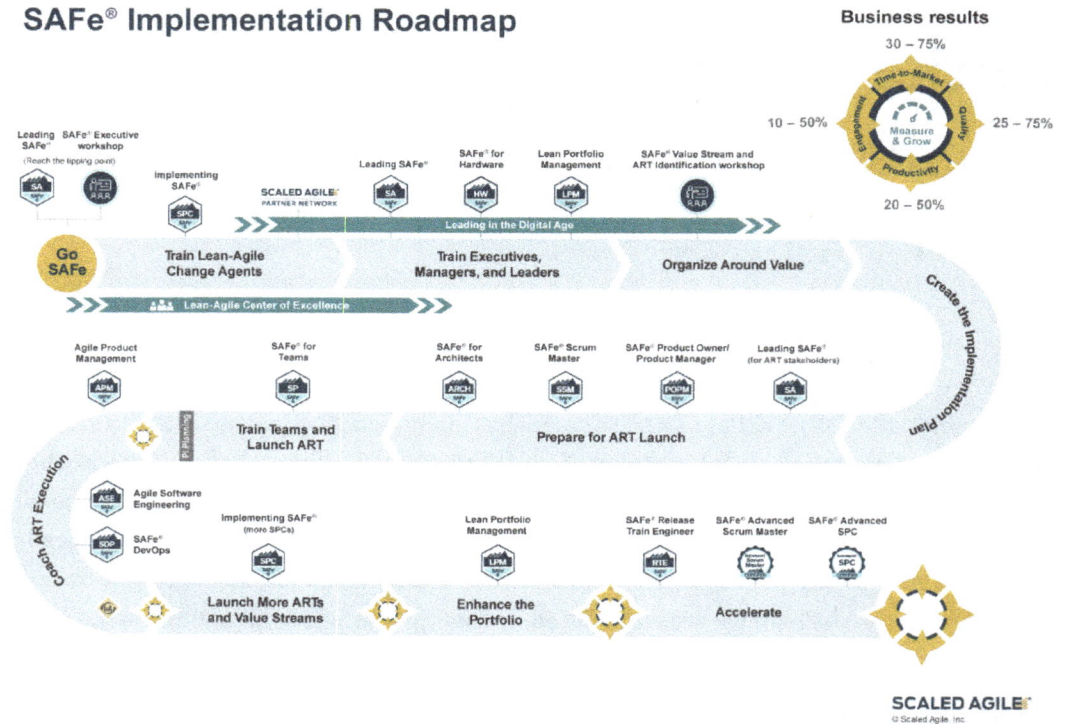

Figure 4.1: The SAFe Implementation Roadmap (© Scaled Agile, Inc. Source: `https://framework.scaledagile.com/implementation-roadmap/`)

The steps are as follows:

1. **Go SAFe:** This is the point when the organization knows there is a problem to be fixed and agrees that SAFe is the solution.

2. **Training Lean-Agile Change Agents:** Enable the change team, referred to as the **guiding coalition** by Kotter (`https://www.kotterinc.com/methodology/8-steps/`), to have the skills needed to support the change.

3. **Train Executives, Managers, and Leaders**: Provide the leadership at all levels with the knowledge of what they are asking the organization to go through and why.

4. **Organize Around Value**: Analyze and design how best to group the organization to maximize value delivery.

5. **Create the Implementation Plan**: The guiding coalition creates a plan for how the changes will happen.

6. **Prepare for ART Launch**: Undertake the necessary steps for the ART to start working.

7. **Train Teams and Launch ART**: Help those on the new ART to know how they will be working and get the ART up and running.

8. **Coach ART Execution**: Once up and running, develop the competency and maturity to deliver.

9. **Launch More ARTs and Value Streams**: Continue the transformation, extending beyond the current ART.

10. **Enhance the Portfolio**: When there are multiple value streams in existence, add the portfolio function to balance the conflicting demands and provide coordination.

11. **Accelerate**: The phase that never finishes—making things better.

As a result, the Implementation Roadmap is actually quite clever. While most people look at it as a single generic approach, in reality, it has to work for various different scales of SAFe® implementation. This means that it can just as usefully be a guide for launching a single ART as it can for improving a whole organization. Of course, it doesn't always fit each scenario perfectly. You personally might not look to use the *Launch More ARTs* step on the roadmap if you're only launching one ART, but it is at least always interesting to consider whether the launching of one ART will, over time, require the launching of others, too. Some key elements in the Implementation Roadmap are well worth considering as an RTE when you're thinking of launching an ART.

The first is the simple statement at the start that just says *Go SAFe*. In essence, this is all about identifying your tipping point, the point at which moving to SAFe, or just launching an ART, makes sense because the current ways of working are not offering results, and you believe SAFe is the answer.

Sometimes, the perfect moment to launch an ART only becomes clear to you after the fact. You may never have all the ideal conditions in place when it's time to act. The important thing is to move forward when you need to, even if everything isn't perfect. Don't wait for all the stars to align—take action as best you can.

Typically, there are a number of things to look for when looking for opportunities to launch an ART. Here are four modes compared against responsiveness to change and the level of dysfunction:

When to Launch an ART?

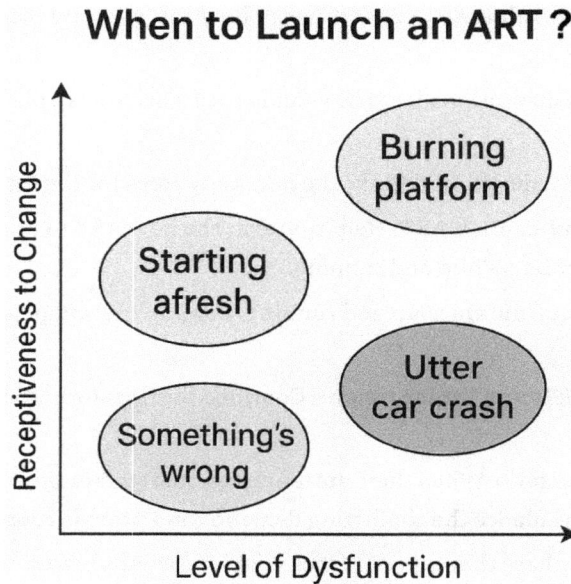

Figure 4.2: When to launch an ART

Let's see what they entail:

- **Starting afresh**: When a new program of work or major initiative is announced in the organization, people begin to prepare for it. New teams may be formed, new individuals may be onboarded to create these teams, or a new department might be established within the organization. Regardless of the trigger event, these changes require some structure, and often, an ART provides a lightweight way to initiate that.

- **Something's wrong**: This situation often isn't as severe and transformative as the others, and it grows over time. Teams are struggling to get dependencies met, or they're being thrown occasional curveballs by the planning impacts of other teams. Whatever it might be that's causing them to keep their heads down, keep on trying to get things done, and generally say "This is fine," even when it isn't. This can often feel like a more risky ART to launch, as you can't be 100% confident that you'll make things better when nothing is terribly wrong in the first place. However, in practice, these teams are generally pretty receptive to someone trying to help them, and have already started on a journey of attempting continuous improvement, so launching these kinds of ARTs can actually work out pretty well.

- **Burning platform:** In this situation, a team or selection of teams is realizing that things just aren't working. Their delivery is slow, they have multiple stakeholders throwing requirements at them at random times and from random directions, and the work they're delivering is taking ages to integrate and release. Often, these teams will pull you toward them to help. They know things aren't right, and they want them to be better, so if you can bring them tools and ideas to improve, then they'll welcome you.

- **Utter car crash:** Most organizations have teams like these, although they will never admit this. These are teams that are struggling so much through their current situation that the dynamics of team behavior have broken down. Nothing is getting delivered. Nothing is even being attempted to be delivered, because everyone is too busy arguing with each other. The rest of the organization just sits there trying not to look at the mess of it all, and no one wants to go and try to fix the situation, as who knows what reputational and emotional damage getting near this mess will cause to someone who tries to help. Oddly, these ARTs tend to be the easiest to launch. The reasons for this are pretty simple. Everyone wants this situation to be fixed, but no one wants to go and fix it themselves. So, if someone volunteers to do so, they often find they are welcomed with open arms and an open checkbook. Also, you don't have to do a lot to make a big difference. A set of teams that are performing pretty well might take a lot of work to get a little bit better. Teams that are performing really badly might just take a little bit of work to get a lot better very quickly. You might have to deal with some dysfunction and disagreement along the way, but if you want to make a name for yourself, fixing big problems is an easy way to do it.

So, that's your tipping point for launching an ART. What might be some signs that push you back, away from that tipping point, and make you think *not yet* or even possibly even *not ever*? There are no hard and fast rules in this space; the final judgment call has to be something you make with your context, but some things to watch out for include the following:

- **The push-based ART:** This is a difficult one, as in some situations, organizations will decide that they're *going SAFe®* and they want to get to the end of that journey as quickly as possible. So, they set an aggressive timeline for launching ARTs, mandate that everyone must be trained, and tell you to *drive it forward* as quickly as possible. The problem is, launching ARTs is a matter of hearts and minds, and this sort of approach wins neither. The teams don't buy into some stranger telling them how to work. Everyone gets *sheep dipped* in a two-day SAFe course, often with many dozens of people attending each course, and in reality, they're just attending remotely with their cameras off while they can get on with their day job. You may find you're hitting the metrics you've been set around the number of people trained and the number of ARTs launched, but on the ground, all you've done is confuse, annoy, and upset people, leading to massive disengagement from you and many of the useful tools within SAFe®. This makes any future attempt at SAFe adoption even more difficult, and it would have been better to have done nothing than to have done this. You may never fully work on a *pull-based* system, where you only launch ARTs that have invited you to do so, and for better or worse, leaders ultimately do have the right to say how they want their organizations to work. But we would strongly advise against going too far, too fast, and without the permission of the people you're trying to take on the journey with you.

- **The malicious compliance ART**: Sometimes, when people oppose ideas within organizations, they don't tell you that they do. In fact, they sometimes tell you the exact opposite—that they're supportive of the change, that they know things have to change, even that they've worked on exactly this kind of change at some time previously in their career. They do this because they know that opposing the change now will look bad on them, and will make them not seem supportive of the way the organization has said that it wants to head. However, when push comes to shove, their behaviors will not have changed, and you have an *ART in name only*.

- **The *over my dead body* ART**: Sometimes, you run into people and teams who are not just a bit skeptical of what you're suggesting; they're vehemently opposed to SAFe, to you, and to everything you ever say or stand for. During one transformation, one manager (we're not sure we could classify them as a leader) warned the change team that if they continued their endeavors to implement SAFe with *their* teams, they would raise a formal complaint with HR!

When you run into these sorts of situations, just walk away. It's a fight you're unlikely to win at this point, and is it really worth all that effort to try to win it anyway?

If someone is that determined to oppose what you do, it's going to take huge amounts of your time and effort to try to change things, and you may lose good people along the way as they look for easier jobs that don't keep them up at night with worry. Sometimes, it's best to stay away from these areas or go around them, and help the people who want help first. Think of a **Weighted Shortest Job First (WSJF)** calculation for the different people you could work with. You're looking to deliver the most value in the shortest amount of time. If something is going to take a lot of time and effort, and may still not return much value, then you have to consider it a lower priority than everything else you could be doing. Sometimes, over time, as new ARTs launch and the organization improves, these areas come back for your help anyway.

In large organizations, no one ever wins a fight, so if launching an ART in an area looks like a massive fight, walk away for now and give it time.

The preceding are all what we might call **practical patterns**: things that have worked for us in the field, things we have experienced, and things to which we have fallen foul.

Launching ARTs typically follows an official pattern, or rather, involves an essential step: **value stream identification (VSI)**, which is usually accomplished through a VSI workshop.

Value stream identification

Before we look at VSI, let us first just check that we understand what a **value stream** is. This is one of those areas that can seem needlessly arcane, technical, and advanced, but it really needn't be. If we can understand it, so can you!

The simplest way to think of a value stream is to think about how work flows through an organization. All work will start somewhere. Maybe it's a customer request, maybe it's an innovative new idea someone thought up, maybe it's an external requirement that someone, such as a regulator, has placed on the organization to deliver. Wherever a piece of work starts its journey through the organization, that is the start of the value stream.

All work then moves through a series of steps to be delivered. Sometimes it moves from team to team, sometimes it moves across entire parts of the organization, and sometimes it even moves out of the organization to a third party and then back in again. Eventually, the work reaches its final state. It has been delivered, put live, communicated, and is now fully operational. That is the end of the value stream.

From this, we can see two things. The first is that all organizations have value streams. If they have ideas, move those ideas through a series of steps to deliver them, and then end up with the thing delivered, that is a value stream.

The second is that most organizations don't realize that they have value streams. Work moves through the organization in a stop/start way, and can hardly be said to flow smoothly. The trick is to recognize and optimize this value stream and its flow of value from start to finish.

So, now that we better understand what value streams are, what do they have to do with preparing an ART for launch?

Why perform VSI

The point of a value stream is to help organizations deliver better products and services to their customers more efficiently. Many different organizational ways of working can block the flow through the value stream, and it is these blockers we want to design out of our system. One of the best ways we can remove those blockers is to make them visible and get the people closest to them to remove them. We do this by aligning our people and processes around delivering this value. This is a lot of what PI Planning, System Demos, and Problem Solving workshops are there as events to accomplish. Get everyone involved in the end-to-end flow of value into the same place, working as one collective team of teams, to optimize the flow of work through their particular value stream.

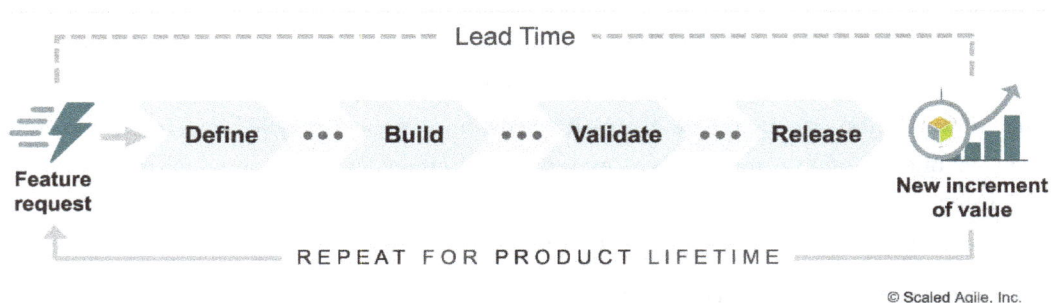

Lead Time

Define ••• Build ••• Validate ••• Release

Feature request

New increment of value

REPEAT FOR PRODUCT LIFETIME

© Scaled Agile, Inc.

Figure 4.3: Optimizing the value stream to achieve the shortest sustainable lead time with the best quality and value (© Scaled Agile, Inc. Source: `https://framework.scaledagile.com/organize-around-value-2/`)

As a result, identifying the value stream(s) that an ART works around is a part of building a successful ART. We will discuss the process in *Chapter 11* briefly, and Scaled Agile provides courses, videos, toolkits, and templates for this purpose; you can easily find them via the SAFe® community portal with a valid membership (`https://community.scaledagile.com`).

> *There is an ART to designing ARTs.*
>
> —*Mark Richards, SAFe Fellow and SPCT*

Let's have a reality check. No ART design is ever perfect. Like real streams, value streams are organic—natural things made up of complex human beings and systems that behave in unpredictable and sometimes irrational ways. Therefore, the answer to the question "Did I get my VSI right or wrong?" is "Yes." You probably got it both right and wrong, because there is no right and wrong. There's just the answer you came up with, and the answer you can work with for now. This is important for two reasons.

First, you can spend too long trying to identify the perfect design for your value stream and never actually get on with applying it and seeing what works. As Agilists, we are all about the **plan-do-check-adjust cycle**, constantly planning something, doing it, seeing what happened, and using that information to decide what to do next. The same is true of ART design. You will never get it perfect the first time, and sometimes you have to apply your VSI in real life to fully understand whether it actually worked or not.

The second reason for not worrying about getting your VSI *perfect* is that if you believe you have got it perfect, then you are less likely to be open to changing and evolving it over time. The ability to inspect and adapt your ART over time is essential to making sure that your value stream keeps flowing.

This is a tension that very often exists between two different factors. On the one hand, you have the desire to build a long-lived, stable ART. One where everyone on the ART knows everyone else, knows what they do, knows how they work, and knows how the team of teams as one collective system best operates. Through this work, the people on the ART develop shared mental models that enable them to shortcut conversations and approaches without the need to debate and discuss them. In short, they become a high-performing collective whole.

On the other hand, nothing stays the same for long. External market conditions can necessitate a change in the size and shape of an ART's solution. Internally, changing strategic priorities, operational demands, and optimizations can necessitate structural changes, too.

For this reason, when we introduce the process, be it in training or the workshop, we make it clear that your VSI and the resulting ART design are never a one-and-done. Next, we will explore when to return to our design and consider updating it.

When to revisit an existing ART design?

When do you redesign an ART? The answer is as often as you need to, but no more than that. The trigger for a change, or at least a review, could come externally from market adjustments or internal changes to strategy, operational improvements, or staffing. The most common patterns we have identified are as follows.

Market conditions

Shifts in customer needs, competitive pressures, emerging technologies, and regulatory landscapes can all compel organizations to rethink how they deliver value. Suppose an ART is aligned with a market opportunity that is shrinking or evolving beyond its current capability. In that case, you must consider whether the ART is still aimed at the proper outcomes and whether its structure, skills, and focus remain fit for purpose.

It doesn't have to be only negative market drivers, either. With growth and increased profit comes more demand. Once an ART has reached the theoretical limit of 12 teams/125 people, splitting the ART becomes necessary. In doing so, you need to understand how best to do this while maintaining flexibility and speed of execution without getting caught up in a dependency nightmare.

In 2007, Netflix pivoted from a DVD rental service to a digital streaming service. The market conditions had shifted, and consumers no longer wanted to wait for DVDs to be posted to them, with a desire for instant, always-on content. This required a massive reorganization of their technology and product teams to focus on streaming infrastructure, content delivery, and personalized recommendations. They moved from a product pipeline aligned to DVD distribution to cross-functional teams focused on streaming and user experience, effectively redesigning the way value was delivered to align with a completely new market landscape.

ARTs exist to provide solutions for customers by delivering the right product to the right customer at the right time. Just because what they did was correct yesterday doesn't mean that it's what is needed today. Adapting to remain relevant is essential. If the market shifts, ARTs must shift as well.

Changing strategy

Enterprises can change their strategy, which has ripple effects on the value streams and ART designs for one of two reasons. Firstly, from a commercial perspective, it is about where and why the organizations want to focus. It could be an increased push for a market segment or geography requiring an increased investment or exiting another to enable a focused effort elsewhere.

Secondly, strategy can change for operational reasons—how they want to operate and deliver their offerings. This can involve bringing in-house delivery, outsourcing, partnering, mergers and acquisitions, or developing new skills and capabilities to service a new focus.

Operational performance

An operational performance change is predominantly required when an ART (or ARTs) is not performing as desired. As the RTE, you may be the one noticing these issues through conversations, metrics, or outcomes of the Inspect and Adapt workshop. Initially, you will do your best to resolve things locally, but sometimes, it is necessary to raise the flag, calling for a more structural rethinking of the portfolio's organization.

Be on the lookout for the following:

- Persistent delivery problems identified in Inspect & Adapt workshops
- An increasing number of dependencies between teams
- Flow metrics showing bottlenecks related to team structure
- Declining predictability across multiple PIs
- Excessive coordination overhead between teams
- Unbalanced workload between teams within the ART
- Missing people or teams on the ART
- PI Objectives consistently not being met
- Burnout indicators showing unsustainable team structures
- Stakeholder dissatisfaction with value delivery cadence
- Difficulty coordinating critical path activities
- Team health surveys showing systemic issues
- Lengthy feature cycle times that cross multiple teams

Periodic review

Beyond these trigger events, we recommend periodically (typically every 18 months to 2 years) doing a light-touch reassessment to confirm whether the way in which the ARTs are constructed is still best suited to the portfolio's needs. Think of this as an insurance policy—spending a day or so with a handful of people from across the portfolio to revalidate, or not, that the portfolio is still structured in the most optimal way.

What to do when the ART does need to change?

Change is work, and like all work, it needs to be planned and accounted for within your capacity. Change is also disruptive, resulting in performance going backward before it gets better. Roadmaps and expectations need to be updated in advance to avoid sad faces!

There are also trade-offs to be considered. Optimizing for one way, often a lead tendency toward flow, can work at odds with technical and architectural robustness. How will you overcome or mitigate this? What mechanisms, processes, events, or people need to be responsible for making this work? Again, once these decisions are made, in the VSI workshop, set people's expectations—and remind them of their decisions later when they (conveniently?) forget.

Once the decision is made that the ART needs refactoring or deletion, portfolio-level changes are necessary to support and guide this. We shall not delve into extensive detail here, as it falls outside the scope of the RTE's role, but it is crucial to be aware of the following implications:

- **Strategic themes**: These will be updated to reflect the change in strategy. These will be created and approved in the **Strategic Portfolio Review** meeting. Changes to the strategic themes will have a ripple effect on the backlog contents from epics through to stories. Work with your Product Managers and Product Owners to adjust the features and stories as is appropriate. Consider whether the new work to be done requires different skill sets from those available.

- **Value stream budgets**: The allocation of portfolio funding within the portfolio could be changing, and therefore, the split of money across the value streams will change. Depending on the trigger, the size of the pot could change, too. The collaborative **Participatory Budgeting** (PB) approach can offer data points on how the split can be made. Once you know the budget for the value stream, the RTE can *balance the books* by aligning capacity to cash.

- Even a minor change will create work for you as the RTE. Don't forget, in addition to the tactical changes being made, spend time with the people on the ART. Be respectful that change creates uncertainty, and this could take them off their game, or they might resist the change. It's an overused term, but bringing people along for the journey is vital for a change to be successful.

What if you do not have a choice over ART design?

There is one final point to make around ART design. Sometimes, the choice is not yours. Sometimes, organizations know that they need to get a handle on delivery and bring people together to plan and resolve problems as one collective whole, but there is a massive red line you must not cross. You are told that the design of the ARTs must exactly mirror the current organizational structure.

This typically happens when senior people have had meetings to set out what they like to call the *strategy* for the department, and have decided on some fundamental ideas around how it operates. For example, we mustn't build any custom APIs to transfer data to and from the mainframe database. APIs are meant to open up data for all, so all APIs must be reusable by all. Therefore, no ART shall have its own API teams; otherwise, they will just try to get specific APIs built for their specific context, and nothing will be reusable. As a result, the solution you must follow is to have an ART made up entirely of API teams that only build APIs.

Let's understand this through an experience Gez had. Faced with the choice of going along with it or having the API teams continue to work in an entirely siloed and project management-driven way, he decided going along with it was probably the better option of the two. The potential third option, getting people to understand the speed and alignment benefits of distributing API teams across the ARTs, then applying a simple coordination layer across them to ensure reusability, provoked an incredibly strong reaction from senior leaders.

So he went along with it, but with one thing at the back of his mind. If senior leaders were so convinced that their model was the correct one, then this correctness must be demonstrated with data over time. Therefore, the ART ran for a while, and it wasn't entirely terrible. It started performing a whole lot better as an ART than it had under its previous project management-based approach. However, after about three PIs, he ran a quick check to see how many of the hundreds of APIs that had been created by that point were actually being reused by any team other than the one that had originally requested them. Even he was surprised by the data that came back. Not a single API was being reused. Not a single API was even capable of being reused. Despite the stated mission of senior leaders to ensure cost savings and speed through API reuse, the practice hadn't in any way translated into reality on the ground.

Armed with this information and other data around how the API ART had been performing, he went back to senior leaders, convinced them that their dream was just not working in practice, indeed it may never work in practice, and explained the significant speed, alignment and dependency reduction benefits they'd get from splitting up the API ART and distributing its teams across the other ARTs that needed APIs to be delivered. It worked, and things got better.

This isn't the only time we've seen this pattern. It's a tricky thing to say out loud as an RTE, as people worry it may lead to bad things happening, but sometimes you make compromises around ART design precisely because you know the design on which people are insisting will be suboptimal or even fail. You make these compromises not because you've given up, but because you're picking your battles. If people won't listen to the theoretical reasons behind what works, perhaps they need to run the suboptimal approach in reality for a while and learn about what does and does not work the hard way. As long as you, as an RTE, take this approach consciously and keep a close eye on the ART in case it blows up earlier or more spectacularly than expected, in essence creating a *safe-to-fail* environment, then this plan B approach can actually be pretty successful.

Once we have a proposal for the design of the ART(s), we need to launch them.

Facilitating ART readiness

There is one fundamental rule in all of this when it comes to training. You can't ask people to adopt a new way of working without telling them what it is. That sounds like a really simple fact, but you'd be astonished at how often organizations try to shortcut this element of launching ARTs.

When you get deep into it, SAFe® is actually not a very complex framework at all. It is just a fractal model, taking ideas that work for a team, and scaling them up to a team of teams, then sometimes scaling them further to a team of teams of teams. However, to explain something in simple terms often takes a lot of learning, as well as a lot of unlearning. Without sufficient time spent helping people to understand what an ART is and why it works, before doing the same for key ART events such as PI Planning, System Demos, and Inspect and Adapt events, then your ART is going to really struggle.

"Of course you would say this," we hear you say. "You run SAFe training for people. Is it any wonder you recommend people be trained in SAFe?"

Well, you can think that if you like, but you honestly would be wrong. We're also Lean and Agile people who are constantly looking to maximize simplicity and cut out non-value-added activities. Why would we run SAFe training when launching ARTs if it didn't add any value?

The simple truth is this. We've launched ARTs after training and coaching everyone on the ART. We've launched ARTs where we've trained and coached 90% of the people on the ART, but some people have been missed due to illness, vacations, and the ever-present *pressure of delivery*. We've also sometimes launched ARTs with zero training and minimal coaching. We've experienced all three of these scenarios multiple times, and can happily tell you that the third scenario, launching an ART without training, is one we never want to relive and gives us nightmares to this day.

Why does PI Planning suffer without training?

The reason for this is simple. To make an event such as PI Planning work, people need to understand *how* it works. Very often, unless time and importance are given to training people in PI Planning, they will go into the event without understanding how it works. At this point, one of three things happens.

They stand around confused for a while, then quickly try to scribble down some sort of plan before leaving the room as quickly as possible, before anyone notices that they don't know what they're doing. Alternatively, they look around at other ARTs in the room, if there are any, and try to copy what they do. This relies on the ART they're copying having been trained and knowing what it is doing, too. Or they follow what is the worst option, and try to invent what PI Planning is from their previous experiences of planning things, which is often a very traditional project management-based approach.

They then decide they only need the team leads there to create the plan; everyone else who actually does the work can go back to work and not waste any more time. The team leads proudly create their plan in an hour or less, declare themselves done, and subsequently go around the organization telling people that PI Planning for 100 people/10 teams, which should take 2 days, can clearly be done by 10 people in just 1 hour. This is music to senior leaders' ears, as it sounds like it will save them time and money and will remove the need for the people who do the work to take time out from *delivering*. How does this happen? Why don't senior leaders push back and explain the importance of the people who do the work getting to plan the work? Because you probably weren't given time and budget to train the senior leaders either.

If this happens, your whole ART-launching endeavor pretty much crashes and burns.

As a result, for the authors of this book, launching an ART without training is a massive red line. Not to say that in certain specific circumstances we haven't done it, because we have. But every time we do, we're reminded what a horrible, costly, and futile endeavor it is, especially when we then spend months undoing the damage the approach had caused.

A personal example

Glenn once experienced this firsthand when the client wanted to offer training, but did not mandate that people attend it because everyone was already busy. On the day of PI Planning, there were lots of confused-looking people. Speaking with people during the event and looking at the feedback afterward, the overarching comment was "Training beforehand would have been useful!" We can unpick later why this cohort didn't attend, but it's never fun to have to say "We told you so."

So, in essence, the old SAFe® mantra of *Train everyone, launch trains* has the highest *truth-to-word count* ratio of anything in the 500,000-word framework. If you want to save time and money by launching ARTs without training at the start, then know that you will end up paying off that initial debt many times over the coming months and years that these ARTs exist. Training matters.

Don't game the metrics

One final thought on this. Sometimes, while trying to cut corners around cost and time or to create vanity metrics for their managers, people decide to measure the *percentage/total number of people trained*. This is a slippery slope, as it can lead to just a handful of people on each team being trained, which hits the metric but misses the point. If only half of a team is trained, you've effectively split the team in half. One half understands the new way of working, whereas the other half does not. At this point, your options are either to press on with a situation where even individual teams, let alone teams of teams, no longer have the shared mental models and common language that is so essential to high performance, or trust that the trained half of the team will pass the knowledge on to the untrained half. This would require both halves of a team to stop doing what they're doing to do some sort of knowledge-sharing session. However, as it is run by inexperienced, poorly trained people, it will struggle to be effective, and will likely use up more time than you would have done if you'd just taken the hit on training everyone in the first place. The idea of a false economy has the word *false* in it for a real reason.

While much of our focus during ART readiness is inwardly looking, we must not lose sight of those on the periphery.

Getting the right stakeholders engaged

You've identified your value stream(s) for your ART. You've assembled the people and teams who will do the work to flow value through the value stream(s). Who else do you need to get involved?

Well, the word *stakeholders* is one of the most common catch-all terms for other people that need to be involved in the delivery of work, and now is the time to consider them. As ever, with any Lean-Agile approach, there's a degree of pragmatism that needs to be applied to which stakeholders to involve and how to involve them. Pragmatism starts with understanding, so let's first unpick this term *stakeholders* to understand how it might best apply to an ART.

In some ways, *stakeholders* has become a very difficult term to unpick. It has become a generic catch-all term to mean *people who want to know what's going on*, or *people who want to tell other people what to do*, or even sometimes just *people we think we need to have notice us and be impressed by our work for the benefit of our annual performance review*. This is especially true in organizations where people are still cursed by the belief that *perception is reality*.

Because of these factors, and others like them, the term *stakeholders* can have a pretty broad meaning; thus, identifying who we want as stakeholders for our ART can take some thinking through. It's a thought process that is well worth it, however, as without it, the ART may get overwhelmed by people, opinions, confusion, and a lack of alignment. As such, the first thing to reflect on is the Agile principle of **simplicity**. How can we strip back and simplify our list of stakeholders such that they don't end up adding additional complexity to the ART and its decision-making processes? There is a good reason a team typically has a single Product Owner prioritizing the work of the team and accepting it as done, rather than a committee of Product Owners all acting as stakeholders. One person on their own rarely disagrees with themselves. A committee of people with competing interests often disagrees with each other.

Choosing stakeholders based on value

Having established that we want to narrow down our list of stakeholders rather than expand it, how then should we choose who to include? SAFe® is centered on delivering value, so it is a good practice to filter potential stakeholders based on the value they bring to the ART itself. If individuals can contribute valuable input to the ART backlog alongside Product Management, then all is well. However, if they merely seek to take value from the ART by insisting their pet projects and personal deliverables are prioritized above everything else, then it's difficult to see what benefit they add to the ART.

This value-based assessment of stakeholders might also lead to some interesting insights. Imagine your ART is developing a new feature for a mobile app that, if successful, could significantly impact call volumes at your customer contact center. Usually, people working in customer contact centers are considered low in the organizational hierarchy. But, given how much the work of the ART will influence their roles, they now become important stakeholders—those who could provide the ART with valuable feedback on the new feature and its design.

With this in mind, you might want to map stakeholders to specific events within the ART. For instance, some stakeholders could offer valuable context, input, and support during feature and story refinement leading up to PI Planning. Others might be most useful during the PI Planning itself. Still, some might be best engaged by attending System Demos, providing feedback on what has been delivered and what could follow.

What we are beginning to see is a more comprehensive picture of stakeholder management across an ART. By reducing the stakeholder list, focusing membership criteria on the value each member contributes to the ART, and guiding those who make the cut on how best they can participate in the events and practices that drive value delivery, we move closer to that core SAFe® principle: **alignment.** We align stakeholders with their roles on the ART and how they can support those roles.

With this in mind, perhaps only one more SAFe core value remains: **transparency.** Once you've thought through and designed your stakeholder interactions, document them clearly and make them transparent. Not necessarily through formal **Responsible, Accountable, Consulted or Informed (RACI)** charts or extensive documentation, but in simple, engaging formats—perhaps pen portraits of stakeholders on the ART, outlining what they do, what they're interested in, and how they can serve the ART to support its continuous value delivery.

What if people are resistant to launching an ART?

It's only fair to acknowledge that getting to your first PI Planning event isn't always easy. You might face resistance from various quarters, and it's important to recognize that people's concerns can stem from many sources. Some individuals are simply uneasy with change, preferring the familiar ways of working they've known for years. Others may resist because PI Planning exposes them and their work to greater scrutiny—the transparency and collaboration it requires can feel threatening to those accustomed to more independence or opacity. Still, some may have valid concerns specific to your organizational context, such as budget constraints, scheduling conflicts, geographical distribution, or previous experiences with unsuccessful change initiatives.

Whatever the reason for hesitation, it's vital to approach these concerns with empathy and practical strategies. In *Chapter 7*, we offer guidance on creating your own elevator pitch for PI Planning—a helpful starting point for building confidence and gaining support. For techniques to address common concerns and help stakeholders trust the process, see *Appendix B: Building Confidence in the Process*.

Summary

In this chapter, we have looked at a number of key areas an RTE will need to consider when involved in launching an ART. We've examined different scenarios you may look for when trying to identify an ART to launch, as well as the more formal practice of value stream identification that goes alongside it. ART structures are never fully fixed and may evolve over time, so we need not worry about whether we have the perfect ART to start with, as there's probably no such thing. As an RTE, your skill is in surfing sometimes rapidly moving waves of evolving situations, and keeping people on board as you do so. Finally, we looked at the crucial importance of training people within each ART and ensuring that a sufficient degree of stakeholder engagement has taken place with those around the ART, too.

Let us now move on to the next chapter, where we will look at how to prepare the ART backlog, ready for PI Planning.

References

Here, you can find the references to expand your knowledge about the specific concepts not covered in this book but mentioned in this chapter:

- Allen C. Ward, *Lean Product and Process Development, Lean Enterprise Institute, Incorporated, 2007 (First Edition)*

Get This Book's PDF Version and Exclusive Extras

UNLOCK NOW

Scan the QR code (or go to packtpub.com/unlock).
Search for this book by name, confirm the edition, and then follow the steps on the page.

Note: Keep your invoice handy. Purchases made directly from Packt don't require one.

5

Pre-PI Planning: Creating and Understanding the Backlog

PI Planning is the seminal event in **SAFe®**, but 125 people do not just turn up and make it up as they go along. We will take you through how to enable the creation of the backlog that they will plan from. From the logistics and backlog creation to the team's readiness, you will discover that many people must prepare for the event to be run successfully, producing a tenable, aligned, and agreed-upon set of objectives that the teams believe they can deliver in the next PI.

Not everything directly falls under the ownership of the RTE, but as the ART facilitator, the RTE is responsible for ensuring that what needs to happen actually occurs. We will explain whom you can call upon so you know what to ask for and how to explain to them the importance of the request and the bearing it holds to successful planning. In this chapter, we will review how the RTE enables successful preparation through looking at these topics:

- What preparation do you need for a successful PI Planning event?
- Understanding the purpose of the backlog and reflecting on its management
- Cadence of creating the PI Planning Backlog
- Preparing PI Planning presentation content

What preparation do you need for a successful PI Planning event?

In SAFe®, the PI Planning event is the cornerstone of the planning cadence for the ART. The objective of the event, held over 2 days, is to create a tenable and agreed-upon set of objectives to deliver for the upcoming 8–12 week planning horizon.

It achieves this by creating alignment between those representing the demand side of the equation, **Executives, Business Owners (BOs), Product Management**, and **System Architects (SAs)**, and the supply side, such as the teams, suppliers, and **Shared Services**.

Something special happens when all these groups work together simultaneously in the same physical or online space. Communication is nearly instant; there is no need to look for an empty slot in another team's diary three weeks in the future. Dependency management and sequencing are mutually agreed upon seamlessly, creating a delivery plan for the ART's **features** and **enablers** backed up by the teams' team-level plans.

The plans become realistic when teams build them based on their expected capacity over the coming PI. The ART then looks only to take on an acceptable level of uncertainty regarding the ask and their expected ability to deliver against it, enabling an acceptable level of predictability at the end of the PI. At the end of the event, the ART will have a set of objectives that the Business Owners accept, and the teams will be confident in their ability to deliver. We will go into the details of the two days in *Chapters 6* and *7*.

Like any act of facilitation, the event becomes much easier if thought and preparation are made beforehand. While the RTE doesn't need to design the event because the **PI Planning Toolkit** (available with a paid SAFe® Studio membership) provides a host of resources to make this easier, including a slide deck with the agenda and instructions for the day, the RTE does need to corral the troops to ensure everything else is in order.

The following are the PI Planning Toolkit contents:

- ART Readiness Workbook (Excel)
- PI Planning Overview for Stakeholders (PowerPoint)
- Preparing Day 1 Briefings (PowerPoint)

- ART Backlog Workbook (Excel)
- ART and Team Events Calendar (Excel)
- Capacity Allocation (Excel)
- ART Canvas (PowerPoint)
- PI Planning Facilitator's Guide (PDF)
- PI Planning Resource Guide (PDF)
- PI Planning Event Template (PowerPoint)
- Coach Sync PI Planning Radiator (Excel)
- Distributed PI Planning Events Agenda (PowerPoint)
- Editable Distributed PI Planning Agenda (Excel)

Just because the framework and this book describe activities that the RTE performs, it doesn't mean the RTE needs to be hands-on with them all. RTEs will do well to have extra pairs of hands to support them during preparatory activities and during the event itself.

During the event's preparation, administrative or junior project management support can relieve the RTE of the burden, allowing them to focus on higher-order activities.

On the day of the event, you will benefit from assistants who can handle logistical challenges, such as building access and food.

With the toolkit in hand to guide us, let's look at what needs to be done.

Areas of preparation

Chapter 4 discussed setting up a new ART, so we will assume that your ART is already in place or that the preparatory activities described in the previous chapter have been completed.

In addition to the content, successful PI Planning events, online or in-person, have logistical needs.

Pre-COVID, arranging PI Planning included ordering copious amounts of sticky notes and marker pens. Planning was always done in person, either in a single location or a distributed manner, with a subset of the ART in as few locations as possible. Since the pandemic, when ARTs were forced to plan online owing to global stay-at-home orders, we now see a greater variety of online and hybrid methods.

Chapter 6 will outline the logistical considerations and actions an RTE needs to perform for in-person and online planning scenarios. To give you a taste, it includes the following:

- Room or tooling reservations
- Attendee identification and invitations
- Attendee access arrangements
- Meeting supplies, sticky notes, markers, and so on
- Food—lots of it!
- Team building activities

Physical and virtual event logistics aside, considerable work remains to be done. We always tell our clients that the heavy lifting in planning preparation is content creation of the features and enablers.

Planning for the next PI Planning event starts the day after the last event. The RTE and Scrum Masters will look at the feedback and their observations from the event while it is fresh in their minds. Then, the focus quickly turns to content creation.

Before we discuss the details of creating the backlog content and the associated briefings for PI Planning, let's step back and reflect on the **backlog** and its effective use.

Understanding the purpose of the backlog and reflecting on its management

As most people see it, a backlog is a list of tasks. Whether it's a backlog for an ART, a single team, or even a personal backlog for a single person, a backlog is a tool and technique for managing the work entering a system.

This definition of a backlog, though, needs to be corrected. A backlog is not a list of things *to do*. A backlog is a list of things that *could be* done. This might sound like arguing over details, but it's essential. As we shall explore more in this chapter, how a backlog is handled can have wide-ranging effects on how a team behaves and how the broader system around the team operates. After all, if a backlog can significantly impact how work enters a system, then the backlog can have measurable effects on how the system as a whole behaves.

Using the backlog to drive team design optimizations

How you structure the demand signals within your backlog will influence how easily it is to realize the value of fulfilling those requests. Creating them so they individually deliver value is vital, as the ART's purpose is to deliver business results.

When organizations are moving from a more traditional project management and delivery way of working, teams are often grouped in silos of disciplines or functional areas, such as a testing or business analysis team. Even in optimized ARTs, delivering a feature's value might still need multiple teams' contributions. Having less optimized team structures results in a *many hands touching it* problem. As we know from the sixth principle, ***Make value flow without interruptions***, requiring different teams to touch work results in a handoff. Where there is a handoff, there is a queue, and where there is a queue, there is a delay.

If the team structure needs to be better designed for flow, avoid succumbing and creating backlog items that pander to this inefficiency. Create features to be end-to-end, or as end-to-end as possible. This forces the teams to work collectively on it. You can use the visualizations in the ART board and the data from the **ART Kanban** to highlight the challenges this creates to manage during delivery and the delays it introduces. Use this data to provide feedback for the future **Inspect and Adapt (I&A)** workshop to change the team structures.

There is no standard template for how you structure your backlog. We can't give you a standard template and say, "Fill in these blanks, and all will be well." As with so many things in this space, context matters, and you will need to craft a backlog that works for you, which contains the necessary information to deliver your features. This may mean your backlog structure changes over time, which is fine, as the SAFe® core value of relentless improvement applies just as much to backlogs as it does to anything else.

However, some basic concepts and principles may help you create a backlog that genuinely benefits the teams on and around the train.

How to record work on the backlog?

As Agile has grown more popular over the years, certain practices from its early days have also grown more popular and survived to the present day. Other practices have fallen by the wayside. Some have survived but mutated so badly that their original purpose can barely be discerned. One massive example of this is the humble sticky note.

Anyone who spends time around an Agile Team will soon come to realize just how many sticky notes they get through over time. Entire office walls sometimes end up covered in hundreds or thousands of them at once. The reasons for this may seem obvious. They're handy, you can move them around when you need to, they're cheap, and they're disposable. However, the reason that has tragically been lost in the mists of time is one of their unique characteristics. They're also small, which means that you can't write much on them. This may sound more like a drawback than a benefit, but originally, their small size was very much intended to benefit their use in the Agile space.

When you can't write much on something, it cannot contain much information. However, the work item that was trying to be represented on that sticky note likely had a good deal of information behind it. So, what happened to that information if it wasn't written down? Well, it stayed in people's heads and transferred from the original head into the new heads that needed to know it through the medium of... talking to each other! As the saying used to go, a user story is a placeholder for a conversation.

Think back to the **Agile Manifesto**. We value *individuals and interactions over processes and tools*. So, which category do the backlog and its items fall into? All it can ever be is a process or a tool. We must make sure that this process or tool doesn't start to replace the individuals and interactions from which true value flows.

One of the real tragedies of the Agile space is that this has been forgotten over the years. The rise of digital tooling has only made the problem worse. For all of its benefits around real-time data capturing and cross-time zone collaboration, one thing most digital backlog management systems have in common is no character limit on what can be written into an item of work, or at least such a high character limit that it makes the whole thing irrelevant.

Not only does this increase the risk of people deprioritizing individuals and interactions, but it also throws open the back door to a backlog that becomes more akin to traditional project management. With no limit to how many words can be written into a backlog item, backlog items can once again turn into requirements or specifications. Rather than setting out a problem to solve from the perspective of the person or people experiencing the problem and then empowering your skilled and creative teams to solve that problem in the best way possible, you can instead write down up front a detailed specification for them to build and tell them to build it. At this point, you may as well give up on this whole Lean and Agile thing, as you're wasting your time pretending it is something you want to see happen.

So, when creating the backlog for your ART, remember the foundational ideas of the Agile movement. We want to give people problems to solve, provide them with the environment and support they need, and trust them to get the job done. If your backlog becomes a long list of requirements or specifications for people to deliver, you're entirely missing the point.

So what format should you use for recording work on an ART backlog?

Well, the short answer is that it's up to you. It's your train's backlog; the train is in charge of what it looks like, so it may look different from train to train. Indeed, whether your backlog is working or could be improved is probably a good topic to pick up in **Retrospectives** and **Problem Solving workshops** over time.

However, while there is no perfect solution, and every train will evolve what its features look like, it is useful to briefly look at the typical anatomy of a feature. This format is a *good enough for now* starting point for many ARTs, acting as a guide to encourage Agile Product Management:

Feature ID	Working at scale can create confusion, so having a unique identifier, often provided by your tooling, is important.
Name	A short name humans can recall and reference, instead of using just a number.
Hypothesis Statement	What the feature is looking to prove or demonstrate by fulfilling the outcome defined.
Acceptance Criteria	Scoping for the feature. Like at the user story level, a way to define the shape of the work, and a test to know when work is done. They also provide a way to validate your hypothesis criteria.

Table 5.1: Anatomy of a feature

What you will notice is that, unlike traditional requirements that convey a tone of *this must be done*, a feature written with a Hypothesis Statement begins with a *we don't know* tone, fostering an environment for experimentation and allowing the option to cease if it turns out to be a foolish idea.

Writing the features down is only the first part of the job. The effort then goes into ensuring that they are aligned with the **strategic themes** and with the desires of the Business Owners, and elaborated so that they are easily planned and delivered.

Don't lead the witness!

Product Owners and Product Management own outcomes, so they should define features using a hypothesis-driven approach that enables the teams to own the solution. If a feature states that the team wants a specific thing in a particular way, that's what you will get. Conversely, defining an outcome enables the teams to explore the best way to achieve it.

As the RTE, you benefit from being a fresh pair of eyes, not getting bogged down in the details of the backlog. You can guide Product Management and Product Owners when you spot features and **stories** that dictate a solution, so that they don't limit the team's creativity and the value they bring to the process.

How big to make it?

The next issue is how big to make your backlog. Now, the temptation is to make it as big as possible. After all, there is doubtless a lot of work to do, and we don't want to forget any of it, so we fill up the backlog with as much work as possible. In addition, we want to prove to those around and above us that we're a dedicated, hard-working team, so if our backlog looks small, our team might look unimportant too.

We're not saying that everyone approaches their backlog this way, but teams worldwide often repeat the preceding phenomena. The problem is that these phenomena make it harder to get work done, increase multitasking, increase risk, waste money, and reduce the value a team or train can deliver. Let us explain.

Big backlogs affect overheads

The first issue is that a big backlog of work increases the overhead of managing the backlog. Imagine you arrive at work one day, get a coffee, and then sit down to decide what to work on that day. If your backlog only has one item, that decision is simple and takes seconds. There's one thing to do that day. You can just get started on it. If the backlog has five items, that decision is marginally more complicated. It's not impossible, but it certainly requires more thought than if you just had one thing to work on. If the backlog has 50 items, the decision becomes even more difficult. Paranoid that among those 50 items, there may be something really important that you haven't noticed, you spend time going through all 50 items, scanning through them, and trying to make sense of the large amount of information you have to process. Agile Teams often do this during backlog refinement or planning meetings. As a result, much more of the meeting is spent deciding what to work on from the backlog, and much less is spent deciding how to work on it. The bigger your backlog, the more time and effort it takes to understand it, meaning the less time you have for doing valuable work.

The problem of working on too many things at the same time

Of course, you could say this is less of a problem because you don't have to make too many decisions about what to work on when you can decide to work on many different items simultaneously, but this then creates a new problem. The more things you work on at once, the more your attention shifts between one thing and the next. When your context shifts between different things, your brain doesn't automatically flip from thinking about work item A straight into thinking about work item B. Instead, it takes time to stop thinking about A and then more time to start thinking about B. As a result, more of your time gets eaten up by dealing with the consequences of a large backlog rather than doing work, which would never have happened if your backlog had just one item on it.

The shelf-life risk

Large backlogs also increase risk. Theoretically, you could have a huge backlog that you burn through very quickly, like some eight-lane superhighway with hundreds of cars whizzing along it at the maximum possible speed. Realistically, your throughput is more like an old English country road, with twists, turns, potholes, and high hedges you can't even see over. Work crawls slowly along it, occasionally stopping for a picnic. If your backlog is more like the latter example than the former, then the chances are that many items on the backlog will have been there for quite some time. The issue is that backlog items have a *shelf life* and go stale and rotten if left sitting around for too long. That user requirement you captured in the backlog 12 months ago—is it something the users still need, or have their needs changed over the last 12 months? Has your regulatory environment changed, meaning that backlog items would no longer be compliant if delivered? In extreme cases, is there still anyone working in your organization who was there when the backlog item was written and could help explain what it meant if anybody needed to ask?

The backlog that time forgot!

Gez's personal best in terms of backlog item age was seeing a client with an item that had sat on their backlog unworked for five and a half years. They didn't delete it, as no one knew why it had been put on the backlog, because everyone who was there when it was written had since left the organization. This also meant that no one was around to approve removing it, so it just stayed on the backlog forevermore.

Large backlogs

This leads us to another problem with large backlogs: the amount of waste they create. The preceding example points to one form of waste. If a backlog item has become old and stale, but we still want to work on it or something similar, we need someone to review it to understand and refine it again. This was already done when the item was first created. Having to repeat the refinement activity with no appreciable new benefit creates waste.

Long backlogs also contain another form of waste. Every item on a backlog is a potential piece of value that could be delivered. However, while an item sits on the backlog, it has yet to be delivered. Indeed, it may be sitting there idle, not even being delivered. As a result, inventory is piling up without providing value, another classic form of waste in a system.

Not only are items in a backlog not delivering value, but they may even be preventing the overall value delivery. This can happen when a backlog ceases to be a list of things that *could* be done and instead becomes a list of things that *must* be done. It is common in a more traditionally minded project-based organization. As a result, people start to work through the backlog in order, creating a long queue of work by committing to delivering the items on it. But what if a new item arrives with an even higher value than those already on the backlog? In an ideal world, those items would jump to the top of the backlog and be delivered next. In a less ideal world, those higher value items get told to wait while the lower value items (around which delivery commitments have already been made) are delivered first. This creates a situation where a long backlog of work reduces the overall delivery of value just through the facts of its size and commitments.

Too small backlogs

Of course, another problem could be on the other side of this *backlog size continuum*. It is a backlog with too little work, leaving people with nothing to work on. That, too, is problematic, and that's not what we would advocate for. Therefore, you're looking for a *Goldilocks backlog*—a backlog that is not too long but not too short for the context. We can't give you a rule for exactly how many items should exist on a backlog, as it will vary depending on your capacity, throughput, and broader context.

As a rough rule of thumb, having about a PI and a half's worth of work on an ART's backlog is probably the right sort of ballpark to aim for. It would be best to prepare enough work for the next PI Planning event. The chances are that some of the work you propose to be planned into the PI won't make the cut when it's taken to the teams. So, having some contingency of additional items ready for planning can help fill the emerging gaps.

Reaching a state of flow

Ultimately, a flow-based system is what you're looking to get to with any backlog. Small pieces of work move through the system at a continuous and sustainable pace, constantly delivering and returning value for customers, teams, and organizations alike. Only once has Gez seen a system running like this, and it took the organization a few years to work toward this state. Interestingly, this organization had started with PI Planning as a two-day event, but once they reached this whole organization flow state, their PI Planning dropped to a single day. All of their teams were continuously exploring, refining, aligning, and delivering as one high-performing system every day, so PI Planning became more of a check and balance on the system for the sake of organizational discipline, to keep things high-performing, more than being an event where everyone gets into a room to work out what on earth is going on. Truly flow-based ARTs and organizations may be rare, but they are definitely possible with enough hard work and dedication.

The backlog versus the roadmap

Of course, you can consider all the benefits of having a small backlog with work constantly flowing into and out of it, but we're sure you're thinking, "My stakeholders will never accept that." More traditionally minded stakeholders want to see grand, impressive initiatives delivered. The sort of thing they can call *<INSERT NAME OF DEPARTMENT> Transformation*. The kind of thing that will get them that next promotion.

The problem is that vast programs of work create large batch sizes that move much more slowly through the system, which is why most *<NAME> Transformation* programs are mostly just people managing external appearances and *optics*, *managing upward* to avoid anyone asking what there is to show for the multi-millions invested. A great RTE would be doing these stakeholders a massive favor by helping them break work down into smaller tasks and keep their queue lengths short with a backlog based on a continuous flow of value, but this can take time for stakeholders to appreciate.

So, what do you do as an interim measure?

Well, the answer lies in two places. The first is **roadmaps**. Sometimes looked down on by members of the Agile community, roadmaps, when handled carefully, are hugely valuable in setting the direction for delivery and helping people make the best use of the present by presenting a clearer vision for the future. Put another way, building a great feature is often more straightforward when you can see the bigger picture this feature may fit into. Another practical benefit of roadmaps when dealing with *transformation*-minded stakeholders is that they become a place where wants, desires, and long-term visions are set out without creating big queues of work that jam up and slow down the delivery of the here and now. In many businesses, the idea that we can only tell people what they might get in two weeks, with no consideration beyond that, just isn't going to fly or even be compliant with an organization's regulatory requirements. Therefore, road mapping is a handy way to align these needs with the imperative of keeping backlogs short and flowing.

The power of no!

The second place we can push back against a large backlog is in a simple word. That word is *no*. So often, humans are tempted to please others or not challenge authority. So when someone turns up with a work request, we immediately assure them that we can help, and too often display that reassurance by telling them, "I've put it on the backlog for you." We know full well the work is unlikely to be delivered, as we're already running all of our teams well above their capacity, but by putting the work on a backlog, we can pretend the world is better than it is.

As an RTE, it is often your job to coach Product Owners and Product Managers on the value of the word *no*. But this is often a hard sell and requires courage and a psychologically safe space for them to say it. As the RTE, you can provide the *covering fire* needed for them to do it. And you need to back them up when someone from on high comes knocking, demanding the super urgent thing they want but couldn't have.

Building the initial backlog

One challenge you often encounter when launching an ART is constructing the initial single backlog for the entire ART. Sometimes, the teams you're bringing together to form your ART have backlogs, and sometimes they don't. Whichever the case may be, creating a single backlog from which all teams on the ART take their work can present a challenge. Over the years, though, we've found a pretty well-proven technique for this.

Over time, work flowing from an ART backlog down into team backlogs is essential for ensuring that all teams on the ART are aligned around the work they're delivering so they can continuously deliver vertical slices of value across the end-to-end product.

To get started, try reversing the flow of work. By reversing the flow, we mean bringing together all the different teams' backlogs into one place and looking through them to see whether you can find user stories or other types of work related to each other. Sometimes, these are different parts of the same feature. After all, whilst ARTs can improve things, people have often found ad hoc ways to deliver things end-to-end across organizational chaos. As a result, you may see teams sharing common features or ideas across their backlogs. It then becomes pretty simple to take these items and write them up into features for the new ART backlog.

Even where creating features from stories across teams doesn't turn out to be as easy, a bit of thought and discussion across the teams can often tease out common goals, joint projects, or shared stakeholders, which you can then categorize into rough approximations of features to start with.

If teams are already working on similar things, why must we artificially create a common ART backlog across them? Looking back to those core SAFe® values of transparency and alignment, we need to check that teams are aligned, make transparent which parts of them are aligned, and, therefore, make transparent which elements of work we are pausing or abandoning altogether.

This last bit is especially important, as the chances are that there are fragments of work that teams will have in their backlog that don't align with anything the organization wants to see achieved in the following PI. In a world where little order has been applied to work prioritization, you often get random stakeholders throwing in weird and wonderful ideas they've had, sometimes based on nothing more than random conversations they've had with their friends. Limiting our Work-in-Process (WIP) means working on fewer things, and often, these poorly aligned, random elements are the things we should abandon first. Prioritization will also help with this, but more on this later.

Creating a backlog for a new ART is similar to a backlog refinement session, so it shouldn't be an entirely alien concept to Agile Teams. However, getting to version 1.0 of the new backlog often takes multiple passes:

1. The first step is identifying each team's backlog and where it is kept. Some may be in digital tooling, some in digital spreadsheets, some on sticky notes on a wall, and some in a team member's head.

2. Having identified all the sources of demand, collating them into a single location that will become your single source of truth is the next step.

3. Next, refine them to unify the format of the requests to make comparison, alignment, and amalgamation easier.

4. Finally, look for patterns and create new backlog items.

Having explored some of the topics regarding what a good and a not-so-good backlog looks like, let's explore what is actually on the backlog.

Types of work on the backlog

What should be in your backlog? As Glenn says, "Work is work, is work," so if you want it done, it needs to be on the backlog.

That may sound obvious, but you'd be surprised how often teams and ARTs don't do this. They put on their backlogs the things they've been asked or told to do, and that's it. If these requests come from business stakeholders, you can bet your bottom dollar that they will be shiny new features.

If you are lucky, enabler work creeps onto the backlog. The business doesn't truly understand it and would prefer you didn't do it, but they've been convinced it's needed to get their shiny new features. Maintenance and technical debt are recorded less often. Be careful here, though. If the work is too visible, you'll have to justify why you *got it wrong* and didn't follow the corporate mantra of *right first time*.

Once in a blue moon, you might even include some process improvement activity in the backlog when the planets align. However, you generally keep that on a separate *action log* somewhere else to avoid interfering with *real work*. To do this is a significant mistake. All work goes on the same backlog and is prioritized in the same way.

Outside of these types of work, there is one extra special category, like having the keys to the executive bathroom reserved for a select few. This category includes work from the side, under the radar, and typically never appears on the backlog. It's the executive who phones the team lead with an urgent request for something to be done that cannot be refused. It's the stakeholder who goes drinking with the Product Owner and has a subtle understanding that they can ask the team to do things for them when they need to.

Whatever form this back channel for work entering the team takes, it generally has one thing in common: the team has no choice about it. They need to do it, and typically, they must do it immediately. You rarely see this sort of work directly, as it doesn't undergo any formal process to be completed, but you can indirectly see it through its impact. Typically, the team reaches the end of an iteration or a PI and reports that they've done far less than they thought they would due to *unexpected work*.

The preceding examples may sound flippant, and they are to illustrate a point. It's straightforward to say things like *all work should be visible on a single backlog*, but many organizational social pressures prevent this. As an RTE, it's your job to surface and resolve these issues to benefit the ART and those around it.

If it's work that the teams on the ART need to do, it goes on the ART backlog, no matter what type of work it is. It really is that simple.

We want to call out some specific advice about recording technical debt on your backlog next.

Technical debt

Making technical debt visible on a backlog might require some coaching of the stakeholders. Explain why tackling technical debt in the short term is essential, even though it's risky, and that the benefits will only be felt in the medium to long term.

The key concept here is that it's called technical debt for a reason. When you have a debt, the debt incurs interest, meaning that unless you pay it off, your level of debt grows steadily over time. You will also need to build an environment where it's okay for people to admit that they've done things that haven't worked perfectly, haven't integrated as planned, or have to take shortcuts due to the pressure of delivery under which they found themselves. In the corporate world of individualized annual performance assessments, technical debt and the bugs it creates in production have a strong incentive to remain hidden.

The naivety of technical debt

When Glenn started his career, he was an embedded software engineer for Motorola, working on their GSM Telecoms equipment. In addition to adding new functionality to the system, he and his colleagues removed defects and fixed corners that had been cut 15–20 years ago. In his straight-from-university naivety, he was astonished that these issues had remained in the code for so long.

However, he realized that Motorola could employ him so long after the product had been launched *because* it was one of the first to market and gain market share. In doing so, it had to make trade-off decisions during launch. They knew a technically perfect solution wouldn't get them the market share they wanted.

If you want to anchor this idea in the SAFe® principles, think about principle 1: **Take an economic view**. Technical debt, like any debt, incurs interest, but sometimes you need to borrow money and accrue debt in order to grow.

Improvement items

Making improvement items visible on the backlog is sometimes even harder. We'll cover this more in *Chapter 9*, but there is a sad pattern of teams and ARTs trying to identify improvement items that would improve how they work and get work done, but too often finding that such activities are of no interest to those above them, so they never get any time given to work on them.

Even if they do, they soon run into some part of the organization that says, "You cannot change that process; it's been centrally decided." As the saying goes, the definition of a bureaucratic organization is one where people can say no, but they can't say yes. So, if you're trying to change something and haven't yet been told no, you just haven't socialized your change widely enough.

The ultimate point is that for the SAFe® core values of transparency and alignment to work, a backlog needs to be the single place where all work is represented, with clear entry criteria. There should be no backdoors, no hiding or avoiding specific categories of work. Just teams and an ART that are empowered to make all of their work visible and be clear about which things they will be working on next.

Where to store the backlog?

The Agile Manifesto, written in 2001, was oriented around a team. Having the backlog on your wall to support the transparency foundation made sense. However, when you are part of a team of teams that may not be in the same building or even country, part of a large enterprise, have regulatory requirements, and sometimes work from home, stickies on the wall won't cut it.

Here, an **Agile Lifecycle Management (ALM)** tool can help if you heed our earlier warning about tooling and face-to-face communication.

ALM tools often receive bad press in the Agile community—some of it rightly so. But let's be pragmatic and take a balanced view. Our consulting experience shows that many tools' poor perceptions are due to poor configuration and permissions. Whatever the reason, if a tool does not directly support your outcomes and help deliver value, it's a failed tool.

In many enterprises, these tools are centrally controlled and configured. They are often administered by people unfamiliar with the actual use of the tool and the working practices of your teams and the ART. Consequently, the installation and configuration are somewhat rudimentary and often near out-of-the-box settings. We can't blame these IT teams, even if we'd like an easy target. Many ALMs are enterprise-grade products and should truly be licensed alongside some initial consultative piece that ensures it is set up as needed. But this costs more, often significantly more, so it doesn't happen.

The result? One extreme or the other, from everything that could be turned on being turned on, which results in a large and complex user interface, or it is limited and generic. On top of that, the admin permissions to modify it are locked away with the IT teams, which are not set up to handle your regular configuration changes out of the back of Retrospectives and the I&A Problem Solving workshop, being better suited to incident management.

So, when you want a workflow changed to match how you actually work, you find you cannot. We will scream if we see another *To Do, In Progress, Done* board.

When set up well and with trusted people within the ART who can adapt the tool as needed, they are worth their weight in gold. Having a scaled digital information radiator and enabling automation to reduce transaction costs are advantages.

Who owns the ART backlog?

Product Management [mic drop!].

Okay, let's be more nuanced. The framework describes different groups as having **content authority** over different backlogs. Solution Management has content authority on the Solution Backlog, Product Management on the ART backlog, and Product Owners on the Team Backlog.

This means they have **delegated authority** to decide what goes in the backlog and how to sequence it through prioritization to achieve the best economic outcome while aligning with the ART's vision and maintaining alignment with the overall portfolio's strategic themes.

Does this mean they are superhumans who know everything that needs to be done? No, but they are the conduits for demand signals sent to the backlog.

So, given that Product Management owns the backlog, how do they prioritize, and how do they involve stakeholders in prioritization?

Prioritizing using Weighted Shortest Job First (WSJF)

Having said the Product Manager has delegated authority over the backlog and the sequencing through prioritization, it doesn't mean they do it all independently. They could, but it will end in arguments. They are also likely to be wrong.

As the human manifestation of the ART backlog, acting as a conduit, they represent many stakeholders, customers, and business demands regarding the solution's future state. Therefore, it would seem sensible not to undertake prioritization alone but with others. The following section discusses some people they may wish to include.

Let's take a quick look at the prioritization process and technique itself. At a team level, no fancy formulas or methods have been widely documented or seen in the wild, and for good reason. As the *Scrum Guide* says, it is up to the Product Owner to order the backlog. When created well, stories are small units of independent value, so having a cumbersome process would be overkill.

However, as soon as we zoom out and get to features, capabilities, and epics, their size enables a closer linkage to business outcomes, and therefore, applying a level of discipline makes appropriate sense.

SAFe® has adopted a modified version of Donald G. Reinertsen's WSJF approach, which is documented in our recommended reading, *The Principles of Development Flow: Second Generation Lean Product Development*. This mechanism is a bit like opportunity cost on steroids: it aims to find the smallest item with the highest value, measured by a **cost of delay** (**CoD**), to work on next.

The calculation is simply the CD divided by job size. Unlike Reinertsen's documented approach, which attempts to assign an actual currency value to the CoD, SAFe suggests using the following three lenses, rated using the modified Fibonacci sequence from 1 to 20. This aligns with how many teams estimate the story size. However, as a general rule in feature WSJF, we do not go higher than 20 to avoid skewing the results, encouraging deeper conversations about where the value originates:

- **User and business value:** What does the end user or our business get from doing this thing?
- **Time criticality:** An often overlooked perspective in prioritization. How does the value of the work change over time?
- **Risk reduction** (**RR**) and/or **opportunity enablement** (**OE**): Forward-looking value, showing how much risk this item reduces in the product or what potential unlocks from doing it. Often, the benefit is indirectly gained from this work. Your enabler features will frequently score higher here.

Using these proxy measures of currency for the value a feature creates, they are summed to create that feature's CoD.

$$WSJF = \frac{\text{Cost of Delay (User and Business Value + Time Criticality + Risk Reduction and/or Opportunity Enablement)}}{\text{Job Size}}$$

Figure 5.1: WSJF calculation

The value assignment to these three elements is then done using relative estimation, in the same way that stories are sized. The first time you use WSJF, you must anchor each lens by finding the smallest and assigning it a *1*.

As an RTE, the Product Manager may ask you to facilitate the prioritization meetings. This has two benefits. First, they can contribute without worrying about facilitation. Second, you are a neutral arbiter who can remove tension from the room.

If you are sizing the initial backlog or a new influx of many features (e.g., from having broken down a new epic), doing this physically on a wall or floor, or a digital workspace equivalent, without numbers, but using space between items, enables the conversations that need to happen, to happen, without people being lost in numbering.

If you use this approach for the two multi-dimensional lenses, *Figure 5.2* demonstrates how to space the items. Of particular note, the top right, with a score of 20, is reserved for when and only when the item is high in both dimensions. As a facilitator or arbiter, use this to your benefit when someone is dogmatically arguing for their pet feature to be at the top of the list.

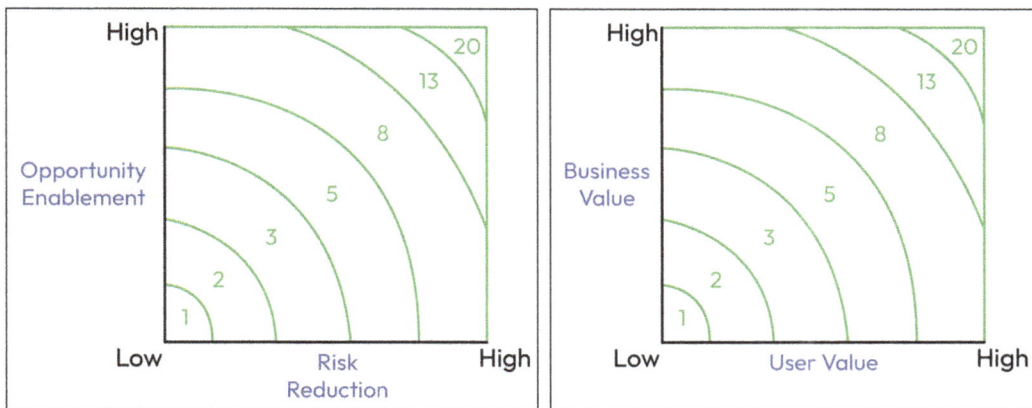

Figure 5.2: How to apply a Fibonacci number to multi-dimensional elements of CoD

Lastly, it's worth stating that the value of holding these prioritization meetings is ultimately the sequencing of the backlog for the best economic benefit of the enterprise. Still, in doing so, the value comes from the conversations held. Do not rush this part.

WSJF as a guide, not to drive

WSJF is a powerful tool for comparing apples to pears. However, you may discover that your Product Manager or Business Owners are frustrated with the orders that result. As long as productive, professional conversations have taken place, and the calculating of the CoD hasn't been gamed to get the *right result*, it is okay to let the Product Manager use their skills and expertise to have the WSJF guide and influence the sequence, and not to follow it mindlessly.

We would prefer that educated, thinking humans balance inputs from WSJF and their experience to arrive at the final order. As the RTE, you can act as their conscience, ensuring they do not mindlessly ignore these inputs. Note when this happens and use it as a reflection point in a future I&A Problem-Solving workshop or coaching session.

Having now considered what goes in the backlog and how to prioritize it, let's next turn to who to involve and when you might do this over the course of the PI.

Cadence of creating the PI Planning Backlog

At the close of PI Planning, as the RTE, you might fancy a relaxing drink and time in a darkened room to decompress after a busy couple of days. Without wanting to ruin your hard-earned rest, planning for the next event starts tomorrow! The good news for you, as the RTE, is that the heavy lifting falls at the feet of the PM and the SA. Their job is to create, refine, prioritize, and socialize the content. It is your job to make sure they balance the needs of delivery in the just-planned current PI while looking forward to the next one.

While they are responsible for preparing the backlog, a suitably constructed backlog will require the involvement of many people. *Figure 5.3* guides the cadence and effort levels the key players will exert over the coming PI ahead of PI Planning.

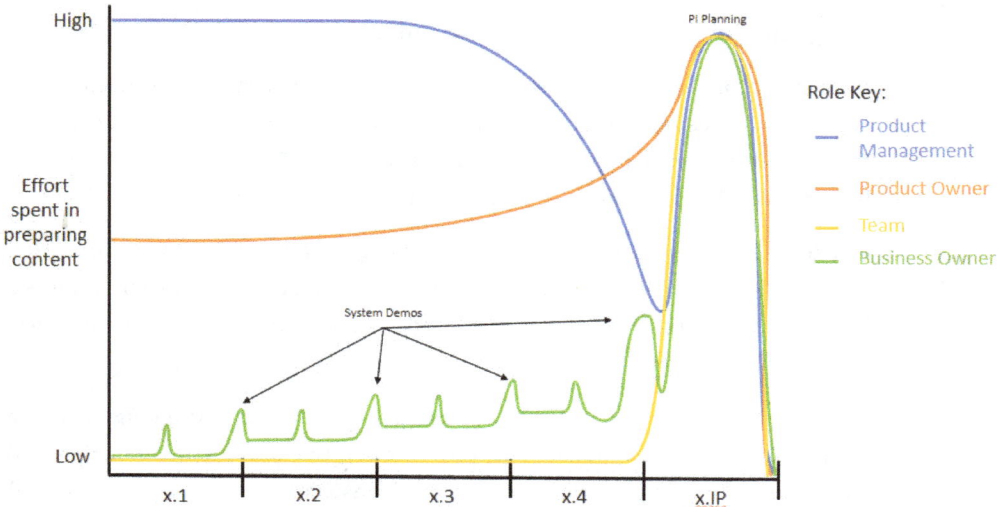

Figure 5.3: Preparation intensity in creating the next PI's backlog

The graph illustrates that early in the PI, the PM leads the finalization of candidate features for the next PI. They collaborate closely with the POs within the teams, as they are part of the broader Product Management function that supports this work. Business Owners increase their involvement during the PI, attending system demonstrations and backlog refinement sessions. Toward the end of the PI, when the features are stable—except for any late-breaking requests—the POs and the teams prepare for PI Planning, primarily during the **Innovation and Planning** iteration.

Now, let's look in more detail on a role-by-role basis.

Product Management and the System Architect

The first point is that the PM and SA should have an effective working relationship. By this, we mean they regularly work together cooperatively and for the greater good of the solution, accepting that only they can constructively guide development together. If you still need to, this is one of your first challenges.

Using capacity allocation when the PM and SA won't play nicely

In a mature, professional relationship, the PM and SA can balance the needs of the customer and business-driven needs with architectural enablement. Unfortunately, this doesn't always happen, and, initially at least, the PM and SA are at constant loggerheads about getting their priorities in the backlog and being worked on.

An effective measure to overcome this constant fighting is to use **capacity allocation** to define how much each party has to use on a PI-by-PI basis. In essence, this is a brute-force prioritization approach. Beyond features and enablers, you might also set allocations for maintenance or technical debt buy-down.

Glenn has found this effective method to stop the arguments long enough to coach the two parties to start playing nicely. Ultimately, the allocation will be removed when the PM and SA can prioritize effectively, ensuring the relevant needs are balanced.

In a typical 10-week PI, with 5 iterations, including the IP iteration, a simple but effective mental model is that the first 4 iterations follow *creating*, *refining*, *prioritizing*, and then *socializing* the features. Like all models, it's right and wrong simultaneously, but provides a mental checkpoint for RTE against progress for the next PI Planning event.

You should expect to see the PM and SA looking ahead early in the PI. The **ART roadmap, Portfolio roadmap,** and **Architectural Runway** will guide the creation of features and enabler features. Epics might need to be decomposed into features, which typically requires involvement from a broader range of stakeholders outside the ART.

As the new features and enablers are documented, they will need refining and elaborating to prepare for PI Planning. Various people will be involved, including technical leads, Business Owners, Product Owners, **Subject Matter Experts (SMEs)**, and so on. Where necessary, the RTE can help unite these people, mainly if they are used to being spoon-fed work and don't necessarily see it as their job to contribute.

Throughout the PI, the PM and SA's efforts will taper off as the features are created, and other parties will take over the responsibility of preparing for PI Planning.

In line with the principle of *flow*, we encourage the PM to run prioritization sessions regularly as new features and enablers are created. This *little and often* approach reduces the perceived effort and indicates highly valuable and urgent work early. We also encourage prioritization to be a *team sport* (i.e., including the SA, BOs, yourself as the RTE, and other relevant parties). It is more effective and can stop future arguments about the placement of a feature on the backlog.

Business Owners

As key stakeholders and critical friends of the ART, they must be included in the entire backlog creation lifecycle. You do not want them to see the features for the first time during PI Planning or state that they are unhappy with the backlog's sequencing.

Unfortunately, a common issue is people volunteering or being told to be BOs but not having the time to do so. It isn't a five-minute job or just turning up to PI Planning. The exact level of involvement will vary greatly. Considering ad-hoc discussions or meetings with the PM and teams, System Demo participation, and PI Planning, it could easily take 25% or more of their time.

Product Owners

POs are part of the broader Product Management function. While their primary focus is at the team level, representing the customer's desires to the team, they also support Product Managers in refining and elaborating the ART backlog. They do not simply consume features; they help define them, too.

Therefore, their involvement in the PI includes refinement and elaboration, followed by decomposition into draft stories to socialize with the team and prepare with them ahead of the PI Planning.

Watch out for POs wanting to be *spoon-fed* work and not contribute. You may need to step in and support the PM to build the required collaborative relationship.

The teams

The teams will likely be more involved in the latter part of the PI as their focus shifts from delivery to preparation for planning. They are often involved in elaborating the features, although this often won't be en masse, with a technical lead or SME from the team participating.

As the features are ready for the POs to decompose, the wider team will see the work likely to come their way in the following PI. Effort levels rise significantly during the IP iteration as they prepare earnestly for and undertake the PI Planning.

Working with their PO, the team must create draft stories ahead of PI Planning. When teams spend a lot of effort crafting stories ahead of PI Planning, they become psychologically attached to them, which generates resistance to adapting them during planning. Encourage simple, often one-liner-style stories to be taken into planning. They will become fully fledged during iteration refinement and planning activities later.

> **Things the RTE wishes to be done**
>
> Just because you are the RTE doesn't mean you won't create backlog items. Based on Retrospectives or the Inspect and Adapt meeting, you may request capacity in an upcoming PI for the ART to make improvements to optimize flow.
>
> If doing something takes time, it takes capacity and needs to be planned by the teams. As a proponent of SAFe®, breaking the rules and not following due process yourself would be inappropriate. It also provides another opportunity to model the behavior you wish the train to follow.

At this point, we now have the feature backlog created and ready for PI Planning. For the event to achieve a positive result, the morning briefing packs need to be made.

Preparing PI Planning presentation content

The content for PI Planning doesn't stop at the backlog creation. On the morning of the first day, a senior leader, the Product Manager, and the SA set the scene and their vision for the upcoming PI through their respective perspectives of the *why*, the *what*, and the *how*, respectively.

As a cohort that should know better, it can still feel like you are herding cats to prepare the backlog ahead of the event. For your sanity, being passed slides that you've not seen on a USB stick at 8:55 a.m. is far from ideal. Getting the content at least 24 hours before the event enables you to compile a master deck. It also lets you double-check the content. Ideally, and especially in the early days of the train, having it a good few days before allows you to review and suggest alterations.

We'll discuss more about facilitating PI Planning in *Chapters 7* and *8*. Let's walk through the three briefings and their purpose so you are better informed about how to help the executive, Product Manager, and SA prepare their briefings.

Executive briefing

The first session is the rallying cry that aligns and invigorates the ART as they plan the following PI. It sets the tone for what is to come and reflects on what has happened. Arguably, this is the most important opportunity to prepare the two days for productivity and positivity.

So, what do you want the executive to cover? It's the view from the bridge, the commander's intent, starting with the current context: what is happening in the market, what customers are telling us, and what our competitors are doing. Beyond the high-level view, sharing what has happened with the outputs of this ART in previous PIs helps those creating the solution understand the impact of their work, which can be both satisfying and motivating.

Too often, leaders believe everyone understands the vision because they emailed them six months ago! Looking forward, both near- and medium-term aid alignment, anchoring the actions today with where the business wants to go. The trick to solidifying everyone's understanding is *little and often* in a way that makes it relatable.

Then, in closing, they must emphasize the importance of the upcoming PI's work and the ART's contribution to the organization's objectives.

Because this initial session is crucial in setting the tone for the entire two days, it helps if you can nudge, influence, or directly provide talking points to the executive. Seeing people's hope and vibrancy drained in the first 45 minutes of the day can be devastating and challenging to recover from.

It's called the **executive briefing**, but does it have to be an executive? While it would be lovely to have someone from the top echelons of the enterprise attend, we need to be realistic. Are you looking for someone senior enough to have the knowledge and gravitas to deliver the required message?

> **What if the leader isn't available on the day?**
>
> Leaders' diaries fill up quickly, and urgent demands on their time can put them far from your office. This doesn't mean you need an understudy, although having one in the wings is a helpful contingency plan. Make plans to conference the leader into the session on Zoom or have a pre-recorded message ready and available to play.
>
> We have managed to get senior leaders, many levels up, to participate virtually in this fashion, which the teams greatly appreciated. The power of a custom, specific direct message to them as a cohort goes a long way toward morale building.

Product Management briefing

While the executive will share views from the enterprise's demand side, Product Management will examine the situation from the supply side. They will answer how the ART plans to deliver the enterprise's desired outcomes.

The Product Manager will cover the following:

- Vision and product strategy
- The features that define the PI's goal and link it to the portfolio's strategic themes
- General updates and relevant milestones

In the same way that the executive regularly shares the vision for the portfolio and enterprise, Product Management periodically shares the product strategy. This anchors the near-term activities with a broader, zoomed-out view.

The core content, however, will be the content the teams will plan for the next two days. While we expect that the features have been socialized with the teams by their POs ahead of time, creating a common understanding in the room in the Product Manager's own words does no harm. There may also be late-breaking new features that need explaining.

Generally, having presocialized the features, there is no need to walk through them individually in detail. It is helpful to do the following:

- Confirm the order of the features in the backlog and why they are in the order they are
- Highlight key points of specific features that are worth noting to support planning
- Discuss changes to features since they were circulated before the planning event
- Provide an opportunity for questions from the teams

System Architecture briefing

In the last slot is the SA. This briefing will cover elements that customers and users typically do not directly notice, but are just as important as the features.

In the same way that the Product Manager outlines the business features to be worked on, the SA provides an overview of the enabler features—again, not going into minute detail (something to watch out for as the RTE; you might need to coach them), creating a high-level view for alignment and understanding.

This briefing will also cover important topics, such as **user experience** (UX) and development updates. It might be appropriate for the **System Team** to share updates to the development platforms, tooling, and pipelines that have happened recently, as well as their upcoming backlog for the PI.

RTE – planning context

Hang on, we hear you say? Didn't we say earlier that you didn't need to create any content for PI Planning? Well, it's not a truly honest statement.

After the three briefings, you will lay out how the rest of the planning will work procedurally. We'll share more about how each section works and your involvement in *Chapters 7* and *8*. But, as part of this, you may wish to bring in some data and feedback from BOs that came out of the I&A session. For example, if the ART has a tendency to be overly optimistic about what it can achieve, then you can remind them, through the data, of the improvement actions they agreed to take and the impact of not being predictable.

Making the presentations impactful, useful, and not boring!

The standard timetable for PI Planning offers nearly 25% of the 2 days to briefings and planning process alignment. This valuable time would not be offered up if there wasn't value in these activities. If you had 120 people in the room, this is equivalent to 45 staff days of cost! While you don't control the content and presentation of the briefings, you do need to make sure the organization gets value for money for the time. This becomes another coaching opportunity for you:

- **Share the feedback from the previous sessions with the presenters:** Knowing that others thought they droned on in a monotone voice for 90 minutes might be useful, even if it's light peer pressure.

- **Video them and share privately so they can review how they did:** Enabling personal reflection and seeing themselves as others did from a different angle can bring new observations.

- **Provide guidance and examples, and offer to review the presentation material:** This is great if they are happy to receive help and want to get better. Some people are less welcoming of help or the self-awareness they need to get better.

Summary

In this chapter, you have learned about the critical pre-PI Planning activities that lay the foundation for successful planning events. You have explored the purpose and management of an effective backlog, recognizing that it is not merely a list of tasks to complete but rather a tool for managing work that could be undertaken—a crucial distinction that influences how teams approach their tasks. You have gained insights into the optimal backlog size, record-keeping methodologies, prioritization techniques using WSJF, and the dynamics of backlog ownership.

We've walked you through the cadence of creating the PI Planning Backlog, illustrating how various roles, from Product Management and System Architects to Business Owners and Product Owners, contribute throughout the PI to prepare for the upcoming planning event. You have also learned how to create effective PI Planning presentation content that establishes the appropriate context and tone for productive planning sessions.

These lessons are essential because the success of PI Planning largely depends on the quality of preparation. A well-structured backlog enables teams to concentrate on delivering high-value items, whereas inadequate preparation results in wasted time, confusion, and, ultimately, less value delivered to customers. As an RTE, your ability to facilitate and coordinate this preparation process directly influences your ART's ability to plan effectively and deliver consistently. Although you may not create most of this content yourself, your guardianship ensures that those responsible maintain a sensible schedule and do not become lost in the urgent demands of today.

Understanding these aspects of preparation will equip you to mitigate risk and uncertainty in your forthcoming PI. Remember that inadequate inputs will inevitably lead to expensive adjustments and rework, which will impact time, quality, and output.

However, we are still not quite ready for PI Planning. In the next chapter, we will examine the event logistics required for both in-person and virtual events to ensure that, when the time comes, it will be successful.

References

Here, you can find the references to expand your knowledge about the specific concepts not covered in this book but mentioned in this chapter:

- Reinertsen, D. G. (2009). *The Principles of Product Development Flow*: Second Generation Lean Product Development. Celeritas Publishing.

Get This Book's PDF Version and Exclusive Extras

UNLOCK NOW

Scan the QR code (or go to packtpub.com/unlock).
Search for this book by name, confirm the edition,
and then follow the steps on the page.

*Note: Keep your invoice handy. Purchases made
directly from Packt don't require one.*

6

Event Logistics for PI Planning

PI Planning is critical for building relationships, establishing trust, and reinforcing ART goals. By fostering a welcoming, collaborative environment, you create an atmosphere where team members can connect, share insights, and work toward common goals. Conversations with leadership about the importance of PI Planning can emphasize that this is more than just an operational task; it's a valuable opportunity for team building, alignment, and long-term ART success.

Investing time and resources into the logistics of PI Planning pays off by creating a memorable, productive experience that empowers teams to do their best work. No matter how you run it, PI Planning is a big event that requires careful preparation. Luckily, this is a well-worn path, and there is a lot of guidance on how to set yourself up for success.

In this chapter, we'll cover the essential logistics to help you prepare for successful PI Planning events. Effective planning ensures smooth coordination, minimizes disruptions, and enables ARTs to align around common goals and objectives, whether in person or remotely.

This chapter will contain the following main headings:

- Evolving PI Planning: lessons from the past and adapting to the future
- Top tips to get ready for PI Planning
- Planning an in-person (colocated or distributed) event
- Considerations for online or remote events
- Planning the agenda

Evolving PI Planning: lessons from the past and adapting to the future

Things have changed a lot over the years. Back in the days before the pandemic, in-person PI Planning was the most common practice. We often had to manage PI Planning with teams in different locations and, frequently, different countries and continents.

The pandemic dramatically changed things. Almost overnight, we had to pivot from our norm of wanting people together to share the same message and grow in relationships. We had to find a way to make it work when we were no longer allowed to meet. In those days, most people hadn't heard of Mural, and tools such as Zoom were far more basic than they are today.

We now have a wealth of technology options to share information more effectively. Most companies use tools such as Zoom or Teams for online calls and digital whiteboarding tools such as Mural, Miro, and LucidChart. You can also leverage dedicated tools designed just for PI Planning. We tend to be tool-agnostic, but we always subscribe to the Manifesto's first value: *Individuals and interactions over processes and tools.*

Why is it essential to review the history? Well, if nothing else, thinking about what is necessary is helpful. It is easy to take a simple idea and overcomplicate it to the point where we don't get what we need or oversimplify it to the point where we don't get what we want, and it becomes a waste of time.

No matter how you run PI Planning, remember that the primary objective is to share information and create a plan, as the name suggests! As the **Agile Manifesto** states, *face-to-face conversation is the best way to share complex information*. It is important not to forget about that as you're planning your event. At every stage of PI Planning readiness, you should consider how the event will help you reach a plan that the teams and stakeholders will be confident in for the following PI.

Top tips to get ready for PI Planning

Over the years, we've tried many ways to make PI Planning more efficient—some more effective than others. It would be fair to say that some were an outright disaster! But we learn more from our failures than successes, and we'll take you through the top tips we've picked up.

Use the toolkit(s)

Our first and most valuable tip is to check out the **SAFe® PI Planning Toolkit** in **SAFe Studio**. It doesn't matter how many PI Planning events we run; we always return to the toolkits as they are invaluable to ensure that we *dot our i's and cross our t's*. The PI Planning Toolkit contains spreadsheets and sample presentations that you can use to brief stakeholders. It also includes one of the most valuable spreadsheets ever in the history of time (that might be a slight exaggeration, but only *slight*).

The *Art Readiness Workbook* contains checklists for everything from a content checklist to a nifty table that, when you plug in the teams and tables, will spit out the number of packs of sticky notes and pens you will need. It helps you build a forward-looking PI and iteration calendar and do the necessary date math to send future invites.

Setting a date

It may seem obvious, but one of the first things you must do is set a date. You may be tempted to wait until you've got all your ducks in a row, but from experience, all the work you've got to do to prepare for PI Planning can quickly expand, and your first PI Planning can drift for months, if not years. This is why putting a line in the sand and setting the date becomes a forcing function for everyone to align around. As the one who may be setting the date, keep in mind the need for an available space; while room availability should not hold you to ransom, if you have a few days' leeway, take advantage of it.

When working with international colleagues, you will need to consider national and sometimes regional holidays, as it's too easy to lose a large contingency of your ART because of a holiday you are unaware of.

In SAFe, all teams must synchronize and work on the same cadence. Their iterations should be the same length (typically two weeks) and start and finish on the same day. We bring this up as it is a critical enabler for planning when your PI Planning events are going to occur. As a result, we can also schedule PI Planning a long way in advance.

Gathering the right people ahead of time

Effective pre-event communication and preparation are essential for a smooth and productive PI Planning session. To ensure that participants are aligned and well prepared, start by distributing the event agenda, session objectives, and pre-read materials at least one week in advance. The agenda should outline each session, its purpose, and the expected outcomes to help participants understand the flow and goals of the event. The PI Planning Toolkit is a great resource to help make sure you don't miss anything.

We need to go beyond pre-read materials, such as summaries of upcoming features, historical metrics, or background on new initiatives, that allow participants to familiarize themselves with the context and come prepared with questions or ideas. We should bring people on the journey and socialize before the event. There is a law of diminishing returns—too much preparation and we risk creating waste by locking down plans that are likely to change, but not enough, and we can find that we won't get to a viable plan at the end of the event. That said, there will always be some people who won't be able to make any planning sessions. Providing this information ahead of time also helps reduce unnecessary explanations during the event, allowing more time for critical discussions and decision-making.

In addition to sharing materials, organize pre-planning meetings with key stakeholders, including **Product Managers, Product Owners**, and **System Architects**. These alignment meetings are critical to synchronize priorities, refine features, and set a foundation for collaborative problem-solving. During these discussions, focus on clarifying high-priority features, understanding dependencies between teams, and identifying potential risks that could impact the planning outcomes. By addressing these points beforehand, stakeholders can enter the PI Planning event with a shared understanding of the objectives and constraints, paving the way for effective planning and a more streamlined process. These meetings also foster early collaboration, allowing teams to build rapport and gain alignment on technical and business perspectives, which will contribute to a more cohesive and successful planning session.

With your checklists and agenda at the ready to guide your planning preparations, a date in the diary, and all necessary attendees invited, let's move on and consider what logistics are required in advance. First up is in-person.

Planning an in-person (colocated or distributed) event

Organizing any event for 125 people presents unique challenges, especially when the event requires breakout areas for smaller team discussions. The following sections will outline the considerations for an in-person event.

The venue

If you're fortunate enough to work for a large company, you might have access to a company auditorium. Still, availability can be limited, especially for the full two days that PI Planning generally requires. Remember that, besides the main planning session, you will likely need additional rooms for team breakouts and quieter conversations or calls for people who can't make it in person. If you don't have the luxury of a suitable venue on-site, you will likely be looking at conference rooms or hotel spaces. Before you go looking for a venue, though, check that there are no security classification or commercially sensitive restrictions on your work that would stop you from going off-site.

Not all space is the same. You need a space to configure the tables in a *cabaret format*, as in one dedicated table space per team, ideally circular, to promote collaboration and communication. Spaces with fixed seating or a boardroom table might look impressive, but are not practical.

It's not just about being able to physically fit everything you need into the room. You are gathering people together for two days to collaborate. To achieve this, they need to move freely around each other. Always double-check the space, as facilities or venues don't need to live or understand the consequences of cramped working conditions. We firmly believe that large rooms inspire big ideas!

Using an outside venue

When I [Tim] first organized an in-person PI Planning session, we considered various venues, ranging from nearby hotels to spaces in the city center. Costs varied widely, depending on location and accessibility, making having a clear budget essential. Consider the cadence of future PI Planning sessions as you book venues. Like all businesses, hotels and conference centers like to remove uncertainty, so you can often negotiate a better rate by committing to multiple bookings throughout the year.

It is always worth asking about their catering options and other venues' services. You could get a better rate if the venue usually partners with catering companies or audio-visual teams. The added benefit is that they will know the venue, and you'll be less likely to encounter unexpected challenges.

Environmental factors

When scouting for a venue, the first factor to consider is capacity. It's crucial to ensure ample space for everyone while maintaining an open environment that prevents overcrowding. One factor often overlooked is the room layout—pillars, for example, can obstruct visibility and disrupt seating arrangements. You need to plan where the presentation will be displayed, ensuring that everyone in the room can view the screen(s).

Environmental factors such as lighting, temperature, air quality, and acoustics significantly affect participant focus and comfort. Studies have shown that natural light and well-calibrated artificial lighting reduce fatigue and improve attention. Similarly, keeping the room temperature around 22°C/71°F supports cognitive function, with deviations causing discomfort and potential distraction. High-quality ventilation and soundproofing reduce background noise and maintain air quality, critical for cognitive performance over extended periods. If the venue is too crowded, it will get noisy, and people will struggle to hear one another.

Consider the lighting, specifically daylight. Some venues have conference rooms in the basement, and a day without daylight can increase fatigue. If this is your situation, have breaks and lunch upstairs in a room with windows.

Breakout areas

It is easy to focus all your attention on the main room for PI Planning, but we also need to consider the spaces for breakout rooms. These areas should be easily accessible yet provide enough separation from the main area to maintain focus during discussions. Moreover, these rooms must have amenities such as audiovisual equipment, whiteboards, and refreshments. Comfort extends beyond furniture; ensuring adequate temperature control and natural light can significantly enhance the attendee experience.

Breakout areas are a double-edged sword. While they provide quieter spaces for teams to huddle, it can generate friction for other teams to find them. Therefore, if you go down this route, make sure you have a map and a legend available to all those planning. Also, if the rooms are not immediately to the sides of the main room, you will lose time walking around the rooms; you might even lose people as they get distracted!

Not everything that shines is gold

I [Tim] was part of PI Planning for a company based in the UK. We had the benefit of an auditorium with fantastic AV equipment. The screen was about two stories high, and the microphones and cameras were top-notch. What we needed was wall space and breakout rooms. The room was great for the briefings and plan reviews, but without wall space for our plans, we had to use a Mural board, and the teams had dedicated rooms to create their plans in different building areas. I was just visiting that day, but I was given a map of the teams' locations. It was nearly impossible for the teams to collaborate. Luckily, in that instance, the teams were primarily stream-aligned with minimal dependencies, but I couldn't help wondering what it would be like if we had all been in the same room and what might have come up if we had found another way.

Wall space

Wall space is another key consideration. Teams need areas to post their plans and sticky notes for easy reference throughout the event. Additionally, ensure enough seating and space for people to move around comfortably. A room crammed with tables and chairs makes moving from one team to another problematic, defeating the purpose of having everyone together to collaborate freely.

Check the walls

Go and check the room the event will be in well ahead of time, and if you plan to build a physical ART board on a wall, check that the wall will work, and the venue will let you put things on it! Many years ago, Gez organized a PI Planning event in London. It was a lovely hotel; the staff were super helpful, and the lunches were fantastic. However, the allocated meeting room for PI Planning had walls covered in rough, hairy fabric. You could not even stick a sticky note to the fabric! As a result, Gez spent two days running around trying to stick people's notes back onto the ART board using pins, sticky tack, tape, and all sorts, as the notes gently rained to the floor like confetti at an Agile wedding.

Your ideal ask on wall space is a large, flat, smooth wall, with plenty of space around it, on which people can make all of their work visible and then easily stand around it to debate and discuss.

When laying out the room, always think about who is in the teams on the ART when you are building it. Some teams have short people, whereas some have tall ones. If you have many teams on your ART, you will have many rows on your board, which means some rows will be high up and others will be lower down. Make sure you assign the higher-up rows to the teams with tall people and the lower-down rows to the teams with shorter people. For your organization's health and safety, people will tend to get annoyed at having to stand on chairs to use the board, and you want to keep everyone safe when using SAFe®.

Effective use of digital tooling

Even at in-person events, teams across the ART can find it useful to have access to digital tooling to support their planning or have digital representations of their planning spaces. This creates an additional set of requirements for the venue:

- Are there enough power outlets, not just around the walls but also on floor plates that are accessible across the room without becoming trip hazards?
- Is there robust Wi-Fi that can support not only the speed and bandwidth requirements, but also the number of connections?

While digital tools offer significant advantages—from real-time collaboration to effortless post-event documentation and integration between systems such as JIRA and Mural—they also come with an important warning: technology should enhance, not replace, human interaction. The primary value of gathering for PI Planning lies in the face-to-face collaboration and relationship building that occurs naturally when people work together. Remain vigilant about preventing team members from becoming isolated behind screens; encourage them to look up, engage directly with colleagues, and concentrate on meaningful conversations that foster mutual understanding and unlock solutions to complex problems. *The digital tools should support your process, not hinder the vital personal connections that make PI Planning truly effective.*

A word on accessibility

Accessibility isn't just a logistical consideration; it's a commitment to respect and inclusion that fosters engagement and equity within the ART. As RTEs, we advocate for inclusive spaces where everyone has an equal opportunity to contribute to the planning process.

A thoughtfully accessible venue provides a foundation for full engagement, removing physical barriers and supporting attendees with diverse needs. For example, accessible entrances, exits, and pathways allow individuals using wheelchairs, walkers, or other mobility devices to move independently and safely. Seating accommodating varying needs ensures that attendees are comfortable and can choose where they'd like to sit rather than being limited to designated areas.

Close, well-equipped, accessible toilets and elevator access for multi-story venues are additional essential features contributing to ease of movement and a sense of autonomy for all attendees.

Equally important are visual and auditory accommodations. For visually impaired attendees, clear, high-contrast signage, accessible presentation slides, and assistive technology can make navigating the venue and engaging with content much more effortless. Similarly, a quality sound system, live captioning, and sign language interpreters are invaluable to participants who are hard of hearing, allowing them to stay fully engaged with presentations and team discussions. Offering assistive listening devices and real-time captioning ensures that auditory information is accessible to all.

Accessibility planning also extends to communication and cognitive needs. Providing materials in various formats, such as large print or screen-reader-compatible documents, ensures that event information is accessible and valuable for all attendees. For those with sensory processing sensitivities, quiet rooms provide a peaceful retreat when needed, allowing everyone to manage their energy and focus effectively. Training staff on accessibility awareness further enhances the event's inclusivity, helping attendees with respect, empathy, and knowledge.

Ensuring equipment readiness

Many conference centers now offer advanced AV setups, but double-checking AV equipment before the event can save time and prevent frustration. On several occasions, we arrived at a venue only to find that the promised microphones or projectors were included, but they still needed to be set up. We now recommend creating a comprehensive checklist to review before each event. Also, consider having simple backup AV equipment on hand.

These days, tools such as Zoom and Teams and devices such as Chromecast and Apple TV allow you to share content quickly and create ad-hoc networks if needed. Sometimes, you may need to broadcast to additional locations or involve remote participants. At the same time, a hybrid setup can work, ensuring that the primary experience remains for in-person attendees, as this is an in-person first event.

An example checklist could be as follows:

- **Understand the room acoustics:**
    - **Size and shape**: Larger rooms with high ceilings or unusual shapes may require additional sound equipment.
    - **Surfaces**: Hard surfaces (such as glass and concrete) reflect sound, while soft surfaces (carpets and curtains) absorb it. Check whether the room has acoustics issues that could impact sound quality.

- **Background noise**: Consider external noise sources (e.g., air conditioning, adjacent rooms, etc.) and take steps to reduce them if possible.

- **Types of microphones:**

  - **Presenter(s)**: Lavalier (lapel) or headset mics are ideal for hands-free use and freedom of movement.

  - **Audience questions**: Handheld wireless microphones should be passed around so everyone can hear. Have *runners* who can move the roaming mics around. We particularly like the cube-shaped *Catch Box*, a foam-covered box you can throw around the room quickly. It lightens the mood when it misses its target!

  - **Backup microphones**: Always have at least one spare mic ready in case of failure.

- **Speakers and amplification:**

  - **PA system**: A portable PA system with powerful, full-range speakers will help cover a large room.

  - **Speaker placement**: To distribute sound evenly, place speakers at the front and additional ones toward the back or sides. Avoid placing speakers directly facing the audience to prevent feedback.

  - **Mixer console**: A mixer helps balance sound levels across microphones and manage audio from multiple sources (e.g., microphones and video audio).

- **Video requirements:**

  - **Projectors or large screens:**

    - **Screen visibility**: Ensure that screens are large enough to be visible from the back. You'll likely need one large screen at the front and possibly one additional screen halfway down the room.

    - **Brightness**: High-lumen projectors (3,000+ lumens) are best for large rooms with ambient light.

    - **Resolution**: Aim for at least 1080p resolution for clear, professional-looking, and readable visuals.

    - **Number**: If you are running a distributed planning event (with multiple in-person locations), having screens and showing the live view of the other locations creates a connection between sites. This means you also need cameras and separate signaling.

- **Screen placement and angle:**
  - **Screen height:** Position the screen high enough so those at the back can see without obstruction.
  - **Projector placement:** Set the projector far enough back to cover the entire screen, or use short-throw projectors if space is limited.
  - **Dual screens:** Consider dual screens if there are large sections of the room at wide angles where some attendees might struggle to see a single central screen.

- **Video playback and connectivity:**
  - **Laptop or device compatibility:** Ensure that your device connects easily to the projector or screen (USBC, HDMI, VGA, etc.). It may be old technology, but we recommend a VGA adaptor! If that is all the venue has, you'll struggle, but better to be safe than sorry!
  - **Remote control or clicker:** A wireless clicker allows easy slide transitions for all the briefings.
  - **Backup device:** Prepare a backup laptop or tablet for use in case of a device failure, and share slides and other content with other stakeholders so they can intervene if necessary.

- **Live streaming or recording (if applicable):**
  - **Camera positioning:** Place a camera to capture presenters and audience (if relevant), ensuring they don't obstruct sightlines to the screen.
  - **Sound feed for recording:** Connect the camera to the PA system for clear audio in recordings or streams.
  - **Stable internet connection:** Check Wi-Fi strength or use a wired connection if live streaming is needed.

- **Pre-workshop AV testing:**
  - **Complete walkthrough:** Walk through each area of the room to check sightlines and sound coverage.
  - **Run a full test:** Test the entire setup with a full trial run, including video playback, audio levels, and microphone sound check.
  - **Backup plan:** Be prepared with backup batteries, microphones, cables, and key equipment.

- **Power and internet:**

    - **Charging and power stations**: Ensure that there are enough power outlets and charging stations for participants' laptops and devices. Test randomly to make sure they work, particularly in the mid-room suspended floor units, as we've found them not to be. Remind people to bring charged devices just in case!

- **Bandwidth and number of devices limits**: Check these beforehand. Do some speed tests in various locations around the room. If possible, it is always safer to have hard-wired internet so that you're not relying on WiFi, especially if you're presenting.

> **Confirm support staff's availability**
>
> You may need to budget for a tech/AV person to set everything up and run it on the day to ensure the event goes smoothly. Venues often use the same people repeatedly, and you may have staff who can help you. Like any other team member, make sure you have their availability.

Managing food and refreshments

Food is often a significant expense during PI Planning, especially if you provide meals over multiple days. Understanding the available budget and expectations around meals is critical. Some events may call for simple catering, such as sandwiches or finger foods, while others might benefit from more extensive options, such as pizza or buffet meals. Always check with the ART about dietary restrictions, including the requirements of gluten-free, vegetarian, vegan, and halal options.

Label meals to ensure that those with dietary restrictions have what they need. Issues arise when standard meals run out, and others inadvertently consume special meals.

One option to save costs is to ask participants to bring their own food, although attendees may perceive this as a lack of investment in the event. Consider the tone you want to set. PI Planning is more than a planning session—it's an opportunity for the ART to unite, build relationships, and foster trust. Investing in a positive environment that includes shared meals can make a difference.

> **A collaborative lunch**
>
> If you ask people to bring their own, try doing it collaboratively with a *potluck* lunch. I [Glenn] have seen this work well, where groups take turns producing a main dish or dessert, such as a large chilli or salad. Yes, you don't know what it will be, but that is part of the fun and creates togetherness because people on the ART make it. You could consider reimbursing people for the ingredient costs, too.

Transportation and parking

Many people will descend on the venue you choose; ensure that there are enough spaces to accommodate the anticipated number of attendees. If parking is limited, negotiate reduced rates for event participants. Provide clear information on parking locations, fees, and any restrictions well in advance. Including a map and directions can save time and reduce confusion for attendees unfamiliar with the area.

Consider alternative transportation options if the venue is in a high-traffic area or lacks adequate parking. Share details on nearby public transportation, such as subway, bus, or train stations, and schedules and stops close to the venue. For additional convenience, arranging shuttle services from key locations, such as popular hotels or transit hubs, can streamline arrival and departure, especially for larger groups. Communicate shuttle schedules and pickup points clearly, ensuring that participants understand their options.

Building access

If you have many people coming as visitors to your office, we suggest talking to the facilities management team and security. Don't be caught out by not having enough visitors' badges. You can speed access by pre-registering people ahead of the event. Pre-registration is a necessity at secure sites, and you may need to collect specific identification details. Moreover, ensure that attendees bring their photo ID with them. Knowing in advance, pre-registering, and providing details to attendees before they travel improves everyone's experience.

Non-local travel arrangements

You may enjoy working within an enterprise where all attendees are local to your office. But even when booking an off-site location, do not assume that everyone is familiar with it. Sharing the location's details, parking or public transit options, and food and refreshment arrangements with attendees is an appropriate response.

When attendees come from further afield, there are more considerations, regardless of whether this is their first trip or whether they've been to the site many times, such as the following:

- Airport or train station details
- Transport from the travel hub to hotels and the office
- Best located hotels, or where there might be a negotiated rate
- Recommended restaurants
- Options for recreation time if they are extending their stay

- Any local safety information
- A local point of contact to answer logistical queries

Facilitation support for distributed events

It doesn't matter whether you are all in a single room or spread over several locations; the RTE needs help on the day to make things as successful as possible. Your first line of support is your Scrum Masters, local or remote. Beyond the standard SAFe® training for Scrum Masters, spend time with them setting out how you plan to facilitate the event and how you would like them to support you.

When running a distributed planning event, we suggest having a lead person at each site. This person can be your eyes and ears on the ground, someone you can easily reach, and someone who will escalate issues before they fester. This saves considerable time and enables you to help overcome any problems that arise.

Depending on your experience and relationships with those at the other locations, it might be best to have someone from your office travel to these locations. A word of warning: reflect on how the teams in the other sites perceive this, so as not to be seen as not trusting them. Balance the perception, real or otherwise, versus the facilitation benefits.

As you can see, running a large in-person event requires a lot of planning and organization. That's why so many people hire a wedding planner for their big day! Our advice is to make sure you have support from others to help with this, as the workload of arranging all of this, alongside making sure that the ART is ready for the planning event, can be too much for one person.

Now, let's look at what is needed if the event is being held online.

Considerations for online or remote events

Whether you're running PI Planning remotely or in person, the goal may be the same, but the logistics are very different. At the time of writing, we are a few years after the pandemic, which changed how we work forever. Most companies now have the capability for people to work remotely and have invested heavily in tooling. As a result, the path of least resistance will be leveraging the tools you likely already have at your disposal.

You will need to consider both the selection and use of tools that support the following:

- **Communication**: Audio and visual, chat, and coordination
- **Agile Lifecycle Management** (**ALM**): For backlog management and planning

- **Collaboration:** To generate SAFe®-specific artifacts, such as the ART Planning Board, and impromptu conversations at a whiteboard

We are generally tool-agnostic and subscribe to the Agile value that individuals and interactions are more important than processes and tools. No matter how fancy your tools are, you will ultimately only be able to create a committed and robust plan if you remember the people. The tools are there to help us collaborate, so don't let them get in the way.

There will be subtle differences if you run a **distributed PI Planning** (i.e., multiple locations with people grouped in person) versus **dispersed PI Planning**, where everyone works remotely at home.

Your objective with *distributed* is to make the experience as close to being a single-site in-person event as possible. If we were to draw a Venn diagram, *distributed* would sit between *in-person* and *online*, with a bigger overlap with *in-person*. We've already talked about this earlier in the chapter, in the in-person equipment checklist in the *Ensuring equipment readiness* subsection, with our most substantial advice to get a remote window into their world, with dedicated screens showing a live camera of the other rooms, an effective tool to do this.

Dispersed creates its own challenges, as you will have little or no control over the tech setup of the attendee's home office. The biggest impact on event facilitation is that it's harder to pull together quick huddles than it would be if everyone were in the same place.

We find that fully remote planning sessions are often tricky to facilitate, as you don't have the luxury of looking around the room to get a feel for effectiveness and progress. Yes, collaboration tooling provides some input, but you cannot see how the collaboration is happening or the loner who's tuned out and needs a friendly nudge to rejoin the activity. While you can do a cycle of drop-ins to the team's video chat channel to see how things are going, it can be time-consuming and disruptive to teams. For your context of people and tooling, you will need to develop signals that provide confidence in progress or the early signs of issues.

Communication

The secret sauce of PI Planning is that putting 125 people in a room for 2 days with the single objective of creating a plan for the next 10 weeks works amazingly well. We all know that collaboration is easier face-to-face. Still, when running a fully remote session with people scattered around the world, you need to create an experience that is as close to in-person as possible, in addition to facilitation.

This section will explore the challenges of tooling and how to overcome them. Most of the answers do not involve using a different tool. This is partly because most corporations dictate which tools are available. More importantly, nothing is perfect, and it's your skill in guiding the ART during these events that will bring back the humanness of the event.

A simple example is when one team needs to speak to another. In person, they can walk over to the other side of the room, and even if the group is in deep conversation, they can tap someone on the shoulder and have a quick chat, all while not disturbing the rest of the team. Compare this to unceremoniously jumping into their online meeting room, thus disturbing everyone. As an ART, what protocols do you want to put in place to enable fast communication and collaboration across teams, but without impacting the overall flow? There are many solutions, all with pros and cons, ranging from interrupting them, sending a team-wide chat message, directly messaging a person, maybe the Scrum Master or Product Owner, to logging your request in a queue.

Audiovisual and chat communication

One of the most critical pieces of tooling is for audiovisual communication. Your enterprise probably already provides one. However, you need to consider a few things based on their functionality:

- **Participant limit**: A large ART can have 125 people before you add Business Owners, the System Team, and supplier representation. Ensure that the limit is large enough for everyone to connect.

- **Large group tooling**: You'll never appreciate a single-click mass mute option until you've had to find the 3 people out of 125 who have connected and not muted, then take a phone call or make dinner for the kids! Also, does it provide a webinar-style, central Q&A feature?

- **Breakout rooms**: Most tooling provides this capability, but not all tooling is built the same. Can you easily create or remove breakout rooms? Can participants self-navigate around them without needing someone to act like an 1890s switchboard operator, moving them around rooms on demand? Can you broadcast messages or share a screen with them in the breakout rooms? If the implementation is clunky, a workaround is to create multiple channels instead of using breakout rooms, enabling people to join and leave as needed. If you end up with the latter, make sure the links are shared in a central, known location so other teams are not hindered in connecting by having to hunt for the details.

- **Live captioning**: While recording the PI Planning isn't necessary, and nobody needs to watch 16 hours of people working, live captioning can support people with accessibility needs or those whose primary language isn't that of the speaker.

- **Backup:** What is your plan for an outage during the day? In days gone by, you could use the telephone audio conferencing service, but many enterprises stopped purchasing them some time ago. We have seen some RTEs have an alternative online meeting system account in place to scrape by. If you're considering this, check your compliance with your corporate IT policies. At the very least, think about how you can get a message to attendees if the IT systems do fall over and you need to postpone.

Coordination and assistance

Operating a sizable online event such as this, requiring high levels of communication and collaboration, brings specific challenges compared to everyone in the same room. We have found the following useful to reduce your stress and the event's success:

- **Back-channels:** You will need to speak to different cohorts of people during the event, from Scrum Masters and Product Owners to Business Owners. Tracking them down can be challenging, and the amount of communication they will get via your internal messaging service can be significant, so they may miss your messages when looking for them. Creating a back-channel for these cohorts can overcome this. We've used WhatsApp groups for these effectively before. If this is your intention, plan before the event to get people's numbers and set up the groups beforehand.
- **Create a tech support channel:** To ensure quick troubleshooting and free up your time, set up a dedicated point of contact for tech issues. Staff it with someone tech-savvy in your group or from corporate IT.
- **Virtual noticeboard:** The schedule may need to be adjusted, or the approach may need to be adapted during the event. Instead of broadcasting updates to everyone, like someone virtually shouting, create an advertised noticeboard.
- **Facilitator check-ins:** Have facilitators check in with teams throughout the day to offer support and maintain momentum.

Agile Lifecycle Management (ALM)

The tooling you use to execute the PI will also be a factor in the logistics of PI Planning. In many organizations, you may have no choice of what to use. As the RTE, you do not need to be a tooling expert; you can draw upon the **System Team** to help you. Many of the collaboration tools integrate with the most commonly used tools through plugins, and you can also export in various formats that you can use to import the data.

In person, you need to make the judgment call to use sticky notes and marker pens or go down a tooling approach. There are pros and cons for both. A risk with tooling is having one person in each team *driving* and everyone watching. Not only is this boring for the other teammates, but it's slow, and you likely won't have time to plan effectively in two days. Conversely, less post-planning admin is needed, and it might manage dependency tracking better than humans can.

We could debate the pros or cons of tooling versus paper for in-person, but when working remotely, distributed, or online dispersed, you will have to embrace some level of tooling for your own sanity and to stop things from getting missed. Having one team see in real time what another team is planning becomes a must.

We recommend that you apply systems thinking and facilitate a decision across the ART on which tool teams will use for what activity. Modern tooling provides not just visualization but also dependency linkage and capacity management calculations. There is a strong argument that all teams use the same tool to benefit from the cross-team connectivity provided. Depending on your toolset in your organization, this could be your ALM or a collaboration tool that ideally connects to it.

Also, don't forget the cardinal rule for tooling: it is there to help you, not drive your way of working.

Collaboration tooling

While growing in popularity, collaborative tooling, such as digital whiteboards, is still not part of the core IT service offering in many enterprises. Tooling in this category either resembles a free-form whiteboard with minor templating or is a structured tool with set usage methods. Both have their benefits, and you can even find SAFe®-specific tooling available in the more structured grouping.

We've seen most people utilize digital whiteboards, as they provide greater flexibility for multiple uses, from PI Planning, feature design, and elaboration to the **Inspect and Adapt (I&A)** workshop. At the time of publication, the market leaders are the likes of Mural and Miro. If you have access to these or similar tooling, your life will be considerably easier.

Things become trickier if the company doesn't provide this, as your corporate firewall might even block them. They can be, at scale, expensive to license too, although you may be able to optimize how many full licenses you need versus the often free guest licenses.

> **Controlling the templates**
>
> When we first started using digital whiteboards, people would often move parts of the board around, unwittingly adjusting or even deleting other teams' plans. Nowadays, it is much better; most people have at least some experience with the tooling. However, you will need to spend a lot of time ensuring you lock down the backgrounds and the templates so you don't get into trouble. Then, remind people that *Ctrl + Z* is their friend!

If you cannot access a dedicated collaboration tool, you can get creative with corporate IT-provided solutions such as Microsoft 365. Anything that enables multiple people to interact with something can work, but often with a much smaller canvas size and user limits. Working around the need for proper tooling is inferior but better than nothing.

Here are some functionalities we've found useful:

- **Templates**: Using off-the-shelf or custom templates can save you time. Learning your tool of choice and how to create these is worth the investment, as you have a repeating pattern of work through the Planning Interval and the team's iterations.
- **Voting and polling**: Whether it's PI Planning confidence voting or choosing the most impactful solution in the **I&A Problem Solving workshop**, something that can automatically count, sort, and playback the results is often helpful.
- **Diagramming capabilities**: At times, as adults, we all struggle to draw with pen and paper, and it is even more challenging with a mouse or trackpad on a digital whiteboard. Therefore, built-in drawing elements and iconography, such as flow diagram boxes, can remove frustration and speed up getting ideas down.
- **Facilitation tools**: Facilitation features, such as timers, presentation mode, and private mode for individual brainstorming, can elevate sessions, providing more scope for creative activities.

We've illustrated the challenges of conducting entirely online planning and the additional tools and layers needed for effective communication, collaboration, and coordination. It demonstrates how much more difficult it is when you cannot simply walk across the room to speak with someone. However, with the right set of tools and procedures in place, you can make it work.

Your ALM and collaboration tools serve as replacements for sticky notes and marker pens. You will have to invest time in setting them up correctly for your context and making sure that all the relevant people know how to use them so that PI Planning can be productive and you don't lose valuable time. With physical and tooling logistics behind us, let's focus on the agenda and how, even though a template is available in the PI Planning Toolkit, we may need to modify it.

Planning the agenda

The PI Planning toolkit provides a standard agenda for an ART in the same time zone, whether in person, distributed, or fully remote. For reasons we've already discussed, the latter is tighter on time. The fun begins when multiple time zones are spread over a vast area, or you have travelers aligning around one or more hubs. For this reason, we will explore things to consider and our advice from operating in these situations.

Time zones

With time zones more than a couple of hours apart, you likely need to run PI Planning over three days, not two. If you are lucky, you can have three slightly shorter days with only minimal disruption to working hours.

With disparate time zones, you need to start making trade-off decisions to maximize the length of overlapping time spent collaborating. In extreme situations, you could deliver briefings ahead of time in each time zone, have them recorded and watched before the event, and then do a collective Q&A.

If your teams are geographically colocated, then you may have non-overlapping time with other locations where they can undertake planning for the team, and then use the overlapping time for cross-team collaboration and sequencing. While this optimizes the contact time, it trades off this with potential rework when the team discovers an assumption in their planning will not work.

The SAFe® PI Planning Toolkit includes a presentation deck and a spreadsheet with sample agendas designed for distributed planning events that you can use to adapt the schedule based on the time zones. In *Figure 6.1*, we've created a sample three-time zone agenda for the first day.

India IST	Europe CET	US MST	Subject	Facilitator/Presenter/Participants	Description
6:30 - 6:40 PM	2:00 - 2:10 PM	6:00 - 6:10 AM	Kick Off	Emma Caldwell (RTE)	Introduction, agenda, objectives, and working agreements
6:40 - 7:00 PM	2:10 - 2:30 PM	6:10 - 6:30 AM	Business Context	Liam Harper (Commercial BO)	Planning Context and Deliverables
7:00 - 7:40 PM	2:30 - 3:10 PM	6:30 - 7:10 AM	Product/Solution Vision	Sophia Bennett (Product Manager)	Vision of solution, products/services, and prioritized features
7:40 - 8:00 PM	3:10 - 3:30 PM	7:10 - 7:30 AM	Architecture/TSD	Noah Fletcher (Systems Architect)	Vision for architecture, new architecture epics, common frameworks, and program-level NFRs
8:00 - 8:30 PM	3:30 - 4:00 PM	7:30 - 8:00 AM	Development and Quality Practices	Isabella Reed (Quality)	Updates on project setup, Agile tooling, improvements in engineering practices, etc.
8:30 - 8:40 PM	4:00 - 4:10 PM	8:00 - 8:10 AM	Planning Requirements	Emma Caldwell (RTE)	Specific planning process, draft plan acceptance criteria, etc.
8:40 - 9:25 PM	4:10 - 4:55 PM	8:10 - 8:55 AM	Break for Dinner/Snack/Breakfast		
9:25 - 12:00 AM (India leaves at 11 PM – an hour before other teams)	4:55 - 7:30 PM	8:55 - 11:30 AM	Team Breakouts	Teams (ALL)	Features broken into stories (Each team); PI plan and objectives finished (Each team); Risks and impediments identified (Each team); Program Feature Board continuously updated (Scrum Masters); Architects and Product Managers circulate
	6:00 - 6:15 PM 7:00 - 7:15 PM	10:00 - 10:15 AM 11:00 - 11:15 AM	Scrum of Scrum	RTE and SM	Hourly Scrum of Scrums checkpoint to discuss planning status, program impediments, and dependencies
		11:30-12:15 PM	Lunch in the US - Europe Leave for the day		
		12:15 - 2:15 PM	Team Breakouts	Teams (US ONLY)	Features broken into stories (Each team); PI plan and objectives finished (Each team); Risks and impediments identified (Each team); Program Feature Board continuously updated (Scrum Masters); Architects and Product Managers circulate
		1:30 - 1:45 PM	Scrum of Scrum	SM (US ONLY)	Hourly Scrum of Scrums checkpoint to discuss planning status, program impediments, and dependencies
			END OF DAY ONE		

Figure 6.1: An example agenda for Day 1 showing three time zones.

Finding overlapping time can be hard

A couple of years ago, I was working with a company that celebrated its global status. The leadership wanted to include people from different countries in its ARTs. At first, the intent sounded great, but the challenge was implementing it. In practice, scheduling PI Planning was almost impossible. We had to accommodate different time zones across multiple continents, and finding a three-day slot that worked, considering public holidays, was hard. Not only that, but we had to think about the timing. They had a simple solution: base the agenda around the most senior person. If there is one thing you take away from this book, it is this: please, please, please don't do that!

Things to consider and recommendations when making adjustments for multiple time zone events include the following:

- Always share the load and ensure there isn't always one team that gets up early or stays late. We often rotate so that it is fair for everyone.
- Not all time zones are equal. For example, many people catch the bus to work in countries such as India, where large outsourcing providers are based. If they miss their bus, they won't be able to get home.

- Plan regular breaks. You'll also need to take plenty of breaks to keep everyone fresh when working remotely.

- Check local employment and labor rules. We have seen some jurisdictions that state employees should be provided with hot food if they work late.

- Consider their personal situations when asking people to come in early or stay late. They may have school drop-offs to attend to or a career responsibility for a family member.

Travelers

We've worked with clients who have seen the power of in-person and regularly flew people half-way around the world to conduct in-person PI Planning. If this is the case, and those traveling are doing so long-haul, we need to be respectful of them and the impact on their health and family life.

One way to accommodate this is to run a longer Day 1, enabling a shorter Day 2 of PI planning. If people are due to fly home in the evening of Day 2 of PI planning, even if short-haul, at some point in the day, they will start clock-watching and have in the back of their mind the travel and airport time needed to make their flight. If we can execute planning well, we can maintain their focus and still provide plenty of time for them to make their flight in a relaxed way.

> **Being aware of the human impact of travel**
>
> For one client's transformation, we formed the **Lean-Agile Center of Excellence** (**LACE**) into an ART and undertook PI Planning like the rest of the organization. I [Glenn] was UK-based, but planning was in the Midwest of the United States. I love helping organizations make their world a better place, and I am often amazed at the wonders of PI Planning, but doing 20+ hours and 9,200 miles in a plane over 5 days is no fun, no matter how good the in-flight movies are.
>
> I wasn't alone on these trips, with 10–15 people coming out from Europe, the corporate head office, to Colorado. In an attempt to make this work, we organized the week's agenda as follows:
>
> - **Monday:** Flight, meet up for dinner, and then sleep (if the jet lag lets you!)
> - **Tuesday:** Teams work together to finalize their pre-planning in the morning. I&A in the afternoon.
> - **Wednesday:** PI Planning Day 1. A longer day, starting early and finishing early to get an extended first break out. ART evening social.
> - **Thursday:** PI Planning Day 2. All completed by 2 p.m., when taxis or hire cars took travelers back to the airport.

- **Friday:** Landed around breakfast, not knowing what day of the week it was! US local team members did the post-PI Planning admin, putting stories in Jira, while European team members tried to stay awake!

As a consultant who often stands at the front of the room as an RTE or supports a new RTE, I loved the experience of being part of a team and working through the process. It made me a better coach and consultant, and I have a deeper appreciation for team members.

If you'd like to learn more about using an ART for your LACE, check out this article: `https://scaledagileframework.com/running-the-transformation-using-a-safe-agile-release-train/`.

Going longer

We're now much better at working remotely, but online meetings are much more tiring than in-person meetings. Additionally, it is much less efficient to communicate with a large number of people online. You might be able to send someone a Slack or Teams message, but they may not see it right away, so often, we need to clarify things when we write them quickly. If we're there in person and need to ask a question, we simply walk across the room and have a conversation.

Multiplying the effect of being remote and time zones, we may need more time and will typically spread the agenda over four or five shorter days. As always, there are trade-offs with this approach, as in the time people are not in planning, they may end up going back to their *day job*, which, at the very least, they might mentally bring into the planning session, or worse, get caught up in and miss one of the days!

Communication ahead of the event

After organizing the event, remember to share details with people ahead of time. This means more than sending a single email! For the groups of people attending, work out the different methods of reaching them and then repeatedly use a variety of them to ensure that the information you share with them to improve their experience is received, acknowledged, and understood.

It is helpful to create a central wiki page on your internal systems with the information that can be referred to in all communications. Be mindful of lessons from marketers, including the key information in the communication, as click-through rates can be pretty low.

It is useful to create a communication plan. Simply outline what you will broadly send and by what methods during the PI. Some designing now will make the process repeatable and easy to execute for every PI.

Topics you should consider sharing include the following:

- New tools, including when training or familiarization sessions are scheduled
- New ways of working or process changes
- Travel and access arrangements
- Last-minute reminders
- The technical or administrative support contact on the day

Divide the communications plan into different cohorts, such as the entire train, Scrum Masters, Product Owners/Product Managers, external stakeholders, and so on. Then, target specific information for each group as needed.

There are lots of ways to stay organized when working out your communication plan. These days, there are so many tools like Microsoft Teams or Slack. Even if you *go old school* and use distribution lists, you can save everyone from numerous errors and frustrations compared with the error-prone task of copying and pasting 125 email addresses.

Summary

Effective PI Planning logistics are the cornerstone of a successful ART event, whether conducted in-person or remotely. Effective logistics create the foundation for a successful event; poor planning can undermine even the best-prepared content. This chapter highlighted the importance of meticulous preparation, including venue selection, accessibility, and technology integration, to foster collaboration and alignment.

When it is in-person, it's not a case of finding a space; it's finding the right space. The right space includes suitable factors such as open space to move around, walls, and so on. Having sorted the space, we discussed additional requirements to make the space work, from power and internet to food and drink.

With remote and online planning, toolsets become essential factors. They become your digital walls and virtual breakout areas, which are necessary for teams to collaborate easily as if they were in the same room. We outlined challenges in facilitating such events because, despite improving tooling, their use is slower and not as easy as a casual glance around a room.

We explored how accommodating multiple time zones complicates your agenda planning. We showed how you can share the pain of unsociable hours, along with other considerations to reflect on.

By leveraging toolkits, adapting to team needs, and prioritizing communication, RTEs can create an environment where teams thrive and produce actionable, confident plans. With careful planning and continuous improvement, PI Planning becomes more than an operational task—it's a powerful opportunity to build trust, strengthen relationships, and drive ART success.

Having now planned the event and supported the Product Management and System Architect in building their backlog, it is time for the big day. In *Chapter 7*, we will explore Day 1 of PI Planning.

Get This Book's PDF Version and Exclusive Extras

UNLOCK NOW

Scan the QR code (or go to packtpub.com/unlock). Search for this book by name, confirm the edition, and then follow the steps on the page.

Note: Keep your invoice handy. Purchases made directly from Packt don't require one.

7

PI Planning: Day 1

In this chapter, we'll begin our exploration of **PI Planning**—often referred to as the seminal event in SAFe®, and for good reason. It's a powerful moment where we bring everyone involved in building and delivering value into the same space, whether that's a physical room or a virtual one. It's our chance to connect, align, and look ahead together. That includes our **Business Owners** and those who support the **ART**—it's a real team effort.

It's perfectly normal for people to feel a little unsure the first time they experience PI Planning. After all, it's not every day we get over 125 people collaborating at once! However, while it may feel different from traditional planning methods, it's precisely that shift that unlocks significant value. And more often than not, those early nerves melt away, replaced by a genuine sense of excitement and clarity. Don't be surprised if some of the most skeptical voices end up being its most prominent advocates.

We'll start by setting the scene and helping you build confidence in the process—whether you're facilitating, participating, or supporting others. Then, we'll walk through how the day is typically structured, with some practical tips to help you tailor the agenda to fit your context. The framework provides a solid foundation, and from there, we can shape it to meet our needs without compromising its essence.

Here's what we'll cover in this chapter as we dive into the first day of PI Planning:

- Capturing the magic of PI Planning
- The PI agenda and feedback loops
- The first team breakout
- The draft plan review
- The management review and Problem Solving workshop

Capturing the magic of PI Planning

It helps to have a short and memorable way of describing the event. Something that makes people lean in, rather than feel like they're about to be pitched a methodology. We want to spark curiosity to help people see that while PI Planning might feel unfamiliar at first, it's a compelling way to align, connect, and create momentum.

You'll want to tailor the pitch to suit your organization, of course. But our go-to version, the one that's worked time and again, sounds like this:

> *Let's get everyone in the same place at the same time to talk to each other and work out what to do next.*

It's just one sentence. No jargon. No frameworks. Just people coming together to make sense of what's next. When crafting your own version, keep it simple. Make it relatable. And let your own enthusiasm show through; people respond to that far more than theory or structure.

SAFe® is a *framework*, not a rigid checklist. Think of it like scaffolding—it's there to support you as you build the right approach for your context. You choose the tools you need, when you need them.

We sometimes hear the question, "What are the best bits of SAFe?". But that's like walking into a hardware shop and asking whether paint or a hammer is better. It depends entirely on what you're trying to achieve.

That said, if there's one element of SAFe that consistently has a transformational impact, it's PI Planning. It brings people together, creates shared clarity, and gets everyone pulling in the same direction. It's often the first event that unlocks real change and the one that people remember.

In fact, once someone's taken part in a well-run PI Planning session, they often become its strongest advocates. The value becomes clear not through explanation, but through experience.

Now, let's run through the agenda.

The PI Planning agenda and feedback loops

At its core, the PI Planning agenda is built around feedback loops, a hallmark of Agile thinking. We do some work, gather input, and adjust based on what we've learned. In this case, the *work* is planning itself.

The structure is simple: leadership expresses intent, teams respond with feasibility, and both sides iterate until aligned. This cycle is what turns PI Planning from a one-way planning meeting into a dynamic and collaborative process.

Here is a sample agenda:

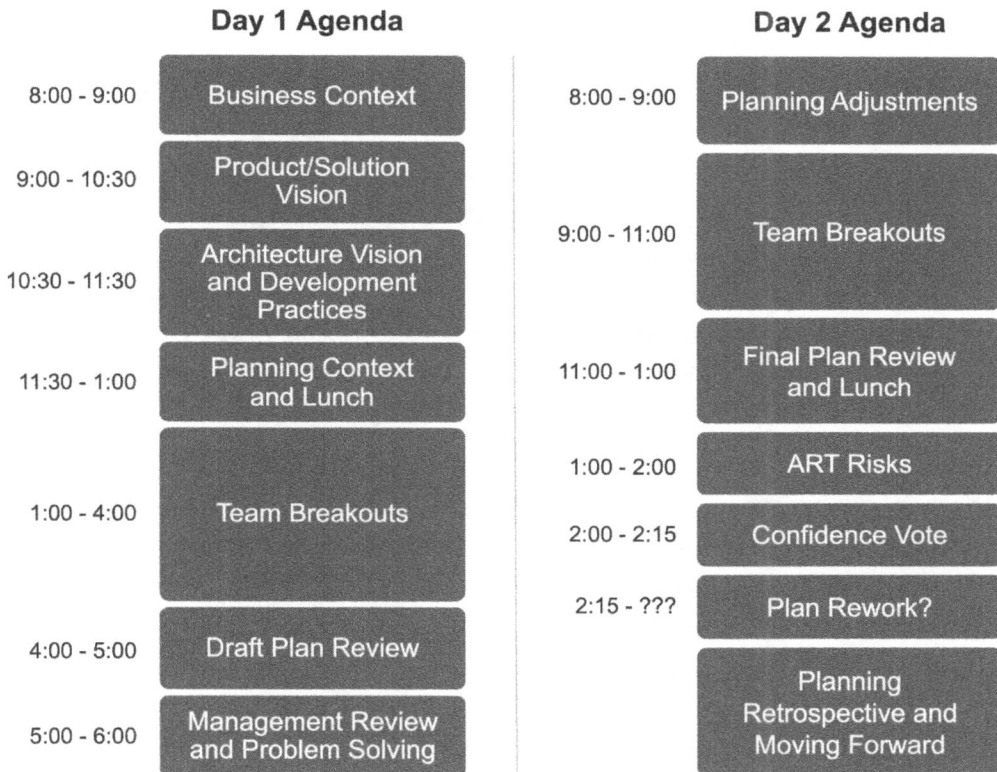

Day 1 Agenda		Day 2 Agenda	
8:00 - 9:00	Business Context	8:00 - 9:00	Planning Adjustments
9:00 - 10:30	Product/Solution Vision	9:00 - 11:00	Team Breakouts
10:30 - 11:30	Architecture Vision and Development Practices		
11:30 - 1:00	Planning Context and Lunch	11:00 - 1:00	Final Plan Review and Lunch
1:00 - 4:00	Team Breakouts	1:00 - 2:00	ART Risks
		2:00 - 2:15	Confidence Vote
		2:15 - ???	Plan Rework?
4:00 - 5:00	Draft Plan Review		Planning Retrospective and Moving Forward
5:00 - 6:00	Management Review and Problem Solving		

© Scaled Agile, Inc.

Figure 7.1: Sample agenda from Scaled Agile (© Scaled Agile, Inc. Source: `https://framework.scaledagile.com/pi-planning/`*)*

You'll notice that there are feedback loops throughout both days:

1. **Start of Day 1**: Leadership shares their goals and vision for the PI in the morning briefings. Teams then begin planning and provide feedback on what they believe is realistically achievable based on their understanding and capacity during the team breakouts.

2. **End of Day 1**: Leadership reviews the teams' initial plans during the **management review** and **Problem Solving workshop**. Based on this input, they adjust their expectations, priorities, or guidance.

3. **Start of Day 2:** The updated leadership perspective is shared back with the teams in the planning adjustments. They revise their plans accordingly, incorporating this new input.

4. **End of Day 2:** Teams present their final plans from late morning. If the business is confident in these plans, the PI Planning event wraps up with a confidence vote. If not, teams and leadership continue through additional feedback loops until alignment is reached.

After running the planning session with a few PIs, you may want to adjust the agenda to suit your context.

> **A note on modifying the agenda**
>
> Before changing the standard agenda, take a moment to understand the purpose behind each activity. Every part of the two-day structure has been tested in real organizations—the agenda exists for a reason. Adjustments are okay, but treat them like experiments. If you make a change, reflect on it afterward: Did it improve things? Did it have unintended side effects? This mindset of curiosity and continuous improvement is part of what makes great RTEs effective.

As a general rule, we don't make wholesale changes to the template agenda unless we can see or experience challenges; after all, it's a well-proven process that has worked many times in many enterprises. We do many minor tweaks, which we'll explain as we take you through the agenda in this and the next chapter.

Let's start the first day with the briefings.

Morning briefings

First impressions matter. Ensure that everything works—including audio, video, screens, and remote access. It's worth over-preparing here. A smooth, professional start builds trust. A rocky kickoff can derail confidence before the real work even begins.

The briefings kick off Day 1 and are designed to orient and energize the group. Although the suggested start time is 8:00 a.m., don't get too caught up in that—start when it makes sense for your context. For example, starting at 9:15 a.m. is common to give people time to arrive and settle. In some regions, traffic patterns or cultural norms might push this later. The important thing is not the clock but the clarity and energy these briefings bring to the room.

Remember, this may be someone's first PI Planning event. It can be overwhelming—unfamiliar people, new processes, and unclear expectations. Great briefings help people feel grounded. They zoom in step by step: from business context, to product vision, to technical constraints—gradually painting a clearer picture before handing the planning over to the teams.

> **Use the toolkits**
>
> We've mentioned this before, but if you have access to **SAFe® Studio**, the **SAFe PI Planning Toolkit** is available to help prepare stakeholders for the briefings. It contains some great coaching questions, templates, and checklists to get you going, and we refer to it every time we work with a new ART.

If you've done an effective job in helping the speakers prepare for the event with content cues and perhaps even a practice run, your role is little more than that of a compere, introducing people, ensuring that the tech is working (and remains so), and enabling the audience to ask questions. For our recommendations on creating the briefings, please refer to the guidance in *Chapter 5*. For now, let's look at what you need to know about the briefings on the day.

Briefing 1: business context

The **business context briefing** sets the stage. A senior leader, someone who can both understand the bigger picture and present it in a way that everyone attending can understand, shares the current state of the business and its future direction. Why does this matter to delivery teams? Because context fuels motivation. People do better work when they understand the *why* behind what they're building.

Even in large organizations, when senior leaders take the time to speak directly to teams (live or recorded), it has a genuine impact.

> **Make the business vision personal and customer-centered**
>
> In one PI Planning session, a senior leader named Priya was asked to open with the business context. Her original slides had all the essentials: strategy updates, quarterly goals, and performance metrics. But during a dry run the day before, it was clear something was missing. The message was informative, but it didn't feel connected to the people in the room.
>
> So, she made one simple change: she started with a story.

At the live event, Priya opened her briefing not with numbers, but with a real customer experience. A small business owner who had been struggling with a clunky onboarding process, lost time, and repeated frustration. She explained how this issue wasn't just costing revenue, it was costing trust. Then, she pointed to how the features in the upcoming PI would directly address that pain.

The room shift was immediate. People sat forward. They could see how their work would solve a real problem, not someday, but soon.

Great business context briefings don't just inform—they inspire. They connect teams to the bigger picture and show how the work ahead creates meaningful outcomes. When people understand *why* they're here and *who* they're helping, they don't just plan—they commit.

We want the people to feel energized and clear about their role in helping the business move forward when they leave.

What if the leader isn't available on the day?

Leaders' diaries fill quickly, and urgent demands on their time can put them far from your office. This doesn't mean you need an understudy, although having one in the wings is a helpful contingency plan. Make plans to conference call the leader into the session on Zoom or have a pre-recorded video message ready and available to play.

We have managed to get senior leaders, many levels up, to participate virtually in this fashion, which the teams greatly appreciated. The power of a custom, specific, direct message to them as a cohort goes a long way toward morale building.

You have to ensure that the business briefing lands:

- **Watch the room**: While the leader is speaking, look out into the room, not the slides. Check people's faces to see whether they are enjoying it and appear to understand the context. This can help you prompt them to ask questions about a particular topic, or you could pose a question, even if you know the answer.
- **Clarify context if needed**: Sometimes, senior leaders are so enthusiastic about their worldview that they forget the curse of knowledge and lose the audience. After they've spoken, to overlay context to the ART, clarify with something like *"For the teams here, that means...."*

- **Listen for soundbites**: Snippets of repeatable elements can help you later in your planning context and during the breakout sessions.

Like all briefings, open it up to the floor for questions to help the ART clarify points of understanding. Having heard the view from the bridge, we move on to the **Product Management** view.

Briefing 2: product or solution vision

If the business context is the *why*, the product vision is the *what*. Product Management outlines the key features and priorities for the PI, ideally linking them back to the strategy. Help them articulate not just what's in scope, but also what's been intentionally left out—and why.

This briefing provides teams with the focus they need to start translating ideas into actionable plans.

Help Product Management bring the backlog to life

A strong product vision briefing does more than list features—it paints a picture of the future that customers will experience if we deliver the right things, in the right way.

Before one PI Planning event, I [Tim] noticed that the Product Management team was preparing to walk through their feature list slide by slide—each one packed with bullet points, acronyms, and delivery targets. It was technically correct, but wasn't very compelling.

So I sat down with them ahead of time and asked a few simple coaching questions to help them think about the customer:

- What problem is this feature solving?
- What would a customer notice if this were live tomorrow?
- What would be missing if we didn't deliver it?

That short conversation unlocked a shift. Instead of reading out feature descriptions, the Product Managers started telling short, compelling stories: what the customer pain looked like, how the feature would help, and how it tied back to the business goals.

Incidentally, in case you hadn't picked it up, we are calling this the ***product/solution vision*** be-cause, for a single ART, you may be looking at one product. However, if you're running multiple ARTs within the same PI Planning event—aligning them as a solution train, or a *team of teams of teams*—then the initial vision may apply to the entire solution rather than to an individual product.

Just like with the business context briefing, it can be helpful for the product vision to review previous PIs, the impacts of delivered work, and lessons learned now that the work is live. This creates a feedback loop within the event: we did something, learned from it, and now use those lessons to plan the next steps. A good product person probably doesn't need much prompting to present a strong product vision. The RTE's role is mainly to provide structure for the event and reassure them that support is available if needed.

Here are some guidelines to improve understanding during the briefing:

- **Summarize themes**: If key messages were buried in the presentation, you can summarize the key elements during the transition to the next speaker.

- **Reflection and questions**: The teams may have immediate questions or may request that the Product Management come to them and discuss a particular topic during the breakout sessions.

- **Link back to business context**: Help make connections by linking the presentation back to what the previous speaker shared.

- **Read the room**: If you think there may be some confusion, prompt for questions: *"Just checking—does everyone have a sense of how these priorities link to their area?"*. You are looking for clarity, not consensus.

Having understood the *what* from Product Management, we move on to the architecture.

Briefing 3: architecture and development practices

This briefing focuses on how we'll work together. That could mean architecture principles, inte-gration standards, technical risks, or evolving ways of working. For marketing or non-technical ARTs, it might cover the tone of voice, regulatory constraints, or branding guidelines.

Giving developers the guardrails they need

I [Tim] remember one PI Planning where the architecture briefing was one of the highlights. In the past, the Architect had fallen into the trap of overloading people with slides—talking about future-state visions and technical diagrams that didn't really help them make day-to-day decisions. This time, he tried something different.

He started by showing the teams where we were trying to get to—our ideal end state. Just a few visuals, nothing heavy. Then, he said, *"Look, if you can do it this way, great—it'll reduce technical debt and get us closer to where we want to be."*

But he knew that not every team was in the same place. So he added, *"If you can't do it this way yet, that's okay. Here's another option that still keeps you moving in the right direction—just make a note of the trade-offs."*

The developers understood that he was opening a conversation with them—they just needed clarity and a bit of flexibility. So, instead of laying down rigid rules, he gave them guardrails—enough structure to stay aligned, but with room to navigate based on their context.

It changed the tone all day. Developers felt empowered, not policed, and there was a lot more conversation throughout the day. We spent far less time later fielding questions like, *"Can we do it this way?"* because we'd already talked through the options together.

Be pragmatic. If nothing's changed since the last PI, that's okay to say. A simple, *"No major up-dates—any questions?"* can be all that's needed.

Technical staff are not always the most polished presenters, so if you feel that they've missed points they previously told you they wanted to get across, you can help extract the information by asking them open questions such as *"Is there anything else you think people might need to know?"*, *"What do you wish you'd told people last time but didn't?"*, and *"How could people misunderstand what is being said here?"*.

Briefing 4: planning context

This is your moment as an RTE to provide structure and support—to create a sense of calm and clarity before the energy of planning kicks in. Use this time to give a concise yet purposeful overview: walk through the agenda, highlight key logistics such as lunch breaks and room locations, introduce attendees, and outline what attendees can expect over the next two days. Even in a mature ART, there are often new joiners or team members who missed training. A clear orientation helps everyone feel grounded, confident, and ready to engage.

To make the most of this moment, a bit of preparation goes a long way. Rehearse your delivery ahead of time so you can speak with ease and avoid reading slides verbatim. Keep your tone welcoming and steady—your calmness sets the tone for the room. Use visuals sparingly but effectively: a clean, high-level view of the agenda, a map of the space if you're in person, or a quick intro slide for key roles (RTE, Product Management, System Architects, and Business Owners) can all help people find their footing.

Most importantly, remember that this short introduction isn't just logistical—it's cultural. You're setting expectations not only for what's happening, but also how you'll work together: open, collaborative, focused, and human. A few minutes well spent here can shape the energy for the rest of the event.

Having now examined the specific sessions, let's consider some general guidance to help the briefings improve over time.

Adapting briefings for complex structures

Some environments need more nuance. You might be working across multiple business units or supporting Product Owners with competing priorities. In other cases, you may be part of a larger Solution Train with several ARTs present. When that's the case, it's essential to adjust the agenda flow to accommodate the complexity.

For example, start with a unified business context that applies across all ARTs. This ensures that everyone begins with a shared understanding of the bigger picture. From there, consider bringing the planning context forward—before individual ARTs split off for their own product and architecture briefings. This helps align expectations early and reduces confusion as the day unfolds.

Whatever adjustments you make, ensure that any competing messages are resolved in advance. The overall story should still feel coherent and consistent for those listening, even if their work is spread across different parts of the organization.

Helping briefings improve over time

Nearly a quarter of PI Planning is dedicated to briefings and planning setup, which is a significant investment of time, especially with large ARTs. As an RTE, your role is to ensure that investment delivers real value. When done well, these sessions set the tone for the event, build confidence, and foster a shared understanding across the room.

There are a few simple but impactful ways to support continuous improvement:

- **Share feedback from the room**: Honest and constructive feedback helps presenters understand what went well and where they might improve. Even small suggestions can help make the next session more engaging and effective.
- **Record the briefings**: Watching their own delivery gives presenters a rare chance to reflect. It can reveal habits they weren't aware of and help them refine their message and presence.
- **Offer light-touch coaching**: Support with structure, narrative flow, or visuals can go a long way. Even seasoned leaders appreciate someone helping them sharpen their story and connect more clearly with their audience.

Regardless of your level of experience with the ART, setting up strong, focused briefings is essential. Prioritize clarity, energy, and relevance, and you'll help unlock the alignment and engagement that makes everything else in PI Planning more effective.

Ready to explore how teams take that input and turn it into a plan? Let's dive into the team breakouts.

The first team breakout

Once the briefings wrap up, it's time for teams to get to work. The first breakout kicks off the real planning. Each team begins to shape its objectives, map dependencies, and explore what's achievable. In this section, we'll explore the structure of the breakout session, the synchronized planning approach across teams that helps overcome impediments, the visualization of deliverables and dependencies on the ART Planning Board, and the practice of surfacing risks early to allow more time for resolution.

For the breakout session, the pattern is simple: about an hour of planning, followed by a **Coach Sync**. As the RTE, you facilitate the sync to check alignment, surface blockers, and assess momentum across the ART.

The sync itself is another feedback loop—a chance to pause, check progress, and make timely adjustments. It's not just about identifying problems; it's about keeping the entire system running smoothly in sync.

The approach each team takes to their breakout will vary. But your role is to stay engaged, spot issues early, and create the conditions for progress. Here's what to look out for:

- **Be present and visible**: Walk the room as if your presence matters, because it does. Listen closely to team conversations. Look for signs of confusion or hesitation. Are teams collaborating or working independently? In remote settings, you can frequently jump between virtual rooms. Be proactive and responsive. Your visibility signals that help is nearby and that this event is essential.

- **Watch for signs of under-preparation**: If a team is huddled in isolation playing endless rounds of planning poker, it may be a red flag. Estimating is fine, but if they're starting from scratch, it likely means they didn't prepare enough. See whether you can help, or at least make a note to support them more before the following PI.

- **Use planning boards as a radar**: A quick visual scan can tell you a lot. Too many risks or dependencies? Team lagging (or racing ahead)? Sticky note colors help keep things readable across teams (and consistent use of colors across teams is an example of *systems thinking*). Balance and visibility matter, especially when others rely on what is planned here.

The Coach Sync

The Coach Sync is a brief yet vital checkpoint during team breakouts—designed to keep the ART aligned and help identify issues early, before they become blockers. Think of it as a radar sweep across the room: a way to quickly understand how planning is progressing, where support is needed, and whether any systemic issues are emerging.

As an RTE, you facilitate the Coach Sync to create visibility and momentum. It's not the place to fix problems—it's where you *find* them. Keep the tone supportive and pragmatic. The goal isn't to critique teams, but to check the pulse of the room and ensure that every team has what they need to keep moving forward.

Here are a few tips to run effective Coach Syncs:

- **Keep Coach Syncs focused**: These sessions aren't for solving problems—they're for surfacing them. Stick to the timebox (15 minutes) and limit the attendees to Team Coaches or Scrum Masters only. When syncs drag on, teams lose access to the support they need. If deeper conversations are required, note them and schedule follow-ups during the next breakout, not during the sync itself.

- **Focus on readiness**: Do teams have what they need? Are blockers emerging? Are dependencies visible? As planning progresses, shift toward output: Are objectives clear? Are risks logged? Is the team ready to present? Use *Yes/No* questions to keep things moving—and watch for long-winded answers, which often mean *No*.

> When Scrum Masters/Team Coaches are answering the questions, if you get an explanation rather than a *Yes* or *No* answer, it's likely a *No*. Also, the longer the explanation, the more the *No* it is! Save yourself and the group some time, and don't let long, drawn-out answers take you down rabbit holes.

The Coach Sync is also your opportunity to spot patterns—for example, if multiple teams are blocked by the same issue or waiting on the same input. Use that insight to bring the right people together and unblock progress. With tight facilitation and a clear purpose, Coach Syncs help the ART stay coordinated, focused, and on track throughout the planning day.

The case for building the plan together

I [Tim] once worked with an ART where one team decided to keep their plans to themselves during the first day of PI Planning. They were confident—heads down, whiteboards full, sticky notes flying. From the outside, it looked like they were making great progress. But they didn't check with other teams. No early conversations. No shared dependencies. Just a quiet focus on *getting it done*.

By the end of the first day, they proudly revealed their plan, and that's when the wheels came off.

They'd missed multiple critical dependencies—some with teams sitting just a few tables away. They'd made assumptions that didn't hold, committed to features that couldn't be delivered, and essentially, built a plan that couldn't work. We had to scrap it and start again on Day 2. To their credit, they took it well—and they *never* made that mistake again.

The lesson? Planning isn't just about building your plan. It's about building *shared* plans. You'll often meet teams that think they've got it sorted—but in a system like this, being done early usually means you've forgotten to talk to someone. The magic of PI Planning isn't in the sticky notes; it's in the conversations. Work with your teams throughout the day. Encourage them to show their thinking, check their assumptions, and update the ART Planning Board as they go. We're not here to build isolated roadmaps—we're here to communicate.

As we are building our plan, we should be visualizing the high-level deliverables and dependencies. We do this using the ART Planning Board.

The ART Planning Board

The **ART Planning Board** is one of the most powerful visual tools in PI Planning. Whether physical or digital, it serves as a shared space for tracking and aligning dependencies across teams, making the invisible visible and helping everyone see the bigger picture. While each team works on its own objectives and plans, the ART Planning Board brings those threads together into a cohesive whole. It is a key outcome artifact from the event.

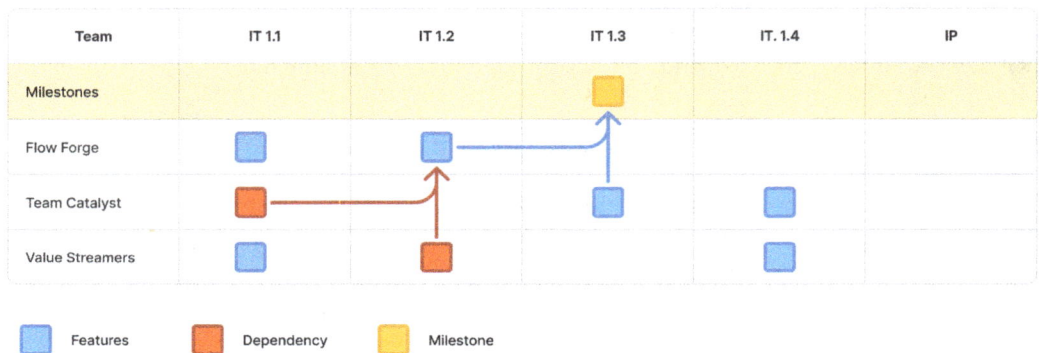

Figure 7.2: The ART Planning Board showing when features are delivered and the significant dependencies

At its core, the board displays features across the iterations of the PI. Across the top of the board are the iterations within the PI, and on the vertical, the teams and external dependencies.

As teams identify dependencies, such as work that another team must complete before they can proceed, they draw connecting lines or use sticky notes to map those links. This simple act of visualization can spark important conversations: Are we depending on work that hasn't been committed to? Is the timing realistic? Are we overloading one team with too many requests? Does the dependency come after a feature is delivered?

A clear, well-maintained board becomes a living map of collaboration. It allows risks to surface early, enabling proactive planning and negotiation between teams. If something critical isn't going to land in time, it's better to know on Day 1 than to be surprised mid-PI. The board also creates a sense of shared ownership—no one team succeeds alone, and seeing the interconnections helps foster that *team of teams* mindset.

As an RTE, your role is to keep this board active and useful. Walk the room (or virtual workspace) regularly, encourage teams to update it as their thinking evolves, and use it as a focal point during syncs and reviews. It's not just a visual aid—it's a coordination engine that helps ensure the train delivers value together.

Update the ART Planning Board incrementally—not at the end

The ART Planning Board is most effective when it evolves throughout the day, not just in a final rush before the review. Encourage teams to update dependencies as they identify them during breakout sessions. Waiting until the end risks missed conversations, unvalidated assumptions, and last-minute surprises that are harder to resolve. An incrementally updated board keeps alignment fresh, supports real-time collaboration, and gives leadership a clearer view of emerging risks and trade-offs. Treat it like a living artifact, not a static deliverable. In fact, if we're in PI Planning and by mid-afternoon, the board is still empty, we begin to worry!

One simple but powerful way to support this is by using a physical or digital **Kanban board** to manage the flow of feature planning across teams. It helps everyone stay aligned and focused, reduces overload, and creates a useful visibility into how planning is progressing.

Your Kanban board can be simple with just three columns:

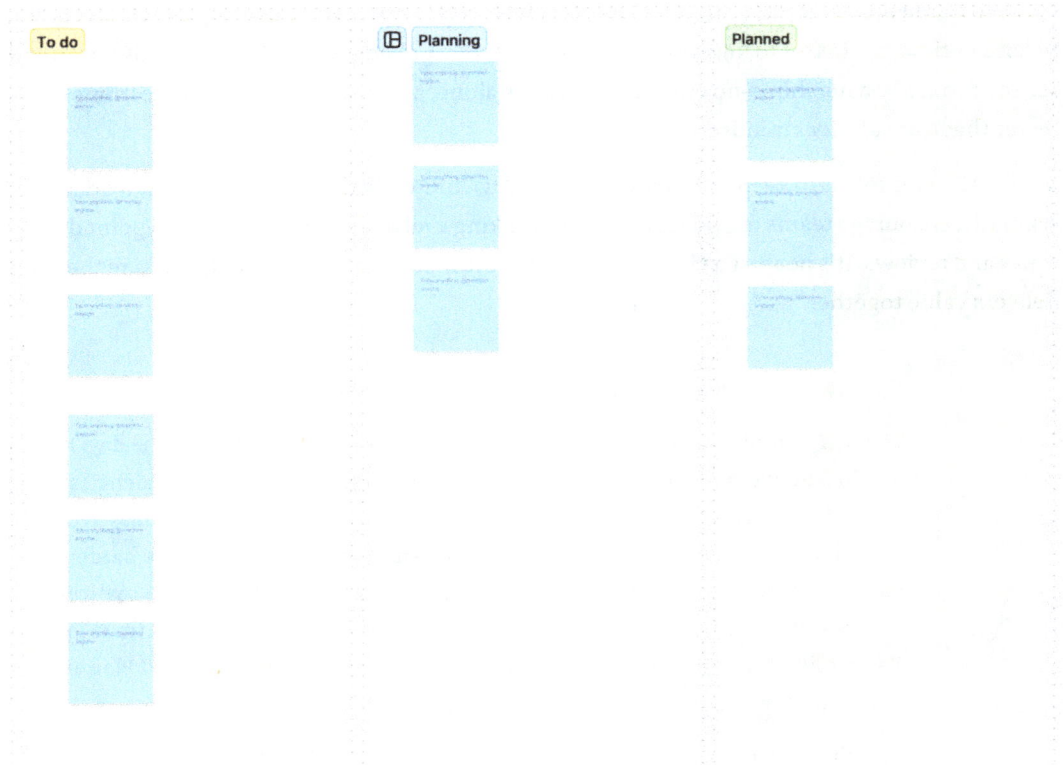

Figure 7.3: Feature planning Kanban

Let's understand them:

- **To do**: Features still pending planning.
- **Planning**: Teams are actively working on this feature, breaking it into stories, considering dependencies, and discussing technical approaches.
- **Planned**: The feature is ready. A Scrum Master or Team Coach has confirmed that the team, dependencies, and risks are reflected on the ART Planning Board, and it's good to proceed.

Product Management will already have prioritized the features. Encourage teams to limit their Work-in-Process (WIP) by picking *one feature at a time* from the top of the *To do* column, moving it through the board as they go. This helps focus energy, reduces context-switching, and avoids a scramble of half-planned work.

As features move into the *Planned* column, the ART Planning Board should reflect that progress. Over time, you'll see the board evolve—not only is it satisfying, it's also a great visual indicator of how the event is flowing and where support might be needed.

New ARTs should update the board only with the RTE and representatives from both ends of the dependency present.

Before the muscle memory is established in the ART for updating the board and validating the placements, I [Glenn] prefer to mandate that the board be updated only when the RTE is present, along with both ends of the dependency.

The RTE can ask the step-back-view questions to test the robustness of the plan. Has everything been done to derisk the dependency and align plans? Having both ends of the dependency present creates a handshake of agreement between the teams that the work placement is correct.

Unfortunately, this lesson came from seeing dependencies added against another team in their swimlane without any discussion or notice that this was needed. The other team simply said, *"We need this thing then."* It was as if they expected magic to happen and the other team to know about this!

By the end of the first breakout, don't expect a finished plan—that's not the goal. What matters is that teams have started to pull the threads together, identify key challenges, and create a shared picture of what might be possible. It's this emerging visibility that sets up meaningful feedback, and that's exactly what the draft plan review is there to capture.

Making risks visible and actionable

As teams work through their planning, they should be actively surfacing risks—anything that could block delivery, create confusion, or cause misalignment. Encourage teams to write these down as they emerge, rather than waiting until the end of the day. The sooner a risk is identified, the more options there are for addressing it. Risks can relate to technical uncertainty, resource constraints, integration challenges, dependency delays, or external factors such as regulatory shifts.

The template agenda only discusses doing this on Day 2, but we like to encourage early identification and addressing of risks during the first day—they become another feedback loop. In *Chapter 8*, we explain how SAFe® recommends capturing and addressing risks by categorizing them as **resolved, owned, accepted, or mitigated**, otherwise known as the '**ROAM**' method.

During your time with the teams or during the Coach Sync, here are some ways to surface the risks:

- Prompt teams during breakout sessions with questions like *"What might get in our way?"* or *"What would need to go right for this to succeed?"*
- Look for invisible risks in overly optimistic plans, large unbroken features, or unclear dependencies
- Review dependency lines on the ART Planning Board—they often reveal where timing or communication might fail
- Look to maintain a psychologically safe space, as people are more likely to raise risks when they feel safe to do so

Identifying and addressing risks isn't just an exercise in risk management—it's a trust-building tool. When people see that risks are not only heard but actively addressed, they gain confidence in the plan and in the team around them.

Keep risk management aligned and visible

You don't have to use the ROAM format if your organization already has another way of managing risks. The important thing is consistency. Align with the approach your teams and stakeholders already understand. *ROAMing* can be a great way to keep things lightweight and transparent during PI Planning, but what really matters is that risks are understood at the right level. Ensure that there's clear visibility, ownership, and follow-up, regardless of the format used.

Now that we have a plan, we need to make sure we're on the right track before it's too late.

The draft plan review

On paper, the **draft plan review** at the end of Day 1 is straightforward. Teams have listened to the briefings, started shaping their plans, and now it's time to share those early thoughts—both with other teams and the stakeholders who helped set the context. It's the first real feedback loop of PI Planning.

But while the format is simple, it's worth facilitating this session with care. Each team is presenting a draft, not a final commitment, to help everyone align and respond to what's emerging. It's a chance for business owners and other teams to understand what's likely to be delivered, offer early feedback, and understand the progress of the planning.

Keep the draft plan review snappy and strategic

When these sessions run for a long time, energy drops and people lose focus. Keep it short, punchy, and valuable; it isn't about being strict for the sake of it—it's about respecting everyone's time, especially at the end of a long day of planning. To keep it valuable and time-efficient, stick to the essentials that help the rest of the ART, Business Owners, and stakeholders understand where things stand.

Each team should aim to cover just the following:

- **Capacity per iteration**: Are we working within our limits?
- **Draft PI objectives**: What outcomes are we aiming for so far?
- **Key risks and issues**: What might get in the way, and are we ROAMing them?

This is not the time to walk through every story or explain technical details. Keep it at the right altitude—high enough to spot alignment issues, missing dependencies, or major concerns, but concise enough to maintain energy across the group. Remind teams that deep dives can happen afterward in follow-ups, not during the review itself.

Questions from the room are welcome and often helpful, but try to keep them relevant to everyone. If someone wants to dive deep into a specific topic, encourage a quick follow-up afterward rather than letting one conversation take over the room. Think of it like a **Team Sync**: it's fine to have a *meet after*, so the whole ART doesn't have to listen to one detailed exchange.

You'll need to use your judgment here. If a discussion is clearly engaging the room and creating real insight, let it run a little. But if things are drifting, feel free to step in and bring it back on track. There's always Day 2 for deeper conversations and fine-tuning the plan.

Getting an early indication of confidence in the plan

Before we wrap up the draft plan review, there is one more thing we would like to bring forward from the template's Day 2 agenda: understanding people's confidence in the draft plan. Again, we will discuss this further in *Chapter 8*, where it appears in the standard agenda structure.

It's simple: run a quick draft confidence vote. You can use a *fist of five*, asking everyone to hold up fingers to show how confident they feel in the plans so far. You might not get a passing average (three out of five is the typical bar), but that's not the point. What you're looking for is an early signal: how confident are the teams now? And more importantly, what would it take to increase that confidence before the final review tomorrow?

You could do this either as an ART as a whole, or get Scrum Masters to ask their teams at their tables.

| No confidence | Little confidence | Good confidence | High confidence | Very high confidence |

Figure 7.4: The confidence vote

If the score is low, that's your prompt to dig a little deeper. Here are some things to look out for:

- What's unclear?
- What's missing?
- Where do people still feel unsure?
- What needs to happen to improve the score?

These are great coaching questions for the leadership team or an opportunity for teams to collaborate overnight to strengthen their plan.

Once the draft reviews are done, the teams are free to go for the evening. In a remote setting, that might just mean logging off—but if you're face-to-face, it's well worth arranging something social. A relaxed dinner, a few drinks—anything that helps people connect as humans, not just roles. After all, building that *team of teams* spirit is one of the most powerful things you can do as an RTE.

While the teams rest and recharge, there's still work to do. Leadership and stakeholders will stay behind just a little longer to tackle the "management review" and Problem Solving Workshop—but more on that in the next section.

The Management Review and Problem Solving workshop

We've put "management review" in quotation marks earlier because there's no fixed rule about who should attend this session. That said, there are a few key roles you'll almost always want in the room.

As an RTE, you'll be there to facilitate. Business Owners, Product Management, and the Architect should also be present—essentially, the same voices who led the briefings at the start of Day 1. This is their opportunity to reflect on what they've heard so far and start shaping the next feedback loop. The cohort of people in the session can do so with fresh eyes, stepping back from a team lens and looking across the ART as a whole.

In practice, you might need a few more people around the table. If someone's closely connected to delivery or has insight into one of the blockers or key decisions on the horizon, bring them in. Some ARTs like to include a representative from each team, such as the Product Owner or Scrum Master. A good rule of thumb is that if someone feels they should be there, they probably should.

This session is about collaboration, not control. It's a space to spot gaps, surface challenges, and explore options, with the aim of supporting the teams to move forward confidently into Day 2.

> **When attendance goes wrong**
>
> Gez once ran a PI Planning event where a representative from the organization's security team was present to advise on security issues. Just before the management review session, they approached Gez and asked whether they needed to stick around. Not viewing them as part of the *management team*, Gez said no and suggested they return the next day.
>
> Naturally, during the management review, a flood of security-related questions came up—and everyone started asking where the security person had gone. Gez found himself looking at the floor, silently resolving never to make that mistake again.
>
> Since then, he's followed a simple rule: if someone thinks they might need to be at the session, they probably should be. Yes, this sometimes means a few extra people in the room who don't end up contributing much, but that rarely causes problems. Occasionally, people are drawn in by the word *management* in the session title and attend to stay in the loop. They may not have much to add, but they tend to observe quietly and cause no harm—and if a critical topic comes up that touches their area, their presence suddenly becomes very valuable.

What's discussed in this session?

This part of PI Planning is where we zoom out and ask, "*What have we learned so far, and does it change what we do next?*".

Many of the people in the room—Business Owners, Product Management, and Architects—were the ones setting the context at the start of the day. They came in with expectations and priorities, and now they've heard what the teams believe is actually feasible. Sometimes, that's a great match. Other times, it might be a little different from what they were hoping for.

This is the moment to reflect and make some smart decisions:

- Are there items we should descope, now that we've seen what's possible?
- Are there trade-offs worth making?
- What do we need to communicate tomorrow morning?
- Is there anything about how the teams are planning that is restricting progress?

This is where Day 1 can be most valuable—not just in creating plans, but in presenting *options*.

For example, leadership might come into the event hoping to deliver three major features of this PI: **Feature A**, **Feature B**, and **Feature C**. After the first day of planning, the teams come back and say one of the following:

- *"We can deliver A and B, but not C—there simply isn't enough capacity"*
- *"We could deliver C, but that would mean dropping A and B"*
- *"If we prioritize differently, we can deliver A and D—a new feature that emerged during planning—which might offer more immediate value"*

This kind of option-based feedback is incredibly valuable. Instead of forcing a yes/no decision on a fixed wishlist, it creates space for meaningful trade-offs. It provides leaders with real, data-driven choices and invites a conversation about what matters most, enabling better alignment and more economically sound decisions.

As the RTE, this is a session to watch closely—not just for what's said, but how. There's one thing we always want to protect here: the teams' ownership of their plans. Leaders are absolutely encouraged to ask questions, challenge assumptions, and explore feasibility—but they shouldn't rewrite the team's work. The people doing the work are the ones who best understand their capacity and context. We will explore how these observations are shared at the beginning of Day 2 in *Chapter 8*.

If a change needs to happen, it should happen as part of a collaborative conversation—and ideally, as one of the first actions on Day 2. That way, the feedback loop stays intact, and the teams stay engaged.

In newer ARTs, this session may also surface concerns about how planning is going overall. Are teams focusing on completing features or just breaking things down? Are risks being addressed or ignored? If plans are looking sparse or fragmented, you can use this moment to reset expectations for Day 2 and help leaders support clearer guidance.

When facilitating the session, consider these points to help it be productive and on topic:

- **Set the tone early**: Remind leaders this is a working session, not a status report. We're here to remove obstacles, not judge progress.

- **Frame it as systems thinking**: Look for patterns in the draft plans. Are we seeing common blockers, gaps, or overloaded teams?

- **Encourage private reflection**: Before jumping into problem-solving, invite participants to take a quiet moment to think about what they've seen: risks, bottlenecks, capacity challenges, and emerging dependencies.

- **Facilitate, don't defend**: You're not here to explain why something happened. Focus on what decisions or support will help teams move forward.

- **Be clear about ownership**: *"Who can take this forward before tomorrow?"* is more helpful than vague action items that disappear overnight.

- **Make trade-offs visible**: Steer the group toward real conversations about scope, sequencing, and feasibility. Avoid falling into *try harder* territory.

Now, the teams can rest and recharge, while leaders and stakeholders head into the management review and Problem Solving workshop. That discussion will help shape a clearer path forward when Day 2 begins.

But before we look ahead, let's quickly summarize what Day 1 was all about—and why it matters.

Summary

In this chapter, we have learned that Day 1 of PI Planning is about alignment and visibility. It starts with a series of briefings—from business context to technical direction—designed to give teams a clear understanding of strategy, priorities, and constraints. The RTE sets the tone with a short orientation, ensuring that everyone knows what to expect. You saw how, without these, the tone and alignment of the planning could be impacted.

Teams then break out to begin planning, surfacing objectives, risks, and dependencies. Regular check-ins (Coach Syncs) help keep things aligned across the ART. We shared how the RTE keeps these activities on track, knowing how to facilitate them to achieve progress and build the draft plan to close the initial feedback loop against the *ask*.

At the end of the day, teams share their draft plans in a timeboxed review—not to commit, but to get feedback and spark conversations.

An optional draft confidence vote can provide an early pulse check. After teams wrap, leadership holds a management review to reflect on what's been learned, explore trade-offs, and prepare for adjustments on Day 2. The RTE is the key facilitator of this, keeping the leadership focused on observations and recommendations to be considered on Day 2.

Throughout, the RTE plays a key role in facilitating flow, creating focus, and helping everyone stay aligned—turning a complex event into a collaborative, high-impact planning experience.

In the next chapter, we look at the second day of PI Planning, which takes the draft plan made on Day 1 through to a final plan, which the ART uses throughout the PI to deliver its objectives.

8

PI Planning: Day 2

Day 2 of **PI Planning** is where it all comes together. The energy of Day 1—where information is shared, options are explored, and initial plans are formed—now shifts toward alignment, refinement, and commitment. Your role as the RTE is crucial here, ensuring that the conversations deepen, risks are addressed, and the confidence in the **ART's** plan grows steadily.

In this chapter, we'll walk through the key elements of Day 2 and explore how you can facilitate each one effectively. We'll look at how to start the day with purpose, how to manage the feedback loop from leadership through planning adjustments, and how to support the teams as they evolve their plans during the final breakouts. We'll also dig into how to run meaningful final plan readouts, navigate the sometimes-tricky art of risk management using the **ROAM** (short for **Resolve, Own, Accept, Mitigate**) technique, and bring it all home with a confident close and next steps.

By the end of this chapter, you'll have a clear view of how to move from draft plans to committed objectives—and how to support your ART to leave the room aligned, energized, and ready to deliver.

This chapter will have the following main topics:

- Kicking off Day 2
- Planning adjustments on Day 2
- Team final plan breakouts
- Facilitating final plan readouts
- Risk management and ROAMing
- The confidence vote
- Event teardown and next steps

Let's get started.

Kicking off Day 2

While you won't see this element on the official PI Planning agenda, it is worth spending a short time thinking about how, as an RTE, you set up for and set the scene for the second day of PI Planning.

Day two agenda

Planning adjustments	8:00 – 9:00	• Planning adjustments made based on previous day's management meeting
Team breakouts	9:00 – 11:00	• Teams develop final plans and refine risks and impediments • Business Owners circulate and assign business value to team objectives
Final plan review and lunch	11:00 – 1:00	• Teams present final plans, risks, and impediments
ART PI Risks	1:00 – 2:00	• Remaining PI-level risks are discussed and ROAMed
PI confidence vote	2:00 – 2:15	• Team and ART confidence vote
Plan rework if necessary	2:15 – ?	• If necessary, planning continues until commitment is achieved
Planning retrospective and moving forward	After commitment	• Retrospective • Moving forward • Final instructions

SCALED AGILE   © Scaled Agile. Inc.   8

Figure 8.1: The Day 2 agenda template (© Scaled Agile, Inc. Source: `https://framework.`
`scaledagile.com/pi-planning`*)*

First, perhaps obviously, you need to get there before everyone else to get ready for everyone's arrival . Ensure that there are still enough drinks, snacks, string, and sticky notes to see everyone through Day 2, as well as perform a quick tidy-up of the room.

Before the event starts, look around the room and examine different team areas. Take stock with a fresh pair of eyes to help you plan how to facilitate the team's best today. A few areas to consider are the following:

- Review any feedback left from Day 1
- Do we have enough stationery supplies?
- Have some teams raced too far ahead?

- Are others too far behind?

- Does the **ART Planning Board** accurately represent the team's plans?

- Are there risks for the ART not captured in the **Draft Plan Review Workshop**?

You can't change things in the team areas—only the teams can do that—but a slow walk around the room with an open mind, just seeing what you might observe, can suggest areas that you might want to investigate further during the rest of the day.

It's worth doing something similar once people arrive. People don't all arrive at once; some come early, some arrive later. Wandering around the room and overhearing conversations that people are having before the day starts can give you another good sense of how the event is going and any changes you might need to consider making over the day.

Begin the day formally with a brief introduction from the RTE to welcome everyone back for Day 2. Doing so can be beneficial, allowing people's minds to focus before the formal parts of the agenda begin. Another good idea now is to share some of the feedback received about the event on Day 1 and describe what has been done to address it. People will gladly give feedback initially when asked, but if they feel their feedback is not being heard or acted upon, they will likely stop providing it. Demonstrate to people what has been done with their feedback, and they will continue to offer more. We encourage you not to overlook this final step, as people's motivation will decrease if they feel their input is not valued despite their efforts to share their views.

After all this, it's time to move on to the main agenda, starting with the planning adjustments.

Planning adjustments on Day 2

You'll remember from *Chapter 7* that PI Planning is all about feedback loops. At the start of Day 1, the organization's business, product, and architectural representatives will present where they want to be by the end of the PI. The teams that do the work then spend the rest of the day exploring what they think they can achieve and how they might do so together. At the end of Day 1, the teams then present this information to the business, product, and architecture sides. After this, these three groups discuss their observations and opinions based on the teams' feedback.

Day 1 is one large feedback loop—information is presented and discussed, and the teams provide feedback. Then, on Day 2, the next step in these feedback loops starts, with the *management layer* presenting their thoughts on the teams' plans so far.

Respecting team ownership

The RTE must ensure that the information is presented to the teams in a way that maintains their psychological ownership of their plans. *Management cannot tell the teams to change their plans*, and there are two good reasons for this.

The first is that the people who do the work plan the work. The management can ask as many questions as they desire about the teams' plans. They can point out things they don't understand, comment on things that may have surprised them, or flag up areas where alignment may have been missed. However, if the management tries to go a step further and change the teams' plans themselves, they will destroy the teams' morale, making future PI Planning events seem pointless. Teams may change their plans after this agenda item and the feedback they have received, but it is always up to the teams to change their plans, not anyone else.

The other reason management can't change the teams' plans is that if they did, both sides would miss the opportunity for something incredibly valuable—a two-way conversation between different parts of the ART that would allow each side to better understand the other.

We also recommend that the playback follow the *Observations and Options* format. This format leaves room for conversation and improvement. For example. "We noticed that Team C has duplicated the work of Team B. Looking at the experience of the teams, this might be a good opportunity for Team B to do this work with Team C's support to grow their skills in this area."

To better understand how this conversation can unfold in practice and how easily it can go wrong without the right facilitation, let's look at a real-world example.

A real-world example of product-talent misalignment

Gez once launched an ART in India, and he, the **Product Manager**, and various others had flown out there to work directly with the teams for their first PI Planning event. At the end of Day 1, the Product Manager became visibly frustrated with what the teams had planned so far, complaining that key features he wanted just weren't planned in, and even that one team had planned in way less work than they were capable of and were borderline being lazy, as far as he was concerned, at least. He started to try to move things around on the teams' boards, but Gez stepped in and stopped him, suggesting we discuss all of this with the teams themselves in the morning.

The following day came, and the Product Manager arrived ready for a big showdown with the teams. The teams had fantastic answers to each question the Product Manager had. The features that had yet to be planned turned out either to have been left for planning on Day 2, or in one case, the feature just wasn't well enough understood by the teams to be able to plan it. Therefore, they requested that the Product Manager spend time with the teams that day explaining the feature. The team, perceived as *being lazy* and not planning enough work, had many holidays coming up that the Product Manager wasn't aware of. And so it went on, and with every answer the team had, you could feel the Product Manager relaxing and moving closer to the teams as more of a collaborative partner than their *senior manager*. At that point, the Product Manager truly understood what PI Planning was all about, and from then on, the ART became one of the most successful and high-performing in the whole organization.

If the Product Manager had been allowed to change the teams' boards without talking to them, none of these conversations would have happened, and all the opportunities for collaborative growth would have been lost.

With that story in mind, let's zoom out and consider what typically gets discussed during this session and why those discussions matter so much.

Trade-offs and opportunity conversations

With the caveats we discussed in the real-world example in mind, we need to think about what is discussed in the Day 2 planning adjustments session. The classic Agile answer is, "Discuss whatever needs to be discussed," but we know that while this is true, it isn't necessarily helpful.

What typically tends to be discussed is the surprises. The management said at the start of Day 1 where they want to be by the end of the PI. At the end of Day 1, the teams often tell management that they can't quite get to the original goal, but they can reach an alternative goal that's still valuable. Sometimes, there are trade-off discussions as well. We've seen situations where the management says they want A, B, and C by the end of the PI. The teams then come back to them and say that they can have A and B but not C, or they can have C but not A and B, so which would the management prefer? At times, you get even more exciting conversations where the management asks for A, B, and C, but the teams say that by focusing on A and C and descoping B, the management could also get D for free. Planning is all about creating the best possible version of the future, and often, this will require trade-offs and compromises on both sides.

Another crucial element of this session is to help the management become more enlisted to support the teams over the rest of Day 2 and the rest of the PI. For example, teams may say they can achieve A and B but not C because C has a massive dependency issue beyond the teams' control. If the management would also like C to happen, can they please sort out this dependency issue? In a related sense, perhaps teams would like to deliver A, B, and C but simply don't have the capacity to do all three. Therefore, the management needs to spend some time thinking through the economics of spending more on capacity, whether that's increasing the number of people or increasing the amount of automation, and decide whether the economic trade-off is worth it to get C. This is an example of applying principle 1 of SAFe®: *Take an economic view*. As an RTE, you can use moments like this to reinforce people's understanding of the underlying principles and develop their skills.

What is discussed in this session will vary from ART to ART, PI to PI, and context to context, but as an RTE, you are looking for conversation to happen and alignment and understanding to grow on both sides. If these happen, you can be confident that the right conversations will occur.

That said, sometimes there isn't that much to discuss, which can also be okay in certain circumstances. We have seen this happen when teams and management have worked together for some time, or at least when the management has spent all of the first day working closely with the teams. Either way, the two sides have built a close and shared understanding. This means there is less need for a distinct feedback loop to be built into the agenda, as the feedback has become flow-based and continuous throughout the event.

Don't ever be tempted to drop this agenda item altogether. While you may think this feedback loop has become continuous for everyone, it may not have become so for every person and every team. So, always keep it on the agenda and allow people to discuss whatever they want. It's far better to spend five minutes checking whether anyone has any questions than to save five minutes but prevent an essential conversation from happening.

Once this session has concluded, the teams will take the new information they have learned back into their breakout sessions to refactor their plans and prepare for a final plan readout.

Team final plan breakouts

The standard PI Planning agenda allocates two hours to the final plan breakouts, which means you have two breakouts with two coach syncs. However, we'd argue that you should probably call a coach sync straight after the planning adjustments session to ensure everyone is okay, understands what was discussed, and has identified everything they need and how they will obtain it to make the agreed-upon adjustments.

In either event, two hours is a relatively short time for these breakouts, especially with new ARTs. Don't be afraid of looking to flex the timeboxes for these agenda items if you feel your ART needs more or less time to get them done to a high enough standard. When people feel rushed, they are more likely to feel stressed. When they feel stressed, they are more likely to feel confused. When they feel confused, you are less likely to get a coherent approach regarding how they intend to commit to and achieve their objectives for the following PI.

If people need more time for something, give them more time. Conversely, you may also run into the opposite situation, where people look like they will be finished ahead of time. This situation also carries risks that you need to look out for. When teams rush through and think they understand, but do not, it carries unnecessary risks to the PI.

Perhaps teams think they are done because they've tagged some stories as happening in different iterations, but haven't yet defined and committed to any objectives. Or they think that because *Agile means you don't ever plan into the future*, they've planned out the next iteration and then refused to plan beyond that. They could think this because they've planned their work but have not yet given any consideration to dependencies they may have on other teams or that other teams may have on them.

It can be helpful to have a mental model of a definition of done for the team's outputs during this breakout session. The **Scrum of Scrums checklist** in the **PI Planning Toolkit** can be a good starting point to build this, having a minimum set of standards that teams would need to demonstrably meet before being considered done with their team breakout sessions. We're not advocating for this as a formal definition of done—heavily documented and turned into a checklist against which each team will be inspected and held to account—because a team's context matters. However, an aide-mémoire you can mentally walk through to pose questions or offer guidance will guide you well in facilitating the event.

As a minimum, we would suggest that the following appear on your list:

- Teams have a rough plan for each iteration of the PI. As you move through the PI, this plan will likely decrease in detail and accuracy. Iteration one might be quite tightly planned out. The iteration before the Innovation and Planning iteration will be much more loosely planned and may contain one or two significant stories.
- Teams have represented their work visually at the feature level on the collective ART board.
- Teams have identified, discussed, and agreed (or disagreed!) on both the dependencies they have on others and the dependencies others have on them.

- Teams have written their committed and uncommitted objectives for the upcoming PI. Ideally, these will be measurable rather than subjective, so by the end of the PI, they will become an effective tool for measuring the ART PI Predictability.

- **Business Owners (BOs)** have circulated and assigned business value points to the objectives.

In addition to creating an iteration-by-iteration plan, during this breakout, teams also need to craft objectives.

Crafting team objectives

Objectives in SAFe® are often misunderstood. Partly, this is because they are less well explained than other elements, but possibly more because the idea of an *objective* already has a meaning elsewhere in the corporate world, which confuses what SAFe means by an objective.

In many organizations, senior leaders give objectives to teams to achieve. Such ideas are well-meaning, for they help remove the habit of senior leaders telling teams precisely what to deliver and by when. As a form of supplying requirements, objectives give the teams more freedom and help increase agility.

However, this definition of an objective lacks an essential element of Agile—the control of the teams themselves. If senior leaders tell teams their objectives, they give teams some degree of freedom to decide how to achieve them. However, they still limit the teams' freedom to achieve objectives even more significantly than the senior leaders might have envisaged. Moreover, teams can more confidently commit to objectives they have crafted themselves, as opposed to objectives others have attempted to craft for them.

As a result, in SAFe, objectives are written by teams and presented to senior leaders for feedback rather than the other way around.

Why should teams write their own objectives?

Think back to the flow through a PI Planning event. The event starts with the management layer presenting their high-level vision and top *X* features that they, ideally at that point, would like to see achieved by the end of the forthcoming PI. Teams then spend time breaking these features down into stories, thinking through the potentially complex interdependencies between teams, and adding in all manner of other details, often in a technical language only the teams involved can easily understand. If the process were left there, the management layer would have a challenging job of making sense of what would be achieved by the end of the PI.

A business person generally won't thank a team that responds to the question "So what am I going to get in 12 weeks?" with a list of 500 stories written in technical jargon.

As a result, in SAFe®, we ask teams to write their objectives in simple, business-oriented language so they can more easily playback to the management layer and see what they will get at the end of the PI:

- Management brings a clear and simple list of what they'd like to achieve in the PI
- Teams break this into hundreds or thousands of small components to determine what is achievable
- Teams then synthesize all of this detail into a clear and simple list of what can be achieved in the PI

While the template agenda shows this happening during the final team breakouts on Day 2, there is no harm if teams start constructing draft objectives at the end of Day 1.

This team-led, feedback-oriented approach to crafting objectives naturally raises a question: what exactly are teams committing to, and how does that commitment compare to other Agile frameworks such as Scrum?

Commitments in SAFe® versus Scrum

Scrum and SAFe have similar perspectives on objectives. In Scrum, a team commits to a sprint goal rather than specific stories. This guiding objective allows for flexibility, enabling teams to adapt their stories throughout the sprint. Teams can achieve the sprint goal by delivering all or some stories. Potentially realizing they can reach the goal with fewer stories, reflecting the Agile Manifesto's principle of *Simplicity, the art of maximizing the amount of work not done.*

The same applies to SAFe. Teams break features into stories and plan them for upcoming iterations, representing higher-level features and dependencies on the ART board, but this work does not constitute a commitment. Teams commit only to their objectives for the upcoming PI, which they believe they can meet by delivering some or all planned stories and features. All scenarios are acceptable, just like in Scrum. From a practical point of view, this makes sense, as it would be unreasonable to expect teams to know exactly what they need to do after two days for an entire PI at this level of detail.

In short, PI Planning is not about creating a committed plan. It is about creating a committed set of objectives to articulate the intent of the PI. Agility means we can change the plan if we need to do so.

Writing clear, business-focused objectives

Teams should write objectives in the language your ART's BOs understand. Context is king here. If they know what "Refactor the XYZ library module" is, this might be a suitable objective, but many won't. Instead, something more akin to "Reduce the escaped defect in the XYZ library to provide better customer satisfaction through refactoring" might be better.

Having it in the language the BOs understand demonstrates that the teams understand their problem domain and offers confidence in their alignment. If the BOs consider this incorrect, they act as a token for a conversation. As Einstein said, *"If you can't explain it simply, you don't understand it well enough."*

Glenn's tip that he likes using with teams is to ask, "What does that get us?" repeatedly. When a team writes a technically oriented objective, you need to chunk up to an outcome, and stepping up to answer this question can get you there. A team once wrote, "Create a customer onboarding template," providing no context or business benefit. However, after several cycles of "What does that get us?" and conversation around the answer, they rewrote the objective to "Support the sales growth by onboarding new customers quickly and consistently with an onboarding template." The joy of the BOs was evident when they came by and discussed the team's objectives.

Before we move on, there's one important concept we need to clarify—especially as it often trips people up the first time they encounter it in SAFe®. Not all objectives created during PI Planning are treated equally, and that's by design. Some objectives the team can fully commit to, while others—although important—carry too much uncertainty to guarantee. That's where the distinction between committed and uncommitted objectives comes in.

This distinction isn't just semantics—it's a key part of setting realistic expectations, managing risk, and building trust with business stakeholders. Let's break it down.

Committed and uncommitted objectives

It is worth pointing out the vital distinction between committed and uncommitted objectives.

Committed objectives are what you would expect them to be. They are objectives that the team has sufficient confidence in being able to deliver, barring *fire, flood, or an act of God*, and they feel able to commit to delivering by the end of the PI. So far, so simple.

Uncommitted objectives are objectives that the team is committing to work on during the PI, just like any other work, but for whatever reason, they do not have the confidence to commit to being able to deliver.

A classic reason for an uncommitted objective is a significant external dependency beyond the team's control. The team is confident in its ability to deliver its element of the work. Still, it is not satisfied that the dependency will be met, so it calls the overall objective uncommitted.

The team may not fully understand the work enough to commit to it now. However, if you are running 10- or 12-week PIs, you can start the work now and learn as you go or put it off for the entire PI before considering revisiting it. The latter option may not be viable, however. We need to get started on this work, and we can't just park it for this long with little to no activity. So, instead, we set expectations to start on it, but we cannot commit to achieving it. These things are the essence of an uncommitted objective.

One final use of the uncommitted objectives is their use as a guardband. Here, the team calls out which work they will drop if the work contributing to committed objectives becomes troubled or grows unexpectedly. In doing so, they help to set expectations and can help to increase their predictability.

> One common anti-pattern to watch out for with uncommitted objectives is being seen as *additional work we will do if we have spare time in the PI*. We cannot state strongly enough that they are never this. A cornerstone of a flow-based system like SAFe® is that we do not put more work into the system than it can deliver. Nor do we build up big queues of work sitting there waiting to be done, but with no work happening on them.
>
> We want small pieces of work flowing continuously through a delivery system to get value and feedback as quickly as possible. If we see uncommitted objectives as *additional work if we have spare time*, they start to form a queue. We risk trying to work on them without factoring them into our overall capacity, which can overload our delivery system and cause it to slow down.

Uncommitted objectives are just like any other form of objective. We think through and plan their work. They all count toward our overall load for the upcoming PI and should not exceed our capacity to deliver work. As a result, the only difference between a committed and an uncommitted objective is that we're clear with our business and other stakeholders upfront about which objectives we can commit to and which we cannot.

Assigning business value to objectives

Assuming teams have written these objectives, the final step in the final team breakouts is for BOs to circulate and assign **business value (BV)** points to each objective. Typically, this is done using a scale of 1 to 10, with 1 being a very low value and 10 being very high. There are several reasons why we do this:

- **Prioritization and trade-offs during delivery**: The first is to give teams a sense of the objectives most valuable to their business stakeholders and why. As a result, if things don't go well over the coming PI and work needs to be reduced a bit, teams already have a good sense of which objectives they should prioritize because of their higher value to the business and which they can cut back on because of their lower value.

- **Encouraging mutual understanding between teams and business**: Running this exercise between the business and the teams aims to help both sides better understand each other's priorities. Sometimes, conversations occur where teams suddenly realize why something they initially did not see as important is hugely significant from a business perspective, or business people realize why something they wanted to insist that the teams deliver might be a lesser priority than something else.

- **Avoiding competition between teams**: Notice we've purposefully used *assigned*, not *scored*, in our language when assigning BV. Teams will be competitive, come what may, but if you use the language of *scoring*, you are more likely to drive an unhealthy competitive environment. It will save you great debate that one team has a higher BV *score* than another.

- **Involving diverse perspectives**: It is often worth looking beyond the black-and-white idea that *the BO assigns BV points to objectives*, and instead, bringing in other people who may be able to provide valuable alternative perspectives.

For example, at a PI Planning event in a major bank, the BO was paired with an architect while assigning BV points to objectives. They came to one team, and the BO looked at an objective written in very technical language and dismissed it as a one-point objective. They didn't know what it was, so they didn't know why they needed it, so they saw it as a massively low priority.

At this point, the architect they had been paired with spoke up, leading to the following conversation:

> **BO**: *I don't know what this is. It doesn't look important, so I'm calling it a one-point objective.*
>
> **Architect**: *Do you realize that if we don't make this architectural change, in six months' time, the whole of internet banking in <country X> will be turned off?*
>
> **BO**: *What?*
>
> **Architect**: *Yes, and if it does get turned off, you'll have to explain to that country's regulatory authority why you allowed it to be turned off.*
>
> **BO**: *Ah. That's probably quite an important objective then...*
>
> **Architect**: *I'd say so, yes.*
>
> **BO**: *Shall we call it a 10-point objective instead?*
>
> **Architect**: *I think that would be wise.*

Just because the points assigned to objectives are called **business value points**, it doesn't mean they can only be allocated by someone from the business. Often, this happens, but various perspectives can be helpful depending on the context. For more technical or platform-based ARTs, we've seen the whole assignment process run by an architect alone with no business involvement, as the architect best understood the work and its value.

- **Turning tension into opportunity**: What if uncommitted objectives end up with a higher assignment of BV than committed objectives? This potentially creates significant tension, as you're saying to a business person, often someone at quite a senior level, that you will only commit to delivering the things they value less and will not commit to delivering the things they value the most. The temptation is to panic and start moving the most valuable things into the committed objective category, but never be tempted to do this.

The value an objective does or does not have makes no difference in whether the team can commit to it. If the team says they cannot commit to something, that is the reality of the situation, no matter how much someone senior wishes it were otherwise. However, when handled correctly, this situation leads to an intriguing possibility. If a senior person sees something hugely valuable being called uncommitted, they will want to change this. So, why not take advantage of the conversation this situation may open up and explain to them why the objective is uncommitted?

Tell them what would need to change for it to move to become committed, asking whether they can help with getting that change to happen. If they can make it happen, tell them that you, as a team, would be happy to move it into a committed objective. You've used a potential issue to turn a problem into an opportunity. Your BO, likely a senior leader with significant control over people and budgets, now becomes someone on your team, helping to get your dependencies and blockers removed for you. If they can help you in this way, you can better help them in return for getting more value delivered sooner. As a result, the ART becomes ever more cross-functional, collaborative, and ultimately, high-performing.

Having completed their planning, the teams collectively share their plans in the readout.

Facilitating final plan readouts

Once teams have finalized their plans, recorded their objectives, and had the assignment of BV by their BO, it's time to bring back those SAFe® core values of transparency and alignment by each team to share their plans with everyone else on the ART.

As an RTE, you're going to have to facilitate this carefully. Not because it is likely to be contentious and cause arguments—hopefully, by now, we've had most of the discussions that we need to have, and most of the disagreements and lack of alignments have been resolved, or at least parked for now into a potential future PI. No, the reason it needs to be facilitated carefully is the opposite of these things. By this stage in the agenda, everyone may be so aligned and *talked out* that this session feels like it drags on forever and kills the energy in an already tired room.

The temptation could be to rush through this agenda item as quickly as possible so everyone can finish and go home early, but this would be a significant mistake. One of the biggest risks to any delivery approach is an assumption or issue that has been overlooked and isn't noticed until its impact has occurred, by which time it is too late. No matter how much discussion has happened over the last two days and in the run-up to the event, there could always be an issue that has been overlooked or people have felt unable to discuss. Therefore, as an RTE, you need to facilitate an in-depth session to ensure no stone has been left unturned, but it is also quick, high-energy, and engaging, without people disappearing down rabbit holes.

Sounds like a challenging square to circle, doesn't it? It can be tricky, but here's how we've managed it over the years:

1. Prep each team for what and how they will present their plan to the rest of the ART. Check that the person presenting is likely to be a good presenter, capable of balancing brevity with both clarity and detail. In essence, someone who isn't going to spend hours waffling technical jargon at people.

2. Create a checklist of items for each team to cover in their presentation, give one to each team, and put one up next to the area where people will be presenting their plans. This way, the audience can hold the presenter accountable for sticking to these points and going off on tangents. Your checklist will be specific to your ART, but for reference, we tend to include the high-level plan (feature level), the team's main dependencies, their objectives, and their risks. Consider what information would be helpful to other teams on the ART, and ensure it is included, but don't ask for more information.

3. Give time for questions, but encourage people to hold *meet-after* sessions for a more in-depth examination of an issue. Remember, PI Planning is just one element of a whole PI. People should continue talking continuously throughout the PI, so not all conversations need to happen in PI Planning. As RTE, keep a list of these *meet-after* topics, along with who is likely to need to attend them, and perhaps offer to set these sessions up for people to help ensure that they happen and don't get lost among the immediate pressure of delivery.

4. As with any facilitation of a timeboxed session, having a large clock or timer in front of the presenter can be hugely helpful. It helps keep them on track and ideally sounds an alarm when their time is up. You may not want to cut them off at this point, but it helps reinforce the fact that there isn't all the time in the world for this session.

As we say, throughout this facilitation, continue to listen to what people say and observe how they react. As the RTE, are you as confident as possible that every hidden assumption, misalignment, and potential risk has been addressed over the two-day event? Don't hesitate to explore this matter with questions during the session if you believe they would assist. Even a simple, "Sorry, I didn't quite understand that; could you clarify?" can reveal a whole world of new information that may otherwise have remained hidden.

Now, let's look at the final aspect of this process involving one of our key stakeholders.

BO acceptance of plans

The final element of this session is to ask the BOs whether they accept the team's plans. This element is sometimes overlooked, but it is hugely important. Very often, the BOs are the people who ultimately fund the ART and the work it produces. If they're not happy with the plans the teams have created, why should they be paying for that plan to happen? At this point, it does boil down to that simple fact. The BOs need to be happy with what they'll get.

In practice, the BOs are happy with the proposed plans for a straightforward reason. They have also spent the last two days in PI Planning, talking to the teams, helping to answer their questions, and asking them questions in return. They've already seen these plans in draft at the end of Day 1 and had a chance to provide feedback at the start of Day 2. They've spent time with the teams discussing and reviewing their objectives and agreeing on BV scores for them. If the BOs turn around and say they're unhappy with the plan, how have things gone so badly wrong?

When BOs have been fully engaged for the last two days, accepting the plan is a formality, which may be why it is overlooked on the agenda. However, it's good to record it formally, particularly in organizations that might need audit trails of decision-making for regulatory compliance. Also, publicly accepting the plans shows commitment and confidence in the teams.

In contrast, the only times we've seen the team plans not to be accepted were instances where BOs appeared at the start of Day 1 to give their briefing, then disappeared off into other meetings for two days, only to reappear again at the end of Day 2 with no idea what the team plans were, or any sense of their alignment to what the BO had hoped to get. As in the portfolio layer of SAFe®, continuous BO engagement is an integral part of successful PI Planning, and it is the RTE's job to ensure that it is happening.

Finally, remember that the BO only needs to accept the plan. This may be different from them being exceedingly pleased with the plan. For example, an ART that served multiple markets worldwide had a BO representing each of those markets at the event. To be fair, all of them remained engaged over the past two days. As Day 2 came to a close, just after the final plan review session, while chatting with a BO, they were asked whether they were happy or not. Their response was intriguing:

> *In one sense, I'm not happy at all, because I'm not going to get all of the things I came here hoping to get. In another sense, I'm really happy, because having spent two days working with the teams for the first time, I finally understand why I'm not going to get certain things, and I have finally have confidence that I'm actually going to get what I'm being told I will get.*

Essentially, the BO discovered different types of happiness arising from PI Planning. One could be getting every feature planned during the event that you went into the event hoping to achieve. Still, another could be having confidence in the predictability of delivery, around which the BO can build their plans.

Now we've accepted the plan, but we're not quite done. We need to make sure that we have captured anything that might trip us up before we can give our **confidence vote**.

Risk management and ROAMing

With the plans now accepted by the BOs, there are just a few things left to do before everyone can go and have a well-earned rest. Next up is to ROAM the risks. You take each risk identified during the PI Planning event and try to place it in one of those four categories:

- **Resolved**: Although the risk may have been identified earlier in the event, it has been discussed and resolved since then, so we no longer need to worry about it.

- **Owned**: The risk has yet to be resolved, so we put someone's name against it so they can own it and keep the ART updated as the PI progresses. Ensure the owner is in the room, as assigning ownership to someone not present typically results in no real ownership or respective action.

- **Accepted**: This is when a risk cannot be resolved or even owned—for example, the COVID-19 pandemic. It may have caused people to go off sick during the PI, causing changes to capacity that may put the objectives at risk. Could the ART resolve the risk of this happening by itself? No. Could someone on the ART have owned COVID as a risk on behalf of the ART? No. COVID was just one of those risks we had to accept, be aware of, and see what happened.

- **Mitigated**: If the risk does materialize, do we have a plan B for what will happen then? What actions could be taken to mitigate the risk even before it occurs?

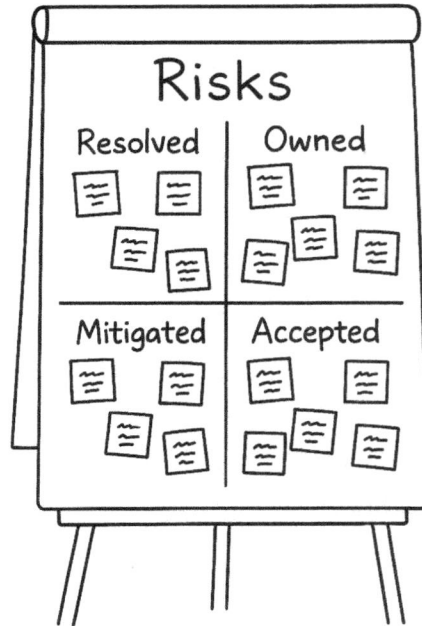

Figure 8.2: An example ROAM board

That's the theory, but what do you, as an RTE, need to look out for in practice? Let's take a look.

Managing energy and engagement during ROAMing

In practice, the first thing to consider is that this can quickly turn into a tedious part of the agenda that may disengage the room. The impact of the risk of the room becoming disengaged at this stage can be highly significant. You're nearing the end of the PI Planning event, so you're in the time when people's final impressions of the event will be formed. If the event concludes with an interminable discussion of uninteresting risks in excessive detail, that impression will linger in people's minds.

Another risk of this ROAMing session losing attendees' energy is that they can start to leave the event altogether. They're tired, and they've worked hard for two days. They have a mountain of work and unread emails building up that they want to get on with, and above all else, they feel like their work at the event is done. If they don't see risks as their problem, why would they want to stay around to listen to them being read out and categorized? Very likely, they won't. The real issue here is that you still have one of the most critical parts of the PI Planning agenda that has yet to happen: the confidence vote. If people start to sneak out of the room during the ROAMing session, you may not get them back for the confidence vote, which is a missed opportunity.

As a result, you can try a few things to mitigate the risk of risk mitigation:

- Encourage teams to share only those risks that are outside their control or that cause an impact outside their area. If a risk exists purely within a team, the team needs to be aware of it and track it, but it likely doesn't need to be shared with the broader ART in a ROAMing session.

- Frame this as a technical activity over a project management one; the latter can switch people off. One way of doing this is to take a leaf from **Six Sigma**, and have the teams think and engage in it from a **Design Failure Mode and Effects Analysis (DFMEA)** point of view, in which they are looking for options where things could go wrong ahead of time, to make their efforts and the product more successful.

- You could move to a more flow-based risk management process. Rather than letting risks build up over two days into a huge batch to process at the end of the event, why not encourage people to categorize risks as they go? If risks get resolved during the event, mark them as resolved as soon as they become so. You will likely still need a ROAMing session at the end of the event, even if you capture your risks as you go, but it can become more about a topline presentation of key risks and things everyone on the ART should be aware of, perhaps calling out some of the risk owners as people to contact about that particular issue if it emerges. There is an added benefit that you may not need everyone to listen to every risk being read out, then shout out its suggested categorization like some surreal corporate game show.

One final item for an RTE to be aware of when it comes to ROAMing is understanding the organization's existing risk management approach, assuming it has one, and ensuring that ROAMing doesn't conflict with it or even unnecessarily duplicate it.

An example from the field

In one organization we worked in, ROAMing didn't work as expected, as there was a straightforward process for categorizing risks, which dictated which job grade in the organization was expected to deal with that type of risk. In another organization, they were still utterly wedded to the **RAID** approach to risk management (short for **risks, assumptions, issues, dependencies**). They were happy to let the *dependencies* piece go, as they could see that tracking them on an ART board was a better solution. Still, they weren't ready to let go of recording and discussing *assumptions* and *issues*, so those had to be added into ROAMing, creating a bespoke *ROAAIMing* (pronounced *roh-ah-ay-ming*) process!

Risk management is one of those areas where a well-meaning RTE can run into the protective spikes and armor of an official organizational regulatory process, so tread lightly around the topic. Focus on doing whatever delivers the most value for the organization with the least amount of effort.

Many organizations we work with can have weak and immature risk management processes. If this is your context, even a basic team-of-team risk identification and ROAM will make the ART stand out. If there are program managers who care about risks, they will quickly become your best friend. Leverage this positivity when you need to ask for help removing an impediment.

When people record their risks, our top tip is to make sure they describe the *impact*, as this helps with classifying and reacting to it. One client got so frustrated telling people to do this, one of their RTEs made up a rubber stamp that created a sticky-note template of **Author**, **Description**, and **Impact**.

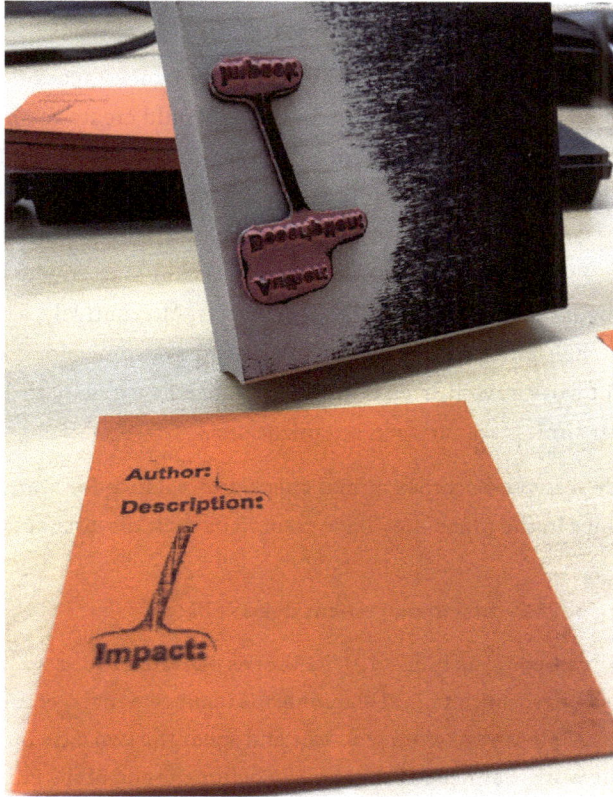

Figure 8.3: A sticky-note stamp that created a template for how risks were to be recorded.

Now, finally, we need to make sure that everyone gets a chance to raise any final concerns, and we do that with the confidence vote.

The confidence vote

We've already called the confidence vote in PI Planning one of the most critical elements of the whole event, and for good reason. At the heart of PI Planning is the belief that the people who do the work should plan the work. As a result, the planning isn't complete until the people who will do the work have agreed that they are happy with the plan. This happiness is expressed via the **confidence vote** agenda item.

Before examining how the vote happens, let's discuss why it happens.

Why does the confidence vote matter?

In more traditional organizations, there may have been many, many years of work being planned on other people's behalf. A project or program manager would create the plan and then assign tasks to different people and teams for them to deliver. In this situation, PI Planning and devolving decision-making down to the teams doing the work is a whole new world—one that may not have initially landed very well. As much as teams may sit there for two days saying that they are planning, they may well be sitting there with a Scrum Master who is a Project Manager with a new job title, being told what their plan for the PI is. Alternatively, a team may have been empowered to create their plans for the PI, but a BO may have come along and insisted they do various other pieces of work as well, even if they don't have the capacity to do so. We're sure you can also think of other similar scenarios in organizations.

Therefore, the confidence vote becomes a final check and balance for teams. It allows them to express their confidence in the plans they have created or their dissatisfaction with them.

What happens when management doesn't listen?

Once, after moving on from an ART one of us had launched, it was entering its fourth PI. For some reason, in this PI Planning, the management layer surrounding the ART had decided to revert to old practices and spent the two days informing the teams of all the work they needed to complete before the end of the PI. The teams, in turn, spent two days telling the management that they couldn't complete that much work in the PI. However, the management wouldn't listen and insisted that the work must be completed. Ultimately, it reached the end of Day 2, and a confidence vote was called. The teams all voted with such low confidence that the votes failed.

The RTE then intervened to resolve the issue, which led to the entire ART returning for a third day and holding a four-and-a-half-hour retrospective on how PI Planning had gone so wrong. It wasn't easy, but by the end, management understood much better why the teams had been saying no to more work than they felt they could deliver, and the teams understood the colossal pressures their management placed on them to get more done. What could have turned into a disaster became a positive and cathartic experience for all concerned. After the mega-retrospective and some adjustments to the plan, a new confidence vote was held and passed, and the teams, working collaboratively with their management, experienced their most successful PI date.

Running the confidence vote

How, then, do we hold a confidence vote? The mechanics of it are pretty simple. Each team on the ART is asked to vote on its confidence in the plan of just its team. Each team member holds up the number of fingers of confidence they have in the plan. One finger is very low confidence, and five fingers are very high. You add up the number of fingers, divide it by the number of people, and the plan is accepted if the average is three or more. Once each team has passed its confidence vote, you collectively rerun the same process across the entire ART. If the average of the fingers is three or more, the ART confidence vote passes, and the PI Planning event ends. If it is less than three, the confidence vote fails, and some rework has to be done before a passing confidence vote can be held.

Let's consider a couple of scenarios you might come across.

The teams have high confidence

The first is that, despite getting a passing confidence vote overall, some people may still vote with a very low confidence level. Perhaps they're holding up just two fingers or even just one. Maybe they've taken matters into their own hands and held up no fingers, just a closed fist of dissent. These people may be lone voices and, therefore, not enough to cause the confidence vote overall to fail, but at the same time, their concerns should never be ignored. Perhaps they've only just noticed a massive issue that wasn't apparent over the two-day event. They may have spent the last two days trying to get someone to listen to their concerns, but they've continuously been ignored. Whatever the reason, this confidence vote is one of those *speak now or forever hold your peace* moments. If someone looks like they have a concern, as an RTE, make sure that the concern is given space to be heard before the event is concluded.

What do you do when you start to see some patterns emerging?

Knowing that the RTE will speak with anyone offering a low vote and that this person gets airtime in front of the entire ART can lead the occasional person to game the process. Over time, you might notice a pattern of someone consistently voting low, sharing an opinion with the whole train, then conceding and changing their vote to three or more after little or no changes to the plan.

Your job, outside of the PI Planning event, is to talk with this person to discover the reason behind this. Could it be they like their 15 minutes of fame, or generally find issues they worry about? How you address this, if at all, depends on what you find. Glenn has seen a dip in the ART's motivation, with moans and groans around the room, when the same person, time and time again, shared a view, typically of items that held little to no value.

Doing this can have different challenges in different contexts. When running face-to-face PI Planning, it is easy to see who the people are holding up low scores and invite them to speak. However, peer- and status-based pressures may make them feel like they can't speak up, causing them to hold up more fingers of confidence than they truly feel. When you're running the confidence vote remotely over a video conferencing system, people can be more anonymous in how they vote, so they are more likely to vote accurately, but at the same time, you, as an RTE, cannot then see who the people voting with low confidence scores are. You can only see that a certain number of low scores have come in. In this situation, it is important to announce that you will give a few moments of silence for anyone with a low score to speak up about their low score and what they think others should know. If they do not speak up even after being given the space to do so, that issue ultimately has to rest on them.

There is low confidence

What if the confidence vote fails, though? In practice, this is quite rare. The earlier example of management forcing the teams to commit to deliver more work than they could manage is relatively unusual. However, we have all been in situations where confidence votes have failed, and often, their failure is relatively simple to fix. In one instance, when the vote failed, the Product Manager stood up and asked the teams why they thought it had failed. The teams all pointed to the same objective and stated that they had failed the vote because that objective was listed in the *committed* category when they didn't feel confident they could commit to it. The Product Manager immediately agreed, suggested moving the objective to *uncommitted*, and called another confidence vote, which immediately passed.

Hopefully, your PI Planning event has run like clockwork. Everyone is aligned, and the confidence vote sails through like a Mirror dinghy on a summer's day. If it does, what then?

Event teardown and next steps

The first thing you may find after a passing confidence vote is everyone running for the door. It's been a long two days, and they have work to do. As far as they're concerned, their passing confidence vote marks the end of PI Planning. Do try to prevent people from running just yet, as there is still a lot more work to do.

Reflecting on PI Planning to make sure we keep improving

From a formal framework perspective, SAFe® states that after the confidence vote, you should call a retrospective across the entire ART to look back at the PI Planning event itself and see what improvements could be identified for the next time. In reality, we very rarely see ARTs do this. After two intensive days of PI Planning, people will not thank you for asking them to stay back for another hour to stick sticky notes on pictures of sailboats. To retrospect only at the end of the event also creates additional problems. If something has been identified as a problem at the start of Day 1, why wait until the end of Day 2 to address it? Why not put a continuous retrospective board up on a wall, or on the doors leaving the planning room, and invite people to add problems to it as the event goes along, addressing them in real time?

We know that there is a risk of recency bias in any retrospective process. That is, you remember more easily the thing that annoyed you an hour ago, but remember less well the thing that annoyed you at the start of Day 1. As a result, a retrospective run only at the end of the PI Planning event will likely only capture recent issues and capture them too late to be resolved. A retrospective run continuously throughout the event will likely capture more issues in more detail and see them addressed more rapidly as well.

That's not to say you shouldn't end the event with a final call out for people to add items to the continuous retrospective board, but doing this is likely to see you collect more feedback than making people stay back for a full-scale retrospective.

As a general rule, we see most feedback about hygiene factors, such as the Wi-Fi speed, room temperature, and the amount of type of food. Some may perceive this as people complaining, but if you can create a positive environment, people can then focus on the real problems at hand, the planning.

Moving the plans to a place where they are useful for the teams

You need to consider how the information in PI Planning is to be taken from the event and stored in its final location. In the odd, unusual situations we've experienced, teams on ARTs have sat together in large open-plan offices with movable glass walls. As a result, the entire PI Planning event is held in the team's everyday workspace, so nothing needs to be moved at the end of the event.

In practice, the information captured in PI Planning must be relocated back to the team area and put in the appropriate tooling.

With regard to physically moving things, consider building ART boards on large sheets of paper, which are removed from the wall, carefully rolled up, and then transported to and rehung in their final location next to the teams on the ART. In other situations, people spend some time on the day after PI Planning sitting and transcribing their plans and objectives into their organization's digital tool of choice. In one memorable situation, in a new ART with low psychological safety, all it took the RTE to do was announce that the teams would be tracked against their delivery of objectives over the following PI for each team member in turn to form a queue to take photographs of the ART board so that they had a record of how the plan would be likely to progress. With over 100 people on the ART, this queue of photographers took a significant amount of time to finish.

The final wrap-up

Other than these things, your wrap-up communications are the final element to consider for PI Planning as an RTE. It's good not just to let the event end and then be forgotten as the day-to-day work takes over again. Make sure it ends with a clear final closure point. Once things such as the ART board, dependencies, and risks have been recorded in their final location, share them with every ART member and the wider ART stakeholders to point people to where these assets are being stored and tracked. Make explicit the dates for the key meetings coming up within the cadence of the PI, ideally with information on how to attend them and get involved. Make sure to also thank those who have taken part and helped to make the event successful. No RTE is an island, and we should always acknowledge our gratitude to those who help us on our way.

Summary

Day 2 of PI Planning is where draft ideas evolve into clear, committed objectives. As the RTE, your job is to guide the ART through a day of focused collaboration, refining plans, addressing risks, and aligning everyone around a shared purpose. We began with the importance of starting the day intentionally—observing the room, acting on feedback, and setting the tone for thoughtful, respectful dialogue.

We explored how to facilitate planning adjustments following leadership feedback, while protecting team ownership and encouraging conversation over command and control. Final team breakouts are where plans are refined, dependencies tackled, and objectives crafted in business-friendly language—not just to communicate better, but to build shared understanding and trust.

Final plan readouts, risk ROAMing, and the confidence vote each serve to validate the work done and surface anything that still needs attention. These moments matter – not just as formalities, but to check understanding, alignment, and collective accountability. The confidence vote, in particular, is a vital checkpoint, confirming the team's belief in their plan and their ability to deliver.

Done well, Day 2 doesn't just end with a plan on the wall—it ends with an ART that's truly aligned, committed, and ready.

As the RTE, your facilitation here sets the tone for the entire PI. In the next chapter, we step into delivery—where your role shifts from orchestrating plans to supporting progress. We'll explore your role in executing the PI in a lot more detail.

9

Executing the PI

PI Planning is done, commitments have been made, what comes next? This is where the real work begins: executing the PI. This chapter is all about how we turn the vision and objectives shaped during PI Planning into real, measurable outcomes.

As RTE, your role is to guide the ART through change, maintain flow, and ensure that you keep delivering. This chapter gives you a practical and people-focused guide to doing just that.

We'll show how to turn PI Planning outcomes into strong execution, with examples of effective practices in the weeks that follow, from managing iteration events and syncs to keeping your stakeholders in the loop. We'll share stories, tips, and tools to help you facilitate well, create alignment, and make sure teams stay connected to the value they're trying to deliver.

You'll learn how to communicate clearly, coach effectively, and make space for feedback and course correction—because plans will change.

This chapter will have the following main topics:

- Moving from PI Planning to execution
- PI cadence of events
- The ART Syncs
- Showing progress and value in System Demos
- Inspect and Adapt workshop

Let's get into it.

Moving from PI Planning to execution

Having explored the ins and outs of PI Planning, we now need to delve into what makes the PI a success. The energy and enthusiasm generated during PI Planning often set the tone for the execution phase. However, without deliberate actions to maintain momentum, the ART risks losing focus. As the RTE, you must ensure that the outcomes from PI Planning (objectives, commitments, and dependencies) are well understood.

We have put a lot of effort into getting a plan that we can commit to, but our work is far from done. As Helmuth von Moltke said, *"No plan survives the first contact with the enemy."* We have made the best decisions that we can with the information that we had in the lead-up to PI Planning, as well as the event itself. The main reason **Agile processes** exist is to help us react to the inevitable changes we encounter during the PI.

Jim Highsmith, one of the signatories of the **Agile Manifesto**, said it brilliantly in his book *Agile Project Management*:

> *A traditional project manager focuses on following the plan with minimal changes, whereas an Agile Leader focuses on adapting successfully to inevitable changes.*

Let's explore that statement in a bit more detail. Our role as an **Agile Leader** is very different from where many of us came from. If you fall into the camp of people who have learned your craft through project management, then it is worth grounding yourself in what we're trying to achieve by thinking about things differently. In the old days, as Jim Highsmith said, we would try to manage our projects with minimal changes. That is what success looks like. Deliver the requirements on time, cost, and quality.

As an Agile Leader, our goals are different. We know and accept that there are going to be changes, and we can't possibly know everything at the start. There is a lot that we can and should do to mitigate changes. We'll come to that toward the end of this chapter, but as we navigate the PI, we must make sure that we keep our eyes on the ultimate goal, which is to deliver value to the customer.

The tools and techniques that we will unpack in this chapter are there to share understanding with teams and stakeholders to make sure that we can deliver the most value. Of course, one of our most useful metrics is predictability: how good are we at seeing these changes coming, and are we getting better at learning from over-committing to work, or under-committing for that matter?

Let's start with what happens immediately after PI Planning.

Post-PI Planning

When you come down from the high of PI Planning, you will be exhausted, though unfortunately, your work is far from over. We often find that you will get a bit of respite as the teams start to focus on delivering the first iteration. You may find during this time that you have a lot of clarifying questions from teams and stakeholders, and it is surprising how little some people remember from the day before.

Your first task will be to write up the plans in a format that is easy to share and monitor throughout the PI. If your PI Planning was in person, then you will likely have to take the objectives from each of the teams and put them somewhere central. There are lots of ways that you can achieve the goal of sharing information, using tooling or simpler methods such as PowerPoint. Like many things, there are pros and cons to each, so now we will explore some of the trade-offs and what we find works best.

PowerPoint or no PowerPoint? That is the question

Most companies use PowerPoint to share information. It is easy because stakeholders are used to consuming information in that way, and most of us have enough skill to produce something that doesn't look too awful, although we have seen some shockers in our time.

There is, however, another way—a better way to share information so that it is more useful than a plan on a page. That isn't to say that every plan on a page is bad; they just don't normally show the information that people think they do, and are normally out of date the moment you send them.

We believe that it is better to keep your plans somewhere where they are useful for the teams and linked to whatever tool the teams are using to plan their work. For example, if you're using Jira (and at the time of writing this book, most people still do), then it is far more useful to keep most of the objectives and write-up in Confluence. That way, you can link to live issues and dashboards in Jira, and the information can be shared in real time. You also have the added benefit of built-in version control and permissions for spaces that will allow you to control the flow of sensitive information.

Jira and Confluence aren't the only options; there are plenty of tools that you can use that are designed to manage the flow of work and have integrations with digital whiteboards, such as Mural and Miro, which we talked about previously.

Regardless of how and where you share the information, the most important things that you will need to capture and be able to share easily are the following:

- **Team PI Objectives with business value**: Some stakeholders will benefit from seeing the details for each team, especially the high-value objectives. You should be able to get the **Product Owners (POs)** and **Scrum Masters (SMs)/Team Coaches** to help you, so you don't need to do the write-up for each team. However, it is sometimes helpful to do it yourself so that you really understand what the teams are doing.

- **ART PI Objectives**: We always summarize the team's objectives into a common goal for what the ART will deliver in the PI. There may be a lot of overlap with teams, and often the practice of distilling what we will accomplish is invaluable. We normally do this with **Product Management** and the **System Architect(s)** so that we're all on the same page. Sometimes, it is as simple as taking all the objectives that have high scores in **business value**. That way, if you're talking to people who aren't close to the ART's work, you can clearly communicate the most important points in a few key messages, rather than sharing 70+ team objectives.

Reviewing and communicating PI Objectives

Once you've summarized your PI Objectives, you will want to share them with relevant stakeholders. Hopefully, they will have been at PI Planning, and we're not sharing anything new. Ultimately, this is the power of well-written PI Objectives; people who aren't close to the ART should still have enough of an idea about what the ART will deliver.

Tim's anecdote

A few years ago, I was on holiday with friends in the British Virgin Islands. On our way home, we had a connecting flight from Beef Island to take us back to London. It was one of those small island airports where you could easily see the whole airfield. We checked in and went through security to the gate. It was quickly evident that none of the light aircraft on the airfield would be suitable to take the 200 passengers safely to London.

After a while, it became clear that our connecting flight wasn't coming. Concerned about making it home for work the next day, I decided to investigate. It was one of those small airports where you could go back through security, so off I went to find an airline representative at the check-in counter.

I asked him for an update, and he replied, "Yes, the flight is delayed until tomorrow. I made an announcement, but the microphone is broken." What the wonderful representative had done was talk to himself in his office. All too often, this is how we communicate. We believe that just because we've sent an email, people are going to read and understand it. Like the airline representative, our method of communication can be broken. Our goal with communication is to make sure that people truly understand the content and what is important.

Effective communication is essential for aligning stakeholders, ensuring clarity of objectives, and building trust within the business setting. Here are a few things to consider:

- **Know your audience and speak their language**: To communicate objectives successfully, it's important to begin by understanding your audience. Different stakeholders have different needs and levels of familiarity with what you're going to deliver. For senior executives, focusing on strategic impacts, high-level goals, and business value will resonate best. Meanwhile, operational stakeholders may require more detail.

  Well-written PI Objectives avoid excessive jargon, unless you're confident that your audience understands it. Be ready to explain terms as necessary.

- **Clarity is key**: Present your objectives in a clear, concise manner, structuring your message logically. Start with what the objective is and why it matters before explaining how it will be achieved. If the objective is complex, break it down into smaller, more manageable components to avoid overwhelming your audience.

- **Demonstrate the value behind the objective**: Connect your message to tangible benefits and illustrate how achieving these objectives addresses stakeholder challenges or supports strategic aims. Stakeholders are more likely to engage when they see how objectives contribute to broader business goals, whether that's increasing revenue, mitigating risks, or improving efficiency.

- **Use visual aids**: Diagrams, charts, and roadmaps help make abstract ideas more concrete, allowing stakeholders to visualize progress, dependencies, and outcomes. These tools can simplify your message and make it easier for your audience to grasp key points.

- **Communication should be a two-way process**: Invite questions, feedback, and open discussion to ensure that everyone fully understands the objectives and feels involved. This approach helps identify potential misunderstandings early and encourages buy-in, as people are more inclined to support plans they've had a hand in shaping.

- **Consistency is essential**: Ensure that your message is consistent across meetings, reports, and updates. Any changes to objectives should be communicated transparently and promptly to avoid confusion and maintain trust.

- **Follow-up is essential to reinforce alignment**: After initial discussions, summarize key points in an email or document that stakeholders can refer back to. Regular progress updates help keep objectives in focus and ensure that everyone remains on the same page.

There may well be other considerations in your context, so it is always worth looking for people who do it well.

> **Learn from the movers and shakers**
>
> Every organization has those people—the ones who always seem to get things done, cut through the noise, and bring people along with them. It's not magic, and it's rarely luck. It's usually down to skill, experience, and a fair bit of emotional intelligence.
>
> Seek them out. Spend time with them. Watch how they communicate, how they build relationships, and how they influence decisions. Ask questions. Be curious.
>
> Chances are, they've learned those behaviors—and if they can learn them, so can you. Once you've figured it out, don't keep it to yourself. Share it. Teach others. That's how we raise the game across the whole business.

Setting up communication channels

One of Safe®'s main strengths is the feedback loops that we have in place to make sure that we're on track to deliver our objectives and incrementally see the value that we're delivering throughout the PI.

It may be sad to say that we have favorite pictures in SAFe, but we do—don't judge! We've said it before, but SAFe is a fractal model, and we draw inspiration from the events and ceremonies we would normally have at a team level in Scrum and simply scale it up to work with our team of teams at the ART level. In the following diagram, the inner circle shows those team-level events; we have corresponding events for the ART and Solution Train that are accomplishing the same goal on a larger scale.

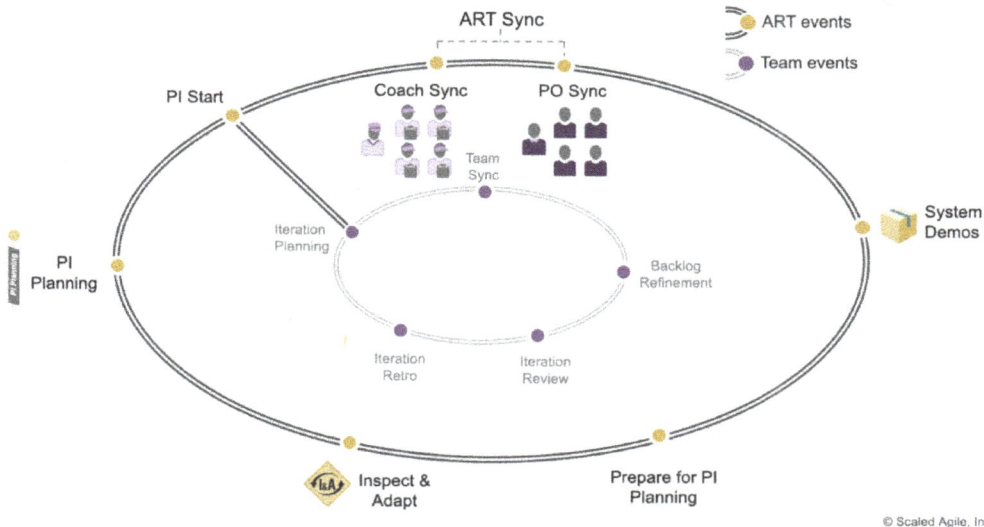

Figure 2. ART events drive development cadence

© Scaled Agile, Inc.

Figure 9.1: ART events drive development cadence (© Scaled Agile, Inc. Source: `https://framework.scaledagile.com/planning-interval/`)

As the RTE, you'll work closely with System Architects, Product Management, Scrum Masters, POs, Business Owners, and other **Subject Matter Experts (SMEs)** to measure your progress through the PI and have the right mechanisms in place to manage risks, issues, and dependencies. For the rest of this chapter, we'll have a look at each of these events to make sure you're set up for success.

PI cadence of events

Cadence plays a vital role in creating predictability and rhythm in Agile, particularly in the context of an ART. We'll start by looking at the events at a team level, even though you won't normally be directly involved, as we leave those events to the teams, and the Scrum Masters and Team Coaches will facilitate them. However, by establishing a series of regular, recurring events—such as **Iteration Planning, Team Syncs, System Demos**, and **Inspect and Adapt workshops**—the ART can reliably synchronize its efforts and maintain momentum.

These events provide consistent touchpoints for teams to align, review progress, and make necessary adjustments. This predictable rhythm helps reduce uncertainty and cognitive load, giving teams a clear structure within which they can confidently plan and deliver. Additionally, cadence ensures that feedback loops occur frequently, enabling continuous improvement and the ability to address challenges before they escalate.

So, now, let's look at what you need to know as an RTE to maximize your chances of success.

Designing great events

Regardless of what level you're looking at, the same principles apply, and running effective meetings and Agile ceremonies is crucial for maintaining team engagement, productivity, and alignment. To ensure that these sessions are valuable, always start by setting a clear objective. Whether it's an Iteration Planning session, Team Sync, or **Iteration Review**, everyone should understand the meeting's purpose and the expected outcomes. Stating this at the beginning helps keep discussions focused and aligned with the goal.

Here are some considerations:

- **An agenda is important**: Prepare a concise outline of the topics to cover and, when possible, share it in advance so participants can prepare. Timeboxing each segment helps maintain the meeting's pace and ensures that you respect everyone's time. For ceremonies such as Team Syncs, adhering to a strict time limit, such as 15 minutes, keeps the meeting efficient and avoids unnecessary diversions.

- **Invite only the people necessary for the discussion**: Having the right attendees promotes efficient decision-making and keeps engagement levels high. Additionally, always start and end on time to create a sense of discipline and trust. If conversations run over, it's often more productive to schedule a follow-up session than to extend the meeting and risk disengagement.

- **Effective facilitation is key**: A good facilitator guides the conversation while remaining neutral, ensuring that discussions stay on track. Encourage quieter team members to participate and gently refocus the group when discussions veer off-topic. Creating a space where everyone feels encouraged to contribute is vital for gathering diverse insights and promoting shared ownership of outcomes.

- **Minimize distractions**: Encourage participants to avoid multitasking and, in virtual meetings, request that cameras remain on when possible. In physical meetings, discourage side conversations and ensure that phones are silenced. These small steps help respect everyone's contributions and keep discussions productive.

- **Visual aids and collaboration tools**: In sprint planning or review sessions, visuals such as Kanban boards, roadmaps, and live demos help convey complex information more clearly. For remote teams, tools such as digital whiteboards (Miro and Mural) and task management platforms (Jira and Trello) facilitate collaboration and keep everyone aligned.

- **Meetings produce actionable outcomes**: Summarize key decisions and tasks, and assign clear responsibilities. For Agile ceremonies such as **Retrospectives** or planning sessions, ensure that these actions are documented, prioritized, and revisited in future meetings to maintain accountability and progress.

- **Gather feedback**: Ask the team what works well and what could be improved. This continuous improvement approach helps refine the process and ensures that meetings remain relevant and valuable.

- **Different ceremonies require different approaches**: Team Syncs should be brief, focusing on progress, plans, and blockers. Sprint planning sessions need more detail and structure to define goals and tasks clearly. Sprint reviews should showcase work completed and gather feedback from stakeholders. Retrospectives, on the other hand, should promote open dialogue, reflection, and opportunities for continuous improvement.

- **Establish psychological safety**: Create an environment where team members feel safe to share ideas, voice concerns, and express themselves honestly. This is especially crucial in **Retrospectives** or **Problem Solving workshops** where candid feedback and reflection drive meaningful improvements.

Your mission as an RTE is to promote a culture where all the preceding points are as natural as breathing to the people on your ART; we want great meetings to be standard culture. While you may not be directly involved, this applies equally to the activities of the teams.

Team-level events

As an RTE, your role is to make sure these events remain focused, efficient, and value-driven. You help maintain the discipline of regular ceremonies, keeping them productive and ensuring they serve their intended purpose. While they will primarily be facilitated by the Scrum Master/Team Coach, it is useful for you to understand their purpose and what good looks like so you can coach the Scrum Masters and teams as needed.

By fostering an environment of collaboration and transparency, you enable teams to inspect their progress objectively and adapt their plans accordingly. Your facilitation helps remove obstacles, promote open communication, and ensure that discussions stay aligned with the goals of the ART. Through a well-managed cadence, you contribute to a culture of continuous improvement, alignment, and sustained delivery, ensuring that the ART consistently delivers value to the business and stakeholders.

Here are the main ceremonies and events that your teams will need to keep themselves on track.

Iteration planning

Iteration Planning is a key event where the team members come together to determine how much work they can commit to delivering during an upcoming iteration. We often get asked whether there is still value in Iteration Planning, as we've already planned stories into iterations during PI Planning. The simple answer is *yes*. In PI Planning, we only plan at a high level, as there is unlikely time to create detailed, iteration-ready stories in the event, which isn't the purpose of it either! We also know from Jim Highsmith's quote earlier in the chapter that changes are inevitable. We will continue to break down work and refine the backlog throughout the PI, and we will plan in more detail as we get closer to the iterations. The main objective of Iteration Planning is to create a shared and realistic plan for what the team intends to deliver in the upcoming iteration—providing clarity, confidence, and alignment on how the work contributes to the team's PI Objectives. It ensures that the team understands the goals, scope, and approach for delivering value in support of the broader Program Increment. Here is a breakdown of the Iteration Planning process:

Phase	What to focus on
Inputs	Team and ART PI Objectives from PI Planning
	Team PI plan backlog (initial stories)
	New work: defects, refactors, and new stories
	Feedback and incomplete stories from the last iteration
Preparation	Scrum Master and PO meet at least 24 hours ahead to confirm priorities
	Team reviews estimated stories from backlog refinement; for the first iteration, make sure backlog items are refined and meet the definition of ready
During the meeting	Remind the team of the PI Objectives and any dependencies
	PO presents prioritized stories
	Team confirms capacity and estimates work
	Stories are planned, and iteration goals created
	Team commits to the iteration goals

Table 9.1: The Iteration Planning setup

The Scrum Master plays a crucial role in keeping the process on track and ensuring that the meeting serves its purpose.

The outcome of a successful Iteration Planning event includes planned stories for the upcoming iteration, committed iteration goals, and a clear understanding of dependencies with other teams.

As an RTE, you will be mostly focused on the high-level outputs: the team goals and any dependencies that come up. We'll look at that in more detail when we review the ART events.

Iteration Review

The Iteration Review is a regular event where the team inspects the increment of work completed during an iteration. It helps the team assess their progress, gather feedback, and make adjustments to their backlog for the next iteration, and promotes transparency, collaboration, and continuous improvement within the Agile Team.

Here is a description of the Iteration Review:

- **Purpose:** The Iteration Review allows the team to assess their progress, demonstrate their work to stakeholders, and gather feedback.

- **Attendees:** It typically involves the Agile Team, the PO, and other stakeholders who are interested in seeing the team's progress.

- **Demo of completed work:** During the Iteration Review, the team showcases the completed stories, spikes (timeboxed investigations), refactors (maintaining and improving existing functionality), and non-functional requirements (constraints that new functionality should maintain) that were worked on during the iteration. They demonstrate the working system to the PO and other stakeholders for their feedback.

- **Feedback and reflection:** Stakeholders provide feedback on the demonstrated work, which is the primary goal of the Iteration Review. The team reflects on the stories that were not completed and discusses the reasons why they were not completed.

- **Iteration goals and Team Backlog:** The team discusses the status of the iteration goals and updates the Team Backlog based on the feedback received during the review.

- **Timeboxing:** The Iteration Review is typically timeboxed to one to two hours, depending on the length of the iteration.

In most cases, you won't be facilitating the Iteration Review, but you will often be a valued attendee as a stakeholder. The challenge that we often find is that, as iterations start and finish at the same time, many of the teams in the ART events will overlap. With that in mind, you will need to think carefully about where you need to be. If you've got a Product Management team, then you can divide and conquer. You may also decide to focus on teams that have significant deliverables or dependencies.

Iteration Retrospectives

Iteration Retrospectives are where the Agile Team members come together to reflect on their work during the iteration and identify areas for improvement. This is one of the events that you should leave to the team, unless they invite you. It is essential that we create a culture of trust, and this is an important time for the team to develop stronger relationships.

Running a great Retrospective is essential for continuous improvement and a collaborative team environment. To create an effective Retrospective, it's important to start by setting the right tone. Create a safe and open atmosphere where team members feel comfortable sharing their thoughts. Emphasize that the Retrospective is a blame-free space focused on learning and improving together. Starting with a brief check-in or an icebreaker can help ease people in and encourage participation.

Following a structured format helps keep discussions focused and productive. Frameworks such as *Start, Stop, Continue* or *What Went Well, What Didn't Go Well*, and *What Could Be Improved?* provide clarity and direction. Timeboxing each section of the Retrospective, such as discussion, brainstorming, and action planning, keeps the session concise and on track. Ideally, Retrospectives should last between 45 and 90 minutes, depending on the length of the sprint or project.

A key outcome of any Retrospective should be actionable improvements. Ensure that the team identifies 1–3 concrete actions to take forward, and assign owners to each action to encourage accountability. Following up on these actions in subsequent Retrospectives helps maintain momentum and demonstrates that the team's feedback leads to real change.

Balanced participation is crucial for success. Encourage everyone to share their thoughts, using techniques such as round-robin discussions, sticky notes, or anonymous contributions to give quieter team members a voice. Additionally, celebrating successes is important for team morale. Acknowledging what went well reinforces positive behaviors and reminds the team of their achievements.

If serious issues or tensions arise, address them promptly. Acknowledge the concern and, if necessary, schedule a separate discussion to explore the issue in more detail, ensuring that the Retrospective remains focused and productive. After the session, share a summary of the discussion and agreed actions with the team. Following up between Retrospectives and reflecting on outcomes in future sessions helps close the feedback loop and reinforces continuous improvement.

It's quite common for teams to complain that they don't have time for all these meetings, especially the Retrospective. From our experience, when people say they don't have time for the Retrospective, that is when they need it more than ever. The Retrospective is a time that we can really focus on continuous improvement and find new, creative ways to get better as a team. Getting better doesn't just magically happen; you need to be deliberate about it.

Here is a description of Iteration Retrospectives:

- **Preparation**: Before the Retrospective, the PO should review outcome-oriented metrics (that measure the benefit achieved over the outputs or work delivered) and gather feedback from customers and stakeholders. The PO should also ensure that the team's commitments are aligned with their capacity to deliver and that the backlog meets the needs of their customers.

- **Conducting the Retrospective**: The Scrum Master leads the Retrospective, which is typically timeboxed to an hour or less. During the Retrospective, the team members participate and share their knowledge and experiences. The Scrum Master establishes transparency and trust among team members, creating an environment where they can candidly share feedback.

- **Topics for discussion**: The team discusses various aspects of the iteration, such as whether they met their iteration goals, their performance reflected in outcome-oriented metrics, and any feedback received from customers and stakeholders. The Retrospective is an opportunity to celebrate successes and recognize what went well.

- **Outputs**: A successful Iteration Retrospective yields both quantitative and qualitative insights about the team's performance. From the discussions, the team identifies one or two improvement areas to focus on for the next iteration. These improvement areas are added as improvement stories to the Team Backlog.

Building trust through Retrospectives

I [Tim] was once working in a team in an airline that was delivering a top-secret new product. Consequently, to help maintain secrecy, we were reporting directly to the CEO, so the stakes were particularly high.

I was acting as the Scrum Master, and in one of our Retrospectives, we were going through the normal agenda and discussing what was working well and what wasn't. It was at that moment that one of the team members got very emotional. He said that he couldn't handle the pressure, he hadn't been sleeping, and it was just all too much. We took the opportunity to stop what we were doing and really dig into what was going on. It was horrible that we had gotten to that point, but this was an opportunity to make it right.

We made an immediate plan for what we could change in the next iteration, and also a plan to address some of the root causes of his feelings. The moment of vulnerability had a ripple effect through the culture of the whole department. We spoke to very senior people about what Agile should be, and what it wasn't. We had the opportunity to tackle some cultural issues that plagued the entire business.

I often think back to that Retrospective. Like many of us, it is so easy to go through the motions and miss the point of what we're trying to achieve. That Retrospective helped me see the power of building trusting relationships within teams and how much of a difference we can make when we get things right, but also how much damage we can do if we get things wrong. If this is something you might be experiencing, we recommend reading Patrick Lencioni's *Five Dysfunctions of a Team*.

By creating a safe space, maintaining structure, and ensuring actionable outcomes, Retrospectives can become a powerful tool for driving learning, collaboration, and meaningful improvements within the team.

To keep things fresh and engaging, consider rotating facilitators. Allowing different team members to lead brings new perspectives and promotes shared ownership of the Retrospective process. Incorporating varied techniques and tools, such as the **Sailboat exercise, 4Ls (Liked, Learned, Lacked, and Longed For)**, or anonymous feedback tools, can also help maintain interest and encourage participation.

There are lots of websites and books that have brilliant and creative ways to run a Retrospective. It is always a good idea to mix things up so that you're keeping things fresh and thinking creatively about how to make things better. We particularly like the book *Agile Retrospectives: Making Good Teams Great*, by Esther Derby and Diana Larsen.

Now, let's look at what happens at the ART level.

The ART Syncs

At the ART level, several ceremonies are designed to facilitate collaboration, alignment, and continuous improvement across multiple teams. These ceremonies provide consistent opportunities for Agile Teams within the ART to synchronize their work, plan and review progress, and collectively address challenges or impediments. By maintaining regular touchpoints, these ceremonies help ensure that teams are aligned with the train's objectives and can respond effectively to changes and obstacles.

Facilitating ART Sync meetings, ensuring that they are productive, focused, and actionable, is central to your role as an RTE. Your job will be to keep discussions aligned with the overall goals of the ART and ensure that any identified risks or dependencies are addressed promptly. As an RTE, you will want to create open communication and collaboration to ensure that teams remain aligned and can collectively work toward delivering value. The RTE also makes sure that action items are clearly defined, owners are assigned, and follow-up happens, maintaining momentum and accountability.

ART-level ceremonies also provide a space to identify systemic challenges that might hinder progress. By regularly discussing dependencies and impediments, the ART can surface issues that require broader organizational support or process improvements. This helps create an environment of continuous improvement, where the ART as a whole learns, adapts, and becomes more effective over time.

These ceremonies are not about reporting status; they are about synchronizing efforts, aligning on shared goals, and proactively solving problems. When executed well, they build trust, encourage collaboration, and keep the entire train moving forward in unison. The predictability and regularity of ART-level ceremonies help maintain a steady cadence, which, in turn, supports the Agile delivery of value, ensuring that all teams are working cohesively to achieve the larger business objectives.

Before we delve into the meetings at the ART level, it is worth spending a few minutes reviewing the ART Kanban board, as it is central to all the syncs and our primary tool for measuring the flow of features delivered by the ART.

The ART Kanban board

The **ART Kanban board** is an essential visual tool for representing work items, specifically **Business Features** and **Enabler Features**, and tracking their progress within the ART. By offering a transparent view of the flow of work, it helps teams coordinate, manage, and monitor their tasks effectively, ensuring seamless collaboration and value delivery.

At its core, the ART Kanban board can be either physical or digital and serves to visualize the progression of features as they move through different stages of development and delivery. These stages are represented by columns that, at the simplest level, might be labeled as *To Do*, *In Progress*, *In Review*, and *Done*. To further organize work, swim lanes can be incorporated to differentiate between teams or specific workstreams within the ART. You will find many examples of the columns people use in various sources, but they should represent the significant states in your organization that help radiate status and manage flow.

Each work item on the board is represented by a card that carries important details, such as its title, description, assignee, and due date. This visual representation allows team members to quickly grasp the status and specifics of each item.

The ART Kanban board also incorporates **Work-in-Process (WIP)** limits. These limits control the amount of work the ART undertakes at any given time, preventing task overload and ensuring that the team remains focused on what they can realistically complete. By setting WIP limits for each stage, teams can maintain a balanced workflow and avoid inefficiencies.

Additionally, the board helps visualize bottlenecks and dependencies. By clearly indicating where work items are stalled or delayed, the teams in the ART can quickly identify issues and take corrective actions to resolve them. This visualization of potential obstacles enhances efficiency and allows dependencies to be managed proactively.

A key advantage of the ART Kanban board is its role in fostering continuous improvement. As a visual management tool, it highlights areas that need optimization, such as reducing cycle times, enhancing workflow efficiency, and improving delivery processes. This ongoing visibility encourages teams to refine their methods and strive for better performance.

Now, we're going to look at where we use the ART Kanban board.

ART-level events

To keep the ART running smoothly, we need regular touchpoints that help us stay aligned, address blockers, and maintain momentum.

The Coach Sync

Just like Team Syncs help individual teams stay on track, the ART needs its own space to coordinate and collaborate. That's where the **Coach Sync** comes in.

This is a critical event for operational alignment—bringing Scrum Masters and Team Coaches together with the RTE to share updates, surface risks, and ensure that teams are moving forward in sync. It's an opportunity, typically once or twice a week, to align around the current state of the PI, maximizing the state of flow. Together, they look to manage dependencies and collaborate on the removal of impediments. As the RTE, you will facilitate this session.

Other team members might also attend if there is value in doing so, but this is normally on a case-by-case basis. Imagine there was an impediment to the test environments. In this situation, the Scrum Master might bring along the tester who knows more about it than being a messenger who doesn't understand the situation as deeply as the tester.

Structure and timing

As this sync covers the entire ART, it takes longer than the team's 15-minute timebox, so it will often be scheduled for 30–60 minutes as needed. Like any other sync or stand-up, you should enable those who need to meet after to do so.

With respect to frequency and the timebox, it is important to experiment to discover how frequently it is helpful for your ART to meet. We've seen ARTs successfully meet once or twice a week, and others who do a quick daily, too. It is cheap and easy to try different approaches to find out what works for you. You may also discover that needs change over time as the maturity of the teams increases, starting to meet more frequently initially before reducing the time or number of sessions as they improve.

The Coach Sync promotes collaboration, coordination, and problem-solving among the Scrum Masters/Team Coaches within the ART alongside the RTE. It helps address dependencies, share progress, and ensure alignment across teams.

In a similar vein to Team Syncs at the team level, we're trying to answer a few key questions to make sure that we're on track to meet our commitments for the PI:

- What have *we* accomplished since the last meeting?
- What do *we* plan to accomplish between now and the next meeting?
- What blockers, risks, or issues do *we* need to address?

As we progress through the PI, we want to keep our focus on the value that we're delivering. With that in mind, it is easy to drift into these meetings and ceremonies, becoming an update on activities rather than what we've completed or the value that we've created.

As the RTE, you may find that you've got a few hats to wear to make sure the teams stay on track. You'll have to listen carefully to understand the nuances and make sure that you ask open questions to make sure that everyone is on the same page. Like all these events, we want to make sure that we, the ART leadership, teams, and stakeholders, have a common understanding of where we are and what needs to be done. Your goal as the RTE is to make sure that if any stakeholder were to ask any member of the team what our biggest accomplishment has been over the past couple of weeks, or what the biggest challenges are, they should give a very similar answer.

You may well be challenged by the teams that you haven't managed to complete something, as there isn't enough time between meetings. This is normally a sign that teams are not breaking down the work into small enough batches. There may also be a cultural issue with people not being confident in making their work transparent. Either way, it is worth taking the time to work with the Scrum Master/Team Coach to find out more and try to get to the root cause. Remember, we don't necessarily need to see things that are finished for every team in every Coach Sync, but if it becomes a habit, then dig a little deeper.

You should use the ART Kanban board and the ART Planning board to focus on what is most important. Although we say 30–60 minutes, in reality, if we're focused on the right level, which is the delivery of features, ART risks, and PI Objectives, you should have a rhythm that looks something like this:

"Team Penguin, you're due to deliver feature X this week. Are you on track? Any issues? Do you need help from anyone else?"

We want to keep all our meetings succinct to make the best use of everyone's time. So, if any blocks or impediments are identified during the Coach Sync, the people involved can stay for a *meet-after* session to problem-solve and find resolutions.

Making time for the meet-after session

We always say that the syncs should be 30 to 60 minutes with a meet-after session. We used to send out one meeting for an hour, and then let people go when we had covered the main agenda. We tend to find that if you set a meeting for 60 minutes, it will take that long, regardless of whether you actually need that time.

For a few years now, we have been experimenting with sending two separate invitations: one 30-minute sync, and one 30-minute meet-after session directly after. The idea is that we want people to hold the time for both, in case they are needed, but see the sync as a shorter session. The main benefit is that people see the meeting as a quick session, and they are less likely to turn up late. The downside is that people may get into the habit of scheduling another meeting over the meet-after invitation if they don't see it as essential. On balance, though, they are grown-ups, and it isn't too much of a challenge to find some time to remove blockers.

Communicating with stakeholders

As the RTE, you are responsible for communication and reporting any major impediments to key stakeholders and the release management team. The Coach Sync also provides an opportunity to highlight progress toward milestones and ensure alignment across teams. It is always worth reminding people of what we set out to achieve at the beginning of the PI and referring to what was in the original vision, the top features that you're delivering, and any changes:

- **Tailor your message to 'stakeholders' interests**: Focus on high-level goals, business value, and mitigating risks. Data-driven insights and concise visuals can effectively highlight the planning's strategic importance without overwhelming them with technical details. Transparency is key—clearly define their roles in the process, such as prioritizing objectives or aligning dependencies, and set realistic expectations for their involvement.

- **Leverage multiple communication channels**: This will keep stakeholders informed, from emails and slide decks to brief calls. Always provide context for decisions, emphasizing how choices impact team execution, budgets, and timelines. Avoid using overly technical jargon and focus on explaining the *why* behind decisions to build trust and understanding.

- **Create opportunities for stakeholder feedback before, during, and after the event**: Structured Q&A sessions or surveys can help capture their insights and ensure they feel heard and valued.

- **Simplicity and inclusiveness are crucial**: Use clear, accessible language and avoid acronyms or technical terms unless everyone is familiar with them. Reinforce shared goals and emphasize the collective success of the ART to create a sense of unity. Regular updates help keep teams informed and aligned. Facilitate two-way communication by encouraging questions and addressing concerns openly. Tools such as Slack or MS Teams can provide instant updates and allow for quick resolution of issues.

- **Take the time to celebrate progress**: Recognize achievements and contributions as they happen and, after the event, highlight successes during Retrospectives to maintain momentum and motivation.

By tailoring your communication to each audience and building an environment of transparency and collaboration, you can ensure a productive and engaging PI Planning experience.

Rotating facilitator

You are typically the primary facilitator of PI Planning and other ART events. However, to get greater engagement and participation, consider rotating the facilitator role among the Scrum Masters or Agile Coaches within the ART. This approach not only diversifies the voices leading discussions but also brings fresh perspectives and ideas to the table, enriching the overall planning process.

When Scrum Masters or Agile Coaches step into the facilitator role, they bring unique insights from their close work with individual teams. These perspectives can identify nuances or challenges that might otherwise be overlooked, helping to improve alignment and problem-solving during the event. Moreover, rotating the facilitation role empowers these leaders, building their confidence and enhancing their skills in guiding collaborative discussions.

To make this approach effective, set clear expectations for facilitators. Provide guidance on the structure of the meeting, the desired outcomes, and best practices for engaging participants. Offer support by staying available as a resource during the event, ensuring that the facilitator feels equipped to handle any challenges that arise.

This practice not only improves engagement during PI Planning but also creates a culture of shared responsibility and continuous learning within the ART. By giving others the opportunity to facilitate, you create a more dynamic and inclusive environment that drives better collaboration and innovation.

So, the Coach Sync covers the *how*; let's look at the *what*—otherwise known as the PO Sync.

PO Sync

Whereas the Coach Sync is primarily focused on operational progress and impediments, the **PO Sync** looks through the progress lens of needed scope and priority adjustment. It allows POs and **Product Managers** (**PMs**) to align and collaborate throughout the PI.

The PO Sync aims to ensure that the POs are working together effectively and that their backlogs are aligned with customer and stakeholder needs. It provides a platform for them to discuss the progress of the ART toward PI Objectives, address issues and opportunities with feature development, and make any necessary adjustments to scope or prioritization.

Again, like the Coach Sync, this event is typically held once or twice a week, for 30–60 minutes. But again, experiment with how often and for how long it's needed.

The PO Sync can be facilitated by a PM, the RTE, or both. The facilitator should provide the agenda to participants in advance and invite Business Owners and SMEs, such as System Architects and System Engineers, as needed. One model we've used when coaching a new ART is saying that we, as change agents or the RTE, will do this, before handing it over to the PM. This provides space for the PM to learn the ropes and concentrate on the content, before having to have their head in content and facilitation. But if the PM never takes over and the RTE keeps helping, that's fine too.

During the PO Sync, various activities take place, including the following:

- **Refining the Program Backlog**: The POs and Product Management work together to refine and prioritize the backlog items, ensuring that they are ready for implementation
- **System Demo preparation and planning**: The POs prepare for the upcoming System Demo by discussing the features and functionality that will be showcased
- **Leading indicators for minimum viable products** (**MVPs**): The POs review and evaluate the leading indicators for MVPs to assess the progress toward achieving the desired outcomes
- **Feature quality evaluation**: The POs assess the quality of the features developed, ensuring that they meet the required standards
- **Capacity allocation analysis with Business Owners**: The POs collaborate with Business Owners to analyze and allocate capacity based on the needs and priorities of the business.

We accept this is a broad list, and on your train together, you need to decide whether you make the sync a working meeting to address this or keep it oriented around a sync that signposts future working sessions to handle these items. A simple way to facilitate this is to break the meeting into two. The first block is the pure sync, and then move on to the agenda items linked to the preceding.

After the PO Sync, the RTE should help coach the POs on any action items they need to take back to their teams. This ensures that the necessary adjustments and improvements are implemented effectively.

The event also emphasizes collaboration among POs. It offers a space to share insights, discuss challenges, and leverage collective problem-solving. This collaborative approach helps create a unified vision across teams while encouraging innovative solutions to common roadblocks. Additionally, the sync serves as a valuable opportunity to share updates and refine priorities, keeping the ART's work on track and focused.

Feedback and continuous improvement are integral to the PO Sync. By establishing an environment of open communication, POs can share lessons learned and identify areas for improvement in both the event itself and the ART's overall processes. Whether it's adjusting the format of the sync to better suit the ART's needs or refining the way backlog priorities are communicated, this iterative approach helps the ART become more efficient and effective over time.

Ultimately, the PO Sync is more than just a meeting; it is a mechanism for ensuring that the ART stays aligned, adaptive, and focused on delivering value. By actively participating in this event, POs contribute not only to the success of their individual teams but also to the overarching success of the ART and the organization as a whole.

Combined ART Sync

You might notice there's a fair bit of overlap between the Coach Sync and the PO Sync. That's where the ART Sync comes in—it's an optional event that combines both into a single session to keep the ART aligned across the PI. Just remember, if you're running an ART Sync, it's instead of the other two, not on top of them!

With so many meetings happening online these days, it's a lot easier to bring people together. Back when we were always in person, trying to get all the Scrum Masters, POs, PMs, architects, and other stakeholders into one room often meant squeezing in like sardines.

Done well, the ART Sync is a great way to align everyone quickly. But a word of caution: the more people you've got, the more important it is to facilitate effectively. Keep the conversation focused and purposeful.

Since it covers both operational delivery (like the Coach Sync) and scope and backlog progress (like the PO Sync), you might need a bit more time—or to split it occasionally—depending on what your ART needs.

As always, experiment. Test different formats and timings to find what works best for your teams. What matters most is that we're staying aligned and moving forward together.

The session gathers a diverse group of participants, including POs, PMs, Scrum Masters, and SMEs such as architects and engineers. This broad audience promotes deeper transparency and collaborative decision-making.

For an effective meeting, make sure you focus on continuous improvement. Feedback from participants is key to refining the meeting's format and ensuring that it remains a dynamic and impactful touchpoint for the train.

Transforming transparency: the story of ART Syncs with Tim

When I stepped in to take over a struggling ART, the issues were glaring. Deliverables were consistently late, morale was low, and predictability hovered at a dismal 40%. It didn't take long to identify one of the primary culprits: a lack of transparency and communication. Teams weren't aligned, risks were hidden until it was too late, and no one felt empowered to share concerns openly.

We needed to rebuild trust, collaboration, and a culture of openness—and fast. To do that, we decided to double down on our ART Syncs, creating a structure that would encourage regular, meaningful communication while respecting the existing sensitivities within the ART.

A new approach: daily ART-level Syncs

We introduced a daily 10 a.m. sync, each with a specific focus, to create consistent touchpoints where issues could be raised, progress shared, and alignment strengthened:

- Monday: Coach Sync—a forum for Scrum Masters and team coaches to align on dependencies, share team-level updates, and surface blockers. It was a safe space where coaches could discuss team dynamics without fear of judgment.

- Tuesday: PO Sync—a time for POs and PMs to review priorities, refine backlogs, and prepare for the System Demo. This ensured everyone was on the same page regarding feature delivery and customer needs.

- Wednesday: ART Sync—the midweek ART Sync brought together the broader leadership group—Scrum Masters, POs, System Architects, and key stakeholders. It focused on progress updates and dependencies, creating an opportunity for cross-functional alignment.

- Thursday: Coach Sync—another Coach Sync gave Scrum Masters a chance to regroup and refine strategies for supporting their teams through the week's challenges.
- Friday: Risk-focused ART Sync—we ended the week with a dedicated ART Sync focused on risks and issues. By explicitly reserving time for this, we encouraged transparency around obstacles and ensured risks were identified early, with action items assigned promptly.

More meetings? Yes—but with purpose

At first glance, it seemed like an overwhelming schedule of meetings. But these syncs were critical to turning the tide. The structured forums provided teams with predictable opportunities to communicate and align, while the specificity of each meeting kept them purposeful.

We also recognized that trust and the transparency it brings would take time to build. In the early days, many participants were hesitant to share openly, fearing judgment or repercussions. To address this, we carefully facilitated the sessions, encouraging respectful dialogue and ensuring that no comment was dismissed. Over time, trust began to grow, and the culture started to shift.

The results: predictability and collaboration

Within a single PI, the impact was undeniable. Our predictability improved from 40% to over 90%. Teams became more confident in raising concerns, and dependencies were managed proactively instead of reactively. Risks were no longer surprises—they were identified, owned, and mitigated.

As the culture of openness solidified, we were able to simplify the syncs. The Friday risk-focused ART Sync became less critical as teams started surfacing risks earlier in the week. Coach Syncs shifted to a lighter cadence as Scrum Masters and team coaches built stronger relationships. What initially seemed like an excessive meeting schedule transformed into a finely tuned communication system that supported the ART's success.

> **The lesson: communication is the foundation**
>
> This experience taught me a vital lesson: transparency and communication are the backbone of any successful ART. While the initial investment in daily syncs seemed intensive, it was exactly what the ART needed to break down silos, rebuild trust, and deliver value consistently.
>
> By listening to the needs of the teams and adjusting as we grew, we created a culture of collaboration that didn't just improve performance—it transformed the ART into a high-functioning, cohesive unit.

In addition to the sync meetings, which aim to optimize delivery, we also need to look to the future by making sure the demand signals in the backlog are in good shape for upcoming PIs.

Backlog refinement

Backlog refinement is one of those quiet but essential practices that can make or break the flow of value across the ART. As the RTE, you're not there to own the backlog, but you *are* responsible for making sure that it's being actively and thoughtfully refined. This means creating the conditions for teams and stakeholders to look ahead—not just get caught up in today's problems. It's easy for everyone to get pulled into delivery mode and lose sight of what's coming next, but your role is to keep one eye on the horizon. Start preparing early. If we wait until the last minute to shape features or stories, we risk making poor trade-offs or slowing delivery because the work isn't ready.

You also play a big part in ensuring the *right voices* are in the room during refinement. Product Management may guide the direction, but they shouldn't be the only ones validating what gets built. Encourage your POs, architects, UX designers, SMEs, and even testers to get involved early. Ask coaching questions that help challenge assumptions:

- "What feedback have we heard from customers that supports this?"
- "What makes this valuable right now?"
- "What would success look like from the user's perspective?"
- "What happens if we don't build this?"

You might even want to revisit some of the tools from earlier in the book, such as empathy maps from *Chapter 3*. These can help teams think beyond the feature itself and back to the people it's meant to serve. What are those users seeing, hearing, saying, and doing? Are we solving a real problem, or are we just adding to the noise?

Use the guardrails to balance your backlog

A healthy backlog isn't just full—it's *balanced*. Make sure you're using the **Lean Budget Guardrails** and capacity allocation to guide how much effort goes into new features, enablers, tech debt, and exploration work. It's easy to let urgent delivery work dominate the backlog, but if we neglect innovation or technical health, we store up problems for the future.

Work with Product Management, System Architects, and Business Owners to regularly review how capacity is allocated. Ask questions such as, "Are we investing enough in keeping the architecture sustainable?" or "Have we set aside time for innovation and exploration this PI?" These conversations help keep your backlog aligned not just with what needs doing now but with what will keep us delivering in the long run.

All this preparation ties directly into the **System Demos**. If we're not refining the right work, we won't be able to demonstrate meaningful progress. And just as importantly, we need to make sure that what we show in demos is *working systems*—not slide decks and not status updates. Refinement lays the foundation; the demo proves we're building something that matters. Let's take a closer look at how we do that well.

Showing progress and value in System Demos

The **System Demo** takes place at the end of each iteration. It brings together stakeholders and ART members to review the integrated work delivered by all teams, providing a clear view of progress toward the PI Objectives. Unlike team-level iteration demos, which focus on individual outputs, the System Demo showcases a fully integrated increment, demonstrating how the various components created by different teams function together as a cohesive system.

Make the System Demo a two-way conversation

The System Demo isn't just a presentation—it's a *collaborative forum*. Treat it as a space for validation and real-time feedback. Invite stakeholders, including Business Owners and customers, and encourage them to actively engage. Their insights help confirm that the ART is delivering what matters most—and just as importantly, they can highlight where things need adjusting.

The goal isn't perfection—it's alignment. A great demo sparks conversation, builds trust, and helps the whole ART course-correct with confidence.

The System Demo creates alignment within the ART. By inspecting the increment in the context of committed objectives, teams and stakeholders can confirm whether the desired outcomes are being achieved. It's also a valuable opportunity for identifying risks or gaps and addressing dependencies early.

The event is led by the RTE, with support from the likes of the System Team, who can help prepare platforms. We like it when the Product Management and the teams collectively run the demo, as it relies on contributions from every Agile Team, and having ownership and being proud of their work is something we like to promote. It's not just about delivering features but about demonstrating real value to the business and validating the work against expectations.

Ultimately, the System Demo is about more than showing what has been built. It fosters trust, encourages collaboration across teams, and reinforces the alignment of daily activities to broader ART goals. It's a crucial step in ensuring that the solutions we deliver meet both technical and business needs. The event itself can become a forcing function in some ARTs, inasmuch that at least once per iteration, the work will be integrated and validated together.

What happens when and who should we invite?

We sometimes hear that Agile Team members do not understand why they need to come to the System Demo when they've been to their own Iteration Review. The simple answer is that the ART is a single system, made up of many teams working together. For it to be effective, the system needs to know the current situational awareness of the rest of the system.

Here are some of the typical attendees:

- PMs and POs
- Members of the System Team
- Business Owners, executive sponsors, customers, and customer proxies
- System Architect, IT operations, and other development participants
- ART Agile Team members

Without the knowledge of how things are being adjusted, the chances of creating a change that will cause issues will rise. In addition, the event is an opportunity to celebrate the success of delivery that has been achieved over the last period while being aligned with what's next.

Typically, the agenda looks like this:

1. Welcome participants and stakeholders.
2. Review the business context and the PI Objectives.

3. Describe and demonstrate each new feature in an end-to-end use case.

4. Identify current risks and impediments.

5. Open discussion for questions and feedback.

6. Wrap up by summarizing progress, feedback, and action items.

To get the most out of a System Demo, we need to be intentional about how we run it. A successful demo doesn't happen by accident—it's planned, facilitated, and delivered with purpose. It should feel like a shared moment of learning and alignment, not just a show-and-tell.

Guidelines for a successful demo

The planned outcome of the System Demo is to gather stakeholder and customer feedback on the integrated solution, ensuring alignment with business goals and facilitating continuous improvement. Follow these guidelines for a successful demo:

- **Timebox the demo to no more than one hour**: A concise, focused session ensures that the demo remains productive and respects the time of all participants, especially stakeholders who may have limited availability. By adhering to a strict one-hour timebox, we keep discussions purposeful and avoid drifting into unrelated topics. This structure also encourages teams to prioritize their contributions, showcasing the most valuable and impactful elements of the increment.

- **Share demo responsibilities among team leads and members**: The System Demo should reflect the collective effort of the ART, so it's important to involve a variety of team members in presenting their work. Sharing responsibilities among team leads and members promotes engagement, accountability, and a sense of ownership across the teams. It also ensures that diverse perspectives and expertise are represented, making the demo richer and more comprehensive. Furthermore, it provides an opportunity for individuals to develop communication skills and gain visibility within the ART.

- **Demo from the staging environment**: Demonstrating directly from the **staging environment** (a production-like environment to test functionality without risking that production gives users unvalidated work) ensures that the capabilities being showcased are as close to production-ready as possible. This approach not only increases credibility but also provides stakeholders with confidence that the increment is robust and ready for further validation. The staging environment mirrors the production setup, so it helps uncover potential integration or performance issues before the final release.

- **Focus on demonstrating working, tested capabilities rather than presentations:** The System Demo is not a PowerPoint session; it's about showing real, tangible progress. Working, tested capabilities provide stakeholders with a clear understanding of what has been achieved and how it contributes to the ART's objectives. Teams should prioritize showing live demonstrations of features or solutions in action, as these provide immediate value and clarity. This approach builds trust and ensures that the focus remains on delivering functional, high-quality increments.

- **Discuss the impact of the current solution on non-functional requirements (NFRs):** NFRs, such as performance, security, scalability, and compliance, are critical to the overall success of the solution. During the demo, it's important to highlight how the current increment addresses these NFRs. For example, teams might discuss how a new feature enhances system performance or how security measures have been integrated into the solution. This ensures that stakeholders understand the broader impact of the work and reinforces the importance of balancing functionality with system quality.

By following these guidelines, the System Demo becomes a dynamic and collaborative event that highlights progress, encourages feedback, and builds confidence in the ART's ability to deliver value.

As we reach the final event in the PI cycle, the Inspect and Adapt workshop gives us the space to close the feedback loop and reflect on how we've performed—not just what we delivered, but how we delivered it. This is where we need to inspect and adapt at scale for the ART, reviewing how we've performed in what we've delivered and how we've worked.

Inspect and Adapt workshop

This is where we need to inspect and adapt, step back, look across the whole ART, and ask the big questions: What's working well? What's holding us back? And what do we want to change going forward?

The **Inspect and Adapt (I&A)** workshop provides an opportunity for the ART to reflect, evaluate, and improve at the end of each PI. The I&A event ensures that the ART embraces a mindset of relentless improvement. By reflecting on the ART's performance and collaboratively identifying opportunities for growth, the workshop creates a culture of accountability, transparency, and learning.

The outcomes of this session often feed directly into the transformation backlog—the place where improvement actions live until they're prioritized and acted upon. This is your opportunity to drive meaningful, systemic change and set the ART up for an even stronger next PI.

The event is made up of three parts: the PI System Demo, quantitative metrics review, and the Problem Solving workshop.

PI System Demo

The workshop begins with a final demonstration of a summary of the ART's accomplishments during the PI. This is the culmination of all the integrated work from the teams, showing stakeholders how the solution has evolved to meet PI Objectives. The demo provides context for the discussion, linking the ART's outputs to business value and uncovering any gaps that might need attention.

But before addressing what didn't go to plan, take time to recognize what *did*. Teams have invested significant effort in solving complex problems, navigating dependencies, and delivering value. The System Demo at the I&A workshop provides the perfect opportunity to acknowledge these achievements. Highlighting successes creates an environment where teams feel valued and are consequently more receptive to discussing areas for improvement.

A balanced approach matters. The workshop will identify issues that need addressing, beginning with recognizing accomplishments and establishing the right context for constructive analysis. Teams that feel their work is appreciated are more likely to engage openly with the improvement process and commit to addressing challenges in the next Program Increment.

Make the PI System Demo matter

Treat the PI System Demo as more than a show-and-tell—it's your moment to *tell a story* about the difference you've made. Focus on showing the product or solution in a production-like environment so stakeholders can see it in action, not just in theory.

Talk through the journey: what was the problem, what did we build, and, most importantly, *how has life improved* for the customer or the business? Anchor your story in metrics where possible and consider framing the impact through the lens of **desirability** (do users want it?), **viability** (does it support the business?), **feasibility** (can we build and maintain it?), and **sustainability** (can we keep delivering over time?).

Always bring it back to **value**. This isn't a status update—it's a value demo. Show what changed, why it matters, and what's next. When done well, it builds trust, reinforces alignment, and energizes everyone for the road ahead.

Once we've seen (and hopefully been able to celebrate) the value that we've created, we can move to the data, where we can take the emotion out of the equation and look at the facts.

Quantitative metrics review

Metrics are important as they help us look at what we've accomplished by taking the emotion out of what we've achieved, or not, as the case may be. Agile is based on empiricism and the practice of making decisions based on what data we've observed. **Data-driven decision-making (DDDM)** is the practice of using factual, objective information to guide and inform choices. By relying on evidence rather than intuition or guesswork, organizations can make more reliable and effective decisions, leading to better outcomes.

The benefits of this approach are both far-reaching and transformative. Let's see how:

- By grounding decisions in data, teams can minimize personal biases and reduce the risk of errors that arise from assumptions or incomplete information. This ensures that decisions are based on clear, reliable evidence rather than subjective opinions.

- Another key benefit is better predictability. Analyzing historical data and trends allows organizations to make more informed forecasts about future outcomes. For example, understanding patterns in customer behavior or operational performance enables proactive planning and more accurate resource allocation.

- DDDM also enhances efficiency. By providing clear insights into what works and what doesn't, it helps streamline processes, reduce time spent deliberating, and prioritize resources on high-value initiatives. Additionally, because decisions are based on measurable outcomes, organizations can track progress against **key performance indicators (KPIs)** and learn from the results to drive continuous improvement.

- Transparency is another strength of this approach. When decisions are guided by data, the rationale behind them is clear and understandable, fostering trust and alignment across teams. This openness is particularly valuable in collaborative environments, where multiple stakeholders need to be on the same page.

- Data also strengthens problem-solving. By identifying root causes rather than addressing symptoms, teams can tackle challenges systematically and develop sustainable solutions. For example, trend analysis or techniques such as the *Five Whys*, supported by data, help uncover the underlying issues that may be hindering progress.

- Aligning decisions with organizational goals becomes more achievable when guided by data. Metrics such as return on investment, customer satisfaction, or operational efficiency can steer teams toward initiatives that directly support strategic objectives. Moreover, leveraging data effectively can provide a significant competitive advantage. Organizations that use data intelligently can respond faster to market changes, identify opportunities, and mitigate risks more effectively than their competitors.

- The ability to manage risk is another compelling reason to adopt a data-driven approach. Data provides a clearer picture of potential outcomes, enabling teams to weigh risks accurately and make more calculated decisions. This reduces the likelihood of costly mistakes and builds confidence in the choices being made.

- Perhaps most importantly, DDDM empowers teams. When individuals have access to accurate data, they can make informed decisions with greater confidence, which helps build a culture of accountability and innovation. This autonomy allows teams to act swiftly and decisively, knowing their actions are backed by evidence.

Measure what matters—avoid measuring everything

Metrics are powerful tools for driving performance and improvement, but not all metrics are created equal. Measuring everything can lead to analysis paralysis, wasted effort, and unintended consequences. Instead, focus on the metrics that truly align with your goals and drive meaningful outcomes.

The Ford Pinto recall story

A cautionary tale of misguided metrics comes from the 1970s Ford Pinto case. Ford engineers discovered a flaw in the Pinto's fuel tank that made it prone to fire in rear-end collisions through insufficient protection. However, the company's decision to delay recalling the cars was based on a cost-benefit analysis metric that compared the cost of repairs against the predicted financial cost of legal settlements for fatalities and injuries. This metric prioritized financial savings over customer safety, leading to public outrage, reputational damage, and eventual recalls. The Pinto story underscores the dangers of measuring the wrong things or prioritizing metrics that conflict with ethical and long-term goals. As the RTE, you will need to sometimes be the organization's conscious if you see the wrong focus.

Insights from Measure What Matters by John Doerr

In *Measure What Matters*, John Doerr introduces the **objectives and key results (OKR)** framework, a system designed to ensure that organizations focus on what truly drives success. The book emphasizes the following:

- **Focus:** Narrow your objectives to a few high-priority goals that align with the organization's vision
- **Alignment:** Ensure that everyone understands and works toward the same objectives to avoid siloed or conflicting efforts
- **Accountability:** Use measurable key results to track progress, but ensure they reflect desired outcomes, not just outputs
- **Adaptability:** Be willing to reassess and refine objectives as circumstances change

Doerr cautions against overloading teams with too many metrics or poorly chosen key results, as this dilutes focus and can lead to unintended behaviors, such as gaming the system.

Now, let's figure out how to apply this tip:

- **Prioritize what to measure:** Select metrics that directly align with your strategic goals and focus on outcomes rather than outputs
- **Avoid perverse incentives:** Ensure that metrics encourage the right behaviors and align with organizational values
- **Review and adjust:** Periodically revisit your metrics to ensure that they remain relevant and drive the desired impact
- **Quality over quantity:** A few meaningful metrics are more powerful than a deluge of data

The Ford Pinto recall story illustrates the dangers of relying on metrics that prioritize cost savings over safety and ethics. It underscores the importance of aligning metrics with values and long-term outcomes that matter most.

By learning from stories such as the Ford Pinto recall and applying principles from *Measure What Matters*, you can avoid the pitfalls of over-measurement and focus on what drives real value and progress.

In an Agile context, the impact of DDDM is particularly evident. Metrics such as velocity, lead time, and predictability can guide priorities during PI Planning, helping teams focus on areas that will deliver the most value. For instance, if data highlights delays caused by dependencies, the ART can address those dependencies in the next PI. Similarly, customer feedback can shape the prioritization of features to ensure that the solution meets their needs.

In essence, DDDM transforms how organizations approach challenges and opportunities. It enables decisions that are not only strategic but also measurable, consistent, and impactful. By embracing this approach, organizations can remain focused on delivering value, even in a fast-changing and uncertain world. RTEs play a crucial role in fostering this culture by helping ARTs select balanced metrics that drive the right behaviors and regularly challenging teams to examine whether their measurements align with customer value and organizational purpose.

Once we've celebrated the wins and reflected on the overall progress of the PI, it's time to shift our focus toward improvement.

Retrospective and Problem Solving workshop

The **Problem Solving workshop** is where the real magic of continuous improvement happens. It gives the ART a structured space to surface the most significant challenges, explore root causes, and, most importantly, take collective ownership of solutions.

This isn't about blame; it's about building a culture where teams feel safe to say, "Here's what didn't work—and here's how we can make it better."

The Problem Solving workshop is designed to tackle systemic challenges within the ART. By focusing on root cause analysis and actionable solutions, this workshop enables the ART to continuously improve and deliver value more effectively. It offers a structured environment for identifying and addressing the issues that can hinder performance, ensuring that the ART becomes increasingly efficient and aligned with its objectives over time. The RTE plays a crucial role in facilitating the event, creating an environment where meaningful progress can be achieved. It follows two cycles of divergent and convergent thinking, as shown in *Figure 9.2*.

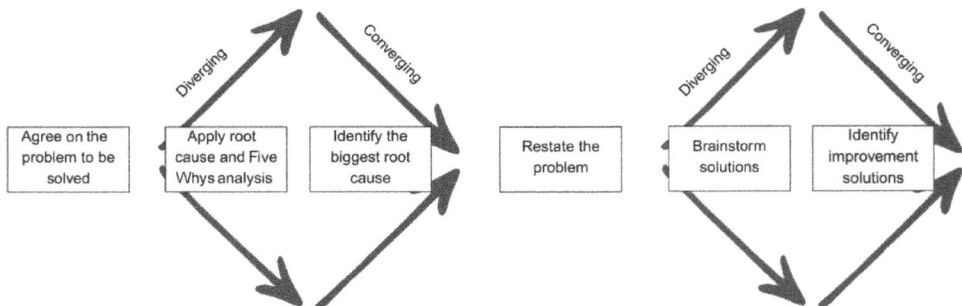

Figure 9.2: The flow of the Problem Solving workshop, showing the thinking patterns of the agenda items

Following the agenda set out in the SAFe® PI Execution toolkit involves finding a problem you want to fix, finding the root cause, and finding ways to fix it. Both finding the root cause and finding solutions involve a divergent and convergent process, much like design thinking.

The workshop begins with Retrospectives across the ART to surface recurring problems or impediments that arose during the PI. These issues might include dependencies, misaligned priorities, or inefficiencies in delivery. Once a list of candidate problems is created, participants—comprising team members and stakeholders—self-organize into groups and collaboratively decide which problem to address. This prioritization ensures the workshop focuses on the most significant issue, one that will have the greatest impact on improving ART performance.

We strongly recommend that you and the Scrum Master practice the skill of writing a well-defined problem statement. Many teams have wasted time having a conversation about a problem, only to find that 20 minutes in, they were talking about a different problem. In crafting a problem statement clearly, not only will people be clear about what problem they are fixing, but it will also encourage a focus on the business impact.

Elements it should include are what, where, when, frequency, and impact. Use these five elements as a mental checklist to test whether the statement is ready to be worked on. Crafting a statement can be harder than you think, and with only four to five I&A events a year, the learning cycle is long. So why not practice this weekly—every time an impediment is raised to you directly or in one of the ART Sync meetings, use this format to record it, thus providing many more opportunities to practice and learn.

With a problem identified, participants conduct a root cause analysis. Techniques such as the **Five Whys** or **fishbone diagrams** are often used to dig deeper and uncover the true source of the issue rather than addressing superficial symptoms. Once the root cause is understood, the group moves on to brainstorming potential solutions. This stage encourages creativity and leverages the collective expertise and diverse perspectives of the participants. The goal is to generate actionable, practical ideas that can resolve the problem effectively and align with the ART's goals.

Jefferson Memorial Five Whys

The Jefferson Memorial Five Whys story is a well-known example of how root cause analysis can uncover the true underlying issue behind a problem. It highlights the value of persistence and critical thinking when addressing challenges, demonstrating the effectiveness of the Five Whys technique. Here's how the story unfolds.

The Jefferson Memorial, one of the iconic landmarks in Washington, D.C., was deteriorating much faster than expected. The excessive wear was attributed to frequent cleaning, which caused significant damage to the stone's structure over time. The cleaning schedule was unusually aggressive because the memorial became covered with dirt and grime far more quickly than similar landmarks. Faced with this problem, park officials sought a solution that would preserve the memorial and reduce maintenance costs.

Instead of simply addressing the immediate issue of frequent cleaning, the team applied the Five Whys technique to uncover the root cause. This systematic method involved asking *why* repeatedly until the fundamental problem was identified.

Q: Why is the Jefferson Memorial deteriorating so quickly?

Because it's being cleaned too often, which wears down the stone.

Q: Why is it cleaned so frequently?

Because it accumulates dirt and grime at a much faster rate than other memorials.

Q: Why does it get dirtier than other memorials?

Because there is an unusually large amount of bird droppings at the site.

Q: Why are there so many birds at the Jefferson Memorial?

The birds are attracted to the large population of insects in the area.

Q: Why are there so many insects near the memorial?

The insects are drawn to the bright lights illuminating the memorial at dusk.

By the fifth *why*, the team had uncovered the root cause of the issue: the timing of the lights. The lights attracted insects, which, in turn, drew birds. The birds then left droppings that required frequent cleaning, leading to the accelerated deterioration of the memorial.

Armed with this insight, the team proposed a simple yet effective solution: adjust the timing of the lights to turn on later in the evening. By delaying the illumination, fewer insects were attracted to the memorial, which led to a significant reduction in the number of birds in the area. This, in turn, decreased the accumulation of grime and dirt, allowing for less frequent cleaning and helping to preserve the memorial's stone structure.

The Jefferson Memorial story is a powerful reminder of the importance of addressing root causes rather than just treating symptoms. Initially, it might have seemed logical to focus on improving cleaning methods or finding materials that were more resistant to wear. However, by digging deeper and asking *why* repeatedly, the team was able to identify and resolve the underlying issue with minimal effort and cost.

This story illustrates the value of the Five Whys technique in problem-solving. It encourages us to look beyond surface-level issues, enabling more sustainable and impactful solutions. Whether applied in business, engineering, or daily life, this approach encourages critical thinking, saves resources, and drives continuous improvement.

The final step in the process is to transform the proposed solutions into actionable items. These actions are added to the ART Backlog, ensuring they are prioritized and executed during the next Planning Interval. By translating insights into concrete steps, the Problem Solving workshop ensures that the ART doesn't just identify issues but actively works to resolve them.

The outcome of the workshop is a set of agreed-upon improvement actions that target systemic problems and enhance ART performance. These actions drive continuous improvement, ensuring that the ART evolves with each iteration. This structured approach creates a culture of collaboration, accountability, and relentless progress, all of which are essential for long-term success.

The RTE ensures the success of the Problem Solving workshop and the broader I&A event. They act as a facilitator, ensuring that the process runs smoothly and productively with open and honest discussions. By creating a psychologically safe environment, the RTE encourages participants to share their thoughts and raise sensitive issues without fear of judgment. This openness is crucial for surfacing the real challenges that need to be addressed.

Perhaps most importantly, the RTE ensures follow-through. An improvement plan is only valuable if it's executed, so the RTE ensures that agreed-upon actions are added to the ART Backlog, assigned to the appropriate teams, and tracked to completion. This follow-up builds trust and reinforces the ART's commitment to continuous improvement.

What do you need to do as an RTE to make it a success?

To ensure that the I&A event is as effective as possible, there are several practical strategies the RTE can employ:

- Preparation is key. Clearly communicating the purpose and structure of the I&A event and sharing metrics or Retrospective prompts in advance helps participants engage thoughtfully.

- Timeboxing the event to no more than three or four hours ensures that discussions remain focused and productive.

- Using visuals and tools to present metrics, Retrospective insights, and problem-solving outputs makes the session more engaging and accessible, particularly for larger or distributed teams.

- Celebrating wins at the start of the session sets a positive tone, motivating participants to tackle challenges constructively.

- Encouraging broad participation ensures that all voices are heard, while aligning improvement actions with PI Objectives ensures the outcomes directly contribute to the ART's broader goals.

Include Scrum Masters and Team Coaches as participants in Problem Solving workshops

Scrum Masters and Team Coaches are often the glue that holds teams together, making them highly sought after during critical events. However, their role in Problem Solving workshops shouldn't be limited to facilitation—they bring invaluable insights into team dynamics, systemic issues, and potential improvements. Ensure that they participate as contributors, not just facilitators.

Sometimes, we ask Scrum Masters to work with their teams ahead of the event to prepare problem statements to work on. This saves time from an already busy event and allows more time to be spent working on finding the root causes and solutions.

If your organization has multiple ARTs, consider trading Scrum Masters for I&A workshops. Having a Scrum Master from another ART facilitate your workshop allows your own Scrum Masters to engage fully as participants. In turn, they can return the favor by facilitating the I&A for the other ART. This cross-ART collaboration not only ensures balanced participation but also introduces fresh perspectives and ideas to the process.

The Problem Solving workshop serves as a vital mechanism for tackling systemic issues that might otherwise remain unresolved. Concentrating on root causes, promoting collaboration, and driving actionable improvements enables the ART to consistently deliver value and adapt to evolving circumstances. Under the RTE's guidance, the workshop transforms into a powerful tool for cultivating a high-performing ART and securing long-term success.

A turning point—the aviation company's Problem Solving workshop

On a crisp Monday morning, the ART teams of an ambitious aviation company gathered in their largest meeting room. Having achieved significant milestones, they faced challenges from operational hurdles and systemic inefficiencies threatening their momentum. The upcoming Problem Solving workshop aimed to tackle these issues directly.

This session had higher stakes. We invited senior leaders, including the CIO and his direct reports. To everyone's surprise—and slight unease—the CIO accepted. His presence signaled the company's commitment to real problems and bridged the gap between the boardroom and the teams on the ground.

The workshop begins

The energy in the room was intense as we began the workshop to identify and resolve pressing challenges affecting the ART's performance. Using the Five Whys technique, we aimed to uncover the root causes of issues hindering us.

The session started with team Retrospectives, where ART members shared experiences and surfaced challenges that had been brewing—dependencies between teams, unclear decision-making processes, and conflicting priorities. We ensured that every voice was heard, encouraging open dialogue.

After consolidating the issues, we invited the CIO and his team to review them. The senior leaders, used to strategic discussions, engaged in the specifics of the ART's daily struggles. For some, it was a revelation.

The Five Whys in action

One of the problems that emerged was the frequent delays in delivering key features. Using the Five Whys, we worked through it:

- *Why were key features delayed?*

  Teams were waiting for critical approvals.

- *Why were approvals taking so long?*

  The approval process involved multiple layers of bureaucracy.

- *Why was the process so bureaucratic?*

  Leaders wanted to control risks at every stage.

- *Why was this level of control deemed necessary?*

  There was a lack of trust in the teams' ability to manage risk independently.

- *Why was trust lacking?*

  There was limited visibility into the teams' processes and progress.

As the analysis progressed, an alarming realization emerged: a significant bottleneck originated from the policies and practices established by the CIO. Credit goes to him for not deflecting or denying this fact. Rather, he actively participated in the conversation, recognizing the unintended effects of these systems and pledging to implement changes.

A turning point

The workshop lasted a couple of hours, with senior leaders confronting the realities presented by the teams. It was a humbling experience for many. The CIO and his direct reports shifted focus from perceived problems to actual team experiences.

By day's end, they outlined actionable steps to resolve approval bottlenecks and other systemic issues. The CIO committed to streamlining approval processes and empowering teams with greater autonomy. The leadership team vowed to stay engaged with the ART, recognizing the importance of ongoing dialogue.

The impact

This Problem Solving workshop marked a turning point for the company. The CIO and his team's involvement addressed critical roadblocks and changed perceptions of what the ART could achieve. They better understood the challenges teams faced and recognized the importance of trust and empowerment.

In the following PIs, the ART's velocity improved significantly. Teams gained confidence, knowing their concerns were heard and addressed. The company reached previously impossible outcomes, highlighting the workshop as a key success driver.

It wasn't just another meeting; it unified leaders and teams in a commitment to improvement. Insights and actions from that day transformed the organization into a more collaborative, agile, and resilient business. Put simply, the I&A is the scaled version of the Iteration Review and the Iteration Retrospective. It enables the team of teams to inspect and adapt on what they've done, what stakeholders think of it, and how they are working. Improvement only comes from deliberate practice.

That brings us to the end of the events that we need to execute the PI effectively.

Summary

In this chapter, we've bridged the gap between planning and outcomes by executing the PI. PI Planning creates momentum, but it is execution that turns PI Objectives into tangible customer value. As an RTE, you guide the ART through optimization while maintaining flow, keeping the team connected to the value they deliver.

We've examined essential events vital for PI execution, including team-level ceremonies and ART-level events such as ART Syncs, System Demos, and the I&A workshop. These meetings serve as feedback loops that help the ART align, tackle challenges, and improve continuously. Effective communication is crucial, requiring tailored messages, transparency, and trust-building with teams and stakeholders.

For an RTE, mastering these practices is critical since even the best plans fail without effective implementation. Your ability to facilitate these events, maintain visibility, promote data-driven decisions, and ensure psychological safety greatly influences the ART's predictable value delivery. By addressing immediate delivery needs and continuous improvement, you lay a foundation for the ART to effectively execute today's plan and evolve for future challenges.

In the following chapter, you'll discover that process execution is merely the starting point. As you assist your teams during the PI, you'll notice chances to mentor and guide teams across roles and throughout the ART. Whether it's aiding a Scrum Master in perfecting their Retrospectives or helping POs sharpen their backlog, your skill to coach with empathy and clarity is what transforms the ART from simply functioning to truly flourishing.

Let's move on and look at how you can coach for lasting, positive change.

References

Here, you can find the links to expand your knowledge about the specific concepts not covered in this book but referenced in this chapter:

- Derby, E., & Larsen, D. (2006). *Agile Retrospectives: Making good teams great.* Pragmatic Bookshelf.

- Doerr, J. (2018). *Measure what matters: How Google, Bono, and the Gates Foundation rock the world with OKRs.* Portfolio/Penguin.

- Highsmith, J. (2010). *Agile project management: Creating innovative products* (2nd ed.). Addison-Wesley Professional.

- Lencioni, P. (2002). *The Five Dysfunctions of a Team: A Leadership Fable.* Jossey-Bass.

Get This Book's PDF Version and Exclusive Extras

UNLOCK NOW

Scan the QR code (or go to `packtpub.com/unlock`). Search for this book by name, confirm the edition, and then follow the steps on the page.

Note: Keep your invoice handy. Purchases made directly from Packt don't require one.

10

Coaching ART Improvements

We've examined how to execute a PI, but the events are just one aspect to consider when coaching an ART. The term *Release Train Engineer* made a lot of sense in the early iterations of SAFe®, but the world has moved on. We can think of the RTE role as more of a chief coach for the train. In this chapter, we will explore the skills and practical steps you need to take to coach the ART to execute well and deliver the organization's objectives. To do this, the RTE is the lead person for improving the performance of the ART and those within it.

Here are some of the topics we will cover in this chapter:

- Becoming a transformational coach
- Creating a transformation backlog

Becoming a transformational coach

There are *coaches* and there are coaches; in our world, many people have taken on the job title of an Agile Coach, but aren't necessarily trained or have the skills to coach people and teams. Unfortunately, this can tarnish the reputation of the coaching world. One of the challenges we face when working in organizations is that many people looking to hire a Scrum Master or an RTE often don't understand the role and the value a great coach can deliver to the business. It is easy to think that by facilitating major events, such as **PI Planning** and the **I&A workshop**, you are adding the most value. Those events are important, but we would argue that the most value you can offer as an RTE is to make a lasting change in the culture.

Before we go into the details, please note that this process takes time. It is easy for an RTE to become frustrated with the slow pace of lasting change. You may be in this role because you understand it and see the value in adopting a coaching mindset. So, don't lose heart; it's better to work on building lasting change than to rush to implement something that will fall apart the minute you leave.

With that said, let's start by examining some of the key areas to consider in coaching lasting transformation.

Building trust and collaboration

As coaches, consultants, and trainers, we work with numerous companies worldwide. Often, when they are interested in implementing SAFe®, these companies are large and come from a Waterfall background, which can lead to a command and control mindset. Frequently, in those companies, people have been there for 20 years or more, and they simply don't know that there is a different way to work.

We also see companies that have been working with Scrum or other frameworks for years and are now looking to scale. Either way, you may encounter resistance from people who dislike change.

Building trust to make connections

I [Tim] was once working with an IT team that supported a SAFe transformation. One of the people that I was coaching had been with the business for his entire career. He understood the mindset at a surface level, but there was always something that didn't seem to click. He was exceptionally skilled at his job as a project and program manager, and he quickly grasped the framework, including meetings, data management, and refining the backlog. However, he struggled whenever we talked about decentralized decision-making or taking ownership.

After a few months working together, he started to open up. He explained that he took comfort in the fact that as long as he followed his boss's orders, he would never be able to mess things up enough to get fired. My heart sank. Over time, we managed to get pockets of that organization to *feel* completely different. It took time and a delicate touch to make sure we didn't make things worse.

> We found that focusing on tangible results removed a lot of emotion from what we were trying to achieve. When we celebrated the value we delivered, we gave people an opportunity to raise their heads above the proverbial trenches and feel more comfortable getting attention in the right way. Looking back, I realize that you never know what is going on in people's minds. If I sense resistance to change, I try to understand the underlying reasons for it. However, if, like me, you're an external consultant, you may be perceived as the enemy. Try not to take it personally, focus on the people and understand their problems, and give them a chance to shine.

One of the most helpful models that we use when coaching teams is *The Five Dysfunctions of a Team* by Patric Lencioni. Lencioni's books are generally written as stories that make it easy for people to digest concepts. Lencioni suggests that trust is the foundation of any high-performing team. Trust comes in two forms: firstly, that you're putting trust in someone or something capable of performing the task at hand; secondly, whether or not they're being honest about the situation and the way they're representing the facts.

In both scenarios, data can be a valuable tool for making decisions based on facts rather than emotions. However, you have to be mindful of how you interpret the information, and don't forget the human behind the machine. Data gathering can quickly start to bypass the first value of the **Agile Manifesto**: *Individuals and interactions over processes and tools*.

We'll look at data and the right way to use it later in this chapter, but let's talk about people first. To help teams perform at their best, we need to step back and consider the broader context.

Psychological safety

Psychological safety is one of the most significant and widely discussed topics within the Agile community. We've got hundreds of war stories about where it has worked and where it hasn't. It is incredible what people can achieve when they are in a place where they feel valued and confident to speak up. As an RTE, you will have to build genuine relationships with people.

One of the most popular books on leadership and feedback is Kim Scott's *Radical Candor*. It is an excellent book that we often recommend to people as we go about our coaching. Kim tells many stories and offers practical advice on how to be a better manager. However, we've seen many people miss the point. They take the title and the idea of giving feedback as a license just to be cruel (and that is the polite way of saying it). The book emphasizes the need to care about the people you are leading.

If you work in an office, it is relatively easy to go for coffee or lunch with your colleagues. You can walk around and get a good sense of how people are feeling. So, if you're in the office, keep your eyes peeled and your ear to the ground. Hopefully, you will be able to build genuine relationships, but you may need to be proactive in organizing social events for the teams. Think about holidays and people's birthdays, when you can get together to learn a little more about the people around you.

Culture can also play a significant role, both organizationally and geographically. It is always good to consider the size of the groups you're talking to and who is in the room. A notable example is whether people are likely to speak up when their boss is in earshot, but it also works the other way around. We have seen many leaders who are new to transformation, and they don't want to appear foolish in front of their team.

Our goal is to break down these barriers, but consider it in terms of removing them one brick at a time. If you take a sledgehammer to the culture, you risk doing more harm than good.

Leading by example and celebrating vulnerability

Tim was once working on an ART in Dublin. It was their first PI Planning, and the team was near the end of their final plan review. As always, we went around the teams and conducted a confidence vote to ensure everyone was committed to the objectives. To provide more context, we were in person, and it involved a large solution with two ARTs in the same room. Most of the teams had voted three or above and were happy with the plan, but then one team stood up and all together gave a two out of five. If even one person gives a two, we should investigate. It was clear that they had agreed to do this as a team and support one another.

What happened next was one of my favorite examples of a leader encouraging psychological safety. The CIO walked from the back of the room and took the microphone. He simply said, *"Thank you, thank you, thank you, this is why we are here."* He suggested everyone take a break while we talked to the team. We worked through the challenges together, and after that, people became much more comfortable speaking their minds.

Creating the right culture is fragile; it doesn't take much to tear down years of work. You have to invest time with people so that even if you mess up, and you will, you've built enough trust with the teams to come back strong.

Imagine the situation: you're sitting in a meeting and you have a nagging doubt that the meeting isn't going as planned. The conversation doesn't seem to be addressing the issue, just dancing around it. There is information you feel like you're missing that everyone else seems to know, or gives the impression they do. What do you do? Speak up and maybe look stupid because you're the only one who doesn't know what is going on, or sit there quietly hoping all becomes clear later?

The reality is, we've all been there, and in many situations, we sit there quietly letting the moment pass. But don't worry, if this has happened to you, it doesn't mean you are a bad person. It's an indication that, at that moment, you didn't feel safe to express your concerns or ask the *stupid question*. Human nature protects us from danger, and at this moment, the threat was loss of respect.

Humans are hardwired for belonging and safety—when these are threatened, our brains prioritize self-protection over contribution. When this happens in the workplace, the team loses countless insights because people choose the safety net or protecting themselves over the danger of speaking up.

The risks to team productivity and collaboration are accentuated in the distributed, virtual, camera-off, always-muted world we now work in, making it harder to read the room. For agility to be successful, we strive for transparent and adaptive teams, yet the working environment doesn't always promote that—it's this paradox that this section examines.

The leadership challenge

Many of our leaders struggle with balancing being *nice* and achieving results, driving the high standards that the enterprise needs. They worry that creating a safe environment will make teams complacent, and standards and work output will drop, despite research showing the contrary.

Depending on people's mental models, a misinterpretation of leadership and management models can cause unintended consequences. Take, as an example, Kim Scott's *The Radical Candor*, mentioned earlier, a book we've been known to recommend to RTEs, which emphasizes challenging directly while personally caring. Some over-index on *candor* with little or no *caring*, taking liberty with the title of the book for abusive, unprofessional behavior. Without an appropriate balance, feedback isn't received, and improvements are not made.

Leaders also fear that exposing their weaknesses and mistakes will undermine their authority. You can understand why they have been conditioned this way, with many organizations operating in an adversarial hierarchical power structure that promotes those who echo the cultural norms.

For the RTE, this means you might inherit teams with years of baggage, and leaders of influence who are working counter to how you want and need to develop the ways of working in the ART.

The research that challenges previous thinking

In 1999, Amy Edmondson at Harvard Business School observed that high-performing medical teams reported more errors than their less-performing counterparts. When she studied this behavior, she discovered it wasn't because they were making more mistakes, but because they felt safe to report them. She coined the phrase *psychological safety*, a place where courage was promoted over comfort.

> *...a shared belief held by members of a team that the team is safe for interpersonal risk taking*
>
> —*Edmondson, A. (1999)*

This isn't just an academic exercise. Google's **Project Aristotle** studied over 180 teams, finding that psychological safety was the single strongest predictor of team effectiveness, being more important than any specific individual's talent, the team's structure, or the resources it had available. The study (`https://www.thinkwithgoogle.com/intl/en-emea/future-of-marketing/management-and-culture/five-dynamics-effective-team/`) stated the following:

> *Our research revealed that sales teams with high ratings for psychological safety actually brought in more revenue, exceeding their sales targets by 17%. Teams with low psychological safety fell short by up to 19%.*

Other organizations have found evidence of the power of psychological safety in various industries worldwide, including aviation, manufacturing, and software development.

Understanding the research is one thing; living it is another.

The RTE as psychological safety champion

It should come as no surprise that deliberate effort is needed to create an environment where people feel safe raising concerns, enabling the team to gang up on the problem, not each other. As the RTE, you are in a unique position to foster this across the ART, and the Scrum Masters encourage this for the teams.

A foundational element of psychological safety is to build genuine relationships. Spend time being present with people, physically or virtually. If you don't spend time with teams apart from ART events, when you do, their behavior will change—we once heard someone whisper "captain on deck" when an RTE came around. Observe who speaks when the team is together and how that changes when leaders and outsiders are present.

Be a catalyst, creating social glue. Celebrating people's birthdays, sharing their holiday experiences, and engaging in coffee chats are simple ways to foster these human connections. Glenn once turned around a dysfunctional team, in part, with Friday afternoon coffee-and-cake team events, featuring a healthy (apart from the sugar) competitive cake-baking challenge.

As the RTE, you can model the behavior you want others to follow:

- **You're imperfect**: Share mistakes you've made and what you've recently learned. If you don't understand what a group is talking about, tell them and ask them to explain—it's almost guaranteed you're not the only one who doesn't know!

- **Inviting questioning**: For example, ask questions such as *"What am I not seeing?"*, *"What would you do differently?,"* or *"What's the biggest risk we're not discussing?."*

- **Small experiments**: Keep trying new things and show constant improvement through trial and error.

In addition to these more tactical actions within your control, you may need to work on influencing broader issues within the organization, such as performance review processes, promotion criteria, or meeting dynamics that inadvertently penalize honesty.

Building a constructive environment is a gradual and ongoing process. Results and behavior change will develop gradually, so you must maintain your focus and not lose faith if you don't see immediate results.

As an RTE, you're not just coaching teams toward better delivery—you're creating the conditions where people can bring their best thinking, their honest concerns, and their innovative ideas to the challenges that matter most.

Giving and receiving feedback

They say feedback is a gift, but that doesn't always mean it's easy to give or receive, for that matter. The adage of the *positive-negative sandwich* doesn't work when you try to bury negative feedback between two compliments. People either see through it or overlook the negative altogether, choosing to focus only on the positive. *Radical Candor* suggests that clear feedback is far more effective when done in the right way. Consider the social capital you need to invest to provide negative feedback without damaging the relationship.

A good rule of thumb is to give genuine, positive feedback 5–10 times as often as negative feedback. Think about it: if you work with someone who is constantly correcting and consistently negative, you're not going to enjoy working with them. They may have a reputation for it around the office, and after a while, you don't even pay attention to them. It's a bit like your children; if you spend all your time shouting at them, they won't even know the difference between something serious and something that doesn't matter in the grand scheme of things.

If, on the other hand, you spend much of your time giving genuine appreciation for the work that they are doing, take the time to ask them questions about their weekend, and listen to their answer—if you take a genuine interest in what they have to say—then when you have to give some course correction, it is much more likely that people will hear you.

Navigating change fatigue

Companies often undergo wave after wave of change. All too often, people become worn down and exhausted by the seemingly endless changes in roles, responsibilities, and processes. As an RTE, you need to be mindful not just of what you're trying to accomplish now, but what has happened before you got there.

One model that can help you understand how people are feeling comes from John Fisher's **personal transition curve**, which visualizes how people can feel at any given moment during a transformation.

THE PROCESS OF TRANSITION
John Fisher's personal transition curve

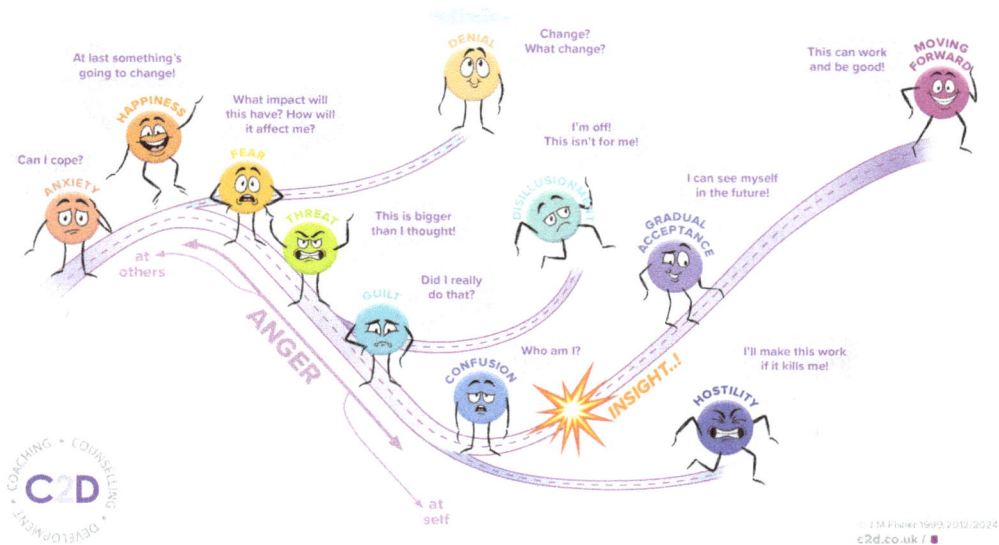

Figure 10.1: John Fisher's personal transition curve (© J. M. Fisher, 1999/2012/2014, c2d.co.uk)

This curve takes you through the anxiety of looming change, through the pit of confusion, and the various states that you might have to navigate along the way. Most people dislike change, and the idea of embarking on something new leaves them wondering whether they can cope or whether it will ultimately be better. As we understand the vision for change, people may have hope that things will change for the better. As you start to implement new roles and responsibilities, you will likely encounter issues that need to be addressed. People may become upset or angry along the way. At this point, you need to hang in there and make sure to listen to how people are feeling.

A common mistake is trying to change too much at once. You, as the RTE, may well see the end goal with such clarity that it is frustrating when people don't see things the way you do. Remember to take things one step at a time and don't try to do everything at once. It's helpful to have a transformation roadmap so that you can share the big picture with stakeholders. However, like any experiment, you should only change one thing at a time; otherwise, you risk not knowing what is working and what isn't.

Making incremental changes

I [Tim] was once working with a support team for a business that wanted to join a **large solution**. The team had undergone numerous iterations of change and transformation, and the consultants who had been there before had had limited success in gaining buy-in from the teams. It became clear quite quickly that the consultants who had worked with them before had tried to *do the change to them* rather than listen and get them on board. One director said, *"They just came in thinking they knew best, and never asked us how we worked, and why we do things the way we do. I've been here for 20 years, and we're not dumb. Their model doesn't work; they're just trying to force us into their mould."*

They were big, dramatic words, and he was clearly upset at how he had been treated. In my mind, it was clear that they needed to adopt **SAFe® Kanban** in their team—it'd have worked much better for them and the teams they worked with, but if I'd said that at the time, I'd have lost them.

Instead, I tamed my advice monster and spent a few weeks getting to know their teams. I got to see what was working and celebrate the things that were working really well. I spoke to their bosses and let them know all the things they were doing well. I used data to demonstrate the control they had in certain areas, while also highlighting areas where waste could be reduced. I looked for ways to highlight the pinch points and presented options to them in their language.

As a result, we implemented a few simple but effective experiments. We made a simple change and showed the results to the director. He loved it and gave us feedback. We listened and then made another adjustment, repeating the process to change the culture within the teams gradually. These days, they surprise me with the insight they offer and how radically different they approach some of their challenges. It all happened one simple step at a time.

Tips for navigating change fatigue

Here are some straightforward ways to help your teams—and yourself—cope with change fatigue:

1. **Acknowledge it**: Start by recognizing how people are feeling. If the team is tired or frustrated, you need to be aware of this. Listening to them builds trust and opens the door to honest conversations; they're more likely to speak out if you show that you're with them.

2. **Remind people why**: Reconnect teams to the purpose behind the work. When people understand the reason for a change, they're more likely to stay engaged.

3. **Encourage support networks**: Whether it's **Communities of Practice**, team huddles, or informal chats, provide people with opportunities to communicate with each other. Sharing the experience makes it easier to carry.

4. **Focus on incremental steps you can test**: Let teams try small changes and learn from them. It gives them a sense of control and reduces resistance. When people help shape the change, they're more likely to embrace it.

5. **Celebrate progress**: When something goes well, no matter how small, acknowledge it. Wins help restore morale and remind us that we're moving forward.

Remember the context, what you're trying to accomplish, and why it is essential. It will help you navigate the challenges from a human perspective.

Let's explore how we can order our efforts with the **transformation backlog**.

Creating a transformation backlog

In the previous chapter, we examined the events we established to execute the PI. As an RTE, there are so many rocks that you can look under, so many places that you could spend your time. In this section, we will have a look at some tools you can use to create your transformation backlog.

You should treat a transformation backlog like any other. Ideas can come from anywhere, so it's best to prioritize them to limit the number of changes you try to make at once.

When you find a problem, we find it helpful to spend a bit of time writing in a clear format, such as the following from Beth Miller (which we use in the **Problem Solving workshop**):

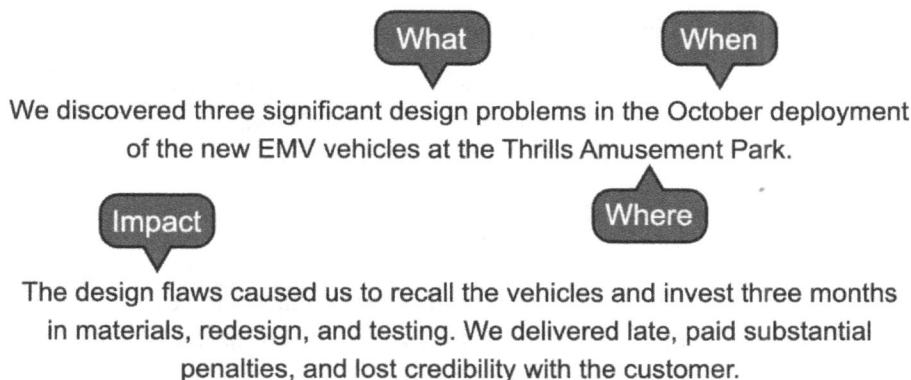

What   **When**

We discovered three significant design problems in the October deployment of the new EMV vehicles at the Thrills Amusement Park.

Impact   **Where**

The design flaws caused us to recall the vehicles and invest three months in materials, redesign, and testing. We delivered late, paid substantial penalties, and lost credibility with the customer.

Concept contributed by Beth Miller

Figure 10.2: Problem statement format by Beth Miller (© Scaled Agile, Inc. Source: `https://framework.scaledagile.com/inspect-and-adapt/`*)*

So often, we find that writing the problem clearly can help to align and demonstrate an Agile value in practical terms. A common challenge when discussing problem statements is that people naturally want to talk about solutions; you, as the RTE, will have to work hard to keep people on track.

I [Tim] was working with a team, and one of the members was keen to put some automated reporting into the dashboards for the teams. The problem seemed straightforward at first, and automating a dashboard made sense. I wanted to delve a little deeper, and we started to try to frame the problem using Beth Miller's statement. After a brief conversation with the team, we discovered that there wasn't just one problem, but rather eight separate issues that we were trying to address. The dashboard was a great idea, but we then decided to work through all eight issues to identify the most significant root cause.

The solution may seem obvious, but it is always worth taking a breath and writing things clearly. The little things do make a difference, and taking the time to have the conversation can lead to some connections that you would be unlikely to make if you're constantly in a rush.

Now, we can explore how to apply this format using some of our favorite tools.

Understanding flow metrics

Leveraging data to drive decisions can be a great way to take emotion out of the equation. No matter where you go, people will have their own agenda for what they want to see in the organization. That said, it is easy to start measuring the wrong things, overloading people with dashboards and reports that are easily accessible from your tool of choice, but offer little meaning.

We aim to utilize the data to tell a story, solve problems, and generate actionable items that eliminate non-value-added waste in our processes and approaches.

Make sure your data is accurate

To make informed decisions based on data, it must be kept current. We're not suggesting that you should be seen as the *Jira police*. However, the simple question of whether the team is updating their work in the tool is the first starting point. You may wish to establish a consistent cadence for data updates. For example, a team Kanban board should not be more than 24 hours out of date, whereas an **ART Feature Kanban**, given its slower pace of work, could be updated a couple of days later.

One of the significant updates in SAFe® 6.0 was the updated metrics article and guidance on how to utilize **flow metrics** at various levels within a SAFe portfolio. Many of these have been around for a while, and some have been incorporated from Mik Kersten's work in his best-selling book *Project to Product*.

The following table shows a summary of what they are and the insight that you can gain from them:

Metric	Description	Purpose/insight
Flow distribution	Categorizes completed work by type over time (features, enablers, defects, etc.)	Understand how types of effort are distributed—are we investing wisely?
Flow velocity	Measures the number of backlog items delivered in a time period	Helps assess delivery trends and team/ART capacity
Flow time	The time from when an item enters the system to when it leaves	Highlights the speed of delivery and areas of delay
Flow load	The number of work items currently in process.	Indicates system overload; helps manage WIP
Flow efficiency	The ratio of active work time to total time	Identifies waste and opportunities to accelerate delivery
Flow predictability	Measures how consistently teams, ARTs, and portfolios can meet their commitments	Builds trust and reveals system reliability

Table 10.1: Flow metrics explained

The SAFe website does a fantastic job of explaining each of these concepts in detail, so we won't duplicate their information here. However, what you should consider are some practical, real-world ways of how you might use them in your day-to-day life as an RTE:

- **Flow distribution**: Take flow distribution. If we review the last PI and see that most completed work was features, with little investment in enablers, technical debt, or defect fixes, that's a great coaching moment. We might say, *"Let's talk about sustainability. Are we investing enough in the system's health, or are we too focused on short-term delivery?"* This opens up a wider discussion with **Product Management** and **System Architects** around balance and long-term resilience.

- **Flow velocity**: If we observe a drop in flow velocity, it can be a prompt to investigate what's happening. Perhaps a team has experienced a dip in availability, or maybe they're struggling with dependencies. Here, we can guide the conversation by asking, *"Has anything changed in the environment? Are we experiencing more blockers or rework?"*

Remember that velocity is a tool for planning capacity management rather than measuring value. You can be busy building the wrong thing.

> **Anecdote from Tim: velocity versus value**
>
> I [Tim] was once working as a Scrum Master for an Agile team. We had an engaged stakeholder who was supportive of Agile, but relatively new to it all. After one of our demos, he pulled me aside and said, *"Tim, all this is great, but I need you to double your velocity in the next sprint."* I had a few options at this point; it could have been a coaching moment to explain the difference between velocity and value, and there were a lot of those moments. In this instance, I went with the *"Yes, sir!"* option. I knew he wanted to show his bosses more value, and it wasn't the time to argue over terminology and make him look silly.
>
> Still, I went back to the team and asked them to, from now on, change anything that they would have given a one today to a two. The result? Double the velocity!
>
> Now, I know that this is an anti-pattern, and I'm not suggesting that you do this to manipulate your data! However, I often tell it as a story to explain the difference between velocity and creating value so that people understand the difference.

- **Flow time**: When we examine flow time and notice that work is taking longer than expected to complete, that's a cue to investigate the hidden delays within the system. We might run a value stream mapping session or simply discuss with the teams: *"Where are we seeing the biggest wait times? Are there approvals or handoffs we can simplify?"*
- **Flow load**: Flow load is particularly useful when we suspect the ART is taking on too much at once. If WIP is creeping up, we can encourage the teams to reflect: *"What's preventing us from finishing what we've started? Can we focus on clearing the board before committing to more work?"* This can naturally lead to discussions around swarming, prioritization, and capacity planning. A higher flow load is likely to negatively influence flow time.

- **Flow efficiency**: If we're seeing low flow efficiency, we know that a significant portion of time is being spent waiting rather than progressing work. This is often where systemic issues come to light—perhaps the teams are waiting on external dependencies or decisions from stakeholders. A coaching response might be, *"Let's look at the journey a feature takes. Where's the work sitting idle, and how might we reduce that?"*

- **Flow predictability**: Lastly, flow predictability gives us insight into how reliably we're delivering what we committed to during PI Planning. If the ART is consistently under-delivering on business value, we might dig into why: *"Were the stories too large? Did our priorities shift mid-PI? Were there surprises we could have planned for better?"* This opens the door to improving estimation, dependency management, and commitment clarity.

The golden rule for optimizing all of these is to create a stable delivery pattern, which improves flow predictability, and then to optimize the speed of delivery as measured by flow time.

You can use the data to set some **Objective and Key Results (OKRs)** to help you focus on what is essential. Here is an example:

Objective:

- Improve our ability to deliver valuable features to our customers in less time

Key results:

- Reduce average flow time for features by 20% by the end of Q3
- Identify and address the top three sources of delay in the feature delivery process by the end of Sprint 3
- Implement WIP limits across all teams' Kanban boards with team agreement and coaching support by the end of Sprint 2
- Conduct at least one value stream mapping workshop per team by mid-Q3 to identify and eliminate waste and handoffs

SAFe® assessments

The **SAFe® assessments** (available through the framework site and SAFe Studio with a paid license) are one of the most useful (and often underused) tools we have to drive meaningful, people-focused improvement. Whether you're looking at *Team and Technical Agility, DevOps*, or *Business Agility*, these surveys help you understand not just where you think you are, but how you compare with others in your industry. They provide us with data, yes, but more importantly, they offer us insight into how our people are experiencing agility on the ground.

Take *Team and Technical Agility*, for example. When you run that assessment with your teams, you get a clear view of how well they're embracing Agile behaviors, technical practices, and cross-team collaboration. The results allow you to benchmark against organizations worldwide. That's incredibly powerful—it helps remove the emotion from improvement conversations. Instead of debating whether you're *good enough*, you can see what's typical, what's working elsewhere, and where your energy might go next.

Tim's first experience with the assessments

A funny thing happened the first time Tim ran the *Business Agility* assessment. One of the teams was led by a couple in a relationship. You'd think if anyone would align on answers, it would be them. They actually had wildly different views on the terminology and where the team landed on the scale.

It was a perfect example of why it's so important to facilitate assessments live, whenever possible. Running a facilitated session not only encourages a richer conversation but also uncovers where misunderstandings or assumptions may lie. The data from a survey is great, but it's the discussion that follows that's truly valuable.

DORA metrics

One of the most significant developments in recent years has been the increased emphasis on DORA metrics. These metrics, initially developed by the **DevOps Research and Assessment (DORA)** team, have become the industry standard for measuring software delivery performance. Backed by years of research and popularized through the annual *State of DevOps* reports, they provide a way to discuss delivery health using data that's both meaningful and actionable.

Incorporating DORA metrics into SAFe® offers a practical and performance-focused approach to connecting Agile and DevOps. These indicators aren't about individual teams or people—they help us assess the delivery capability of our entire system. They can be used at the team, ART, and portfolio levels to make informed decisions, track improvement, and align leadership with delivery reality.

The following table provides a summary of each DORA metric, along with the kind of insight it can offer when used thoughtfully as part of ART-level coaching and improvement.

Metric	What it measures	Insight/why it matters
Deployment frequency	How often changes are deployed to production	Indicates how quickly and regularly the team delivers value
Lead time for changes	Time from code commit to successful production release	Reveals the speed of delivery and efficiency of the delivery pipeline
Change failure rate	Percentage of deployments that cause a failure in production	Reflects the quality and stability of releases
Mean time to restore (MTTR)	Average time to recover from a production failure	Measures resilience and the team's ability to respond to issues quickly

Table 10.2: DORA metrics explained

These four metrics together help us gauge the balance between speed and stability. As RTEs, they provide us with a systems view—how well our ART is performing in delivering, how safe our releases are, and how quickly we can recover when things go wrong.

Ways you might use them as an RTE include the following:

- **Deployment frequency**: If deployment frequency is low, it might suggest large batch sizes, long testing cycles, or a lack of confidence in the release process. As RTEs, we can ask, *"What's stopping us from releasing more frequently? Is it tooling, process, or trust in the quality?"* This opens the door to discussions around automation, **continuous integration/continuous delivery (CI/CD)** maturity, and whether the **definition of done** includes deployability.

- **Lead time for changes**: When lead time is long, it often means there's waste in the pipeline—waiting for approvals, long-lived branches, a large batch size, or delayed testing. We might coach by saying, *"Let's walk through a change from commit to production. Where's the work sitting idle?"* This is ideal for mapping the delivery pipeline and identifying handoffs or blockers.

- **Change failure rate**: A high failure rate may indicate that releases are brittle or that testing is insufficient. But it can also flag cultural issues—perhaps teams are reluctant to report failures. We might reflect, "How safe do we feel to experiment and learn from mistakes? Are failures becoming learning moments or just pain points?" This helps build psychological safety and encourages more robust testing strategies.

- **MTTR:** If MTTR is high, recovery processes might be manual, unclear, or under-practiced. We can start by asking, *"What's our approach when something goes wrong in production? How confident are we in our rollback or recovery plans?"* It's a great way to highlight the value of observability, chaos engineering, and well-rehearsed incident responses.

Understanding how the ART is performing

To quickly gather insights using DORA metrics across your ART, run a 15-minute pulse survey with each team, using a 1–5 scale for each metric.

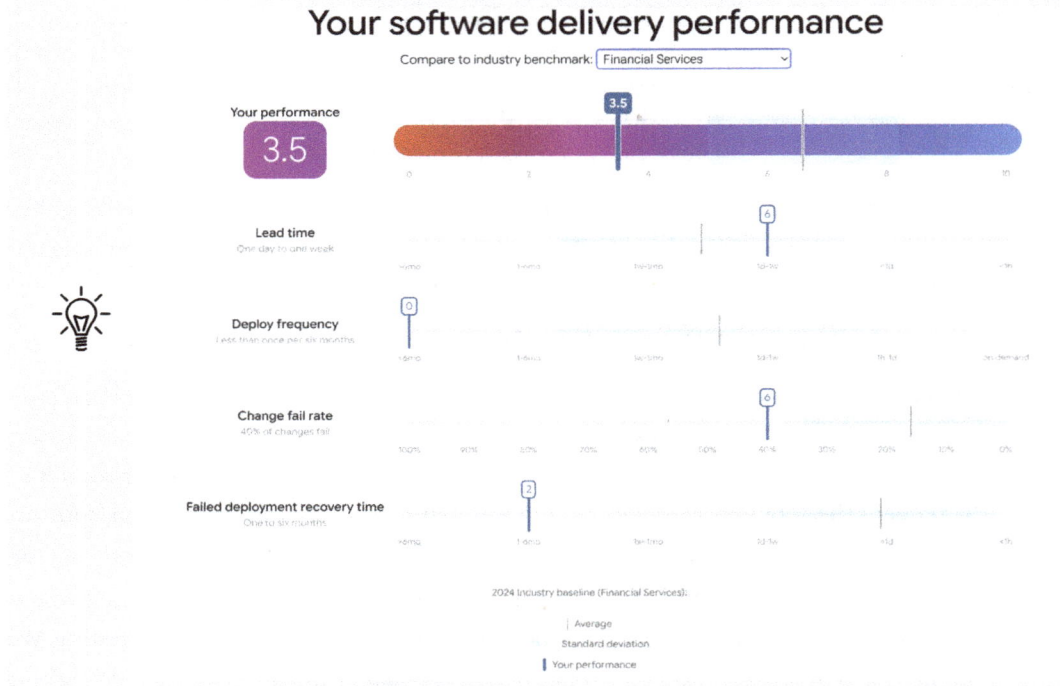

Figure 10.3: A client DORA self-assessment result compared against the Financial Services benchmark

Keep it lightweight and conversational—no need for perfect data. Use the responses to spot consistent pain points and translate them into quick wins for your transformation backlog. For example, if several teams score low on deployment frequency, consider taking actions such as improving CI/CD pipelines or reducing batch sizes. It's a fast, inclusive way to focus your efforts where they'll matter most.

You can also compare your results against a worldwide benchmark, which helps you see how you compare to your competitors.

Team health checks

Just like velocity or predictability, team health is one of those things that's easy to measure badly. But when done well, a health check can be one of the most valuable tools in your kit as an RTE. Not because it gives you a pretty chart to show leadership, but because it opens the door to honest conversations about how teams are feeling. And let's be honest—most of the challenges we face aren't technical. They're about clarity, trust, motivation, and people trying to do their best in a system that often gets in the way.

Before we go too far, let's set expectations. A team health check isn't a silver bullet. It won't fix years of dysfunction overnight or magically turn a struggling team into a high-performing one. However, it does provide a starting point. When teams feel safe enough to say "we don't know what success looks like," or "we're not getting the support we need," that's gold. That's where coaching begins. As the RTE, your job isn't just to surface those insights—it's to do something useful with them.

One of the most powerful things you can do with a health check is to connect it to your system-level change. Not by publishing league tables or calling out red scores in a big room, but by asking: what's getting in the way of flow? What's eroding trust? Where is the system too fragile to support good Agile delivery? Use that insight to inform your transformation backlog, shape your coaching, and engage in more effective conversations with leadership. Because healthy teams don't just deliver more—they stay resilient, they adapt, and they help build the kind of culture that makes agility work.

Here are some examples of health check metrics that are commonly used—and more importantly, meaningful when used well. They're designed to help teams reflect on their working environment, not just what they're delivering. You can score them on a simple red-amber-green scale, or use a 1–5 scale for a bit more granularity.

The key is to prompt honest reflection, not perfection:

- **Clarity of purpose**: Do we understand why we're doing the work, and how it connects to the bigger picture? A low score here may indicate that the team is disconnected from the strategy or customer value.

- **Flow of work**: Can we move work smoothly through our system, or are we constantly stuck waiting for others? This ties in closely with flow time and load—if it's red, there's likely a bottleneck somewhere.

- **Team morale**: How are we feeling as a team? Are we energized and supported, or burnt out and firefighting? This one often reveals deeper issues, such as sustainable pace, recognition, or team dynamics.

- **Collaboration**: Are we working well together, or are we operating in silos? This can reveal dependency pain, poor backlog refinement, or even just a lack of shared rituals.

- **Decision-making**: Can we make decisions quickly and locally, or are we waiting on approvals and unclear priorities? Slow or centralized decisions are a huge source of waste—this is a great metric to highlight it.

- **Support from leadership**: Do we feel we're getting the right level of support from outside the team to succeed? This one often points to structural blockers, such as tooling, skills, and stakeholder engagement.

- **Continuous improvement**: Are we learning and adapting regularly, or are retros and reviews just going through the motions? It's a sign of maturity—teams who feel safe and supported tend to give this a green without prompting.

Employee Net Promoter Score

Employee Net Promoter Score (eNPS) is a straightforward yet powerful way to measure employees' overall satisfaction with their workplace. It's based on a single question: *"How likely are you to recommend this company as a place to work?"* Respondents answer on a scale from 0 to 10, and their answers are grouped into three categories: **Promoters** (9–10), **Passives** (7–8), and **Detractors** (0–6). You then calculate your eNPS by subtracting the percentage of Detractors from the percentage of Promoters. The score ranges from -100 to +100.

It's deliberately simple—and that's its strength. When used effectively, eNPS provides a quick pulse on sentiment across your ART or the wider organization. But the magic is not in the score—it's in what you do next. Always pair the question with an open-text follow-up, such as *"What's the main reason for your score?"* That's where the real insights lie. As RTEs, we're not HR, but we are system coaches, and how people feel about working in the system tells us a lot about its health.

To get the most from eNPS, run it regularly—quarterly tends to work well—and keep the survey anonymous. Use a consistent format and give teams time to reflect. If you're introducing it, explain the intent clearly: this isn't about judgment, it's about learning. Combine the scores with qualitative feedback, and look for patterns: Is morale lower in teams with more external dependencies? Are Detractors flagging a lack of autonomy or unclear priorities? Share insights at ART Sync or with leadership, but keep the focus on action, not accountability.

> We suggest that you don't track the eNPS for individuals, as RTEs, we're much more concerned about the teams. Ask teams how likely they are to recommend the ART or the team environment. It shifts the focus from individual satisfaction to collective experience—and that's something you can influence directly.

Encouraging transparency

Encouraging transparency is one of the most critical parts of your role as an RTE. Without it, all the metrics, cadences, and events in the world won't help. Teams might be delivering, but if we're not seeing the whole picture—if issues are being glossed over or disguised—then we're not leading, we're just treading water. Transparency isn't about blame or exposure; it's about allowing ourselves to learn, adapt, and improve people's working lives.

We've all come across what we jokingly call *watermelon projects*—those that look green on the outside in every dashboard and status report, but are bright red inside once you talk to the team. These projects are ticking along in theory, but beneath the surface, there's confusion, blockers, stress, and unmet expectations. As RTEs, our job is to create an environment where people feel safe enough to say, *"Actually, we're struggling,"* before the system breaks down.

> **Story from Tim**
>
> I was supporting an ART transformation in a large insurance firm. They'd just started using health checks and flow metrics, and during one of the early review sessions, a team member quietly pulled me aside. She looked worried and asked, *"What if leadership sees this and thinks we're failing?"*. The data they'd just shared showed clear delivery delays and a noticeable dip in morale. It was honest, but understandably uncomfortable.

I didn't brush it off. That moment was critical—she wasn't just worried about the numbers, she was worried about trust. So, I used it as an opportunity, not just to coach her team, but also to bring leadership into the conversation. I explained that the point of the data wasn't to assign blame or spotlight underperformance—it was to show where the system needed help. This wasn't about red flags as warning signs; it was about red flags as invitations. Invitations to lead, support, and remove obstacles.

That conversation shifted the tone for the entire ART. Once people saw that the data would be used to make things better—not to tighten the screws—they began to share more openly. And that's when the real transformation started.

Because here's the truth: we don't want to hide problems under a rug. We want to see them—openly and early—so we can respond. Transparency gives us the gift of time. It lets us intervene while there's still room to improve, rather than waiting for things to fall apart. If we aim to create high-performing, resilient ARTs, then our objective measure of success isn't how smooth everything looks on the outside. It's how quickly we surface the red and how effectively we respond to it, together.

Summary

In this chapter, we moved beyond events to explore what truly made an ART successful over time: coaching. We argued that the real value of an RTE is not in running PI Planning or managing the calendar, but in acting as the chief coach—a catalyst for lasting cultural change.

We reframed the role through the lens of transformational coaching, focusing on building trust, creating psychological safety, and providing feedback that encourages growth. Drawing on models such as Lencioni's *Five Dysfunctions* and lessons from *Radical Candor*, we showed how meaningful conversations help people feel valued rather than judged.

We also explored how to spot improvement opportunities, from change fatigue to morale. Tools such as health checks, eNPS, and transformation backlogs offer practical ways forward. Flow and DORA metrics guide improvement conversations and shape actionable OKRs.

A recurring theme was transparency. We 'can't improve what we 'can't see, and false *green* dashboards only create trouble. Through real stories—including challenging but transformational moments—we showed how openness builds trust and allows truth to surface safely.

Ultimately, the chapter reminded us that success is less about processes and more about people. Coaching ART improvements is about creating the conditions for outstanding work and honest conversations.

In the next chapter, we will look at how SAFe® can scale to even bigger sizes beyond a single ART using the Solution Train construct.

References

Here, you can find the references to expand your knowledge about the specific concepts not covered in this book but mentioned in this chapter:

- Edmondson, A. (1999). *Psychological Safety and Learning Behavior in Work Teams. Administrative Science Quarterly, 44* (2), 350–383. `https://doi.org/10.2307/2666999`

- Edmondson, A. (2018). *The Fearless Organization: Creating Psychological Safety in the Workplace for Learning, Innovation, and Growth.* Wiley. `https://fearlessorganizationscan.com/the-fearless-organization`

- Fisher, J. M. (2000, June). *The process of transition.* Paper presented at the Human Resource Development Conference, University of Leeds, UK.

- Tamiru, N. (2023, June). *Team dynamics: Five keys to building effective teams.* Think with Google. `https://business.google.com/in/think/future-of-marketing/five-dynamics-effective-team/`

- Kersten, M. (2019). *Project to Product: How to survive and thrive in the age of digital disruption with the flow framework.* IT Revolution Press. `https://flowframework.org/ffc-project-to-product-book/`

- Lencioni, P. (2002). *The Five Dysfunctions of a Team: A leadership fable.* Jossey-Bass. `https://www.tablegroup.com/product/dysfunctions/`

- Scott, K. (2017). *Radical Candor: Be a kick-ass boss without losing your humanity.* St. Martin's Press. `https://www.radicalcandor.com/our-approach`

Get This Book's PDF Version and Exclusive Extras

UNLOCK NOW

Scan the QR code (or go to packtpub.com/unlock).
Search for this book by name, confirm the edition,
and then follow the steps on the page.

*Note: Keep your invoice handy. Purchases made
directly from Packt don't require one.*

Part 3

Beyond the ART

Our final examination of the RTE understands the scope of the role, both when the solution delivery expands beyond the ART to a Solution Train and when working within a portfolio. At this level, the RTE enters a broader arena where alignment, coordination, and visibility become even more important. It is no longer just about ensuring that a single train runs smoothly; it's about supporting multiple ARTs to work in harmony, managing dependencies, and keeping delivery aligned with enterprise strategy. We will explore how the RTE collaborates with Solution Train Engineers, Epic Owners, and portfolio leadership to extend the same Lean-Agile principles across a wider landscape, ensuring that the flow of value scales without reverting to heavy governance or control.

This part of the book includes the following chapters:

- *Chapter 11, Working with a Solution Train*
- *Chapter 12, Connecting the RTE to the Portfolio*

11

Working with a Solution Train

Sometimes, 125 people just isn't enough to build and maintain large, complex solutions. When this happens, we need to scale beyond the **Agile Release Train** (**ART**) construct. In **SAFe®**, this manifests as a **Solution Train** at the **Large Solution layer** and the **Large Solution Integration and Delivery** competency. We've previously mentioned that SAFe is a **fractal model,** and once again, the Solution Train is a variant of the practices employed by the team and the ART, creating a team of teams of teams. If your organization is working on some of the most significant and complicated solutions, or especially if it is using third-party suppliers, you are likely to see the benefit from using a Solution Train.

This chapter will guide you through the complexities of operating within Solution Trains, equipping you with the knowledge to navigate scaled Agile environments effectively. You'll learn what constitutes a Solution Train and the critical decision factors for when your organization genuinely needs one, avoiding the common pitfall of premature scaling, which can create overhead without benefit. We'll explore how your role as an RTE evolves when your ART becomes part of a larger Solution Train, including the additional coordination responsibilities and new stakeholder relationships you'll need to manage. Finally, you'll gain clarity on the distinct role of the **Solution Train Engineer** (**STE**), understanding how their responsibilities complement and differ from yours, enabling more effective collaboration and clearer boundaries.

This chapter will have the following topics:

- The structure of the Solution Train
- Being an RTE in a Solution Train
- Being an STE in a Solution Train

Let's start by understanding what the Solution Train is and why you might want to use it.

The structure of the Solution Train

As we mentioned in the introduction, a Solution Train is necessary when hundreds or thousands of people work simultaneously on delivering a solution. Typical examples include, but are not limited to, banking, insurance, space, automotive, and governmental, to name but a few. When you start considering cyber-physical systems (i.e., products with software, firmware, and hardware) being delivered at scale, it often becomes essential. The common thread is a need for more than the practical limit of a single ART of 125 people, as well as potentially utilizing suppliers, to plan, collaborate, and deliver together at scale.

As you can see from *Figure 11.1*, the Solution Train serves as a container and coordinator for multiple ARTs and, if needed, suppliers.

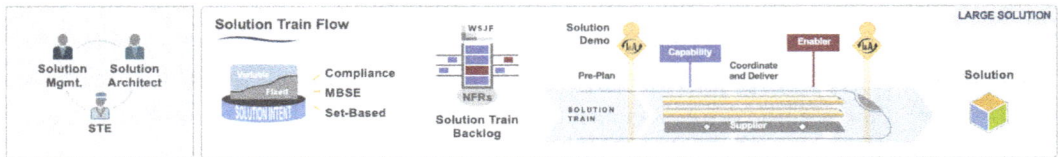

Figure 11.1: The Large Solution layer in SAFe® (© Scaled Agile, Inc. Source: `https://framework.scaledagile.com/large-solution/`*)*

A Solution Train doesn't have any direct delivery capacity; teams still reside within the ARTs, and the ARTs in a Solution Train program work similarly to those in a standalone one. It does have three unique roles:

- **STE**: They facilitate and coach the execution of the Solution Train.
- **Solution Management**: They are responsible for product management for the solution that the Solution Train delivers. They own the vision and ensure that the most valuable work is delivered to best serve its customers.
- **Solution Architect**: They own the technical and architectural vision.

At a simple level, they are all scaled versions of the RTE, Product Management, and **Systems Architect** within the ART. But as you might expect, there are nuances, which we will explore later. Working at this scale demands a disciplined approach to establishing and sustaining alignment across the breadth and diversity of ARTs and teams. From their respective domains, they guide the execution to ensure that value flows unobstructed through the value stream, delivering the right thing to the right people at the right time.

So, if this is when you *would* use a Solution Train, what about when you *shouldn't?* You shouldn't use a Solution Train when someone wishes to bypass the design of the ARTs and value streams and says, "Oh, we have 500 people in the IT department, we need a Solution Train." The Solution Train, much like an Agile Team and an ART, consists of the people, resources, systems, and funding necessary to align around a common objective. It is not a container for people merely doing tasks! Effective working will only come when the Solution Train is aligned around a common mission and vision.

Looking at the SAFe® big picture, you'll notice the shaded chevrons that shadow the image, just as they do the ART for Essential SAFe. That's because we are grouping people around a value stream—specifically, a **development value stream** (**DVS**). A DVS is the sequence of steps we go through to create and maintain the systems, products, and solutions we use to serve our customers.

As we've mentioned previously, the first rule of scaling is not to scale. Consequently, if we don't need the size, complexity, and associated coordination costs of utilizing a Solution Train, we shouldn't. Implementing a Solution Train doesn't come for free; you incur an increased cost of alignment through the extra roles, the effort spent coordinating at scale, and the natural inertia of operating at this magnitude, all of which add up.

After reviewing some of the Solution Train's constructs, it's essential to reflect on the process of designing one for optimal value flow.

Solution Train design

Before we discuss the optimizations and trade-offs involved in designing a Solution Train, it's worth reflecting to briefly revisit how these structures are initially formed through the **Value Stream Identification** (**VSI**) workshop. Understanding how ARTs are grouped and aligned to value streams is essential for any RTE working within a Solution Train. Why? Because if the design assumptions made during VSI don't hold true in practice—if teams are misaligned, dependencies are excessive, or value isn't flowing smoothly—then you, as the RTE, will feel the consequences every day. Coordination becomes more difficult, planning becomes less effective, and delivery slows. By understanding how these trains were designed, you will better recognize where friction originates and what options might exist for improvement.

There are five steps in the VSI workshop that we need to walk through to design the ARTs.

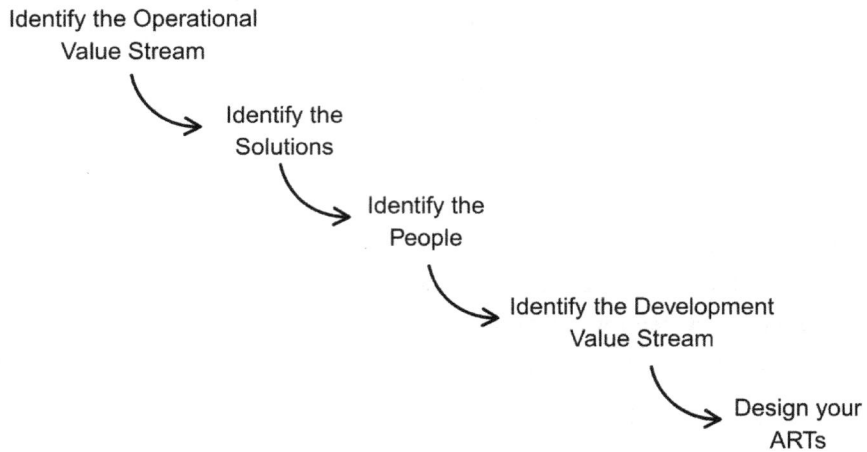

Identify the Operational
Value Stream

        Identify the
        Solutions

                Identify the
                People

                        Identify the Development
                        Value Stream

                                  Design your
                                  ARTs

Figure 11.2: The steps to identify your value streams and design your ARTs

Let's understand these steps:

1. **Identify the operational value stream**: We start with an outside-looking-in view from the customer's perspective, which is the sequence of steps we take to serve them. Be clear on the trigger that starts the process and the value both they and the company receive.

2. **Identify the solutions**: Next, what solutions, systems, or products exist to serve and operate the value stream?

3. **Identify the people**: Who creates and maintains these solutions? Who from around the business supports this process?

4. **Identify the DVS**: Look at which solutions typically get updated in unison with feature requests, creating logical groupings.

5. **Design your ARTs**: Lastly, with the knowledge of the DVS and remembering the first rule of scaling, which is not to scale, how can we construct the smallest, most autonomous group of people possible?

It is during the last step of designing your ARTs that you will realize whether your DVS is large enough to require a Solution Train. When this is the case, there is a sub-stage step of designing the ARTs within the Solution Train, which involves more than simply grouping 125 people into ARTs, akin to filling cups with coffee. Doing so requires consideration of how the ARTs will interact and collaborate with each other.

Before we delve into the considerations and trade-offs, let's examine some design patterns.

ART design patterns

We have three design patterns based on the principles from *Team Topologies* (a book written by Matthew Skelton and Manuel Pais) that SAFe® has implemented for the Solution Train. By using these proven patterns, organizations can dramatically reduce the burden of designing complex **ART structures** from scratch while establishing shared terminology that enables more explicit conversations about solution intent among stakeholders. Decision-makers can more efficiently explore options by focusing on established approaches rather than reinventing the wheel. Also, adding a level of structure to the thinking helps manage what can be an overwhelming task. Let's briefly go through the patterns:

- **Stream-aligned ARTs**: Often the first choice, particularly when the enterprise desires faster time to market. As a scaled version of the cross-functional team, it promotes the flow of value by having the people and the ability to deliver end-to-end, or a sub-part of a product or solution. A stream-aligned ART is linked directly to the value stream steps.

  Taking the example of an e-commerce company, this could be the **Customer Shopping Experience ART**. It would deliver the end-to-end buying journey for customers, from search and product detail pages through to checkout and order confirmation.

- **Complicated subsystem ARTs**: Used where there is a slice of the product or service that requires specific knowledge and skills to work on, owing to its complexity. Breaking this out enables people to focus, reducing the cognitive load.

  Our e-commerce company may utilize the **Recommendation Engine ART**, which develops and maintains machine learning algorithms that generate personalized product recommendations based on customer behavior, inventory, and trends.

- **Platform ARTs**: Provide commonly used services that other stream-aligned ARTs utilize to build the product or service. By offering a building block, the other ARTs can extend and build upon these reusable elements, gaining the benefits of economies of scale through re-use and reduced duplication.

  For our e-commerce example, this could be **Commerce Platform Services ART**, which provides shared services such as pricing, tax calculation, inventory management, and promotion engines used across multiple storefronts and seller portals.

Our advice is that the go-to pattern should be stream aligned, as it offers the most significant benefits in terms of flow, reducing coordination and collaboration costs. It's also most likely the furthest away from your existing organization and technical structure, which, if you're moving to SAFe®, has been identified as lacking (or why would you be changing it?). There are legitimate reasons for using complicated subsystem ARTs and platform ARTs, but do so for good reasons, not just because they are similar to what you currently do or because people feel more comfortable in these patterns.

Trade-offs for design decisions

Before you can decide on a design, you need to consider the trade-offs that such a decision will entail.

Trade-off	Considerations
Alignment vs. autonomy	Alignment is crucial at scale to ensure that everyone is working toward a common objective and is moving in the same direction. It offers reduced friction for coordination and collaboration. But if you overdo it, it hampers localized decision-making and impinges on creativity. Autonomy promotes faster execution and decision-making, which is crucial for a shorter time to market. However, left unchecked, it will result in a fragmented and misaligned solution. The goal is to find a sweet spot where teams are aligned enough to work together effectively, but also have the freedom to innovate and respond to changes quickly.
Complexity vs. simplicity	The solution's complexity and the cognitive load it represents suggest that a complicated subsystem ART is needed. Remember, implementing one increases coordination costs and likely slows flow.

People skills and location	Every ART needs the people and skills they bring to execute effectively. Creating the right blend cannot be done purely on a skills matrix alone. Geographic location and the time zones involved can reduce overlapping working hours, which can impede collaboration and increase travel costs for face-to-face meetings and events.
	Do you have existing, highly performing teams? Splitting them will have a short-term impact on delivery. Does this impact and the cost of change outweigh the expected benefits?
	When you have limited capacity in specialist roles, consider their placement carefully. Spreading them over multiple ARTs might serve the ART, but it could weaken the discipline; therefore, a **Community of Practice (CoP)** may be necessary to address this issue. Alternatively, you might form this group as a shared service supporting any ART that needs them, but this can create commitment and prioritization challenges.
	Finally, reflect on the employee well-being of the design—are you creating undue stress or challenge?
Flow vs. control	Optimal flow states occur when teams and ARTs can work with minimal friction, bottlenecks, and delays. To avoid sub-optimization and find that one ART works well at the cost of others, how will the appropriate controls be implemented and used to enable effective integration and alignment of shared delivery milestones? Many elements come naturally from SAFe®, but, as is often the case, how you implement it can affect the outcomes.
Customer needs vs. technical feasibility	Your customer-centric, stream-aligned ARTs focus on delivering features to customers quickly and efficiently. While this serves customers and the business's commercial needs with ease, it can create technical and architectural pain points, resulting in technical debt.
	If you are optimizing for speed of delivery, what mechanisms need to be put in place (e.g., CoPs, design authority working groups, architectural governance, etc.) to mitigate the risk?
	Conversely, create a complicated subsystem or platform ART. It can often have a technical focus and require coordination and alignment with other ARTs to complete work in a flow state. Therefore, your communication and collaboration costs will be higher, likely necessitating more frequent touchpoints to maintain synchronization.

Table 11.1: ART design trade-off considerations

Let's take these concepts and reflect on a customer story to demonstrate the trade-offs and decisions made.

Evolving ARTs for new UI platform development: a case study

Our client was modernizing their product by transitioning from a traditional desktop application to a web-based point-of-sale interface. This new UI promised numerous advantages, including improved usability and a more contemporary experience.

Initial approach

We faced a critical decision: should we distribute UI development teams across multiple ARTs, or create a dedicated ART focused solely on the new interface? While distributing teams would have made it easier for individual ARTs to integrate with the new interface, we ultimately chose to establish a dedicated ART. This decision was driven by the fact that the point-of-sale system was not yet production-ready and required a significant investment to bring it to that point. Even after initial deployment, maintaining a singular ART enabled a strong technical and architectural focus, creating a stable foundation for the future platform.

Reassessment and evolution

Approximately 18 months later, we conducted another VSI workshop to reassess the ART design. After carefully considering the trade-offs, we decided to disband the dedicated UI ART and distribute teams across the other ARTs. This reorganization optimized workflow and made it easier for teams to implement UI features within their specific domains. However, we recognized that this approach risked introducing architectural and technical debt to the platform.

Mitigating risk through a hybrid structure

To address potential inconsistencies while maintaining the flow, we established several dedicated teams outside the formal ART structure, but following the portfolio cadence introduced by SAFe®. These teams held technical and design authority over the architectural patterns for the new interface. They functioned as consultants rather than implementers—other teams would approach them for guidance on adding functionality, but would generally implement the features themselves. This hybrid approach balanced domain ownership with architectural consistency.

> **Key learning**
>
> This case study demonstrates a fundamental principle of Agile architecture: what works today may not be optimal tomorrow. By periodically reflecting on our organizational design and willingly evolving our approach, we ensured that our structure remained optimized for current needs rather than historical requirements. The journey from centralized to distributed UI development, with appropriate guardrails, highlights the importance of adaptability in scaled Agile transformations.

Taking all of these factors into account enables the design process to proceed. However, as SAFe® Fellow Mark Richards says, *"There is an art to ART design,"* and you won't know how effective your choices are until you start using them. Before implementation, though, you can reduce risk by conducting a tabletop simulation exercise with real or simulated **epics** and **features** to determine which ARTs need to work on them. Your objective is to have as few ARTs working simultaneously as possible. If you find that every ART needs to be involved for every change, assuming this isn't just a highly complex solution, then you might realize your design isn't well optimized.

Finally, during the design phase, for ARTs of all sizes, whether standalone or within a Solution Train, they are designed with the people to be included. However, for now, you don't need to create and optimize the team design; the RTE can address this later.

With the designs in place, we now need to understand how planning and alignment work.

Using multiple planning horizons

We've met some people who believe that when they look at the SAFe big picture, it is a management hierarchy with top-down control, but the reality is that it is a Product Management hierarchy with aligned autonomy.

Let's consider this through the metaphor of an airplane.

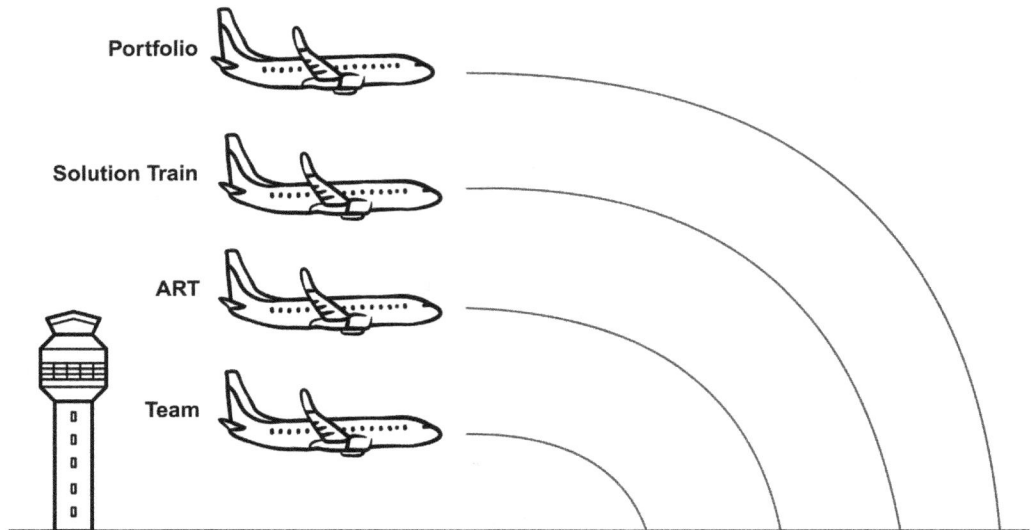

Figure 11.3: Planning horizons using an airplane metaphor

The aviation metaphor works on distinct levels, each representing a different planning horizon.

At the *Team* level, like a plane taxiing at the airport, there is high visibility and definition of the immediate surroundings—the field, gate, and even the marshal with their guidance panels. The planning horizon is short and detailed, likely extending only to the end of the runway. The pilot can see the terminal clearly, but anything beyond the airport's boundary remains vague and undefined.

As we ascend to the *ART* level, at a few thousand feet, the aircraft can still make out the airport below, albeit with less detail, but its focus extends further across the surrounding area. At this altitude, the terminal is visible, but with little detail. This level connects to detailed ground operations and broader journey planning, as ART Product Management knows the destination but not the specific runway or gate.

Climbing higher at the *Solution Train* level, we reach an intermediate cruising altitude where we're now flying a larger aircraft—perhaps a wide-body jet carrying multiple crews (akin to ARTs), working together on a complex, multi-faceted mission. At this altitude, the Solution Train can see across broader regions and coordinate the various specialized teams within the same aircraft, ensuring that their combined efforts align toward the shared destination while managing the dependencies between their interconnected work.

Rising to the *Portfolio* level, akin to cruising altitude, the airport's visibility has long gone, but the view encompasses the ultimate destination country. The ground below shows little detail, but **Epic Owners** and the fiduciaries within the **Strategic Portfolio Review** (**SPR**) can see terrain and weather patterns to navigate over a considerable distance into the future. At this level, a major city might be the target, but lower-level details have minimal impact on the journey planning.

Connecting all four levels is the golden thread of how to reach the destination, with each level working within its appropriate detail and planning horizon to achieve the overall outcome.

When applied to SAFe®, this multi-layered perspective takes concrete form. At the *Portfolio* level (cruising altitude), the most significant pieces of work—**portfolio epics**—are prioritized and sequenced, typically looking ahead over an extended planning horizon of 18 months to 3 years. The epics provide the strategic *country* destination and a broad navigation path.

Working down through the layers, at the *ART* level, the focus narrows to creating plans for a **Planning Increment** of 10 weeks, with visibility extending to a roadmap for a couple of PIs beyond that. This is analogous to seeing beyond the airport while maintaining awareness of the broader journey.

At the *Team* level (taxiing), planning becomes increasingly detailed and immediate—teams plan for the entire PI but focus intensely on their two-week iterations and ultimately refine their path during daily **Team Syncs**. Here, like a pilot navigating the immediate surroundings of the runway and terminal, teams have a high definition of near-term work.

SAFe thus operates as a series of loosely coupled planning horizons, operating independently while being influenced by and influencing those around it. Each level maintains autonomy with delegated decision-making authority to define the most valuable work within its scope while remaining aligned to the ultimate destination set out by the portfolio's strategic themes. **Strategic themes** create a coherent thread from high-level strategic themes, providing direction down to day-to-day execution, with each level maintaining the appropriate level of detail for its planning horizon.

Consequently, each level in the framework creates roadmaps, showing the indicative direction of travel, demonstrating what it believes will be delivered when. These roadmaps are indicative as they are only a forecast based on what is known today. While each level, e.g., portfolio, Solution Train, and ART, is independent of the others, they are connected through the golden thread of strategic themes and the decomposition of high-level demand signals. As the Product Management function at each level—**Solution Management**, **Product Management**, and **Product Owner**—has content authority at their respective level, their roadmaps will incorporate both work derived from the local context and linked work to the next level up. As an RTE, you sit in the middle of this. You're helping Product Managers manage their ART-level roadmap, ensuring it aligns with both the broader solution plan and the reality of team capacity and delivery. Your role is to facilitate a two-way conversation, supporting both top-down alignment and bottom-up realism, so the roadmap becomes a tool for insight, not just aspiration.

At the **Large Solution** layer, the unit of work is the **capability**. Capabilities can span multiple ARTs within a Solution Train, but are still delivered within a single PI. Remember that anything longer than a PI is an epic. Capabilities are programmed through features in ARTs and delivered by the teams through the stories they provide. However, while these delivery-focused roadmaps add value, a different perspective of the work can also enhance value by demonstrating what will be achieved at the product or solution level. These product and solution roadmaps articulate the evolution, aligned with the product vision, often through a consumable lens to your customers.

With ARTs designed and a roadmap in place, it's time to move on to how planning in a Solution Train operates.

The planning cycle

By now, you've hopefully experienced and begun to master the skill of facilitating PI Planning for your ART. Doing so as part of a Solution Train adds additional layers of complexity and co-ordination due to the scale and cross-ART alignment involved. As with any human endeavor at this scale, there is a cost of alignment. For a Solution Train to be successful, it comes down to effective *stage management*.

Pre-planning

The roadmaps, as discussed earlier in this chapter, offer some insight into the answer. However, more often than not, a few weeks ahead of PI Planning, the STE is likely to bring the leaders of the ARTs together to confirm agreement on the work that will be planned and which ARTs, and potentially which teams (particularly where integration is complex or timing is critical), will be working on it. The outcome of this will be an agreement on the capabilities to be planned and an initial view of where dependencies will occur, needing teams to collaborate and align during the planning event. *Table 11.2* shows an example of what this might look like, although a scaled ART Board with string and sticky notes can work just as well.

ART	Team	Capability 1	Capability 2	Capability 3	Capability 4
Customer Shopping Experience	Code Red	x			
	Fern	x		x	
	Trekkies		x	x	
Recommendation Engine	AI Nerds	x			
	Data Warehousing				x
Commerce Platform Services	Compliance				x
	Banking		x		

Table 11.2: Example pre-planning capability to ART and team mapping matrix

This is an example output from a pre-planning meeting, mapping capabilities to ARTs and their respective teams. It shows which teams are expected to contribute to which capabilities in the upcoming PI, helping to coordinate delivery across the solution. For example, within the **Customer Shopping Experience ART**, the **Code Red** and **Fern** teams are aligned to **Capability 1**, while **Trekkies** support **Capability 2** and **Capability 3**. This mapping provides early visibility into cross-team collaboration needs and potential dependencies, ensuring better alignment during PI Planning.

View Solution Train pre-planning as a dependency reduction system rather than just dependency management. It allows ART leaders the time and space to resequence work, modify scopes, or align on shared architectural patterns that lessen the need for handoffs later.

Having created alignment through the pre-planning activities, each respective ART and their teams undertake a pretty standard preparation process, albeit sometimes talking to teams on other ARTs.

PI Planning

There are subtle nuances in PI Planning itself, but for most people involved, the differences are not dramatic. At the start of the day, to maintain alignment, the Solution Train will present some information through the **Business Context** briefings to all ARTs.

Here's a visualization of how the Solution Train and ARTs PI Planning is set out over the two days:

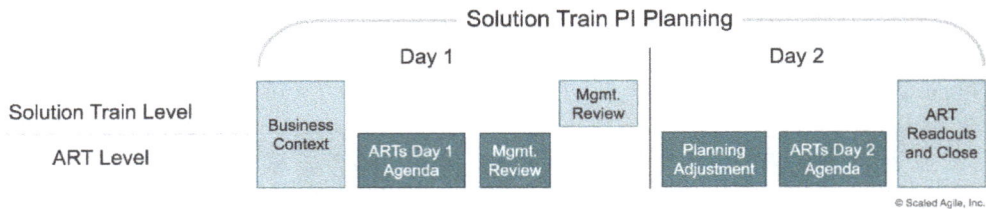

Figure 11.4: A typical Solution Train PI Planning agenda pattern (© Scaled Agile, Inc. Source:
`https://framework.scaledagile.com/coordinate-and-deliver/`)

Then, during the team breakout periods and if the ARTs are all planning simultaneously, in addition to the ART-level Scrum of Scrums that you, as the RTE, with the **Scrum Masters** hold, the STE will host similar sync sessions with all the RTEs. When there isn't simultaneous planning, you still need to maintain alignment, utilizing whatever options you have at your disposal, even if this is asynchronous and non-verbal, e.g. roadmaps, planning progress, Solution Intent, chat or messaging systems (e.g., Slack of Teams) and tooling that shows plans and planning artifacts, such as the ART Planning board and draft PI Objectives.

During team breakout sessions, teams may need to communicate with other teams on a different ART to address dependencies, schedule and align deliveries, as well as the features within the ART.

At the end of the day, after the ARTs hold their local **Management Review**, the Solution Train runs a scaled-up version. Typical conversations occur, but they are *zoomed out* at the ART level rather than the team level.

Finally, at the end of the second day, a combined **Final Plan Readout** session happens.

Having planned, we will move on to look at a specific point of execution, applying a disciplined approach to engineering that maintains alignment while promoting agility at scale.

Need for disciplined engineering practices using the Solution Intent

At a small scale, engineering decisions occur naturally: over a desk, in a chat, or scribbled on a whiteboard. We actively encourage this behavior, as does the **Agile Manifesto**, encouraging face-to-face interaction. Yet as we scale across multiple ARTs into Solution Trains, these more personal approaches, such as picking up the phone to talk to the architect, while still valuable and desirable, begin to face practical challenges. The cost of misalignment grows, and the ripple effects of the disconnect between decisions, assumptions, and delivery spread far and wide.

So, we need to be more disciplined in our approach when working at a larger scale. Not in a bureaucratic, traditional way, but in a way aligned with Agile and Lean principles. One that honors the context of hundreds or thousands of people working collectively toward a common objective. Scaling comes at a cost—the cost of creating alignment, maintaining a common understanding, and coordination. These costs are one of the reasons why we encourage people not to jump into launching a Solution Train unless they need to and will get the benefit from it.

The Solution Architect, or in reality, the team of Solution Architects working with the System Architects in the ARTs, is critical to setting standards and creating the basis for alignment and understanding. The practices within the framework create a structure to support the coordination alongside artifacts such as the **Solution Context** and **Solution Intent**. The Solution Context, while not specific to Solution Trains, becomes more critical as it documents the environment in which the solution is created, maintained, and used. We will see what the Solution Intent is and how it links to the context in the next section.

Understanding the Solution Intent

The Solution Intent is the central, evolving artifact that provides a single source of truth regarding what the solution is today and what it will be tomorrow, as well as how it will be built. It uses the language of **fixed intent** and **variable intent**. Fixed items are behaviors that the solution must deploy, such as regulatory or must-have functionality, alongside capabilities already deployed. Variable intent is the art of the possible—things that the Solution Train might deliver in the future. The Solution Intent works in unison with the Solution Content, which describes the environment and users of the solution.

A disciplined approach doesn't mean rigid thinking. Encourage teams to challenge assumptions about what is truly fixed. It's easy to fall into the habit of labeling things as non-negotiable—especially when words such as *regulatory* or *compliance* are used—but often it's the *outcome* that must be achieved, not a specific implementation. By separating the *what* from the *how*, teams can explore more flexible, innovative, and efficient ways to meet requirements without unnecessarily locking down the solution too early.

The following figure shows how the Solution Intent brings together specifications, design, and tests to provide a structured yet flexible view of the current and future solution.

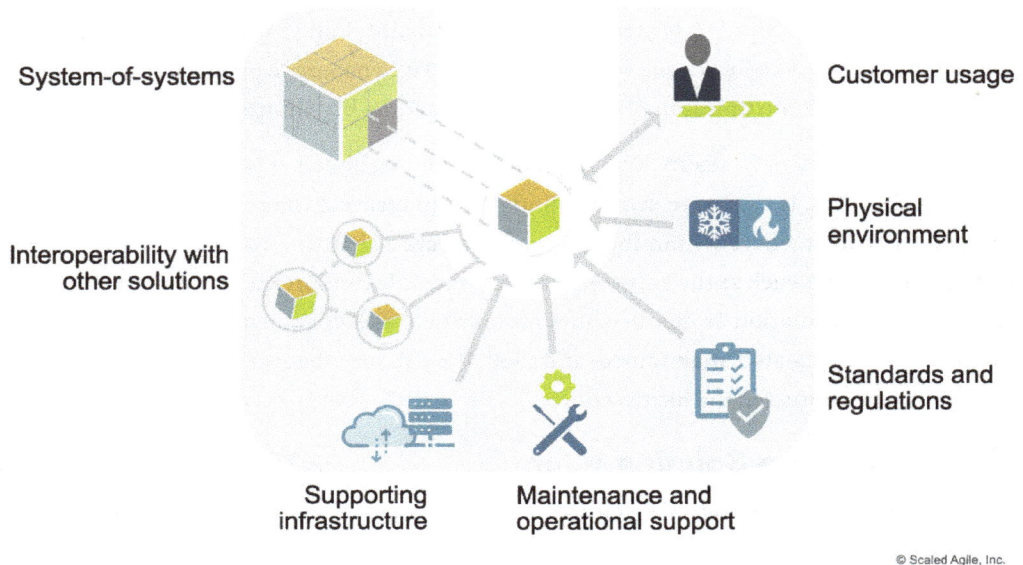

Figure 11.5: The Solution Intent, the artifact that holds current and future states of the solution (© Scaled Agile, Inc. Source: `https://framework.scaledagile.com/large-solution-integration-and-delivery-discipline`*)*

There is no specificity on how an organization captures the Solution Intent, just that the three critical elements (**Specification**, **Design**, and **Tests**) are captured. As a consequence of scale alone, your organization will likely already have tooling in place that captures this information. The challenge comes when this is a legacy toolset that is not supportive of Agile, iterative development. That being said, the tooling doesn't have to be fancy; if you have a small Solution Train, capturing it in tools such as Jira and Confluence could be effective enough, although it might not meet your regulatory requirements if relevant. We highly recommend that whatever tool you use, it supports **model-based systems engineering** (**MBSE**).

Regardless of how it is documented, an investment is required to maintain it so that it aligns with both the current and desired future state for every PI. Like any information store, it will need curation and regular maintenance to keep it in effective working order; the moment you cannot trust the documentation, its value depreciates immediately. We would expect this to be led by the Solution Architect and Solution Management, with facilitation and coaching from the STE. Updates to it should be shared widely and often; the **System Demos** are a perfect opportunity to do so.

Why does the Solution Intent matter?

At scale, traceability and auditability become a necessary economic consideration. Nobody can hold a mental model of the entire solution, so it must be documented as a lasting body of knowledge to support those working on evolving it. These large solutions have a life well beyond the typical tenure of staff in the modern workforce, so it also becomes a continuity issue as people come and go.

When it comes to solutions that operate in regulated environments, these elements become non-negotiable demands on how you operate. With the right tooling in place, you can operate with agility at scale and always be compliance-ready, unlocking frequent deployments. These regulatory and compliance activities act like a tax on your business operations, so it's imperative to reduce the cost and enable the time to market that you and your customers demand.

These factors make architecture the backbone that answers the question, "How will the solution be built?", evolving over time as understanding is achieved and demands adapt based on market needs, balancing intentional and emergent designs. Maintaining this balance is one of the primary objectives of Solution Architects. Endeavoring to avoid impinging on fast feedback and continuous learning, while maintaining alignment to reduce rework and accelerate time to market. In essence, it's the balance between speed of execution and risk, without constant hand-holding from the Solution Architect.

Disciplined engineering in practice

Given that teams won't have the luxury of being able to chat with the Solution Architect every time they have a query, the Solution Intent as a repository of knowledge enables teams to act with autonomy, making informed decisions that are aligned with the solution today and the direction of travel.

Teams can reference the Solution Intent to understand the rationale behind architectural decisions, see what has already been tried, and why specific approaches were chosen or rejected. In doing so, it reduces the likelihood of teams inadvertently working against each other or duplicating effort across ARTs. When a team encounters a technical challenge, they can first consult the Solution Intent to see whether similar problems have been solved elsewhere in the solution or whether their proposed approach conflicts with established patterns.

The variable intent proves to be a helpful guide here. By seeing not just what must be delivered but also what might be delivered, teams are helped in making tactical decisions that keep future options open. For example, a team working on a payment system might discover that future variable intent includes support for cryptocurrency transactions, influencing their current API design choices without over-engineering for uncertain requirements.

Cadence offers value here, too. Referring to Solution Intent during PI Planning ensures that what teams are planning aligns with both fixed and variable intent. This isn't about approval or control, but about surfacing potential conflicts early when they're cheap to resolve rather than expensive to unpick later.

The real test comes when teams face the inevitable trade-offs. With Solution Intent as their guide, they can make decisions that serve the broader solution context rather than optimizing locally. When teams do need to reach out to the Solution Architect (and they should when facing significant decisions), both parties are working from the same shared understanding, making those conversations more focused and productive. The investment in maintaining this living documentation pays dividends by enabling distributed decision-making that remains coherent across the solution landscape, while keeping the Solution Architect engaged where their expertise adds the most value, rather than being consumed by constant clarification requests.

Let us examine a case study that explores the challenges and costs associated with failing to apply this disciplined approach. The aerospace industry provides exceptionally compelling examples because the stakes are so high, both in terms of safety and commercial success. What makes these failures particularly instructive is that they rarely stem from a lack of technical capability or innovation. Instead, they highlight how the absence of coordinated practices—the very coordination that Solution Intent is designed to provide—can derail even the most sophisticated engineering efforts. The costs of retrofitting discipline into an already complex system invariably exceed the investment required to embed it from the outset.

Case study: The implications of not following a disciplined approach

In 2008, Boeing's flagship 787 Dreamliner encountered a highly publicized delay. This delay was not due to hardware or mechanical failures but to insufficient traceability and documentation of critical software components. Pat Shanahan, vice president and general manager of Boeing's 787 Dreamliner program, explained, *"It's not that the brakes don't work; it's the traceability of the software."*

Boeing recognized that adding traceability to demonstrate software compliance retroactively would be challenging and prone to errors. This predicament compelled engineers to make the costly and time-consuming decision to rewrite extensive sections of software from scratch.

This costly example shows that disciplined engineering practices are essential safeguards at scale. Without traceability, compliance, and documentation—core to effective systems engineering—complex R&D projects risk disruptions and rising costs.

Boeing's experience demonstrates that rigorous engineering practices from the outset prevent costly rework and regulatory risks. Engineering discipline is not bureaucratic overhead; it is foundational to managing complexity and achieving predictable, sustainable success as solutions evolve.

Applying a disciplined approach maximizes economies of scale and resilience, while also helping to optimize workflow, mainly by avoiding the introduction of waste into the system. Ways you can promote this include the following:

- **Anchor the use of the Solution Intent during PI Planning**: Do this both in preparation for and during the event itself, as the single source of truth. Teams on the ART should use it to maintain alignment and understand the situational context of how the solution arrived at its current state.
- **Spot cross-ART duplication**: In large, complex solutions, it is challenging, if not impossible, for teams to mentally model what every other team or ART is doing. Encourage Product Management and System Architects to use it to verify that their plans are not duplicates or conflicting with other ART.
- **Use Solution Intent as a first-stop reference**: Guide Scrum Masters and teams to review the Solution Intent before escalating queries to the Solution Architect, reducing bottlenecks and encouraging autonomy.
- **Keep it updated**: Check in with System and Solution Architects periodically to ensure that this repository of knowledge is being maintained, curated, and edited.
- **Reinforce alignment over approval**: Frame Solution Intent not as a control mechanism but as a guide that helps teams make better decisions in line with long-term strategy.
- **Use it as a catalyst for a conversation between Architects and teams**: Help different cohorts use the Solution Intent as a focal point of their conversations, instead of reinventing the world.
- **Embed it into your ART events**: Include periodic walkthroughs or recaps of the Solution Intent in Inspect & Adapt, ART Syncs, or System Demos to keep it visible and relevant.

Next, we turn to the suppliers and how enterprises can maximize delivery outcomes and value by their strategic inclusion on a Solution Train.

Suppliers on a Solution Train

Suppliers are part of the Solution Train's construct on the big picture. We find that this can confuse two fronts. Firstly, some think the supplier construct is for when they have an outsourced partner working alongside their teams. Secondly, some portfolios without Solution Trains use suppliers and don't understand how to work with them when they don't have a Solution Train.

Let's address the construct of what it is and isn't. As modeled on the big picture, a supplier is a vendor you are using to provide an element of your solution that operates as a black box. By this, we mean they have a contract to provide you with an element of your solution, but you have not specified, or did not specify, how they would work. They have the autonomy to work as they see fit. It is counter to what many believe it shows, that of an outsourcing partner who provides staff to work alongside your own teams. With an outsourcing partner, they effectively act like employees of your own company, with access to your IT systems and adherence to the processes and ways of working you stipulate. The only difference is the company's name at the top of their paycheck.

The outsourcing of staff in the augmentation model would result in either team members, entire teams, or an entire ART working seamlessly within a portfolio. A supplier, however, will unlikely share their staffing profile and working practices in delivering their part of the solution.

So, what if you don't have a Solution Train, but are using a supplier as we've outlined? We encourage you not to overthink it. SAFe® is a framework, and therefore, you should not follow it without consideration; it can be adjusted as needed. If you have a supplier who works alongside an ART, ask yourself whether you can coordinate your deliverables simply and reliably enough through the ART leadership (the RTE, PM, and SA). If so, they can sit adjacent to the ART. If you feel that the complexity and coordination effort required are greater, you might find that the Solution Train construct offers value, but it wouldn't be your first choice.

When might we use a supplier? There are various reasons why you might consider this operating model:

- **Lack of skills to build it**: Scaling up a delivery capacity, let alone achieving the point where it performs efficiently, can be challenging. Either because of time to market or a lack of desire, you may find a supplier who can create the thing you need faster.

- **Avoiding upfront investment**: When the element you need is a variation of something already existing, working with a supplier who has built it before can reduce the need for costly upfront development. You're leveraging their existing capabilities, tools, and expertise, saving time and initial expense. While the long-term unit cost may be higher, the trade-off often brings faster time to market, a higher level of functionality, and improved quality by building on a proven, mature solution.

- **Lack of capacity**: If you are undertaking a transformation or business refactoring, there may already be too many moving parts. Handing the delivery to another provider offers the organization headspace to focus on other higher-value improvements.

- **Not strategic**: You need the thing, but it is more of a commodity than the rest of your solution. It can make sense to focus your efforts on the elements of your solution that contribute to your distinctiveness.

- **Legacy contract**: Operating at scale with partners will create multi-year contractual agreements. If you are moving to SAFe®, you might inherit legacy contracts and working methods. Here, you simply need to do the best you can within the constraints of the contract and the vendors' appetite to adjust their ways of working.

- **Regulatory or compliance requirements**: In some industries (e.g., aerospace, defense, or healthcare), pre-approved suppliers may be required for compliance, audit, or certification purposes.

- **Access to intellectual property (IP)**: If another organization owns IP protected through patents, you have no option but to source through them if they will not license it.

Regardless of how the contract is structured, we encourage you to work collaboratively with them operationally and treat them like partners rather than adversaries, which will yield dividends unless specific circumstances dictate otherwise.

> **The power of asking**
>
> Once, while working for a utility company, Glenn encountered a potential roadblock to their Agile adoption—their outsource partner, whose teams were in India, had been contracted traditionally, working on specific, scoped, and sized delivery items. He met the on-site contact for coffee one day and outlined the transformation's objectives to see what might be possible within the existing contract. The response from the outsourcer shocked him. They responded that they would love to do Agile; in fact, they had already done so. They had been taking the fixed elements of work presented to them from the utility and using Agile in their teams to deliver it for some time. Going forward, the outsourcer sought ways to expose the working methods while remaining true to the contract, mindful that renegotiating was well above everyone's pay grade and not something that could be accomplished quickly between two large international enterprises.
>
> As Glenn's father used to say to him, *"If you don't ask, you don't get!"*

Having looked at some of the differences and challenges of running at scale using a Solution Train, let's look next at what being an RTE as part of a Solution Train is like before moving on to the STE role.

Being an RTE in a Solution Train

An RTE operating on a Solution Train retains fundamentally the same core responsibilities as their counterparts on standard ARTs, with the primary distinction being the expanded scope and complexity of their coordination efforts. They continue to serve as the chief facilitator for aligning the teams on the ART toward common objectives, ensuring that each team understands their role within the broader solution context while maintaining clear communication channels across all participating teams. This alignment becomes increasingly critical on Solution Trains due to the increased number of stakeholders and the interdependent nature of the various ARTs contributing to the overall solution.

The essential activities of conducting PI Planning sessions and managing team dependencies remain central to the RTE's role; however, these responsibilities scale significantly when orchestrating across multiple trains. The RTE must facilitate cross-ART coordination during PI Planning, ensuring that dependencies between different release trains are identified, prioritized, and effectively managed throughout the Program Increment. Despite the added complexity, the fundamental focus on delivering value to customers remains unchanged. The RTE continues to drive the elimination of impediments, foster continuous improvement, and ensure that all teams maintain their commitment to delivering working solutions that meet customer needs and business objectives.

However, when an RTE transitions to working within a Solution Train environment, the scope and complexity of their coordination responsibilities expand considerably. Rather than orchestrating activities within a single ART, they must now support coordination in partnership with other RTEs and the STE across multiple release trains, each with its own culture and delivery commitments. This multiplication of moving parts requires the RTE to utilize the dependency mapping identified during pre-planning and PI Planning, which spans the trains across the Solution Train. This mapping identifies not just the traditional team-to-team dependencies within one ART but also the more complex inter-train dependencies that can create significant bottlenecks if not adequately managed. Consequently, the communication and synchronization requirements increase, as the RTE must support the establishment and maintenance of effective channels between diverse teams that may have different working practices and technical approaches.

The alignment responsibilities also broaden significantly from ensuring that teams within one train work cohesively to orchestrating multiple ARTs into a coherent solution roadmap. This requires closer collaboration with peer RTEs, moving beyond occasional coordination to regularly working together, ensuring system-wide flow. The RTE must shift its focus from ART-level PI Objectives to solution-level OKRs, requiring a deeper understanding of how individual train contributions aggregate into meaningful customer and business outcomes.

Perhaps most significantly, the RTE's perspective must evolve from the relatively short-term focus of one to two Program Increments to a much longer strategic horizon, often spanning three years or more. This extended timeframe requires the RTE to help guide the long-term evolution of the solution architecture and delivery capability, moving beyond immediate delivery concerns to consider how the solution will adapt and scale over time. Consequently, the role evolves from primarily tactical facilitation to strategic oversight, with less direct interaction with individual teams and greater focus on enabling entire ARTs to deliver effectively. The RTE becomes responsible for maintaining alignment and coherence at the solution level, ensuring that the collective efforts of multiple trains result in a unified, valuable solution rather than a collection of disparate components.

To better understand this, we interviewed Annette Gomez, of CVS Health, about her tips for working effectively across the Solution Train with the other RTEs.

Working across ARTs and interviewing Annette Gomez, CVS Health

In a Solution Train, the role of an RTE shifts from orchestrating a single ART to contributing to a broader network of coordinated value delivery. Annette shared in her interview that success comes not just from structure and tooling, but from trust, relationships, and steady rhythms of communication.

Start with relationships, not just roles

Working across ARTs begins with building genuine connections. Annette described how she and her fellow RTEs would hold informal weekly catch-ups—not merely to exchange status updates, but to remain close, discuss challenges, and simply get to know one another as individuals. These weren't polished stakeholder syncs—they were open, candid, and often unstructured by design.

"There was a great collaboration between the RTEs. We were very closely connected and shared a lot of stuff."

—Annette

In practice, this meant being transparent about difficulties, remaining calm under pressure, and creating an environment that fosters honesty. Establishing psychological safety among peers enabled the RTEs to challenge one another constructively, admit when things weren't going as planned, and co-create solutions without ego.

Coordinate through shared understanding

Formal coordination mechanisms still matter. Annette highlighted how OKRs provided a common north star for multiple ARTs, and how shared planning boards—whether physical or digital—made dependencies visible and actionable. Keeping all ARTs on the same cadence was essential, not only for synchronized delivery but to maintain a common planning rhythm and pace of feedback.

Documentation also played a role. It wasn't heavy or bureaucratic, but it was reliable. Plans and dependencies were recorded and updated to ensure continuity and clarity between trains.

Make time for collaboration and support

Collaboration didn't stop at alignment meetings. RTEs would regularly join each other's meetings (with permission) to observe, support, and spot improvement opportunities. Some even experimented with joint office hours or cross-train **Retrospectives**, which helped create a sense of shared ownership across ART boundaries.

These interactions weren't just functional—they were social, too. Opportunities to build camaraderie—through shared lunches, coffee chats, or just checking in—proved invaluable when navigating the complexities of large-scale delivery.

The mindset that makes it work

Ultimately, what set these RTEs apart wasn't a process—it was a mindset. They showed up as peers, not competitors. They balanced confidence with humility. They brought their experiences to the table, but never presumed to have all the answers. And they remained willing to learn from each other, from their teams, and from the system as it evolved.

As Annette shares, the RTEs within the Solution Train will perform best when they work together as a team. It demonstrates that Annette and her colleagues demonstrated systems thinking by working together for the broader benefit of the solution. Some other suggestions for activities RTEs can undertake together to strengthen the links and outcomes are as follows:

- **Industrial tourism**: Undertake a **Gemba walk** (a Lean approach where you learn about a situation, the place where work is actually done) by visiting other RTEs to see how they fulfill their responsibilities, such as PI Planning. But don't just observe, take part, maybe even lead.

- **Collaborate on defining standards**: There may be opportunities to create alignment and improve cross-ART working through defining standard artifact formats or definitions of done.

- **Work together to solve cross-ART challenges**: Many hands make light work! And many heads come up with creative, intelligent solutions. Chances are, if one ART is experiencing a systemic problem in the organization, others are too.

- **Create a CoP**: Improvements only come from being deliberate. Create a time and space for the RTEs to foster shared learning, separate from their day-to-day operational work.

Working with the STE

Working with the STE is a scaled-up version of the RTE-Scrum Master relationship. Just as a Scrum Master clears the path for a team and facilitates flow, the STE operates across the entire Solution Train—enabling collaboration, supporting delivery, and ensuring alignment across multiple ARTs. The difference lies in the altitude from our earlier plane analogy: the STE takes a strategic, longer-term view, focusing on multi-PI Planning horizons and system-wide health, while RTEs remain closer to the tactical realities of implementation. The STE acts as a stage manager for the whole production, ensuring that all moving parts, people, and objectives come together in harmony. This isn't to say that the STE doesn't care about the current PI and its deliveries; they very much do. However scale dictates, they need to rely on their RTEs in the same way the RTE relies on their Scrum Masters, while also stepping back and looking into the future.

In our interview with Annette, she emphasized the importance of maintaining open communication with her STE, even when it required making difficult decisions. That trust enabled her to speak up when she disagreed with an approach, offering insights from the ART level that might not have been apparent at the solution layer. The STE isn't there to direct; it serves a support role, empowering RTEs to succeed by establishing expectations, offering coaching, and keeping the bigger picture in mind.

For an RTE, this relationship works best when it's built on transparency and mutual respect. The STE relies on you to provide a clear view of what's happening on the ground; you rely on them to shape and sustain the broader system. Just as Scrum Masters guide teams while enabling autonomy, STEs guide RTEs—creating clarity without constraining progress.

Participating in the Solution Train syncs

As we've already outlined, coordination, collaboration, and communication at scale become harder; therefore, it is essential to be intentional in your practice to promote effective working patterns. Similarly, as the ART scales the Team Sync to the **Coach Sync** and **PO Sync**, the Solution Train scales these to the **RTE Sync**, **PM Sync**, and **Architecture Sync**. You may not be directly involved in all syncs, but you will need to support the facilitation of their effectiveness, just as you rely on your ART Scrum Masters to help you.

RTE Sync

In this meeting, you will engage with the STE and other RTEs to ensure alignment, enhance operational efficiencies, and address any challenges. Although these meetings are typically held weekly, the frequency may vary based on necessity. They are particularly effective when coordinated with ART events, held just after, as the RTEs can collectively tackle any arising risks and issues.

Don't see these meetings as just formal working sessions; make the most of building connections, too. Annette told us that in her Solution Train, the RTEs have weekly informal sessions to not only provide time for collaboration but also to develop the personal relationships so critical for successful working.

The session might follow the following running order:

- Blockers and impediments
- Review actions and outcomes
- Progress updates
- Review risks

PM Sync

Primarily for the Product Management and Solution Management communities, you are welcome to attend if needed. You will support removing blocks that arise from the meeting and collaborate with your Product Management team to communicate changes in scope and upcoming work to the teams on the ART.

Topics covered include the following:

- Issues and opportunities
- Action progress from the last sync
- Progress updates for the current PI
- Scope and prioritization updates
- Backlog and roadmap preparation for future PIs

Architecture Sync

Unlike the ART level, the Solution Train level also has the Architecture Sync. It ensures consistency in designs and trade-offs across the Solution Train. It is not just for System and Solution Architects but also for other key technical stakeholders as needed. Again, your involvement will likely focus on resolving issues and promoting constructive participation.

The architects will follow a running order similar to the following:

- Review action items
- Current PI trade-off and design decisions
- Addressing issues or risks
- Architectural general updates
- Enabler backlog for upcoming PIs

Now, instead of being an RTE for an ART on Solution Train, what if you were to become the STE yourself?

Being an STE in a Solution Train

The transition from RTE to STE is more than just a change in job title — it's a change in altitude. Where the RTE is immersed in delivery detail, cadences, and team dynamics across a single train, the STE operates on a broader level. They look out across the entire Solution Train, shaping alignment, fostering strategic flow, and creating the conditions for multiple ARTs to move in concert.

This role isn't about controlling the trains—it's about enabling them to run smoothly.

Consequently, the STE can spend approximately 50% of their time working beyond the boundaries of the Solution Train itself, focusing on the interface between the solution delivery capability and the broader organizational ecosystem. This external focus recognizes that Solution Trains operate within complex organizational environments where success depends as much on effective stakeholder management and organizational alignment as it does on internal coordination and delivery execution.

Much of this external work centers on education and preparation activities that create the conditions for Solution Train success. Key activities include the following:

- **Stakeholder education and alignment**: Teaching organizational leaders, business stakeholders, and external teams about Solution Train principles, working methods, and delivery cadences to ensure realistic expectations and appropriate engagement patterns

- **Dependency management and work preparation**: Identifying and managing external dependencies that could impact solution delivery, while preparing work and stakeholders well in advance of PI Planning to prevent last-minute disruptions or poorly defined requirements being pushed into ARTs

- **Organizational impediment removal**: Working with leadership and support functions to create flow by addressing structural, procedural, or cultural barriers that prevent the Solution Train from operating effectively

- **Strategic alignment facilitation**: Ensuring that organizational strategy translates coherently into Solution Train goals and that feedback from solution delivery informs strategic decision-making

The STE faces particular challenges in getting the organization ready to work effectively with the Solution Train model, often requiring significant cultural and procedural changes in how external groups engage with delivery teams, plan work, and measure success.

From doer to enabler

One of the hardest shifts for new STEs is stepping back. As an RTE, you were often the glue holding planning, teams, and progress together. But as an STE, you can't—and shouldn't—try to do everything yourself. Instead, your job becomes enabling others to do the work. That means asking the right questions, not giving your opinions, creating space for people to learn and figure things out, and not solving it for them. Your strength lies in connecting the dots between people, plans, and perspectives.

> *An RTE is glue—and the STE just becomes the bigger version of that. You don't do the thing, you help others do it.*
>
> —*Maarten Sterrenburg*

It's easy to default to solving problems directly, but the better move is usually to empower others to do so and hold the system accountable for enabling it. Let's observe this in practice through a case study featuring Maarten Sterrenburg, an STE from the Dutch Tax Office, who transformed the planning process of the Solution Train.

Case study: How 450 People found their rhythm

When the Dutch Tax Office decided to merge multiple ARTs into a Solution Train, they quickly discovered that coordination was becoming their biggest enemy rather than their greatest asset. The organization had grown to include teams scattered across the Netherlands, working on the citizen-facing front end of the tax system—essentially, the business card of the entire organization to Dutch society. With separate PI Planning events running simultaneously, stakeholders found themselves torn between multiple venues, trying to be in several places at once, while critical alignment conversations simply weren't happening.

The challenge intensified when Maarten Sterrenburg and his team realized they were facilitating 450 people across multiple ARTs who needed to coordinate quarterly. The traditional approach of separate planning sessions was creating more silos than bridges, with stakeholders missing crucial conversations and teams making assumptions about dependencies that didn't hold. Something had to change, and it needed to be bold.

The solution was as simple as it was ambitious: bring everyone together under one roof. The team found a venue, a massive cycling hall in Apeldoorn, where they arranged tables throughout the center of the space. Every quarter, all 450 people, teams, stakeholders, and leadership would converge for their PI Planning. Yes, it meant arranging hotel rooms for people traveling from Utrecht and other Dutch cities, and yes, the budget conversations were challenging, but the investment proved worthwhile almost immediately.

The transformation was remarkable. Stakeholders could finally visit every team they needed to see, while also connecting with other stakeholders in natural conversations. Team members could walk across the hall to coordinate with dependencies in real time rather than sending emails or scheduling follow-up meetings. What emerged wasn't just better planning; it was a social event that strengthened relationships and trust across the entire Solution Train. The alignment achieved in those two days each quarter was extraordinary, with everyone finally understanding each other's priorities and how their work contributed to the broader strategy.

Benefits achieved included the following:

- There was a dramatic improvement in cross-ART alignment and dependency management
- Stakeholders could efficiently engage with all relevant teams in one location
- Stronger relationships and trust were built through face-to-face interactions
- Plans made sense because everyone understood the bigger picture
- There were fewer follow-up meetings and coordination overhead between planning sessions

The success of big room planning at the Dutch Tax Office demonstrates that, sometimes, the simplest solutions (e.g., placing people in the same space) can address the most complex coordination challenges. While the logistics required investment and commitment, the payoff in terms of alignment, relationship building, and execution quality rendered it an essential component of their Solution Train's success.

Strategic thinking, not tactical control

An RTE typically helps the **Product Management** and System Architect to look one or two PIs ahead of them. The STE helps the Solution Management and Solution Architect to look out across a longer horizon, often two to three years or more, connecting solution-level outcomes to portfolio goals, product direction, and architectural evolution. This entails developing a more in-depth relationship with portfolio management, product leadership, and enterprise architecture. It also means making sure cross-ART dependencies are surfaced early, anticipating organizational bottlenecks, and shaping shared initiatives that steer the system, not just the teams.

For the RTE, using this look-ahead lens means reflecting on the capability needs of upcoming work when compared with those of the current team members. For example, if a future epic will require lots of data analytics, and you only have a couple of team members who can do this, it is your job to find a solution to bolster these skills, be that hiring permanent or contingent labor or even partnering with a vendor, creating an enabling team for a short period.

Supporting new STEs

If you're stepping into the STE role—or helping someone else do so—the first thing to let go of is the idea that you need to be in control. The most effective STEs aren't the ones making all the calls; they're the ones who've learned how to facilitate alignment without centralizing decision-making. Here is how this should be done:

- Shift your mindset from delivery detail to longer-term system health and direction.
- Focus on coaching servant leadership, especially if you're mentoring a new STE.

- Encourage collaboration over hierarchy. Resist using your role to force outcomes.
- Build working relationships between architecture, product, portfolio, and line management, and help others do the same.
- Visualize and manage cross-ART dependencies—not just the ones today, but the ones coming in 6–12 months from now.

Leading cultural change

The STE isn't just a coordinator; they're a cultural signal. In many organizations, this role becomes the linchpin of the transition from command-and-control to decentralized leadership. If the STE defaults to hierarchy, the system around them will follow. But if they model facilitation, psychological safety, and open feedback, it unlocks the potential for collaboration at scale.

Ultimately, the STE makes agility possible at the highest levels of enterprise delivery. It's a role of influence, not control—one that thrives on humility, clarity, and trust.

Summary

In this chapter, we've explored the complexities of scaling agility beyond the ART through Solution Trains—the large-scale coordination mechanism for hundreds or thousands of people working on complex solutions. We've examined the structure of Solution Trains, including the three core roles (STE, Solution Management, and Solution Architect), the integration of suppliers, and the critical design patterns that determine how multiple ARTs work together effectively. Understanding when and why to implement a Solution Train is crucial, as the coordination costs are significant and should only be undertaken when the complexity and scale genuinely require it.

For RTEs operating within a Solution Train, the role fundamentally remains the same while expanding in scope and complexity. Your coordination responsibilities now extend beyond your ART to include cross-train dependencies, multi-horizon planning, and alignment with solution-level objectives. The relationships with peer RTEs become critical, requiring regular collaboration, shared understanding, and coordinated problem-solving. We' also introduced the STE role as the scaled version of the RTE—a servant leader who enables multiple ARTs to work in concert, operating at a higher altitude with strategic focus rather than tactical control.

These concepts are vital for RTEs because they represent the natural evolution of Agile scaling in complex organizations. Understanding how Solution Trains work—whether you're operating within one or potentially stepping into the STE role—prepares you for the realities of large-scale Agile delivery. The principles of disciplined engineering, Solution Intent, and multi-horizon planning become essential tools for maintaining coherence and quality when hundreds of people contribute to a single solution, positioning you for effectiveness in your current role while preparing you for potential enterprise leadership opportunities.

In the next chapter, we will scale again to the portfolio, examining how, when multiple solutions are delivered across various value streams, the RTE must manage different levels of complexity due to even more moving parts.

References

Here, you can find the references to expand your knowledge about the specific concepts not covered in this book but mentioned in this chapter:

- Reuters. (2008, July 15). Brake software latest threat to Boeing 787. *Reuters.* `https://www.reuters.com/article/us-airshow-boeing-787/brake-software-latest-threat-to-boeing-787-idUSL1559730020080715/`

- Skelton, M., & Pais, M. (2019). *Team topologies: Organizing business and technology teams for fast flow.* IT Revolution Press.

12

Connecting the RTE to the Portfolio

In this chapter, we'll explore how we, as RTEs, are not just leading trains—we are a valuable part of the **value stream network**. One of the significant challenges that we have in scaling agility is understanding how we and our teams fit into the big picture. We've said it before, and I'm sure we will say it again, **SAFe®** is a **fractal model**. We take what is proven to work at the team level, then scale it up to the **ART**, our team of teams, and, where appropriate, large solutions and portfolios.

In the last chapter, we explored scaling using a **Solution Train**, which offers a single solution. A **SAFe portfolio**, however, scales to multiple solutions with multiple ARTs delivering them. In this chapter, you will learn not only what a portfolio is, but also how, as an RTE, you need to work with other RTEs and portfolio stakeholders. This chapter will focus on your role as an RTE and some of the most critical areas that will impact you daily.

Here are some of the topics that we will cover:

- What is a SAFe® portfolio?
- Understanding the Portfolio Backlog
- Breaking work into value streams and ARTs
- Coordinating with the Value Management Office
- Working with the **Lean-Agile Center of Excellence (LACE)**

Let's get cracking!

What is a SAFe® portfolio?

Before we go any further, we need to ensure we're aligned on what SAFe® defines as a **portfolio** and why we may need one in the first place. At the start of this chapter, it is essential to point out that your company may or may not benefit from being structured as a portfolio. If you're part of a start-up with just one ART, you may find that that is enough. We don't want to create governance for governance's sake. However, for most of the companies that we work with that have adopted or are in the process of adopting SAFe, we find that structuring your teams in a portfolio is helpful to get a holistic view of the work and make decisions about how to link the **enterprise strategy** to the work that the teams are doing on the ground.

In many traditional portfolio approaches, especially those rooted in Waterfall, the center of gravity is the constant trade-off between *running the business* and *changing the business*. While this framing can be useful, it often becomes a trap. It sets up a zero-sum game where innovation competes with operations, leading to short-term firefighting rather than long-term value creation. In SAFe, the portfolio shifts the conversation. Rather than slicing work into projects that battle for budget, the focus is on aligning multiple ARTs around value streams and strategic themes. This makes dependencies and synergies visible across teams, encouraging organizations to fund persistent capabilities instead of one-off initiatives. The result is less about defending today versus building tomorrow, and more about enabling a continuous, adaptive flow of value that keeps pace with both.

The role of value streams in a SAFe® portfolio

If we were in a training class at this moment, it would be the time that we say, "Listen up, these definitions are important!" By its nature, Agile is full of terms and patterns that often sound the same. As a result, we have to ensure that we're all on the same page. Let's start with the textbook definition of a portfolio and then unpack it.

A SAFe portfolio is a collection of **development value streams**. The first logical question after that statement is, What is a development value stream?! In SAFe, we have three types of value streams, and you can see where this gets tricky. Here are some definitions and examples:

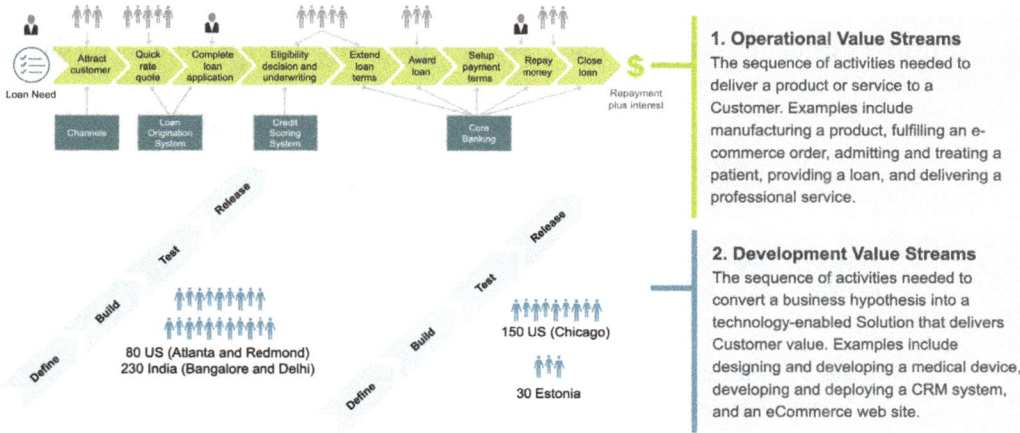

Figure 12.1: Operational and development value streams showing how the latter serves the former (© Scaled Agile, Inc. Source: `https://framework.scaledagile.com/organize-around-value-2/`)

- **Business Agility Value Stream**: Business Agility Value Streams help the organization move fast enough to thrive in a changing world. Here is the example from Scaled Agile:

Figure 12.2: Business Agility Value Stream (© Scaled Agile, Inc. Source: `https://framework.scaledagile.com/business-agility`)

- **Purpose**: Enables rapid sensing of opportunities, making decisions, and delivering solutions faster than competitors
- **Who it involves**: Leadership, Agile teams, and every part of the enterprise
- **Example**: Quickly adapting to a new regulation by updating systems and training teams

- **Operational Value Stream**: Operational Value Streams are the steps we take as a business to deliver existing services and products to customers, internal or external, every day:

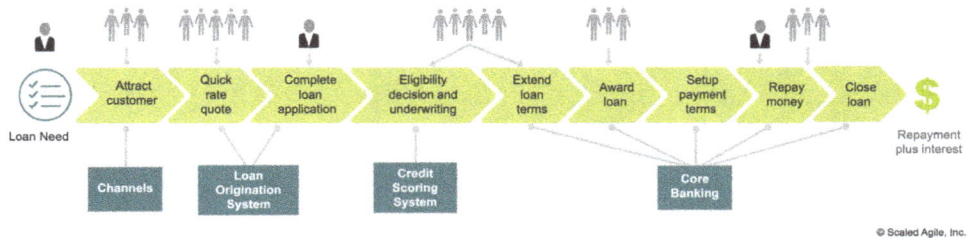

Figure 12.3: The Operational Value Stream serves the user or customer, offering value to them and the organization (© Scaled Agile, Inc. Source: `https://framework.scaledagile.com/operational-value-streams/`*)*

- **Purpose**: Runs the day-to-day activities that deliver value directly to the customer
- **Who it involves**: People and systems that operate solutions built by development value streams
- **Example**: Processing an insurance claim or fulfilling an online order

- **Development value stream**: These are how we create and maintain our solutions that are used to serve our customers in the Operational Value Stream. This is where we will spend most of our time in this chapter, as it is where you live as an RTE:

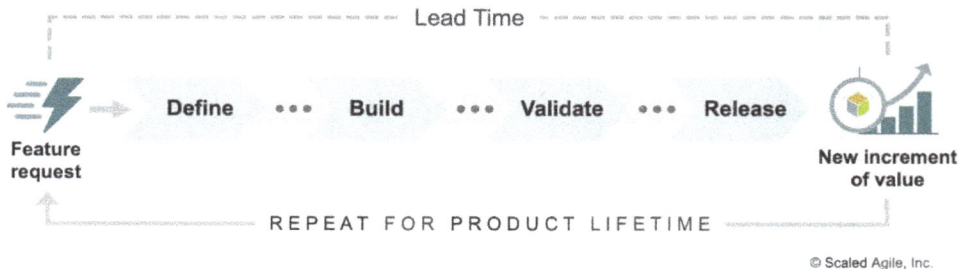

Figure 12.4: Development value stream (© Scaled Agile, Inc. Source: `https://framework.scaledagile.com/development-value-streams/`*)*

- **Purpose**: Creates and maintains solutions, systems, or products for customers. It is worth noting that customers can be either internal (such as HR) or external (a consumer). We define a customer as whoever consumes your work.
- **Who it involves**: Agile Release Trains, Solution Trains, and suppliers.
- **Example**: Building a new mobile banking app.

You can read more about the different value streams on the SAFe® website (`https://framework.scaledagile.com/development-value-streams`). Let's delve a little deeper into the development value stream. We've described a SAFe portfolio as *a collection of development value streams*, but what does that really mean in practice? If a value stream is developing a solution made up of lots of products, they will be related in some way, shape, or form. We need to manage any dependencies between those different products.

> **Creating a cadence and synchronization in the portfolio**
>
> I [Tim] once worked for a major airline. There were a lot of teams that needed to interact with each other. There was one ART that developed the website, one for the app, another for the iPad app, and so on. There were also a few teams working on distributing tickets to travel agents, which is just scratching the surface. Essentially, all the teams found it difficult to plan anything without being seen as a portfolio. Even though some teams were using SAFe and getting pretty good at **PI Planning**, others were using a different framework. As a result, an ART would plan something, and then a couple of weeks later, a requirement would come in from one of the other areas. When a new director came in to lead the portfolio, whom I'd worked with in the past, one of the first things she did was to align all the teams to SAFe. We found that after just a couple of PIs, the teams aligned more, and we accelerated the ability to deliver her strategy.

Imagine that you were an RTE on one of those trains. You struggle to make tangible improvements despite your best efforts because things keep changing. That's what we're trying to do with **Lean Portfolio Management** (**LPM**) and a SAFe portfolio: bring a bit more structure to how we make decisions. Now, look at the main concepts you need to understand as an RTE.

Understanding the Portfolio Backlog

One of the central concepts for any team is that we want to have a single prioritized backlog from which to pull our work. Working with large numbers of teams is particularly challenging, and we've already seen the concept through managing the features on our ART.

Our largest initiative within SAFe are **portfolio epics**. An epic is a major initiative that begins as a hypothesis, tested through a Lean business case. Unlike a project, it isn't tied to a fixed scope or temporary teams; instead, it adapts as evidence emerges and is delivered through existing ARTs and value streams. Epics are broken down into **capabilities**, capabilities are broken down into **features**, and features into **stories**.

Unlike capabilities and features, epics don't have the constraint of fitting into a single PI. They are larger pieces of work that will typically be broken down and delivered across multiple value streams and ARTs. As an RTE, you must keep a keen eye on the epics and the **portfolio roadmap**, as it will give you much insight into what your teams will likely deliver over the coming months. As we'll see later in this chapter, you and your Product Managers will work with **Epic Owners** to shepherd the new initiatives from their initial inception to delivery to deliver your part of the epic. Your most useful tool will be the **portfolio Kanban**, so let's look at that now.

The flow of epics through the Portfolio Backlog

The portfolio Kanban is one of the most straightforward yet powerful tools for managing the flow of epic-level work across an organization. At its heart, it's just a visual system for tracking how big pieces of work move from idea to implementation—but as with many things in SAFe®, the magic is in how we use it to foster alignment, transparency, and collaboration. When we work at the portfolio level, we often deal with vast, complex ideas that require significant investment. Without a way to capture and visualize the status of these initiatives, it's easy for things to get stuck, become invisible, or—even worse—be pushed forward without enough shared understanding.

The portfolio Kanban gives us a structured way to manage that flow. We can see what's being considered, what's being validated, what's being approved, and what's actively being worked on. It allows for disciplined decision-making; just because something has been proposed doesn't mean it automatically gets funded or prioritized. We can engage in the necessary conversations around strategy, value, and readiness without losing sight of the bigger picture.

As RTEs, we live and breathe flow. The portfolio Kanban is where we extend that principle upward, helping our leaders and stakeholders see work as a flow system rather than a series of disconnected projects. It gives us a place to introduce lightweight governance, ensuring that big decisions are made with the right amount of rigor—not too heavy or loose. And because it's a visual system, it invites participation. Anyone standing around the Kanban—virtual or physical—can ask questions, challenge assumptions, and offer insights. That's the kind of openness we want in a Lean-Agile environment. If we nurture it carefully, the portfolio Kanban becomes more than just a board; it becomes a central meeting place for organizational learning and alignment. We can spot bottlenecks, uncover dependencies early, and create a sense of collective ownership over the portfolio's success.

It reminds us that strategy doesn't happen far away in a boardroom—it's a living, breathing conversation. Strategy is executed through the delivery of the **strategic themes**, with the significant initiatives being delivered as epics, all of which will have an Epic Owner assigned to be the custodian for them through delivery. Let's next look at the Epic Owner role, so you know how to collaborate with them as an RTE.

Understanding the Epic Owner role

When we talk about guiding big pieces of work through the portfolio Kanban, we naturally meet the Epic Owner. Think of the Epic Owner as the champion and shepherd for a particular epic. Their role is to guide that idea from a rough concept to a clear, validated, and actionable piece of work. They're not doing this alone—far from it—but they are responsible for pulling together the right people, gathering the evidence needed to make good decisions, and ensuring that the epic's progress stays visible and aligned with strategic priorities. The responsibility wheel from the framework shows the key elements of their role:

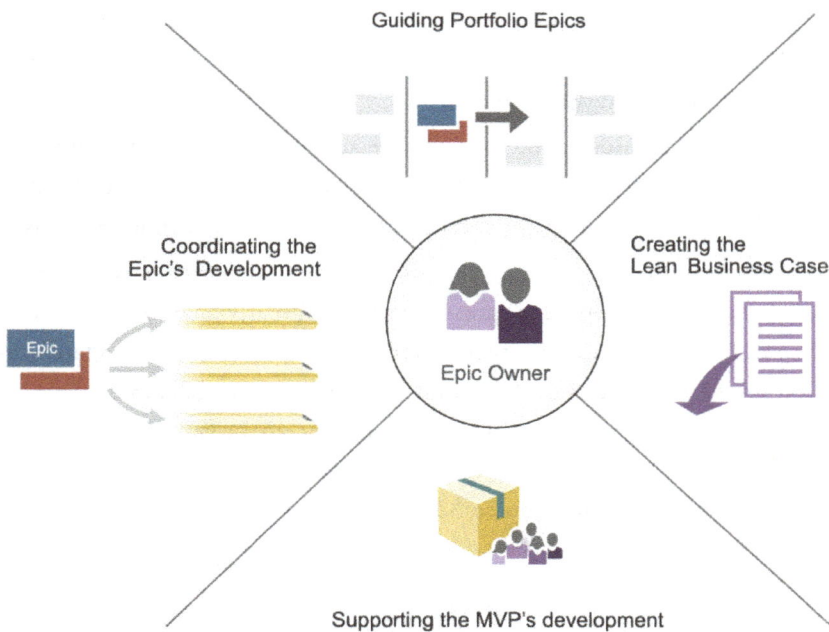

Figure 12.5: The Epic Owner's primary responsibilities (© Scaled Agile, Inc. Source: `https://framework.scaledagile.com/epic-owner`*)*

A good Epic Owner isn't just passionate about their epic; they're deeply collaborative, seeking feedback, listening to different perspectives, and always keeping an eye on the bigger picture of value delivery. They work closely with Enterprise Architects, Business Owners, and, of course, us as RTEs to keep the flow healthy and the portfolio of Kanban vibrant.

In some organizations, we get challenged by some who think the Epic Owner is no more than a sponsor. The trouble with this thinking is that in many organizations, a sponsor can often be no more than a figurehead and not as active as we would want an Epic Owner to be.

The following are some tips for collaborating with Epic Owners:

- **Build a partnership, not a process**: We should approach our relationship with Epic Owners as a true partnership. They bring passion and a deep understanding of the idea; we bring flow thinking and facilitation skills. Together, we can shape the epic thoughtfully rather than rushing it through the system.

- **Make the Kanban your shared workspace**: Encourage Epic Owners to see the portfolio Kanban not as an administrative task but as a dynamic tool they actively use. Invite them into conversations about **Work-in-Process (WIP)** limits, bottlenecks, and prioritization. Make it a living, breathing board you both own.

- **Support evidence-based thinking**: Epic Owners can sometimes fall in love with their ideas (and that's not bad!). Our role is to gently challenge assumptions, encourage small experiments, and keep them thinking about data and outcomes rather than opinions.

- **Create regular touch points**: Rather than relying on formal meetings, have informal check-ins where you review the epic's progress together. Regular, relaxed conversations help you catch risks early and connect the work to strategy. While Product Managers work closely with Epic Owners to understand the *what*, as RTEs our strength lies in coaching. Use these touchpoints to help Epic Owners clearly communicate the value their epic aims to deliver, support the ART in understanding that intent, and coach teams on how they can best contribute to achieving those outcomes.

Coaching questions for Epic Owners

While the role of an Epic Owner is more on the product ownership, or for enablers, the architecture side, you are still going to want to support them in their role. Here are some questions you may find helpful to connect with them, supporting their thinking on the epic and how your ART can best deliver it:

- What problem are we really trying to solve with this epic?

- How do we know this is the right problem to solve?

- Who will benefit from this epic, and how can we engage them early?

- What small experiments could we run to validate our assumptions?

- What would we focus on if we had to achieve 80% of the value with half the investment?

- What risks have we spotted, and what might we be missing?

- How will we know, as early as possible, whether this epic is on the right track?

- What dependencies might slow us down, and how can we surface them now?

- How does this epic align with our current strategic themes?

- If this epic wasn't approved, what would happen? (What's the real cost of delay?)

Now, let's look at how to get an early view of what's coming up.

Understanding the steps in the portfolio Kanban

Portfolio flow starts with understanding how work—specifically, portfolio epics—moves through the portfolio Kanban. Each epic follows a lifecycle, from **funnel** to **reviewing** to **analyzing** and beyond. Our job as RTEs is to make that flow visible, ensure healthy movement between stages, and highlight when things get stuck. The portfolio Kanban is a pull-based system, not a push. That means we should resist the temptation to overload it. Ideas are reviewed and validated thoughtfully before they are allowed to move forward. We help maintain discipline here by being a strong voice for flow efficiency, not just getting *more stuff* in progress.

Each stage of the Kanban represents a key point in the life of an epic, from the very first idea to when it is fully delivered—and sometimes even when it's deliberately stopped!

As RTEs, we have a crucial part to make sure that value doesn't just get planned—it gets delivered steadily and predictably across the portfolio. Portfolio flow is all about how epics move through the system, from the earliest idea to real-world outcomes. It's not just a question of tracking work; it's about managing the system to reduce delays, spot risks early, and keep everyone aligned with the bigger picture. To do that well, we need to understand how the portfolio Kanban works, how to respect WIP limits, and how to bridge the communication gap between strategic thinkers and delivery teams.

Let's walk through the typical stages together:

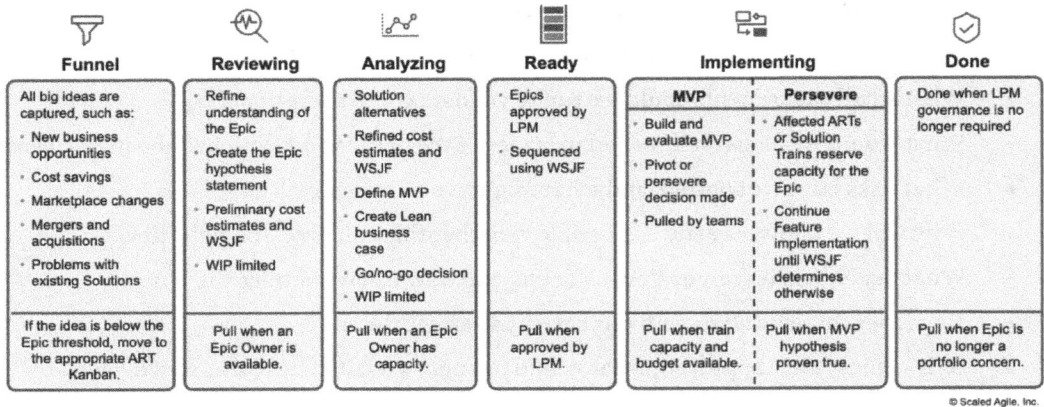

Funnel	Reviewing	Analyzing	Ready	Implementing		Done
All big ideas are captured, such as: • New business opportunities • Cost savings • Marketplace changes • Mergers and acquisitions • Problems with existing Solutions	• Refine understanding of the Epic • Create the Epic hypothesis statement • Preliminary cost estimates and WSJF • WIP limited	• Solution alternatives • Refined cost estimates and WSJF • Define MVP • Create Lean business case • Go/no-go decision • WIP limited	• Epics approved by LPM • Sequenced using WSJF	**MVP** • Build and evaluate MVP • Pivot or persevere decision made • Pulled by teams	**Persevere** • Affected ARTs or Solution Trains reserve capacity for the Epic • Continue Feature implementation until WSJF determines otherwise	• Done when LPM governance is no longer required
If the idea is below the Epic threshold, move to the appropriate ART Kanban.	Pull when an Epic Owner is available.	Pull when an Epic Owner has capacity.	Pull when approved by LPM.	Pull when train capacity and budget available.	Pull when MVP hypothesis proven true.	Pull when Epic is no longer a portfolio concern.

© Scaled Agile. Inc.

Figure 12.6: Portfolio Kanban (© Scaled Agile, Inc. Source: `https://framework.`
`scaledagile.com/portfolio-backlog/)`

The funnel

This is where all new ideas land. At this point, we're simply capturing potential epics. Nothing is filtered yet, and we mustn't stifle creativity too early. Think of it as a place for possibilities, where anyone with a substantive idea can record it. We're early in the process, but keeping an eye on what is coming in is always helpful.

Having a single place in the organization for these ideas to be captured can be quite an achievement in itself. We've seen organizations where, when we asked about the things needed to do, we were given a handful of sticky notes, an Excel spreadsheet, and a filtered list of stuff in Jira!

Reviewing

Now, we start to filter. In the reviewing stage, we assess whether the idea aligns with strategic themes and is worth exploring further. We might look at the initial **epic hypothesis**, rough value estimates, and early feasibility. We'll also perform preliminary prioritization using **Weighted Shortest Job First (WSJF)**.

One of the most critical aspects of keeping the portfolio flow healthy is respecting WIP limits. Without clear WIP limits, the portfolio Kanban can easily become a traffic jam of half-started, half-finished epics. We support leaders by gently reminding them that starting fewer things often results in finishing more—faster. Healthy flow happens when the system isn't overwhelmed, and Epic Owners have the focus to drive their work forward. WIP limits aren't a constraint; they are an enabler of better outcomes.

As an RTE, watch for any ideas that might relate to your area. You might want to have an informal catch-up with potential epics to understand what might be required.

Analyzing

This is the exploration phase, where we start adding more meat to the bones. We create our **Lean Business Case** and start thinking more about what's involved in delivering the epic.

You may find that people in your team are approached to *put a bit more meat on the bones* in refining their understanding of the epic by the Epic Owner. As an RTE, you should make sure that people such as architects and development leads have the right capacity ring-fenced. This sort of work isn't often considered during PI Planning. A certain amount of support is acceptable, but when this becomes too much, it will need to be planned into a future PI under an **Enabler feature** or a conversation with **Product Management** about dropping an uncommitted commitment. How much is too much? While there is never a simple answer, you would always step in and have a conversation when the demand was jeopardizing the deliverability of the PI Objectives.

Ready

If the epic is approved by LPM fiduciaries in the **Strategic Portfolio Review** after analysis, it moves into the **ready** phase. This is the pool of validated, prioritized work that is waiting for capacity and the right moment to be pulled into execution.

You should be aware of anything that will touch your ART at this stage. You'll need to work with Product Management to ensure that all your bases are covered. Hopefully, this was all taken care of, but you should consider the following:

- **Look for the testability of the epic**: A good epic should have clear success criteria—things we can observe, measure, and test against. If you're struggling to define what *done* looks like, it's a strong sign that the epic needs more refinement.

- **Ask for risk spikes or early experiments**: If an epic contains significant unknowns (technical risk, compliance risk, market risk, etc.), check whether the Epic Owner has proposed small, fast experiments to reduce those uncertainties. We want to shrink the unknowns before committing lots of money and people.

- **Challenge assumptions about sequencing**: Sometimes, an epic looks huge because it bundles too many steps together. Help Epic Owners separate *what must happen first* from *what could happen later*. Often, there's a small early slice of value that can be delivered independently while learning along the way.

- **Watch out for "everything and the kitchen sink" epics**: If the epic reads like a wish list, it's a warning sign. Guide the Epic Owner to find the core of the value: what would we deliver if we only had half the time or half the budget? Focus on that first.

  In a similar vein, how quickly will the epic hypothesis be proven or not by the MVP? Is it testing the riskiest element of the hypothesis, or trying to prove what the Epic Owner is trying to approve to continue delivery?

- **Check dependencies**: Big, messy webs of dependencies suggest that the epic might not be sliced cleanly. Suppose every team or every supplier is involved from day one, then it might need to be broken into more manageable, loosely coupled pieces.

- **Size should be right-sized for commitment**: A portfolio epic shouldn't be so big that it locks up the Portfolio Backlog for a year. Suppose it's so large or risky that the organization hesitates to commit. In that case, it's probably a candidate for further breakdown before approval. Encourage short feedback cycles; if the epic can't deliver a meaningful piece of value in a single PI or two, it's too big. Help Epic Owners focus on how they could get early feedback from customers or internal users.

A few good coaching questions to use

These more delivery-oriented questions will help you guide the ART during planning and delivery:

- Is there a way to deliver value without waiting for all the dependencies to line up?
- How quickly can we get honest customer feedback on part of this idea?
- Which part of this epic creates the most risk or cost—and can we shrink it? The golden rule we often remind ourselves of is that big batches mean significant risks. If we break the epic down wisely, we reduce the risk, speed up learning, and increase our chances of delighting customers. It's always better to make 10 small bets than 1 gigantic one!
- What part of the hypothesis statement is the MVP trying to prove?

Implementing

The ARTs and solution teams are actively delivering the epic, which can only happen when the contributing value streams have sufficient capacity. The portfolio Kanban is a pull system like any other. The **implementing** stage is about tracking progress against the Lean Business Case, monitoring key metrics, and adapting as necessary. As an RTE, you should watch out for misalignment between the epic's intent and what's being delivered. Also, ensure that you have a regular review with the Epic Owners. You should consider whether they must be invited to your **System Demos** and **PI System Demos**.

We always like to collaborate with our Product Managers to ensure we can demonstrate progress. Suppose you're working with other ARTs in the portfolio or as part of the same value stream. In that case, you may need to work closely with other RTEs to understand any risks and issues, which we covered in more detail in *Chapter 11*.

Done

According to SAFe®, the epic is completed when it is *no longer LPM's concern*. That doesn't mean that our work is over. You may still be supporting aspects of it through your delivery. Product Managers may continue adding new features to the epic until WSJF results in them prioritizing other features not from the epic. While the portfolio may seem distant from day-to-day ART activities, we're closer to it than we think—critical connectors between strategy and execution.

So, as an RTE, there is a lot of benefit to familiarizing yourself with what may be coming down the pipe. We'll be more specific in other formal areas, so let's unpack that a little more now.

RTE's touch points with the portfolio flow

As RTEs, we have several essential touch points where we can actively support the portfolio flow:

- **Ensuring visibility from portfolio to ART level (and back again)**: Ensure the teams understand the bigger strategic context behind the work they are picking up—and help escalate real delivery risks back up to Portfolio Leaders.

- **Feeding up data (risks, progress, and dependency concerns)**: Leaders need more than green traffic lights. They need real, honest views of what's happening, where risks materialize, and where support is required.

- **Feeding down context, strategic themes, and investment focus**: Translate portfolio strategy into a language that ARTs and teams can use. Keep reminding everyone why this epic now matters.

- **Helping teams understand the bigger picture (why this epic matters)**: Make sure that ARTs can see the customer, business, or technical outcomes behind the work. It's easier to stay motivated and deliver better solutions when you know the real *why*.

- **Highlighting misaligned work early**: Watch for teams or trains drifting away from the epic's intent. Catch misalignment early through regular check-ins, demos, and informal conversations.

- **Supporting the Lean Governance function (budgets, guardrails, and feedback loops)**: Help link real-world delivery to strategic financial management. Participate in feedback loops that help refine budgets, inform guardrail reviews, and improve investment decisions.

- **Connecting to the LPM function**: As RTEs, we sit in a powerful place—close enough to delivery to see reality and close enough to leadership to influence decisions. One of our most important contributions is ensuring that decision-making at the top is informed by what's happening on the ground.

- **We are the connectors**: We bring delivery data, risks, and learnings up to the portfolio level. We carry context, investment priorities, and strategic focus back to the ARTs. When we do this well, we help build a portfolio that isn't just full of good ideas but of real outcomes, delivered predictably and with purpose.

Having looked at the flow of work through the portfolio, let's next explore what happens when the work to deliver an epic spans value streams or ARTs.

Breaking work into value streams and ARTs

We've already talked about flow at the ART level, and as an RTE, that will be where you focus your energy. That said, it is worth noting that the same concepts will apply at the portfolio level. The work you do in reporting your work on your ART will flow up to the portfolio, so accuracy will be critical. Ideally, each value stream will operate independently, delivering value without relying on anyone else. However, reality is often more tangled. Dependencies between value streams are common, and while they do introduce complexity, they also present opportunities. **Value Stream Coordination** is about managing these dependencies thoughtfully and exploiting the hidden potential in how different streams connect.

Although dependencies are sometimes seen as a problem, applying **systems thinking** reminds us that value often flows through these relationships. Well-coordinated value streams can deliver unique, differentiated solutions that competitors struggle to match. As RTEs, we play a key role in helping these connections flourish rather than becoming bottlenecks. Several essential practices underpin successful value stream coordination. Firstly, coordination roles appear across the portfolio, such as the triads we recognize at the team and ART levels. **Enterprise Architects** guide technical alignment, **Solution Portfolio Management** oversees large solution sets, and RTEs, STEs, and the **Value Management Office** (**VMO**) help facilitate smooth execution across trains.

Cadence and synchronization are crucial, too. Suppose multiple value streams are to collaborate effectively. In that case, they must operate on a shared heartbeat—synchronizing PI Planning, Inspect & Adapt, and Demos to create natural integration points. This regular rhythm supports faster learning, makes dependencies visible early, and lowers the cost of change. Importantly, new portfolio-level work is introduced at fixed, predictable intervals rather than sneaking in mid-PI and disrupting focus.

Integration is another big theme. Complete integration across value streams might not be possible in every iteration, but partial integration is vital. Frequent integration points help reduce risk, catch issues early, and accelerate learning. Good DevOps practices become essential here, enabling small, incremental changes to move safely into production without building up risky large batches.

Finally, the portfolio roadmap ties all these moving parts together, showing how individual solutions align to a broader picture and helping coordinate the timing of significant milestones. And underpinning it all is the principle of releasing on demand—ensuring that when integrated value is ready, it can be deployed quickly and reliably, whether by individual ARTs or through wider system-level releases.

As RTEs, we must foster the habits of coordination: encouraging shared cadence, highlighting cross-stream risks and opportunities, supporting integration efforts, and always thinking about how the whole system delivers value, not just its parts. By helping people connect beyond their immediate teams, we make the whole greater than the sum of its parts.

Tips for the RTE: supporting Value Stream Coordination

Here are a few ideas to consider when coordinating with other value streams:

- **Champion the cadence**: Help value streams align their PI Planning, Inspect & Adapt, and demos. A shared rhythm makes collaboration so much easier.

- **Surface dependencies early**: Encourage ARTs to visualize and discuss cross-stream dependencies during PI Planning. Use tools such as dependency boards and System Demos to keep them visible.

- **Facilitate integration conversations**: Check in regularly. Are we integrating across streams early enough? Where can we experiment with partial integrations before the full system comes together?

- **Protect focus during the PI**: Be a strong voice for managing new portfolio work responsibly. Push back kindly when people try to sneak major changes halfway through.

- **Promote DevOps thinking across streams**: Support efforts to reduce batch sizes, automate integration, and improve release practices. Small, regular changes lower risk and accelerate learning. Think about how you can use the **flow accelerators** that we reviewed in *Chapter 10*.

- **Connect people, not just plans**: Sometimes, conversation is the best coordination tool. Create spaces where teams from different streams can talk, share insights, and solve problems. Of course, coordination is vital, but it's not enough. We also need to think about how value moves to keep the whole system healthy. Flow is the lifeblood of a Lean portfolio, and this is where the RTE steps forward again: not just connecting people but actively guiding the flow of work across ARTs to keep things moving smoothly and predictably.

RTEs are key people in supporting flow at the portfolio level, but they are not alone in doing so. Next, we'll look at the VMO who actually runs some of the portfolio functions.

Coordinating with the Value Management Office

As RTEs, our day-to-day is rooted in execution—facilitating alignment, enabling flow, and helping teams deliver value. But to lead effectively, we must also lift our gaze and connect with the strategic engine of the organization. That's where our relationship with the VMO becomes critical.

The VMO plays a central role in the Lean-Agile enterprise. It helps manage LPM, ensures lean governance is in place, supports operational excellence, and helps the organization continuously adapt to change. While we're supporting execution at the ART level, the VMO is looking across the broader system—shaping strategy, funding, and enterprise flow. When we work closely together, we create a seamless connection between strategy and delivery.

One of the VMO's key responsibilities is facilitating LPM. This involves making sure the most valuable work is being funded and prioritized at the right time.

As an RTE, you can provide the VMO with essential insights from the ground:

- Which teams have capacity?
- What dependencies are emerging?
- How confident are we in delivering certain features or capabilities?
- What systemic impediments are we seeing that will impact others?

This helps the VMO ensure that investment decisions are grounded in real delivery data—not just wishful thinking.

The VMO also plays a strong role in operational excellence—promoting best practices that make delivery smoother and more efficient. As an RTE, you're in a great position to test and refine those practices in the field. Your feedback is vital. Share with the VMO what's working well on the train and where process friction still exists. This partnership helps evolve the system, improving how governance, planning, and execution align across the enterprise.

Another key responsibility of the VMO is implementing Lean Governance. This isn't about heavy-handed control—it's about ensuring transparency and alignment while reducing bureaucracy. As an RTE, you're on the front line, helping teams stay aligned with Lean budgeting, milestone tracking, and metrics. By working with the VMO, you can ensure that governance mechanisms are enabling delivery, not slowing it down. Together, you can identify old policies or approval steps that are no longer fit for purpose and collaborate to remove or modernize them.

Under the banner of Lean Governance, the VMO will, ideally collaboratively, set standards for reporting KPIs and ensuring transparency of execution—for example, defining how value streams and ARTs document on the internal wiki what they are, who is involved, and what they're doing. This isn't about imposing work on you, but applying systems thinking to the portfolio so that all those who need to understand what is happening can do so easily through a base level of consistency. Part of this equation is for you to provide feedback on improvement opportunities and the cost in time and money to provide this information, so the VMO can make an economic trade-off decision around the cost versus the benefits.

The VMO is also focused on optimizing value delivery and reducing waste at scale. You bring insight into where work gets stuck: duplicated effort, rework, unclear ownership, or overloaded teams. These issues are often symptoms of larger system problems. When you share these patterns with the VMO, they can help drive broader improvements—whether that's clarifying value streams, fixing funding flows, or reshaping how work is prioritized.

Lastly, the VMO plays an essential role in breaking down silos and improving communication across the enterprise. While you work across teams within the train, the VMO works across trains, portfolios, and business functions. When you stay tightly connected with them, you amplify your impact. You help ensure that the ART isn't just moving fast—it's moving in the right direction, aligned with strategic priorities and contributing to enterprise outcomes.

While the VMO supports the execution across the portfolio on a day-to-day basis, the LACE works initially during the transformation to SAFe® and then becomes the internal coaches and consultancy to support continued improvement. Utilizing their expertise offers the RTE allies someone to bounce ideas off.

Working with the Lean Agile Center of Excellence

Alongside your partnership with the VMO, another key relationship in your role as RTE is with the LACE. While you focus on the successful delivery and continuous improvement of a single ART, the LACE is responsible for enabling Lean-Agile transformation across the entire organization. It's a natural alliance—one grounded in shared values, common goals, and complementary perspectives.

The LACE is typically made up of a small, cross-functional Agile team, acting as the guiding co-alition for change. It includes people who understand the 'organization's structure, culture, and strategy—and who are committed to embedding Lean-Agile thinking at every level. As RTEs, we often serve as the eyes and ears of the transformation at the delivery level. When we stay connected to the LACE, we help ground the transformation in real-world insights from the teams doing the work.

One of the strengths of the LACE is its structure. Like any Agile team, it has a Product Owner who prioritizes the transformation backlog, a **Scrum Master** or team coach who supports flow and removes barriers, and members from across different business areas. This diversity means the LACE can look at transformation challenges from multiple angles—technical, cultural, processes, and people.

As RTEs, we bring essential context to these discussions. We know where Agile practices are thriving and where they're just ticking boxes. We know which teams need support, which patterns of dysfunction are holding back flow, and where leadership behaviors are either enabling or hindering agility. By sharing this with the LACE, we help steer the transformation in a meaningful and grounded direction.

The LACE's mission is to keep the transformation aligned, both in terms of purpose and progress. In fast-moving organizations, it's easy for different areas to drift off in their own direction. By working with the LACE, you help ensure that the ART isn't just improving in isolation, but contributing to a wider movement. That alignment is critical when scaling Agile across multiple trains and portfolios.

LACE members are also often SAFe® experts or experienced change agents. They can offer guidance, tools, and perspective on how to tackle difficult transformation challenges—from shifting mindsets to reshaping funding models. Tap into their expertise. Bring them into workshops. Invite them to *observe, inspect, and adapt*. Your collaboration helps close the feedback loop between strategy and execution, and between theory and practice.

Finally, the LACE plays a key role in communicating the vision. Agile transformations can feel confusing or even threatening for people across the business. The LACE helps tell the story—why we're changing, what's working, and where we're going next. As an RTE, you can help amplify that message. Share your stories. Highlight success. Use your voice to show what "great" looks like on the ground.

You're a coach, a connector, and a catalyst for change. Whether you're mentoring Scrum Masters, clearing systemic impediments, using flow metrics to guide improvement, or partnering with the VMO to align strategy and execution, you are shaping how your ART grows, delivers, and thrives. Let's take a moment to reflect on the key ideas we've covered.

While many LACEs operate as a single team, there have been occasions where we have scaled them to a team of teams, as this case study shares.

Case study: Scaling the LACE beyond a single team

A multinational enterprise with 3,000+ staff across three continents was struggling with its Agile transformation. After launching three successful ARTs, tensions emerged as the transformation was perceived as US-led and engineering-centric, lacking broader enterprise engagement. The traditional small LACE team model wasn't providing the reach or influence needed to address dependencies and misaligned ways of working across diverse functional groups.

Glenn and the transformation consultancy team, working alongside internal change agents from a recent leadership development program, proposed an unconventional approach: transform the LACE itself into an ART.

The LACE-as-ART structure

Rather than the typical 5–8 person LACE team, this approach scaled to 70 people across multiple functions, including marketing, sales, communications, HR, account management, and corporate development.

The structure maintained all traditional ART elements with a dedicated RTE who was an Agile convert, effectively modeling behaviors for newcomers to Agile practices. A System Architect role was filled by a senior SPC to provide consistency and standards across the transformation work. The seven teams each had Product Owners and Scrum Masters, though many weren't full-time roles and required significant coaching as team members transitioned into these responsibilities.

Critical to success was aligning with the existing ARTs' cadence and synchronization, enabling cross-ART collaboration and allowing other teams to predict and plan for the transformation's impact on their work.

RTE interaction model

The RTE role within the LACE-ART required significant behavior modeling for Agile newcomers while managing the complexity of non-traditional Agile work. The RTE became crucial in demonstrating servant leadership to functions unfamiliar with Agile practices, extending beyond traditional facilitation to become a bridge between Agile-native and Agile-curious parts of the organization.

Coordination became essential with other ARTs' RTEs, as the LACE-ART's mission directly impacted their teams through training, process changes, and organizational shifts. Regular synchronization allowed other RTEs to predict and plan for transformation impacts, creating a collaborative network of RTEs managing enterprise-wide change.

Practical challenges emerged around scheduling, particularly for coaching teams within the LACE-ART whose ceremony times often clashed with the ARTs they were supporting, requiring flexible timing adjustments and creative scheduling solutions.

Outcomes and legacy

The LACE-as-ART successfully launched over 15 ARTs while creating lasting organizational capability. Beyond the immediate transformation deliverables, it established the following:

- A durable cross-functional network capable of rapid collaboration
- Organizational muscle memory for working across boundaries
- Pull-based demand for Agile adoption in previously resistant areas
- Internal capability through trained SPCs who could support new teams independently

Key insight for RTEs

While LACEs are typically small, focused teams, creating a large cross-functional team of teams can provide the scale and influence needed for complex transformations. The ART structure becomes particularly valuable when the LACE must manage multiple dependencies across diverse functions while maintaining the coordination and predictability that enterprise-scale change demands.

> The RTE role in this context extends beyond traditional facilitation to become a crucial bridge between Agile-native and Agile-curious parts of the organization, requiring enhanced change leadership alongside standard RTE capabilities.

Summary

In this chapter, we stepped back to see how we, as RTEs, connect to the wider SAFe® portfolio. We explored what a SAFe portfolio is, how development value streams fit into it, and why understanding the flow of portfolio epics through the Kanban system is so important to achieving real business outcomes. We unpacked the crucial relationship between RTEs and Epic Owners. We looked at how we can support portfolio flow by respecting WIP limits, surfacing risks early, and helping teams see the true purpose behind their work.

Most importantly, we reinforced a key theme: our impact stretches far wider even when our day-to-day focus is at the train level. By helping manage portfolio flow, coordinating across value streams, and bringing real-world feedback into LPM conversations, we move beyond simply running ceremonies—we become key drivers of organizational agility and enterprise success.

Throughout this handbook, we've journeyed from the fundamentals of the RTE role to the practical aspects of launching and sustaining ARTs, the key events that establish cadence and alignment, and how the role connects to the wider enterprise. You now possess the knowledge, tools, and perspectives to truly make a difference as an RTE.

Remember, being an effective RTE isn't about achieving perfection—it's about continuous learning, adapting, and maintaining a relentless focus on enabling your teams to deliver value. We hope this handbook serves as a trusted guide as you navigate your RTE journey. For those pursuing formal certification, the appendix that follows provides guidance on preparing for the RTE exam.

Get This Book's PDF Version and Exclusive Extras

Scan the QR code (or go to packtpub.com/unlock).
Search for this book by name, confirm the edition,
and then follow the steps on the page.

*Note: Keep your invoice handy. Purchases made
directly from Packt don't require one.*

13

Appendix A: Preparing for the SAFe® RTE Exam

Achieving the **SAFe® Release Train Engineer (RTE)** certification is a significant milestone, representing mastery of the **Scaled Agile Framework® (SAFe)** and a commitment to fostering organizational success. However, passing a SAFe exam requires more than simply attending a course or reading materials. It demands strategic preparation, practical understanding, and a confident approach to the exam process.

The SAFe exams assess your ability to demonstrate a solid grasp of principles, roles, and practices, and apply them effectively in practical scenarios. This chapter will guide you through the process of preparing for and completing your certification, from understanding the exam structure to celebrating your achievement and planning your professional growth.

It is important to note that Scaled Agile changes the format of its exams based on feedback. With that in mind, the tips in this chapter are more generic for multiple-choice exams and the general principles and ethos of SAFe, as they are more likely to stand the test of time.

Here's what we'll cover:

- The SAFe® exam structure
- Using the study guide for targeted preparation
- Celebrating your achievement and looking ahead

Let's make sure your certification path is clear, focused, and, ultimately, successful.

The SAFe® exam structure

The SAFe® exam is carefully structured to assess your theoretical knowledge and practical application of the framework. Although it is a multiple-choice test, its focus on scenario-based questions requires a deeper level of understanding.

The questions often emphasize core areas such as Lean-Agile principles, value streams, and roles within SAFe. High-priority topics, such as PI Planning and the role of the RTE, form a substantial portion of the exam. Scenario-based questions challenge you to connect theory with practical situations, requiring an understanding of *what* a principle is, *why* it matters, and *how* it's applied.

Multiple-choice exams frequently assess your grasp of principles and how they can be applied to solve problems. Understanding the *why* behind key ideas is crucial—don't just memorize what happens during PI Planning, for instance, but consider why the process exists and how it supports alignment across teams. Connecting theory to practice will deepen your understanding and make it easier to identify correct answers. Patterns also play an essential role in frameworks such as SAFe, as many of its roles, ceremonies, and principles follow consistent logic. Recognizing these patterns can help you quickly identify relevant information in the exam.

Knowing this, you should tailor your preparation to focus on key topics while building your ability to think critically about their application. Additionally, the timed nature of the exam means you'll need to work both accurately and efficiently. Practicing time management during preparation will help you balance speed and accuracy on exam day.

> **Don't just practice—reflect and review**
>
> When Tim was recently supporting someone preparing for a SAFe exam, they flagged the questions from the practice exam (available after you attend a course) that they weren't sure about—not just to guess and move on, but to make a note of the concepts they needed to come back to.
>
> They didn't leave it there, though. They took time to go back through each of those flagged questions and dug into the underlying principles behind them. They weren't just memorizing answers—they were building confidence in the thinking.
>
> The result? A fantastic 98% on the real exam. Not bad at all.
>
> Now, you might not have someone like Tim on hand, but the real takeaway is this: find a peer, a classmate, or someone else who's been through it. Talk through the bits that aren't landing for you. Use each other as sounding boards. It's one of the best ways to turn "I think I get it" into "I know this."

Preparing for the multiple-choice format

Preparing for multiple-choice questions involves more than simply memorizing facts. It requires a strategic approach that combines a deep understanding of the material, the ability to interpret questions effectively, and techniques to identify the best possible answers. With thoughtful preparation and a clear strategy, you can confidently tackle multiple-choice exams.

First, it's essential to familiarize yourself with the exam format. Multiple-choice questions often test your ability to apply knowledge in context rather than just recalling facts. Many scenario-based questions present real-world situations where you must decide how to use a framework or principle. These scenarios often include keyword clues such as *best*, *most likely*, or *always*, which can hint at the answer. Practicing with sample questions or past exams will help you understand the structure and style of questions and prepare you to interpret them effectively.

Techniques for answering questions

When faced with a difficult question, the process of elimination can be a lifesaver:

- Start by ruling out any incorrect options. Look for contradictions or answers that don't align with the framework's principles—these can usually be eliminated immediately. Be wary of distractors, which are plausible-sounding options that may not fully align with the framework's principles. Even if you're unsure of the correct answer, narrowing your choices improves the likelihood of guessing correctly.

- Paying close attention to the wording of questions and answers can also provide valuable clues. Qualifiers such as *always* or *never* are often too rigid to align with real-world practices. They may indicate incorrect answers, whereas terms such as *most often* or *usually* are more likely to be correct.

- Context is key. Consider the scenario described in the question and how it connects to foundational principles such as alignment, value delivery, or continuous improvement.

- Don't rush—ensure that you understand the question and all the options before selecting your answer. Some questions seem obvious initially, but take a breath before making your selection, and then move on confidently.

Understanding rather than guessing

It's also essential to prioritize understanding over guessing. Some questions challenge you to apply broader principles rather than recall specific details. In these cases, foundational ideas such as Lean-Agile leadership or value streams should be considered. Visualizing framework elements, such as the **SAFe® Big Picture** or a particular ceremony, can help ground your thinking and guide you to the right choice. Take time and reflect on the question's intent, avoiding hasty decisions.

If you're stuck and have been through all the preceding steps, try applying the scenario to a real-world situation. SAFe is based on common practices from companies; choose the one that sounds like you can deliver the most value to the customer/business without breaking people in the process!

Getting in the right mindset

When you're ready to sit the exam, you'll find that managing your time effectively is a crucial aspect of success. Balancing speed and accuracy is essential, as spending too long on one question can prevent you from completing the exam. Practicing timed exams during your preparation will help you build confidence and improve your pacing, ensuring that you can allocate your time wisely on the day.

Effective study habits also play a key role in preparing for multiple-choice exams. Active study methods, such as using flashcards, summarizing concepts in your own words, or explaining ideas to someone else, are far more effective than passive reading. These techniques help reinforce your understanding and improve retention. Additionally, breaking your study sessions into manageable chunks, using techniques such as the Pomodoro method, can keep you focused and prevent burnout.

Finally, staying calm and focused during the exam is vital. Even with excellent preparation, nerves can undermine performance if not managed effectively. Use deep breathing techniques or brief moments of mindfulness to center yourself if you feel overwhelmed. After completing the exam, revisit flagged questions and review your answers if time allows, ensuring that you've given each question your best effort.

You can confidently approach multiple-choice exams by combining a thoughtful study approach with strategies for interpreting and answering questions. Preparation isn't just about knowing the material—it's about equipping yourself with the tools and techniques to demonstrate that knowledge effectively. Trust in your preparation, stay calm, and tackle each question methodically to achieve success.

Scaled Agile has provided some very useful content to help you prepare and set up for success.

Using the study guide for targeted preparation

The SAFe® study guide (`https://support.scaledagile.com/en/articles/9791380-exam-study-guide-rte-6-0-safe-release-train-engineer`) is your most valuable resource, offering a clear roadmap to the knowledge and skills you'll need to succeed. It's more than just a list of topics; it's a focused summary of what matters most in SAFe. To make the most of it, start by identifying core concepts such as roles, ceremonies, and the flow of value through the organization. These foundational topics often underpin the majority of exam questions.

Having reviewed the study guide, you will have an overview of what the exam will cover. Let's look at some additional items that will help you prepare and take the exam successfully. We'll outline the following:

- How the glossary supports you with terminology
- How the practice exam lets you test your knowledge and focus your revision
- How to prepare yourself for the real exam

The glossary

Understanding the precise definitions of terms is crucial because the exam often includes nuanced questions where the correct answer depends on subtle distinctions. Beyond memorization, however, connecting these terms and concepts to real-world applications is vital. For example, when studying PI Planning, consider its purpose and how it fosters team alignment. Relating theoretical principles to workplace scenarios or case studies will deepen your understanding and help you recall information during the exam.

Supplement the study guide with official resources on the Scaled Agile website. SAFe Studio now has a treasure trove of videos, e-learning, blogs, and talks. The questions will most likely be based on the framework articles. These include detailed explanations, diagrams, and case studies that bring the framework to life. Combined with the study guide, these materials provide a comprehensive foundation for your preparation.

Harnessing the power of the practice exam

The practice exam is an indispensable tool for exam preparation, and taking it early in the process can provide valuable insights. It serves as a measure of your current knowledge and a diagnostic tool for identifying areas that need more attention.

By attempting the practice exam, you'll familiarize yourself with the format and types of questions you'll encounter. It's a chance to understand how SAFe® principles are presented in a test context and to sharpen your critical thinking skills. When reviewing your results, consider the questions you answered incorrectly. These are opportunities to pinpoint knowledge gaps and refine your understanding.

Treat the practice exam as part of a feedback loop. Use your results to guide further study, focusing on weaker areas. Revisit the study guide, explore additional resources, and discuss challenging concepts with colleagues. Each round of practice and review will bring you closer to exam readiness.

> **Warning!**
>
> You can easily get very good at taking the practice test as you start to recognize the questions and answers.

Now, let's shift our focus to the big day itself.

Focusing on the exam day

When you're ready to take the exam (at the time of writing, you've got 30 days from the date that you finish the course), start by setting up a quiet, distraction-free environment where you can focus entirely on the test. A reliable internet connection is essential, as the exam is online, and it's wise to test your setup beforehand to avoid last-minute technical issues.

Scheduling the exam during peak productivity hours can also make a big difference. Some people are most alert in the morning, while others perform better in the afternoon or evening. Choose a time that aligns with your natural rhythm to maximize focus and clarity.

During the exam, stay calm and focused. If you encounter a challenging question, avoid dwelling on it for too long. Instead, move on and return to it later if time permits. Often, a fresh perspective can make the answer more straightforward. Remember to read each question carefully, as the phrasing usually provides clues about the correct answer.

Trust your experience, not just terminology

A senior manager preparing for an exam found herself struggling with complex terminology in the questions. Tim suggested that she should translate the scenario into a real-life situation; she immediately grasped the core concept: *"Oh, basically tell the person they're wrong without breaking the relationship."*

This moment highlights a crucial lesson for experienced professionals facing exams or assessments: don't let unfamiliar jargon intimidate you. Your years of practical experience are invaluable. When confronted with complex questions, try to do the following:

1. Visualize a real-world scenario that fits the question.
2. Consider how you'd handle it based on your experience.
3. Trust your instincts and practical knowledge.

Remember, exams often use specific terminology, but they're testing your understanding of concepts you've likely encountered in your career. By relating questions to real-life situations, you can cut through academic language and showcase your true expertise. Your ability to apply concepts in practical settings is often more valuable than memorizing definitions.

Celebrating your achievement and looking ahead

Passing the SAFe® exam is a significant accomplishment and one worth celebrating. Once certified, you'll receive a digital certificate and badge to proudly display on LinkedIn, your resume/CV, and even email signatures. These credentials validate your expertise and demonstrate your commitment to professional growth.

Sharing your achievement with your colleagues and network is more than just a moment of pride—it's an opportunity to inspire others. Announcing your success within your organization can encourage others to pursue certifications, fostering a culture of continuous learning and improvement.

Looking beyond certification

Certification is not the end of the journey; it's the beginning of a more profound commitment to professional development. As an RTE, your role requires you to stay current with evolving Agile practices and deepen your understanding of the framework.

Consider joining **Communities of Practice (CoPs)** or attending Agile meetups where you can discuss challenges, share insights, and learn from others. Exploring advanced certifications or specializations, such as **SAFe® Practice Consultant (SPC)**, can further enhance your expertise. Additionally, staying engaged with resources such as blogs, webinars, and Agile conferences ensures that you remain informed about the latest developments in the field.

Reflect on your certification journey and how it has enhanced your understanding of SAFe. Use this momentum to set new goals for yourself and your organization. Continuous improvement is at the heart of Agile, and your journey as a certified RTE is an opportunity to embody that principle every day.

By taking a strategic approach to your preparation, effectively leveraging resources, and maintaining a growth mindset, you can confidently pass the SAFe exam and set the stage for ongoing success in your Agile career.

Summary

Preparing for and passing the SAFe RTE exam marks a key milestone in your career and your growth as a leader. It's not about ticking a box; it's about proving your ability to lead with purpose, to apply Lean-Agile principles in real-world situations, and to support your teams with clarity and care.

This final chapter has walked through the practical steps to help you get there: understanding the exam format and focusing on *why* the principles matter, not just what they are; using the study guide and glossary to anchor your preparation; taking the practice exam early to identify weaker areas and aim for depth over memorization; preparing both your environment and mindset to ensure a calm, confident experience; and finally, celebrating your success—and using it as a springboard for whatever comes next.

Certification isn't the end of the journey. It's the beginning of a richer commitment to relentlessly learning, leading, and improving. You now have the tools, mindset, and community to guide you.

We hope this book has supported, encouraged, and even challenged you. Whether you're preparing for your first PI or coaching your second train, we're cheering you on every step of the way.

Get This Book's PDF Version and Exclusive Extras

UNLOCK NOW

Scan the QR code (or go to packtpub.com/unlock).
Search for this book by name, confirm the edition, and then follow the steps on the page.

Note: Keep your invoice handy. Purchases made directly from Packt don't require one.

14

Appendix B: Building Confidence in PI Planning

The power of **PI Planning** is undeniable, and if you can get a PI Planning event set up and run it successfully, then very often, you won't have to keep trying to persuade people of its value. Once people see it, they tend to understand and decide they never want to go back to their previous approaches for getting people and teams aligned with each other.

However, getting permission and buy-in to run a PI Planning event can be a difficult thing, as it is very different from what many organizations have used before.

In this appendix, we'll look at how to build support for PI Planning and address people's uncertainties to get you to that all-important first event, after which people rarely look back.

Let's start by looking at some of the common concerns around the event before we move on to looking at some of the better ways of getting buy-in for it.

Concern: PI Planning is too theoretical—we need to be more pragmatic

Some people argue that PI Planning may look like it works on paper, but it will never work in practice, especially not in their organization, which, as we all know, is a unique snowflake entirely different from every other similar organization in the same industry that has had PI Planning work perfectly well many times before. Instead, we are told, we need to be *pragmatic*.

There are two problems with this argument. The first is that the definition of pragmatism being used here is very often wrong. The concept of pragmatism is all about trying something out and seeing how it works in practice, rather than just keeping it as a theoretical concern. In reality, this means that the pragmatic approach is just to run a PI Planning event and see how it works in practice.

However, this explanation is less useful in reality because of the second problem with the pragmatism argument. Often, what people really mean when they use the *pragmatism* excuse isn't anything to do with pragmatism at all. It is all about the desire to prevent the event from happening and make you look like the unrealistic one in the whole situation, while making themselves look like the sensible ones who are protecting the organization from the chaos of crazy theories.

You then need to set off on a much more difficult quest—that of trying to understand what is really behind their worry and address that. We don't know what specifically the source of the concern in your context might be, as it could be any number of things, but over the years, we've found that two common reasons sit behind it, which you might find helpful to validate first.

A lack of understanding

This reason often occurs because someone has looked at the **SAFe®** big picture and been overwhelmed by it, or they've heard a bit about SAFe, enough to become confused by it, but not yet enough to understand it. As a result, if they don't understand it, they feel pretty sure that other people won't understand it either (for what person doubts the superiority of their own knowledge in comparison with others?). Therefore, they see it as their duty to shut the whole idea down before it causes more confusion and potential damage. Besides, shutting it down means that no one ever has to realize that the original person didn't understand it, allowing them to save face in the competitive corporate climb of the ladder.

A misunderstanding

A misunderstanding is slightly different. Perhaps someone has learned about SAFe second or third hand from someone who didn't understand it well either, or perhaps they've read comments online that are not entirely accurate. Either way, it is not uncommon to find someone believing that *SAFe says we must X*, even when SAFe says no such thing.

If a simple misunderstanding is the issue, then it is your job as an RTE to help people understand. Sometimes this can mean one-to-one coaching to understand someone's specific knowledge gaps or misconceptions. At other times, this may mean looking to run a larger workshop or more formal instructor-led training around SAFe more generally.

If you do take this latter approach, look for a SAFe® course that has a PI Planning simulation exercise in it, such as *Leading SAFe* or *SAFe for Teams*. Out of all of the SAFe training content available, it is very often the PI Planning simulation exercise that provides the penny-drop moment of realization to people.

The second reason for arguing against PI Planning on the grounds of pragmatism is to make sure that not too much attention is turned toward existing organizational problems. Delivery is difficult in many large organizations, and larger programs and initiatives can run into real problems as they progress. When the senior leaders of these pieces of work get into trouble, the last thing they want to do is invite other people in to see that trouble, as all it will do is create yet more trouble—for them at least.

So, offering to hold an event where up to 125 people all meet, physically or virtually, to look at everything that's going on sounds like the very last thing they want to see happen. Faced with this risk, as they see it, they attempt to shut the risk down by arguing that it is just not pragmatic to hold the event, on the grounds that it will be too disruptive to a program already at risk.

If this is what's really going on, then you have an even harder job on your hands. You need to win someone's trust and convince them that far from making things harder for them, what you will actually be doing is making their lives easier, and making the leaders look more successful in return. Whether people will give you the time of day to even start to have these conversations is always something you have to discover for yourself. Sometimes they don't, especially when the initiative is heavily involving a third-party supplier who sees an increase in scrutiny around their work as a contractual or even existential risk. Give it time, but also be aware that, sometimes, if you're getting real resistance like this, then there may be easier ARTs to launch first.

Here are some coaching questions to start a conversation to help create movement:

- I'm curious, when you say PI Planning feels too theoretical, what experiences or examples come to mind?
- What would help PI Planning feel more grounded or relevant for the teams here?
- When you imagine the event in our context, what concerns you most about how it might unfold?
- What kinds of alignment or insights do you wish our current planning approach provided that it doesn't today?
- If we approached the first PI Planning as a learning experiment rather than a finalized process, what could that enable?

Concern: PI Planning is too expensive

This concern around PI Planning is more grounded in reality and, therefore, sometimes harder to overcome. We don't mean that it is too expensive in terms of people's time.

If you need to bring together up to 125 people into a single venue to run a face-to-face event, then unless your organization already owns an event space, you're going to need to spend some money hiring a large venue to use. Once you've hired it, you have all of the costs that go with it. Do you pay for drinks and snacks for everyone who attends over the two days? Do you even pay for them all to have lunch together? What if they want to hold a social event together in the evening? You might be able to put the occasional team-building drinks through your expenses process for your immediate direct reports, but how do you buy an evening out for many dozens of people?

That's just the cost for the event itself. Does your organization have everyone working in the same building in the same city all the time already? Probably not, as most organizations that benefit from SAFe® do so in part because their people are not co-located and are often globally distributed. Therefore, to get everyone together for PI Planning, you're going to be spending another load of money on travel and accommodation for people as well. It can't be denied, the costs of a face-to-face PI Planning event can soon add up. However, there is a very useful technique for helping to resolve this problem, as Gez once discovered, almost by accident.

Example of data-driven decision-making on expenses

Many years ago, Gez was working with some teams that he had formed into an ART over time. However, the organization was still quite traditional, and so it had also assigned a more traditional project manager to the teams. The problem was, no one on the team was really sure why the project manager was there. After looking around a bit and getting to know people, the project manager wasn't entirely sure why they were there either. However, there they were, and they needed things to do. So, one job they decided to take on was tracking blockers around the teams. They got team members to log any time they were blocked during each iteration, which he then collated and presented at each iteration review. Again, no one really understood why this information was being collected, but it didn't do any harm, and as it happened, it turned out to be invaluable.

Eventually, as is so often the case in large organizations, a change of senior leadership led to a sudden change of direction around PI Planning. From being an event that the teams had recently started running as standard, it suddenly looked like it was now going to become an event that was totally forbidden, due to how much it cost in travel, accommodation, and venue hire.

The RTE, the teams, and Gez were all a bit stumped by this at first and didn't know quite how to respond. But then something occurred to them. How could you object to the cost of PI Planning if you could prove that it was more expensive not to run it? What if you could prove that the savings the event created more than offset how much it cost to run?

They remembered that the project manager had been gathering data on time blocked across the teams for some time, around 18 months by that point. They got hold of this data and calculated how many hours in total all of the people on the ART had been blocked on average across their PIs. They then compared this data with the average hourly salary cost of the people doing the work, and worked out how much wasted spending the blockers across the teams on the ART were creating on average.

Finally, they compared this cost with the cost of PI Planning as an event.

They found that if PI Planning reduced hours blocked in the next PI by just 10%, then the event would have paid for itself. They were therefore permitted to run the event one more time and track the time blocked for the next 12 weeks. In the end, PI Planning helped the ART reduce its time blocked by around 15%, and the argument was won.

PI Planning, despite its cost to run, was overall cheaper for the organization than not running PI Planning at all.

Feel free to repeat this experiment yourself with your own teams and your own data. If nothing else, it helps focus the conversations of the ART around meaningful business outcomes, such as cost reduction, which is always a good habit to have.

Glenn once experienced something similar. One of his international clients, which ultimately put in place 17 trains during his time with them, saw high travel costs. However, they welcomed these with open arms. One day, Glenn had a chat with one of the VPs and said how pleased he was that the costs of PI Planning were never really challenged. The response was simple, *"I'm spending the best part of $10 million a year on these teams, and I'm getting nothing for it. If $500,000 unlocks that spend and gets results, it's a good investment!"*

These questions might help you have a conversation about costs:

- What is the cost when misalignment is caught late and we need to work together to overcome it?
- What might we learn, or avoid wasting, by having everyone align at the same time and place?
- When we've held large events or workshops before, what benefits or outcomes made them feel worthwhile?
- Where could the most significant value from a shared planning event come from: clarity, connection, commitment, or something else?
- If cost wasn't the main issue, what other worries might still be in play about bringing everyone together?

Concern: PI Planning is too chaotic

As some people see it, how can getting up to 125 people into a single room to talk to each other for 2 days create anything other than noise and confusion? Surely it would be better to just get the team leads into a room for an hour or two, have a proper, formal business meeting, and agree between them what everyone should be doing and by when?

This is a common argument against PI Planning, especially from people whose job it has previously been to be those team leads who used to get to decide everything between themselves. You could look at that from a perspective of bias, and think that the too chaotic argument is just another way to shut down something that threatens established power structures, and sometimes you may be correct, but it seems far more useful to take it as an objection at face value and assume that the person objecting really does see a chaotic event as both likely and harmful.

On the face of it, especially if you've never been to one, PI Planning may well seem chaotic—so many people in a room, all expected to run around and talk to each other when they may never have even met before. How on earth can that result in clarity of direction and common alignment around it?

There are often two things to emphasize here. The first is that it needn't be chaotic. There is a clear structure and agenda to follow if people want to follow it. Individual sessions are timeboxed and facilitated to make sure that we're all working toward the outcomes that we're after. People can be trained in it all beforehand so that they go in with a good understanding of what to do. While a great PI Planning event is generally more organic than that, emphasizing structure, especially at the start, can help give people enough initial comfort to get started.

If there is chaos in PI Planning, that chaos was not created by PI Planning. That chaos already existed in your organizational system. Here are some examples, but we're sure you could list many more that happen in your organization:

- The chaos of finding that two teams were both working on the same thing without realizing or talking to each other. That's something PI Planning has uncovered, not created.
- The chaos of finding that different people from the business have different strategic priorities that oppose each other. That again is something already existing that PI Planning has just brought to light.
- The chaos of finding that a team has more scope to deliver than they can actually achieve by the target date. That's something PI Planning can fix, and is the exact opposite of something PI Planning would cause.

The issue isn't PI Planning causing chaos. The issue is PI Planning making all of that existing chaos visible. On top of this, it takes this chaos, which is usually only popping up to be visible now and again over the course of delivery, and crams it all into two days, making the total volume of chaos appear to be much larger by condensing the size of its container or timebox. Cramming 12 weeks of continuous low-level chaos and confusion into just 2 days can make things seem very chaotic indeed. This isn't the fault of PI Planning. The way we tend to look at it is that the chaos you're experiencing already exists anyway. You can either experience it slowly and constantly, or you can get it all out of the way in just 2 days, so that you don't have to experience any more chaos over the next 12 weeks.

These questions might help you engage in a conversation about this concern:

- What would make it safe for people to raise issues openly without it feeling like disorder?
- If we could design the experience so that people leave feeling clearer than when they arrived, what would it look like?
- What might it tell us about our system if things felt chaotic during the event?
- Where have you previously seen large groups work effectively together, and what contributed to it feeling organized and purposeful?
- If the event revealed hidden conflicts or overlaps, how could that assist us in making better decisions in the future?

Concern: PI Planning takes too much time away from delivery

This objection to PI Planning can have two different reasons behind it. As with other concerns, the first reason may be that the objector has a deeper motive for preventing PI Planning from taking place, such as a desire to avoid interference in or scrutiny of their work. At other times, though, this may be a more neutral objection, since the program or initiative is already significantly late, people are under huge pressure to hit deadlines, and taking everyone away from work for two days, plus all that time spent being trained and preparing backlogs, will only make things worse.

No better was this mindset exemplified than the time we were launching some ARTs in an organization, and a traditional project manager was assigned to work alongside us to project manage the Agile transformation (yes, really!). To be fair, the project manager was very helpful in many ways, but we were struck by the fact that whenever some teams were identified to be offered training before forming an ART, the project manager always described them as the *impacted teams*, the *impact* in this instance being taking some time out to do some training.

We tried to convince them that learning new skills wasn't an impact on the teams; it was actually something really positive and beneficial, but we never really got through. In that project manager's world, time spent away from delivery was seen as having a negative impact on delivery, even if the impact was intended to be massively beneficial to improving the speed and quality of the delivery itself.

The other problem with this objection is that it becomes horribly self-sustaining through this vicious cycle. Teams are under pressure to hit delivery dates, so they can't take time out for PI Planning. Because they're not taking time out for PI Planning, they find it harder to get things delivered. This puts more pressure on delivery dates, which means they can't take time out for PI Planning. When you step back and look at it, this is a bit of a strange objection to PI Planning, as it is basically saying that things are so bad, you don't want to improve, but you'd be surprised how often it works.

Sometimes, you have to leave these teams to themselves until their burning platform becomes so serious that calls for improvement cannot be ignored. At other times, though, if you can win the trust of people to run a small experiment around PI Planning, the value and benefits of it soon become obvious, and people take to it more wholeheartedly.

> We were once working with some teams that would have benefited from PI Planning, but were under constant colossal delivery pressures. As a result, we proposed running their first PI for just 6 weeks, rather than the more usual 10 to 12 weeks. The deal was that they would run it for six weeks and see how it went. If it went well, they were welcome to carry on and perhaps make the next PI longer. If it didn't, they could walk away at that point, and they'd only have put six weeks of work at *risk of being impacted.*
>
> In the end, the 6-week PI was hugely successful, and they immediately stepped up to 12 weeks and carried on running PI Planning for many years after.
>
> Sometimes, making the experiment small makes it safer to risk failing, makes the risks seem smaller, and generates real learning earlier around what works and what does not.

Conversations aimed at overcoming the time away from delivery could be started with the following:

- What might happen if we treated the event not as time away from delivery, but as time invested in making delivery more efficient or quicker?
- How might the cost of 2 days of planning compare to the cost of rework or misalignment over the next 12 weeks?
- What would make it feel worthwhile for the teams taking part? What outcomes would justify the time spent?
- How does the pressure to deliver right now affect our ability to plan and deliver effectively in the next few months?

Concern: PI Planning is too big

We've touched on this worry to some degree when looking at the previous ones, but this concern is so common that it is worth calling out by itself. When you look at it from the perspective of the person who raises it, PI Planning does look like a really big event. These are people, often project or program managers, who are used to decisions being taken by a small group of senior people. It's not necessarily about PI Planning taking this power away from them, although it can be. It's more often the simple fact that some people plan on behalf of other people who do the doing; this has been the way that their world has worked for years, and they don't see how the world could be any different.

Others may say that getting everyone into a room to spend two days planning may seem expensive, chaotic, and take up a lot of time, but for the *too-big* objectors, the whole purpose of the event makes no sense. They plan the work, and they tell other people what work to do and when. The other people who do the work don't have these specialist skills and experience in project planning, so why would we ask them to take the role on?

> We saw this once when we had a queue of ARTs to launch in an organization. One day, a program manager got in touch to ask about launching their program as an ART. We agreed, but said that we wouldn't be able to get to them for around 10 to 12 weeks, as we had other ARTs to launch first. They seemed okay with this answer, but the next week, we happened to bump into the program manager again, who said, *"Oh, don't worry, we've done PI Planning now. We won't need your help."*

On inquiring some more, it turned out that they had got the team leads into a room for an hour, created a plan for the next 12 weeks, then emailed it out to the teams, calling it PI Planning. Is it any wonder SAFe® sometimes gets a bad name in organizations? Two risks tend to come out of this objection. Let's look at them.

When only half the team shows up, and it's the wrong half

Even if you think you've got agreement to run the event, you may find that only a small handful of members from each team turn up to the event on the day. Perhaps a tech lead, a design lead, and a **Scrum Master** (who is actually a **Project Manager**). For a team of seven people, you may look at this and think, "Well, I've got half the team here, good enough," but the reality is that you may only have the management half of the team. The people who do the actual work are all absent. Sometimes, only one person from the team turns up; even if the whole team turns up at the start of Day 1, later on Day 1 and into Day 2, you begin to notice that lots of the team are no longer there, as they've been told to go back to work. You may then find you only get the full team attending again at the end, when they are called back into the room to be told what their plan is.

This *too-big* thinking sometimes doesn't necessarily stop PI Planning from happening. It does, however, chip away at it, reducing its effectiveness and the benefits that it can create, especially around predictability. The mantra always has to be that *the people who do the work plan the work*.

Consequently, if you were to uninvite anyone from the event, it should be the team lead and project manager, not the team!

The dangerous illusion of PI Planning

Too-big thinking often doesn't stop PI Planning from happening; it allows it, but makes it sub-optimal. In some ways, preventing it from happening altogether may have been the better outcome.

This is because a PI Planning event that doesn't happen doesn't set any bad examples. In contrast, a PI Planning event that happens badly sets bad examples that can then spread far and wide. It only takes one ART to do a quarterly planning meeting for an hour with just the team leads for all of your other teams and ARTs to look at it and ask why they can't do the same. Everyone wants to save time, and it looks like that ART over there just saved nearly two whole days, so let's all copy them for the next event. Rot like this can spread quickly, and is, we believe, another reason that SAFe® has gained a poor reputation in some situations.

The risk of this problem is further compounded if you end up being stretched too thinly as an RTE. If you're having to launch and run an ART for a short time, before being moved onto a new ART being launched, you never have time to make sure that the first ART you worked on hasn't accidentally derailed itself. Once it does, others may then look to it rather than you for examples of what to do.

Always be careful when you see this *too-big* thinking around PI Planning. It may not stop PI Planning initially, but it can chip away at it over time. The people who do the work plan the work. If the people who do the work aren't involved in PI Planning, it is not PI Planning. You can let people do quarterly planning meetings with the team leads for an hour—their choices are their choices—but you really must insist that they don't call it PI Planning when they do so.

The PI Planning that wasn't planning at all!

A client of Glenn's once had one ART, which wasn't much more than some people grouped together, holding a shortened half-day PI Planning meeting. Glenn dutifully went along to learn about their optimizations. He found that it was no more than **Product Owners**, who were actually Project Managers with a new title, sharing their wish list of items to work on over the next quarter with the ART leadership. No teams, no planning, and done in a strict scheduled order, so the Product Owners never met or talked to each other. Consequently, while high-level priorities appeared loosely aligned, the lack of collaboration among Product Owners and teams meant detailed plans were misaligned, poorly prioritized, and inadequately sequenced, making it difficult to deliver valuable, complete work.

Attempt to overcome this concern with these conversation starters:

- When you imagine a PI Planning event, what feels *too big* about it? Is it the number of people, the scale of decisions, or something else?

- What benefits might be gained by involving the people who actually do the work in the planning process?

- How might decisions change if those closest to the work had a say in shaping the plan?

- What concerns you most about involving a larger group in the planning process?

- How can a bigger planning event help minimize surprises or escalations later in delivery?

Concern: PI Planning is not agile enough

On the face of it, we can see the appeal of this argument. Gez used to believe it himself, funnily enough, and the reason for this was simple. Up until then, Gez's main experiences with Lean and Agile were at a small technology start-up, which grew out of someone's bedroom. Even after he'd moved on from that experience, he only tended to work with individual people and teams, never at enterprise scale. So, when he first heard of the idea of creating a plan for the next 12 weeks, he instinctively felt that that was the opposite of the Agile he'd come to know and love. In his world, you would plan two weeks of work, do the work for two weeks, show it to some people at the end, and only then decide what to do over the next two weeks. That's what agile was for him: the ability to continuously inspect and adapt, to learn and plan by doing.

So, why did he change from this passionately held belief into becoming a **SAFe® Practice Consultant (SPC)**, then a **SAFe Practice Consultant-T (SPCT)**, and now a **SAFe Fellow**? Well, he didn't change his mind; he just broadened it. If he were still working in a start-up, he wouldn't look to use SAFe, as it is the *Scaled* Agile Framework®, and a start-up tends not to have much organizational scale. Returning to our hardware store analogy from earlier, for a start-up, SAFe would be the wrong tool for the job. Even as the start-up grew, he would have been hesitant to rush to use the framework, because the golden rule is that *the first rule of scaling is don't*. If you can do things with fewer people in a simpler way, just do that.

However, some organizations are far beyond this point. They have already scaled. They have hundreds, thousands, even tens of thousands of employees distributed all over the world, and their current systems for handling that situation tend to be poor. The logical extension of this then follows into the world of their planning. In a small start-up finding its way in a new marketplace, a 12-week plan may lack sufficient agility. But for a large organization, having a plan that only lasts for 12 weeks might be incredibly agile—in fact, the most agile they have ever been. These sorts of organizations typically tend to have plans that last for years at a time. Not just aspirational, roadmap-based plans, but detailed plans full of specifications and specific deliverables, to be delivered relentlessly for many years to come.

In this type of all too real organizational context, deciding to plan for just the next 12 weeks, then deciding what to do next based on feedback from the 12 weeks, is incredibly agile. Indeed, people sometimes object that it is too agile, and that a PI should last far longer than 12 weeks to make any sense.

The agile/not-agile argument is all about context and your starting point as an organization. For some organizations, PI Planning may not be useful and might just add overhead rather than benefit. For others, it may be the most radically agile they have ever been.

Agile and *agility* are concepts, and concepts have to be applied to contexts in order to make sense. Don't ask whether you have *become agile*, because agile isn't a destination you can reach. Ask whether you are being more agile than you were, or gaining more agility than you once had. If you are, then you're really getting to the heart of what agile and agility are. If you get your planning horizon down to 12 weeks from 2 years, then you have become significantly more agile than you were.

To overcome the *it's not agile enough* concern, these questions or prompts might help you:

- Is it the number of people, the scale of decisions, or something else?
- What does *being agile* mean to you in practice? What kinds of behaviors or decisions would you expect to see?
- In our current context, what would feel *more* agile than how we plan today?
- If our teams only planned 12 weeks rather than 12 months, what might that make possible?
- When you say PI Planning isn't agile enough, what does *agile enough* look like to you?
- What signs would tell you that PI Planning was helping us *respond to change* rather than *lock in a plan*?
- Can you think of a time when a bit more structure actually helped a team be *more* agile? If so, what made that work?
- How can a bigger planning event help minimize surprises or escalations later in delivery?

The hidden concerns

Sometimes, concerns about PI Planning may exist, but remain hidden. For whatever reason, it does not feel safe for people to voice their concerns with the new approach to delivering work, so rather than flagging their issues, they remain silent. As an RTE, this can sometimes catch you off guard. The start of Day 1 is often when you will find out that this has been happening.

We don't mean to sound melodramatic, and it doesn't always happen, but it's happened often enough that it's worth recommending that you watch out for it.

The late grenade

One time, Gez was launching a new ART in India. Everyone had been trained, the teams and key ART roles were all genuinely excited to get started, the event space had been built, and it was all looking really positive. Five minutes before the start of the event, the RTE walked up to Gez with a look of shock on their face and said that their line manager had just told them that they needed to work on something else that day, and they weren't allowed to attend PI Planning. A PI Planning event with no RTE, especially an RTE that had been so closely involved in getting the ART to a great place, would have been a PI Planning event that would have struggled to get off the ground, and the RTE's line manager clearly knew it. They waited until the last possible moment to try to bring the whole thing down. Thankfully, Gez was technically in a more senior role than the line manager, so he went and had a word and got the situation reversed, but still, it wasn't the most useful thing that could have happened just as the event was about to start. As an RTE, you need to have it clearly expressed in advance that there is leadership support for the event, and know that if last-minute issues are placed in your way, you have the ability to call upon leadership to step in and resolve the issue on your behalf, if you find yourself unable to do so directly.

We've already planned

At one client where Glenn worked, during a multi-year transformation effort, there were a few entrenched teams who didn't buy into the Agile dream and saw no benefit to them in attending PI Planning. Many conversations had been had—listening to their views, and offering help and guidance, both from Glenn, other change team members, and the client's leadership—but many months in, it still felt like Day 1 with them.

At their last PI Planning event, they had turned up and refused to plan—until a leader had educated them on the errors of their ways. So, in contrast, for the next event, they went out of their way to plan extremely proactively. This resulted in them pre-planning their entire PI ahead of PI Planning, printing their stories and tasks on a template they had made, cutting them out, and taking fully populated planning sheets to the event.

At the first team breakout, they sat at their table, away from their planning area, and just chatted among themselves. After all, they had nothing more to do; they had fully planned! The RTE and Glenn had spotted this and probed, but the team insisted that they knew best. So, it was agreed to let it play out and undertake an intervention when it was needed.

Ninety minutes later, it was needed. Multiple teams had come to the RTE saying they had needed that team to help them deliver a feature, but they had been dismissed because the team had already planned and fully loaded their iterations. So, the RTE, with one of the leaders, went and spoke to the team. They asked about their plan and how it linked to the priorities for the PI, then observed how some of their work wasn't aligned, especially with the requests from other teams. They asked the team what some options might be to help the ART be successful. Through a mix of common-sense prevailing and a little nudge from seniority, the team started to engage with other teams and were soon removing some of their pre-planned work to accommodate the needs of other teams.

Hopefully, these sorts of things won't happen to you, but as an RTE, you must be aware that it might happen, and think through options for what to do if it does. Solving a problem you can see is one thing. Solving a problem you haven't yet seen but that you might suddenly encounter with no notice at a critical time requires a slightly different approach. The question to think of is "If I wanted to undermine the purpose, process, and outcomes of this event, how would I do it?". Think of the different ways someone could do so, and think through what your different plan Bs would be if any of them occurred.

Summary

Getting to that first PI Planning event is often the hardest step—but also the most powerful. Once people experience it, the value becomes clear: alignment, momentum, and decisions made by the people doing the work, not just those managing it. The challenge is overcoming the early resistance, which often comes not from malice but from uncertainty, misunderstanding, or fear of disruption.

Throughout this chapter, we explored the common concerns people raise, from cost and chaos to *"It's not agile enough."* We've seen that these objections often mask deeper issues, such as unfamiliarity with SAFe®, discomfort with visibility, or reluctance to share decision-making. As RTEs and leaders, our job isn't to argue people into submission—it's to create the safety and clarity needed for them to try it for themselves.

The stories we shared show how to respond with empathy and data, when to stand firm on principles (such as *the people who do the work plan the work*), and how a well-run event can quickly win over even the staunchest skeptics. Sometimes, a small experiment is all it takes to shift perception and build trust.

If you come up against a concern we've not mentioned, you can head to the SAFe Studio forums and ask the global community for input (`https://community.scaledagile.com/`).

Once you've built that confidence and run that first event, the conversation changes.

15

Unlock Your Exclusive Benefits

Your copy of this book includes the following exclusive benefits:

- ⓒ Next-gen Packt Reader
- 🖿 DRM-free PDF/ePub downloads

Follow the guide below to unlock them. The process takes only a few minutes and needs to be completed once.

Unlock this Book's Free Benefits in 3 Easy Steps

Step 1

Keep your purchase invoice ready for *Step 3*. If you have a physical copy, scan it using your phone and save it as a PDF, JPG, or PNG.

For more help on finding your invoice, visit https://www.packtpub.com/unlock-benefits/help.

Note: If you bought this book directly from Packt, no invoice is required. After *Step 2*, you can access your exclusive content right away.

Step 2

Scan the QR code or go to `packtpub.com/unlock`.

On the page that opens (similar to *Figure 15.1* on desktop), search for this book by name and select the correct edition.

<packt>   Q Search...   Subscription 🛒⁰ 👤

Explore Products   Best Sellers   New Releases   Books   Videos   Audiobooks   Learning Hub   Newsletter Hub   Free Learning

Discover and unlock your book's exclusive benefits

Bought a Packt book? Your purchase may come with free bonus benefits designed to maximise your learning. Discover and unlock them here

●————————————○————————————○
Discover Benefits   Sign Up/In   Upload Invoice

Need Help?

| ✦ 1. Discover your book's exclusive benefits | ︿ |

   Q Search by title or ISBN

   CONTINUE TO STEP 2

| ⧖ 2. Login or sign up for free | ﹀ |

| ⬆ 3. Upload your invoice and unlock | ﹀ |

Figure 15.1: Packt unlock landing page on desktop

Step 3

After selecting your book, sign in to your Packt account or create one for free. Then upload your invoice (PDF, PNG, or JPG, up to 10 MB). Follow the on-screen instructions to finish the process.

Need help?

If you get stuck and need help, visit `https://www.packtpub.com/unlock-benefits/help` for a detailed FAQ on how to find your invoices and more. This QR code will take you to the help page.

Note: If you are still facing issues, reach out to `customercare@packt.com`.

‹packt›

`packtpub.com`

Subscribe to our online digital library for full access to over 7,000 books and videos, as well as industry leading tools to help you plan your personal development and advance your career. For more information, please visit our website.

Why subscribe?

- Spend less time learning and more time coding with practical eBooks and Videos from over 4,000 industry professionals
- Improve your learning with Skill Plans built especially for you
- Get a free eBook or video every month
- Fully searchable for easy access to vital information
- Copy and paste, print, and bookmark content

At `www.packt.com`, you can also read a collection of free technical articles, sign up for a range of free newsletters, and receive exclusive discounts and offers on Packt books and eBooks.

Other Books You May Enjoy

If you enjoyed this book, you may be interested in these other books by Packt:

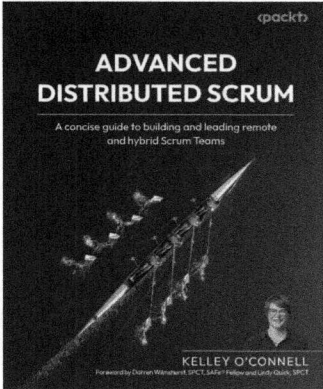

Advanced Distributed Scrum

Kelley O'Connell

ISBN: 978-1-83546-854-8

- Define and align remote roles for seamless collaboration
- Set up tools, workspaces, and team agreements for success
- Recruit, onboard, and integrate remote team members
- Build a strong team culture and resolve conflicts remotely
- Facilitate remote Scrum events across time zones
- Implement CI/CD pipelines in distributed environments
- Ensure security and compliance in remote Scrum setups

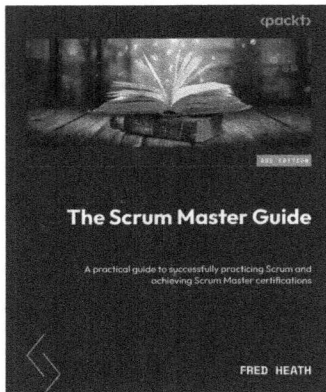

The Scrum Master Guide

Fred Heath

ISBN: 978-1-83588-502-4

- Understand the benefits of Agile development and the application of Scrum values
- Discern the roles and accountabilities of Scrum Team members
- Conduct Scrum events and manage Scrum artifacts effectively
- Recognize Scrum anti-patterns and implement best practices to prevent them
- Master techniques and tools for effective planning and forecasting
- Discover when and how to provide support to the Scrum Team as a Scrum Master
- Familiarize yourself with the format of certification exams to prepare for success

Packt is searching for authors like you

If you're interested in becoming an author for Packt, please visit authors.packtpub.com and apply today. We have worked with thousands of developers and tech professionals, just like you, to help them share their insight with the global tech community. You can make a general application, apply for a specific hot topic that we are recruiting an author for, or submit your own idea.

Share your thoughts

Now you've finished *The Release Train Engineer Handbook*, we'd love to hear your thoughts! Scan the QR code below to go straight to the Amazon review page for this book and share your feedback or leave a review on the site that you purchased it from.

https://packt.link/r/1836205236

Your review is important to us and the tech community and will help us make sure we're delivering excellent quality content.

Index

www.ingramcontent.com/pod-product-compliance
Lightning Source LLC
Chambersburg PA
CBHW081039220326
41598CB00038B/6928